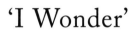

'I Wonder'

'I Wonder'

The Life and Work of Ken Inglis

Edited by
Peter Browne and Seumas Spark

MONASH
UNIVERSITY
PUBLISHING

'I Wonder': The Life and Work of Ken Inglis

Monash University Publishing
Matheson Library Annexe
40 Exhibition Walk
Monash University
Clayton, Victoria 3800, Australia
www.publishing.monash.edu

Monash University Publishing brings to the world publications which advance the best traditions of humane and enlightened thought.

ISBN: 9781925835717 (hardback)
ISBN: 9781925835724 (pdf)
ISBN: 9781925835731 (epub)

www.publishing.monash.edu/books/iw-9781925835717.html

Series: Australian History

Design: Les Thomas

Cover photograph courtesy of the Inglis family.

Cover painting by Oseha Ajokpaezi. Ken Inglis as Vice-Chancellor of the University of Papua New Guinea. Photograph of painting by Ian Maddocks. Reproduced with permission.

A catalogue record for this book is available from the National Library of Australia.

CONTENTS

CONTENTS

CONTRIBUTORS

Annette Becker is a professor at the University of Paris-Nanterre. After focusing mostly on the Great War, her last book *Messagers du désastre: Raphaël Lemkin, Jan Karski et les génocides*, is a history of the concept of genocide from the Armenians and the Jews through to today. Wisconsin University Press is to publish the book in English.

Frank Bongiorno is Professor of History at the Australian National University and Head of the School of History in the Research School of Social Sciences. Ken Inglis was one of his PhD supervisors.

Peter Browne is editor of the online magazine *Inside Story*. As editor of *Australian Society*, he published a series of Ken Inglis's articles between 1986 and 1992.

Martin Crotty is an Associate Professor at the University of Queensland, where he teaches history. His primary research interests centre on masculinity, sport, and Australians at war. His interest in Ken Inglis's work stems from research into Australian commemorative pilgrimages, specifically the Gallipoli pilgrimage of 1965.

Joy Damousi is Professor of History at the University of Melbourne. Her current research is on child refugees and Australian internationalism, 1920 to the present.

Robert Dare graduated in history from the universities of Melbourne and Oxford. He later taught history at the University of Adelaide, where he was successively Head of the Department of History, Dean of Arts and Head of the School of Politics and History.

Glyn Davis is Professor of Political Science at the ANU, and Chief Executive Officer of the Paul Ramsay Foundation. His doctoral thesis examined the political independence of the ABC.

Graeme Davison is an Emeritus Professor of History at Monash University. His most recent books are *Lost Relations: Fortunes of My Family In Australia's Golden Age* (2015), and *City Dreamers: The Urban Imagination in Australia* (2016).

Gavan Daws had Ken Inglis as his history tutor at the University of Melbourne in the early 1950s, and they were colleagues at the Australian National University in the 1970s and 1980s. He has published sixteen books.

Raelene Frances is Professor of History and Dean of the College of Arts and Social Sciences at the Australian National University.

Bill Gammage is a member of the Humanities Research Centre, Australian National University, mostly studying Aboriginal land management. He was a student of Ken Inglis's at ANU, and a colleague at the University of Papua New Guinea.

Judith Keene, Associate Professor in History at the University of Sydney, has written widely on the Spanish civil war and contemporary warfare and cultures. With Liz Rechniewski, she edited the transnational collection, *Seeking Meaning, Seeking Justice in a Post-Cold War World* (2018).

Diane Langmore worked for the *Australian Dictionary of Biography* at the Australian National University. From 2003 to 2008, she was General Editor of the ADB. She worked with Ken Inglis in the History Department at the University of Papua New Guinea.

Shirley Lindenbaum is an anthropologist whose research includes the study of cholera in Bangladesh and of kuru in Papua New Guinea. She is a member of the Graduate Faculty, City University of New York.

Janet McCalman is a social historian, best known for her books on private and public life: *Struggletown* (1984) and *Journeyings* (1993), and for her history of the Royal Women's Hospital *Sex and Suffering* (1998). She is Redmond Barry Distinguished Professor at the University of Melbourne.

Stuart Macintyre was a professor of history at the University of Melbourne, connected to Ken and Amirah Inglis by friendship, shared political and intellectual interests, and admiration.

Ian Maddocks is a retired physician who worked in Papua from 1961 to 1974. From 1970 to 1973, he was Foundation Dean in the Faculty of Health Sciences at the University of Papua New Guinea.

Marian Quartly is Professor Emerita in the Monash School of Philosophical, Historical and International Studies. Recently she has worked on the history of Australian feminism and the history of adoption. Currently, she is writing a history of her own family.

Bruce Scates is a professor based in Ken Inglis's old department in the Research School of Social Sciences at the Australian National University. He has written extensively on the culture of commemoration and the much-contested memory of war.

Seumas Spark is a co-author of *Dunera Lives* (Monash University Publishing, two volumes, 2018/2020). He had the privilege of working with Ken Inglis on these books.

Peter Stanley is a professor at UNSW Canberra. Formerly, he was Principal Historian at the Australian War Memorial, where he worked from 1980 to 2007, and where he first met Ken Inglis. His *Bad Characters* (2011) was joint winner of the Prime Minister's Prize for Australian History.

Bob Wallace and Ken Inglis became friends as students at Melbourne and Oxford. Bob taught economics at Adelaide, Stanford and Flinders universities, and in 1969 as a visiting professor taught the first University of Papua New Guinea economics graduates.

Sue Wallace, Bob Wallace's younger daughter, has tertiary qualifications in journalism and library science, and has extensive experience in the public sector.

Jay Winter is the Charles J. Stille Professor of History Emeritus at Yale University, and an Honorary Professor at the Australian National University. In 2017, the Austrian state awarded him the Victor Adler Prize for a lifetime's work in history.

BIOGRAPHICAL NOTE

Kenneth Stanley Inglis was born at Airlie Hospital in Ivanhoe, Melbourne, on 7 October 1929, to Rene Inglis and her husband Stan, a timber merchant. Ken attended Tyler Street State School in Preston (1935–39), Northcote High School (1940–44), and Melbourne High School (1945–46) for matriculation. Too young to enrol for an arts degree in 1946, he repeated his matriculation year.

From 1947 to 1949 Ken studied for a Bachelor of Arts at the University of Melbourne, where he was a resident of Queen's College. He was awarded first class honours in history and English. From 1950 to 1953, he worked as a tutor: by day in Max Crawford's history department, and by night teaching English at Queen's. In this period Ken started a MA thesis, which later was published as *Hospital and Community: A History of the Royal Melbourne Hospital* (Melbourne University Press, 1958).

In May 1952, Ken married Judy Betheras. They travelled to Oxford in 1953, where Ken read for a doctorate. His DPhil was published as *Churches and the Working Classes in Victorian England* (Routledge & Kegan Paul, London, 1963).

In 1956, Ken and Judy left Oxford for the University of Adelaide, where Ken had been appointed to a position in the History Department. His second book, *The Stuart Case*, prompted by his reporting for the fortnightly magazine *Nation*, was published by Melbourne University Press in 1961.

Ken spent the American academic year 1961–62 at Brown University in Providence, Rhode Island. On returning to Australia, he was appointed to the Australian National University, where Manning Clark had created a second chair in history with Ken in mind.

Judy Inglis died in a car accident in 1962. In 1965, Ken married Amirah Turner, nee Gust, and they combined their families: Ken and Amirah, Deborah Turner, Judy Turner, Jamie Inglis, Kate Inglis, John Henry Turner, Louise Inglis.

From 1967 to 1975, the family lived in Port Moresby, where Ken was the University of Papua New Guinea's inaugural professor of history (1967–72) and second vice-chancellor (1972–75). *The Australian Colonists: An Exploration of Social History 1788–1870* was published by Melbourne University Press in 1974.

Ken returned to the Australian National University in 1975, where he remained until his retirement in 1994. For a time he was the W.K. Hancock professor of history. He spent part of 1982 at Harvard University as Professor of Australian Studies, and in 1985 held a visiting professorship at the University of Hawaii. *This Is the ABC: The Australian Broadcasting Commission 1932–1983* was published by Melbourne University Press in 1983, and two years later came *The Rehearsal: Australians at War in the Sudan 1885* (Rigby, 1985).

After retiring from ANU in 1994, Ken wrote *Sacred Places: War Memorials in the Australian Landscape* (Miegunyah Press, Melbourne, 1998) and *Whose ABC? The Australian Broadcasting Corporation 1983–2006* (Black Inc., Melbourne, 2006). *Dunera Lives: A Visual History*, co-written by Seumas Spark and Jay Winter, with Carol Bunyan, was published by Monash University Publishing in 2018.

Ken edited a number of books, including the eleven-volume *Australians: A Historical Library*, and published hundreds of book chapters and journal, magazine and newspaper articles. His publications span nearly eighty years. His first, a poem, appeared in the *Preston Post* in 1942. His last was another volume on the *Dunera* and *Queen Mary* internees, entitled *Dunera Lives: Profiles*, released by Monash University Publishing in 2020. The same co-authors, and Bill Gammage, worked on this book.

Ken died on 1 December 2017, two-and-a-half years after his beloved Amirah.

INTRODUCTION

The idea for a colloquium on Ken Inglis's life and work arose in 2015. When one of us, Seumas Spark, suggested it to Ken, he responded with a chuckle and a firm "no." Ken liked talk and ideas, but not about himself. Some months later, the idea was put again, but this time Seumas had powerful help. Over coffee and cake, Bill Gammage and Jay Winter, two of Ken's closest friends, gave him good reasons to agree to a celebration of his place in Australian life and letters. Ken remained unconvinced, so Bill chose bluntness: nobody was leaving the table until Ken said yes. Ken didn't so much agree to the colloquium as relent.

Nobody else needed convincing. Rae Frances, Dean of the Faculty of Arts at Monash University, gave her support immediately, and the colloquium was set for November 2016. The two-day program was soon filled. Ken knew each of those invited to present a paper. If he were unsure about the colloquium, they were not. The community of scholars in which Ken had made his life wanted to honour him and his work. Shirley Lindenbaum, distinguished anthropologist and Ken's younger sister, flew from New York to speak. Annette Becker came from Paris, Jay Winter from Connecticut. Several speakers travelled from interstate. Sylvia Lawson, a friend of Ken's from the earliest days of the fortnightly magazine *Nation*, was to contribute to the colloquium, but ill health prevented her speaking; her enthusiasm and erudition were missed.

To the delight of the hundred or more participants, Ken contributed to each session, answering questions from speakers and listeners, posing questions of his own, and drawing on his remarkable memory to offer new glimpses of his methods, experiences and work. Like the long postscripts he wrote for the revised editions of *The Stuart Case* and *Sacred Places*, and his revisiting of themes, places and institutions through his working life, these contributions were a reminder that Ken's major works were always works in progress, and also left behind fertile ground for other scholars. His was an enquiring approach, posing questions, probing conventional wisdoms and pulling at loose ends.

A few days after the colloquium, Seumas asked Ken if he had survived all the attention and enjoyed the occasion. He was frail, and two days of sitting upright and listening closely to thousands of words had drained his energy. The physical toll was evident for the next week. 'Loved every minute of it', he said quietly, and with just a hint of reluctance. One of his happy memories was of the colloquium dinner, where guests sang several of the songs he composed to be sung on long family drives. Ken liked thinking about the vice-chancellors of Melbourne and Monash universities singing along to 'Beware of Falling Rocks', an Inglis family classic.

With some exceptions, the chapters in this book were presented as papers at the colloquium. Three other papers, given by Graeme Davison, Ian Maddocks, and Bruce Scates, appeared in 2017 in a *History Australia* retrospective dedicated to Ken and his scholarship. Graeme and Ian wrote fresh chapters for this volume, while Bruce and fellow historian Rae Frances wrote about Ken's early life, a subject not covered at the colloquium. The chapters by Frank Bongiorno, Martin Crotty, Marian Quartly and Peter Stanley were commissioned for this book. Their contributions enable us to present a fuller picture of Ken's scholarly life – an appreciative but appropriately questioning view, we hope – than was possible at the colloquium, where time was limited.

INTRODUCTION

The chapters appear in roughly chronological order, some dealing with Ken's work, others mainly with his life, and a number balancing the two strands. The colloquium papers have been revised for publication, with our authors' style and wishes in mind. The contributions of Bill Gammage and Gavan Daws remain in the present tense, as they were read on the day. Some contributors referred to Ken as by his first name, others by his surname, and we have retained their usage.

Our biggest debt is to our authors, who so willingly gave their time to write of Ken. It was a pleasure to work with such learned and agreeable contributors. Additional thanks to Rae Frances, Bill Gammage and Jay Winter for support and advice over several years; without them, there would have been no colloquium and no book. The publication of this book was aided greatly by a grant from the University of Melbourne: our thanks to Glyn Davis, Jillian Constable and Stuart Macintyre. Thanks to Kate Manton for saving us from errors and inconsistencies; Nathan Hollier and the staff of Monash University Publishing for taking on the volume, waiting patiently, and seeing it through to publication; and Rhiannon Tanner, who has brought much to this book.

Thanks to Ken's many friends and admirers who helped make the colloquium such a happy, convivial and rewarding occasion. It was a special pleasure to welcome Dick Manuell, Ken's oldest friend, who later shared his recollections of Ken's schooldays with Bruce Scates and Rae Frances for this book. Ken and Dick were friends for more than eighty years. And thanks, finally, to the Inglis, Turner and Gust families, who knew the joys of time spent with Ken better than any.

Peter Browne and Seumas Spark
November 2019

Chapter 1

A LACONIC COLLOQUIUM

Bill Gammage

Welcome to our laconic colloquium. It's an arresting title, isn't it? It's among the many things Seumas and Jay did to bring these days to fruition. It prompted me to a Ken-like wonder about what it means. In 1953, when I was ten in Wagga and Ken was twenty-four in Oxford and the Queen had just been coronated, Mum gave me a Concise Oxford Dictionary. It says that 'laconic' means 'brief, concise, sententious.' 'Sententious' had me flicking pages: it means 'aphoristic, pithy, given to the use of maxims, affecting concise impressive style; (of style) affectedly formal; (of personal) fond of pompous moralising.' I couldn't reconcile 'concise impressive' with 'pompous moralising,' so I battled on to 'aphoristic.' Not there. I was allowed only 'aphorism: short pithy maxim; definition.' This could nearly do for 'laconic,' or 'laconicism' as the noun is, but it simply reverse-cycled 'sententious.' In Oxford Ken was neighbour to some odd people.

I looked for rescue with 'colloquium.' Not there. That's right, my dictionary says it wasn't a word in 1953. The nearest it allowed is 'colloquy: converse, a conversation.' There is also 'colloquial: in or of talk, oral; belonging to familiar speech, not used in formal or elevated language.' So for these two days we can be as formally familiar, impressively pithy and informally pompous as you like.

Via my dictionary, 'laconic' allows me a maxim, and I have one: when speaking or writing of a friend, don't. You're bound to be sandwiched between a job reference and an *Australian Dictionary of Biography* entry. But Ken is also an inspiring teacher, generous mentor, creative style guide, unmatched explorer of Anzac, and fellow pioneer at the University of Papua New Guinea (UPNG) in Port Moresby. Neither he nor I welcome so many adjectives, but I'm being informally pompous.

In 1963 Ken taught us undergraduates American history, among other things from such documents as *The Federalist Papers*, the Emancipation Proclamation and the Gettysburg Address. They taught me detail – things ain't what they seem. Ken spoke too of Mother's Day, of 4 or 2 July, of Thanksgiving and other curious innovations, and for our honours course he led us in studying American religion. I was home in Wagga that September, reading the Book of Mormon, when two Mormon missionaries knocked on the door. They left shell-shocked, but so were we all soon after, for John Kennedy was shot that November – as Ken knows, fifty-three years ago yesterday Australian time. That murder shook a course devoted to beliefs and ideals.

In March 1965 I learnt that Ken was going on the RSL's jubilee return to Gallipoli, Ken sponsored in part by the *Canberra Times* (remember those days?). I had begun an honours thesis on the Australian Imperial Force (AIF) in France, and till then had got only sideways looks, so it was very pleasant to find someone else interested in Anzac. I offered to carry Ken's bags, but I doubt he had any, just a notebook and pen which he put to good use then and after. I called my thesis 'Genesis of the Anzac Ethos,' 'identity' not being used that way then (in Australia, I think, not until by Ian Turner in

1968). Ken read it and said he was pleased. That and Ken's flood of Anzac insights gave me a life-changing boost. He told me, in effect, this subject matters.

Ken mostly explored Anzac at home; I studied it mostly abroad, though I started at a country war memorial. And like most Australians who weren't there, Ken wrote of Gallipoli, whereas I took up the soldiers' word, Anzac, or Helles occasionally. In spite of these geographical tandems, the flow of ideas was pretty well always from Ken to me.

Ken thought Anzac a secular religion. I think he began so in public as 'John Kemp,' in his 1960 *Nation* article, 'Anzac: The Substitute Religion.'[1] His editor conferred that title, I guess from the phrase Ken used: 'Anzac religion.' In the *Canberra Times* K.S. Inglis called the 1965 trip a 'pilgrimage' to a 'holy land.'[2] Such words are axiomatic now. They voice a potent allegiance, and Ken gives 'secular religion' great exploratory power. Still, I'm not entirely comfortable with their attachment to Anzac. 'There is without doubt a tension between Christianity and the Anzac tradition,' John Kemp wrote in 1960.[3] True, yet they also coexist readily enough, and Anzac is not why Australia is so secular. You are taught religion; no one was taught Anzac in 1965. And Christians missionise, as Ken found for his doctorate on the churches and the working classes in Victorian England, and as he showed us of America's numerous sects at about the same time. Neither of Australia's two great secular faiths, Anzac and the bush, missionised. On the contrary, they barred it. In 1965 you had to be a returned soldier to be an Anzac: that is, you had to have been a soldier, and you had to have returned from overseas. Service in Australia, even in 1942–43 Darwin, didn't count. You had to qualify. In this regard a closer religious parallel to Anzac, if you want one, is not Christianity but Judaism: it does not missionise, except that it is taught.

3

Only place and occupation also qualified a bushman. Others might adopt the values and the gospel, but they remained outsiders, at best fellow travellers. You could imitate, but you couldn't be missionised. Ken remarked in 1977 that 'monuments and ceremonies go together,' but the bushman had neither, despite spawning what has been called a secular religion: unionism.[4] Henry Lawson famously remarked, 'Unionism came to the bushman like a religion,' a remark since wrongly attached to the bushman. One missionised; like Anzac, the other didn't.

Ken elaborates on the tension between *secular* and *religion* in his *Sacred Places*. His early articles use neither *sacred*, nor *places*, nor memorials in the way *Sacred Places* does. I don't think he wrote seriously of memorials (as distinct from ceremonies) until *The Australian Colonists* in 1974. I think they became important to his thinking after he met or read George Mosse. Certainly they were important on 30 April 1999, when he sent my wife Jan and me a card from Paris: 'Came across this local war memorial last night on way to concert with A[mirah]. Thought you'd like a pic.' The card shows the Arc de Triomphe.

Might Anzac become a religion? While no one was taught Anzac in 1915 or 1965, today it missionises. Ken has shown how readily it uses religious language and symbolism, and the civic establishment has taken it up and over, a transfer of the sort that led all the world's major religions to dominance. But Anzac is not yet offering salvation: it's simply widening allegiance, building on genealogy, even just pulling a crowd. I tracked its widening reach during twenty years' commenting, or commentating as they say ('commentate' is not in my dictionary), on Adelaide's Anzac Day march and services. Last July I saw on TV how wide that reach now was, in Australian schoolboys at Pozières, no names, simply labelled 'Anzac pilgrims.' In 1965 the RSL would have taken offence at that use of both those words.

This touches an aspect Ken and I got wrong. In 1965 and later we didn't think Anzac would last. Neither of us studied this closely: I hope I may include Ken when I say that we simply watched Anzac's decline through the sixties and assumed it would continue. Today that decline is almost entirely forgotten. Teachers who ask me to explain Anzac's centennial continuity are surprised, sometimes disbelieving, to discover the doldrums of the thirties, fifties and sixties, and that when I was a student neither world war was taught at any level. Students today assume they are continuing an unbroken tradition of study and homage. I can imagine Ken wondering in his inimitable way what might become of Anzac under such smothering delusions. That's what an establishment doctrine, a substitute religion, does to you.

Yet thanks to Ken many more people probe Anzac now than in 1965. It is one of his skills to ask a question and leave it hanging in the mind. His Anzac sequence, from *The Australian Colonists* in 1974 to *Sacred Places* in 1998, locates *sacred places* in stone, wood and paper, on ground, and in minds and hearts, and in so doing asks a big question: what do Australians believe in?

Which Australians? Whitefellas. Despite my comments on Anzac, I'm trying not to pinch anyone else's brief, so I wander now into a personal byway. In September 1998 Ken, Amirah, Jan and I went camping in central Australia: Chambers Pillar, Rainbow Valley, Uluru, Kata Tjuta, Watarrka, across Tempe Downs station to Illamurta Springs police station ruins, up the Finke past Running Waters and Boggy Hole, to Hermannsburg, Palm Valley, Gosse Bluff, Glen Helen, the West MacDonnell gorges and Alice Springs. Illamurta Springs was the base Constable William Willshire used in the mid 1880s to kill local Luritja people; Carl Strehlow followed the Finke on his last journey to Horseshoe Bend in 1922; Boggy Hole was Willshire's base when in February 1891 he shot two Western Aranda men and had their bodies burnt. He was tried for murder but acquitted and sent north to Victoria River, no doubt taking with him the Aboriginal skull he used as an ashtray. So we camped in most beautiful country with a most murderous past, in the open – no tents, but blankets of stars. Another Australia, and a small reproach at how often Australia's historians prefer its Eurocentric parts. On that trip I determined to call 1788's Aborigines 'people,' and the rest of us 'newcomers.'

'For the education of a historian,' Ken might have said of the trip, 'the gains of living on the edge of such a different world, at such a time, were large.'[5] He did say this about going to Papua New Guinea. In February 1966, the wheat harvest over, I was picking up bindii seeds in the orchard of a farm, the same I was on when Kennedy was shot. These bindii were dinkum seeds, with multiple spikes for puncturing bike tyres. They were the colour of the dust, so my method was to pat my palms in the dust, fill them with bindiis, and gently scrape the seeds into a bucket. I had both palms nicely studded when the boss sang out, 'Bill you're wanted on the phone – trunk call from Canberra.' Naturally I jumped to it. We all do when technology commands – a shop assistant will always answer the phone before the customer in front. I raced into the house and delicately grabbed the phone in two fingers.

'Hello Bill, this is Ken Inglis. How would you like to teach at the university in New Guinea?'

'There isn't a university in New Guinea.'

'There will be when you get there.'

Ken had been appointed UPNG's inaugural history professor, but couldn't go in 1966, so was looking for a one-year stand-in. I must've been a fair way down his list because UPNG's preliminary year was to start in two weeks, but I was tempted, and when in my first week at Yass High School I was put on first-form girls' softball, I was persuaded.

In 1966 I spoke to students of PNG's independent future, never imagining how quickly that would materialise. In 1972, after I had worked for five months as Ken's research assistant in Canberra in 1971, Jan and I went back to Port Moresby at Ken's invitation. PNG opened a wonderful world: a beautiful country, the people of 900 languages on the cusp of political change, each day stimulating. In 1966 I was abused for working in a Mau-Mau factory and saw many examples of racial discrimination. A decade later PNG was independent and it was hard to find a European who had ever been discriminatory. In 1972 Ken followed John Gunther as vice-chancellor, and in 1975 paved the way for a Papua New Guinean, Gabriel Gris, to succeed him. Yet in 1966, so shortly before, we were refused entry into the Boroko Hotel dining room because, in our socks and shorts, our legs weren't fully covered. It was one of the few times I've seen Ken angry.

PNG was generous to me. Hank Nelson became a good mate, and Ken's history department was the most diverse and harmonious I've been in. My visiting lecturers were a roll of honour – Ken, Manning Clark, Geoff Blainey, John Legge, Jim Griffin, Charles Rowley, Margaret Mead. Ken widened his publications, notably on war, race and loyalty, and Amirah wrote wonderful books on Papuan race relations. I got an opportunity to see first contact, as we put it in PNG, from the other side of the frontier, as Henry Reynolds put it in Australia. Particularly while working on the 1929 Rabaul Strike and later the 1938–39 Hagen–Sepik Patrol, I had privileged access to that other side in a way not possible anywhere in the world then, and rare at any time. Ken allowed that, as he allowed Hank, Amirah, Jim Griffin, Di Langmore and others to pioneer PNG history and commentary.

Later came the bicentennial history project, which was Ken's idea. It had five source volumes which widened immeasurably the ground floor of Australian historiography, and five volumes, including the 'slice' volumes, which were opportunities to put byways on the main road, and were Ken's innovation and commitment. It was the humanities' largest-ever collaborative project, balancing colleagues diverse in both dictionary senses. I prize its emphasis on language, typified by John McCarthy's laconic maxim, 'Short sentences, small words.' Couldn't we use that today! I worked on the 1938 slice, and often now come across things that should have gone into it. We did have a scarifying interview with an Aboriginal lady who had been in Cootamundra Girls' Home, but the final draft was too distressing for her, and she told us to leave it out. On the other hand, Marcia Langton led some Aboriginal scholars who forcefully told the 1938 editors very early on that Aborigines had nothing to celebrate in 1988, but in the end she wrote a fine chapter with Jack Horner on the 1938 Day of Mourning. I haven't forgotten that generosity. Other Aboriginal scholars refused to take part in the 1938 volume, which sharpened a dilemma I first felt in PNG: in the university, let alone the wider society, since we were doing so much for Papua New Guineans, why so little for Aborigines?

I can't recall Ken and I sharing much about the bicentennial history since 1988, but you can read what he thought of it in 1988 and 1999 in his and Craig Wilcox's 1999 *Observing Australia*.[6] The History showed how much historians and their disciplinary allies hadn't looked at, and the rewards when they did, and it was fortunate in its authors and its publisher, Kevin Weldon. But it was too big to sell by word of mouth, the fairest way. Most people bought it on trust – not so uncommon I daresay, but eleven volumes was a big commitment. It did not become establishment – it got no help from the Australian Bicentennial Authority – and it is cited less than it should be.

Nineteen eighty-eight was a shared anniversary. There were birthdays in October and November, Jan born on 16 May, and Ken and Amirah married on 19 May, they twenty-two years after the Dam Busters' raid and 1365 years after Pope Gregory the Great decreed that saying 'God bless you' was a correct response to a sneeze. So now you know what year Ken and Amirah married. Ken knows those anniversaries, of course, and that later popes fiddled with the calendar, though apparently not the sneeze.

We often play 'what happened when.' Here's an example from Ken: 'For Bill … a token of appreciation … King's Birthday 2006.' He meant George III, naturally. Another: 'No doubt you're thinking today, as I am, of the Commonwealth Senate's passing the Naval Agreement on this day in 1903, and, in the wider world, of the Prince of Wales opening the Victoria Bridge in Montreal in 1860 [25 August].' And: 'Welcome back, on the anniversary of the proclamation of the dogma of the Immaculate Conception in 1854, and of Victor Emmanuel as king in 1867 and, of course, the Prince of Wales' visit to Rawel Pindi in 1905, not forgetting (as you won't have, Bill) the first action of Australian troops in S. Africa 1899 [8 December].' And one for Ken: on this day in 1642, Abel Tasman first met Tasmania.

I hope I haven't sharked too much from speakers to follow, or from Craig Wilcox's fine portrait of Ken's work in *Observing Australia*. He titled that tribute 'a vernacular intellectual.' Without reaching for my dictionary, that seems laconic enough.

Finally, Amirah. I go gently, for Amirah died only in May 2015. But two thefts from Ken. On the move to PNG in 1967, Ken recalled, 'Amirah, always ready for adventure, was keen on the move, undaunted by the challenge of raising all those children in a colony on the edge of another civilisation.' Early that year Amirah grilled me on what Moresby was like, as if a barrage of questions could momentarily convert me from an ignorant transient into a world expert. She was indeed always ready for adventure. We four used to go on short walks around the ACT – Square Rock, Nursery Swamp and so on. Amirah made those walks sound the greatest things that had ever happened to her. The second theft: to dedicate his and Craig's book in 1999 Ken wrote, 'For Amirah, who has shared nearly all these years.' She still shares, Ken, as you do.

Endnotes

1   J Kemp [KS Inglis], 'Anzac: The Substitute Religion,' *Nation*, 23 April 1960, pp. 7–9.

2   KS Inglis, 'Letters from a Pilgrimage: Ken Inglis's Despatches from the Anzac Tour of Greece and Turkey, April–May 1965', *Inside Story*, Melbourne, 2015.

3   Kemp [Inglis], 'Anzac: The Substitute Religion,' p. 8.

4   KS Inglis (ed. C Wilcox), *Observing Australia: 1959 to 1999*, Melbourne University Press, Carlton, 1999, p. 117.

5   Inglis, *Observing Australia*, p. 115.

6   Inglis, *Observing Australia*, pp. 174–85.

Chapter 2

MELIORA SEQUAMUR

The early education of Ken Inglis

Bruce Scates and Raelene Frances

Northcote High School's fine facade is clearly visible from St George's Road: solid red brick walls, tall Georgian windows, an arched entrance crowned with fanlight window. Its initial letters, NHS, are entwined in iron lacework, recalling an age when the ideals of civic education were literally inscribed in its buildings.[1] Established in 1926, it was one of only six publicly funded schools to offer what was called 'higher education.' Most children's schooling ended at fourteen, and in that less equitable age the elite private colleges and the handsomely endowed church schools opposed the 'troubling' move to mass education. Frank Tate, Victoria's first Director of Education, believed new schools like Northcote signalled the beginnings of a fairer social order. They would extend the principle of free, compulsory and secular education, train a modern workforce and create an informed and responsible citizenry.[2] Even so, fees were set at six pounds per annum from year nine. The onset of the Great Depression, rising fees and sinking incomes dashed hopes that any boy – or girl – could succeed through hard work and merit alone.[3]

Visitors approach the main building along a sweeping circular drive. The trees that line, which now reach almost to the roofline, would have been saplings when K.S. Inglis first arrived at the school and stepped through the marble-clad entrance hall into the privileged world of secondary education. The young Inglis (as the slightly patrician 'masters' sometimes called him) would have noted a sturdy wooden board proclaiming the achievements of past scholars. His own name would be added when he graduated dux of the school several years later. But he was especially taken by another roll of honour, recording the names of Old Boys who had died for King and Country. There was only one memorial to The Fallen in Ken's student days; now, no fewer than seven plaques commemorate four separate conflicts. Clearly many a lad heeded Tate's urgings to 'put "self" aside and place his duty and responsibility to the State first.'[4]

What was the young Inglis thinking as he climbed the elegant staircase to his classroom? As a local boy now of some standing (the Inglis family had moved to Preston from Heidelberg as the Depression took a toll on his father's timber business)[5], he possibly knew that NHS was built on the site of an Old Inebriate's Home.[6] It was an irony he may well have savoured. We certainly know that in later life he reflected with some glee on the school's steadfastly self-improving motto. 'Meliora Sequamur,' he reminded an old school chum, Dick Manuell, meant 'Let us follow the better things':

> I see in my dictionary of quotations that Ovid wrote in his
> *Metamorphoses*;
> *Video meliora, proboque:*
> *Deteriora sequor*
> = I see the better things, and approve; I follow the worse.
> No wonder we didn't have the whole quotation on our badges![7]

As Ken would have been the first to acknowledge, the classics accommodate many readings. Armed with a copy of *The Aeneid*, a text often set in Latin classes, the authors of the official school history opt for a shorter and more uplifting interpretation. Even so, they concede that boys quickly vulgarised the motto. 'Let us follow the Preston Girls' became the vernacular version.[8]

Those girls were nowhere to be seen within the school's boundaries. NHS had begun with mixed classes in 1926, but two years later – with the establishment of Preston Girls' High and a push for separate girls' education – only boys were admitted. For all Ken's time at the school, it was a masculine enclave, with all-boy classes run by an all-male teaching staff. 'There were two ladies in the school office,' Dick Manuell recalled, 'performing secretarial duties and at least two ladies (volunteers?) in charge of the school tuck shop, where a standard order of a Noon's pie and sauce cost sixpence.'[9] But that – and the occasional school ball – was the total female presence. Later in life, Ken recalled what pursuing the Preston girls involved:

> I've been remembering our going to bible classes together [he wrote to Dick] and taking sixpenny train rides in the afternoon on the lookout for sheilas, among other adventurous intentions …[10]

Where those adventures led is a matter for speculation, but in church fellowship and school socials, interaction between the sexes was both restrained and closely regulated. There was 'never a hint of improper practices,' Dick later insisted, but boys being boys 'all sorts of outrageous claims were made about girlfriends.'[11]

NHS offered schooling to boys of mixed social origins. Parents' vocations spanned a range of lower-middle-class and middle-class occupations. Among the fathers mentioned in a class list from 1944 are a research chemist, a watch-maker, a bank manager, a grocer, a policeman, a hotel licensee, and a public servant. There is one munitions worker on the list and one textile worker, two of several men who worked in industries directly related to the war effort, and the AIF and the RAAF also appear as 'occupations.' Only two women feature on the list, one a 'draper,' the other a 'domestic.' Supporting their sons through higher education may well have been a challenge. 'Stanley Inglis, 3 Southernhay Street, Regent,' is listed as a manager. Many of the childhood homes of those boys stand to this day, modest but comfortable dwellings stretching all the way from Northcote to St Kilda.[12]

'We were nearly all of Anglo-Saxon and Celtic origin, and Protestant,' Ken recalled in a reflective piece sent to the school archives:

> In five years at Northcote I don't remember knowing any Catholics, and the only boys I recall whose parents were born outside the British Isles or Australia were three Jews, who were among the minority who travelled to school north from Fitzroy, Collingwood or Carlton. Those three seemed very exotic.[13]

This was a white, insular and inward-looking world, where portraits of King and Queen gazed with stern dignity from children's exercise books.

So how did the son of a timber merchant, a child who grew up through the Depression and the Second World War, pursue 'the better things' at NHS? First and foremost, through discipline and application. Every day at the school was highly structured. Tom Bremner, a student some years Ken's senior, recalled a life of order and regimen.

> The school day started at nine each morning when the school door opened and the school gate was closed. You had six minutes to get your books for the next two periods. Those who were shut out at nine o'clock were not allowed inside the grounds until six

past nine and, consequently, they were marked 'late' … The school finished at four in the afternoon. We had eight periods, each lasting forty minutes on Mondays and Tuesdays, six periods with a short lunch period on Wednesday, which was sports afternoon except when examinations were being held. School assembly was held for the first period on Thursday morning followed by religious instruction.[14]

Ken himself, after a visit to the school in the early 1980s, recalled such assemblies and the way unruly boys were marshalled into marching order:

> We used to be paraded every Monday morning to salute the flag … Looking at the old Education Department Gazettes, I find that the headmaster had to get us to remove our caps, 'spring to attention with the eyes on the flag,' and salute 'with a semicircular motion of the right forearm, thumb close to the forefinger, palm to the front, and in position above the right eye, elbow in line with the shoulder, and hold it for five seconds.' It was easier than it sounds when you were brought up to it. The hands by sides and eyes on the flag, as 600 broken and unbroken voices chanted: 'I love God and my country; I honour the flag; I will serve the King, and cheerfully obey my parents, teachers, and the laws.' By the end of my school days I used to resent that 'cheerfully': wasn't it enough that we made all those dreary promises, without having to recite them with a docile smile?[15]

Those 600 boys meant crowded corridors and classrooms. The war years had brought modest prosperity to some, including the Inglis family, who kept their children on for further schooling. By 1944, the school was seriously understaffed, and often irritable teachers struggled with spiralling workloads. 'No wonder I recall so many masters remote, preoccupied and snappy,' Ken recalled, 'Having to teach subjects beyond their competence, one master would bluster and bluff, another would tell us frankly and shrewdly that he and we must learn together.'[16] To their faces, Ken addressed these men as 'Sir'; out of hearing even a model student preferred a range of popular nicknames. 'Daddy' Day, who 'taught us the rudiments of woodwork,' 'Fluffy' Brennan, 'our Latin teacher [who] gave a sharp dig in the ribs to anyone not paying attention,' and the formidable 'Basher' Horsbury, master of algebra. 'He impressed us greatly with an unerring aim of chalk,' Morris Scott recalled more than half a century later. There was a high turnover of teachers in the war years.[17] 'Poppa' Oke, 'an avuncular elder statesmen … with a head of wiry, snowy hair' was brought out of retirement to teach geography as younger men enlisted.[18]

For the most part, the NHS faculty seems to have been highly regarded by their 'Boys' – we were blessed, one recalled, with 'experienced, skilful, well respected teachers.' But there were exceptions. At the height of the war years (with some of the best and youngest off fighting) even Northcote High harboured dodgy characters: 'Butch' or 'Killer' Cummins, one old boy recalled, may have taught Latin but he was also 'a man's man and part-time SP bookmaker.'[19] Others, like the actor Noel Ferrier, were nothing short of scathing. NHS, he asserted,

> was a place seemingly dedicated to bringing out the worst in *all* its pupils. Granted it was wartime (the Second World War, if you *don't* mind) and all the able-bodied teaching staff had gone off to save the Empire, or what was left of it. In their place all sorts of amazing old fogeys had been brought out of retirement to fill the bill when the other chaps were being killed off at Tobruk, et cetera. Added to these geriatrics were the too sick and the too lame for active duty. So as our teaching staff we had an interesting mixture of senile decay, raging alcoholism and one or two who coughed blood quite often. I came out of Northcote High even less literate and more scholastically hopeless than when I left the junior school at Miller Street.[20]

Ferrier's response was both extreme and exceptional. Were *all* the school's pupils so ill served? Presumably not the crop of celebrated poets, scientists, writers and performers NHS nurtured through the war years, Ferrier among them.

Ken himself left several evocative caricatures from his time at NHS. One was of 'Daddy' Day, the woodwork teacher who 'got us to make trains and hobby horses to be sold to buy comforts' for soldiers: 'He taught by scolding, and when my chisel slipped …would abuse me scornfully for hindering the war effort.'[21]

> From the stage of the Assembly Hall Daddy Day – in charge of music and sport as well as woodwork – hectored us into singing…
> 'Advance Australia Fair.' Leading us through its second verse.
>
>> When gallant Cook from Albion sailed
>> To trace wide oceans o'er,
>> True British courage bore him on
>> Till he landed on our shore …
>
> He would stop us and shout 'who's this Tilly who landed on our shore? Some GIRL? Let me hear TILL HE!'[22]

As for 'that genial old man' 'Poppa' Oke, Ken was mesmerised by that 'crest of white hair.' He (and several other equally imaginative boys) were convinced 'Poppa' was a communist.

Nor was it just the teaching staff that made a strong impression. Even then Ken was a close observer of character and possessed a canny eye for the irregular or unexpected. On a visit back to Northcote in 1984, he searched for an old bike shed adjoining nearby playing fields and remembered the brooding presence of old Diggers on the fringes of his school life. The shed was fiercely 'guarded by "Fishy" [Gall], the bullying caretaker, with collarless shirt, cotton wool in ears, RSL badge on lapel.'[23] 'A pompous little fellow, imperious in manner,' 'Fishy' lived with his wife 'in a cottage at the south-west corner of the school grounds.'[24] This was not Ken's first or last encounter with returned men.

Despite or perhaps because of such company, Ken plunged into study. Dick and Ken had first met at Tyler Street State School in Preston, and became lifelong friends. Was Ken the sort of lad to tug the hair of the girl in front of him? No, says Dick:

> He was ... a good boy. We were both very strictly brought up. My family were all Methodists and his were all Presbyterians although our parents didn't go to church as frequently as some ... The people in that area were fairly upright[;] there were a few scamps of course and a few hooligans, but ... Ken was well behaved at school, attentive, never wagged it ... Always did his homework [and] liked music.[25]

By the time, Ken and Dick reached high school it was clear young Inglis liked almost all his subjects. 'Ken excelled,' Dick recalls, mastering arithmetic, Latin and spelling.

> He was top of the class in English, he was especially good at French. Monsieur James, the French master who had spent time in France, was thrilled to have Ken as his leading French student, he had an excellent accent ... [In] our final year, 1944 ... Ken [graduated] eighty marks ahead of his nearest rival.[26]

And even then the power of words and the construction of language fascinated him. Ken was a champion of the school debating team, and a formidable public speaker. From an early age, he relished the vernacular:

> Yes, we all liked [C. J.] Dennis and Ken was good at capturing what we thought was close to the accent Ginger Mick or the Sentimental Bloke might have used (rather like the Fitzroy/

Carlton accents of the 1920s). He could recite sections from *[The Songs of a] Sentimental Bloke*, as I recall. As for the extensive range of Ken's [literary] skills, has anyone told you of his participation in Melbourne Uni revues performed by the Tin Alley Players? He actually wrote words and music for a sham hymn for one of the productions.[27]

Those later halcyon days are the subject of another chapter. For now, we note that 1944 was the first year that the Leaving Certificate was not sufficient to matriculate to university, so Ken went to Melbourne High, 'the Tudor-towered school of the Yarra.'[28] Then came the University of Melbourne, then Oxford. In the immediate post-war years, few public school boys from the lower middle class followed that trajectory.[29]

Not that academic progress was ever easy. Quite apart from the bulging size of the classes, NHS was poorly resourced, especially in regard to its library. Many of the texts were hopelessly out of date – the physics primer, for instance, omitting over three decades of scientific advances. The books were battered and there were not many of them. The exasperation of a 'quick and avid reader' is clear in an 'animated' address Ken gave to a class reunion:

> Can people at the school today believe that we didn't HAVE a library? … Do you remember that the library was a row of shelves along the side of room 15, and that the books didn't even fill the shelves? Do you remember the two most visibly used items on the shelves? The photographic volume in the Official History of Australia in World War I, and the article in the *Encyclopaedia Britannica* on prostitution, marked by a black line made over the years by grimy fingers. Nowadays I suppose when we look at an encyclopaedia we're likely to pass over the entry on prostitution and pause at the one headed prostrate [sic].[30]

It seems there was only one area in which Ken did not outshine his classmates. As Dick recalls, 'He and I were not particularly good at field sports, at football and cricket.' In the 1940s (and still today), sporting competition was an integral part of school life, with houses led by prefect 'princes' jousting for coveted trophies.[31] Though never likely to be chosen for the School XI in cricket, Dick and Ken found other outlets for their energies:

> We were both long-term members of the school tennis team and played many matches against other state high schools. We also participated in athletic events between the four schoolhouses. One event I recall was called 'Tunnel Ball.' Teams would line up in rows with each boy grasping the boy in front of him and bending down to form a tunnel. On the signal, heavy medicine balls would be propelled between our legs, with [the] last boy bending picking up the ball and [running] to the start, repeating the process until we were back in our original positions.[32]

In a school where academic excellence was (and is)[33] prized alongside athletic prowess, this was deemed a worthy if modest contribution to a vigorous sporting calendar.[34]

In school and out, Dick says, Ken was 'great fun.' Dick remembers their earliest days at Tyler Street, playing marbles and 'Saddle the Nag' across the school playground. Empire and Guy Fawkes nights were cause for riotous celebration. The boys built bonfires from 'old car tyres [and] trailer load[s] of shavings and sawdust from [Ken's father's] timber mill.' And as they grew so too did their adventures. After school they rambled through the wilds of Darebin Creek. On weekends, joined by a gang of varying size, they roamed the streets of Northcote and beyond on ramshackle secondhand bicycles. Saturday afternoons they sometimes set forth to Reservoir. It was quite a distance away, but a theatre there screened a threepenny matinee: 'there was lots of whooping and whistling and cheering very loudly at those serials,' Dick remembers.[35]

In his early days at least, there was little sign Ken would become 'a history buff.' Instead, he read comics, like most boys his age: 'Dick Tracy' and 'The Phantom.'[36] Comics, Dick recalled at Ken's 80th birthday, even prompted young Ken's first unfortunate foray into business.

> An entrepreneur even in the difficult times of the great depression, he established a second-hand, swap or buy shop in his parents' garage, making at the most 1/6 profit over the first six months, for most of his customers simply read the comics they wished to and departed without buying or swapping anything.[37]

Above all, from the early days at Tyler Street, to the day he 'duxed' Northcote High, Dick says Ken was a boy of 'spirit': creative, sometimes rebellious, and always inquisitive. 'We both showed socialistic tendencies which were not necessarily supported by our parents … My memory is not entirely clear on this, but we both tried to join the Eureka Youth League.' Ken was never one to toe the party line and this brief flirtation with the comrades ended badly. 'When they discovered Ken's father was a manager of a timber mill, and my father was the secretary of an ink manufacturing company, they wouldn't let us join … Class enemies!'

For all its stress on tradition and service, Northcote High encouraged boys like Ken and Dick to think for themselves. Contrary to Ferrier's jaundiced impressions, it encouraged questioning, curious minds – the practised scepticism that became the hallmark of Inglis scholarship. Ken, like E.P. Thompson, came to view history as 'a discipline of attentive disbelief.'[38] Dick describes his friend as 'a seeker and a doubter,' one slow to judge, but keen to 'observe everything.' Ken also 'did a lot of poking his tongue out at authority.'[39] Sometimes, perhaps, literally. Among Dick's treasured possessions is a group photograph of Ken, himself and three other boys taken in 1936. Most are wearing ties, and smiling warmly and broadly at the camera. Ken, by contrast, looks the other way, over his mate Wally's shoulder, mouth wide open, tongue protruding. His mother – always more a friend to Ken than a figure of authority – took the photo regardless.[40]

That restless intellect and rebellious spirit meant Ken sometimes fell foul of the authorities. Recollections of his first extended visit back to the school confirm even 'a good lad' had his lapses:

> Though the headmaster's office looks much the same as it did more than forty years ago, it _feels_ different. Is it just because my memories are of being sent to it in disgrace for some offence provoked by boredom, or by the urge of an unathletic adolescent to show off some physical activity, like hurling a compass from the back of the room and trying to make it stick in the blackboard? (Badly timed: the terrible deputy headmaster came in just as I threw, and marched me off to the office, where the harassed, arthritic and on the whole kindly old boss magnified my crime by mishearing it: 'You threw your compass at a boy!' 'No, sir. I …' But his appalled words hung in the air). No, the office _has_ changed. A lad saunters in and asks Mr Nelson to give him the money for lunch. 'Make sure you give it back tomorrow, Philip,' says the headmaster. I don't know which surprises an old boy more, the transaction itself or use of the Christian name.[41]

In what other ways did schooling offer an historian's apprenticeship? Ken's 'wonderfully wide vocabulary and skill at putting words together' led to the writing of newsletters and, so Dick thinks, a founding role in _Ripples_. Though Ken would move to Melbourne High before the NHS magazine was properly established, early editions have an Inglis ring. _Ripples_ was a reference to the various school houses – Darebin, Diamond, Merri and Plenty, all tributaries of the

Yarra. Currents joined them together but they also 'connected with a mysterious past,' the paper's first issue proclaimed, and with a rich and complex Aboriginal cosmology.[42] Few school boys thought like that in 1945. Ken would have been acutely aware that rivers were a corridor along which Aboriginal people traded and travelled, a conduit for community.[43] 'This,' the school history acknowledges, 'was a rather progressive commentary given that historically the "white-man" was regarded as "superior" and there was great emphasis on Australia as part of the British Empire.'[44] It is tempting to suggest *Ripples* signalled the course of future Inglis scholarship, an early essay, perhaps, in the work of 'one of Australia's most creative, versatile and influential historians.'[45] Dick puts it perfectly: from early youth to his final days, Ken was both insightful and 'compassionate.'[46]

And even at NHS war loomed large in the future historian's interests. How could it not? '[The war] ruled our lives at school,' Ken told a reunion of classmates, 'and am I right in remembering that we all expected to be in it as soon as we turned 18?'

> Remember the slit trenches and the air raid alarms; the searchlight company at the back of Merri Park; war saving certificates; making wooden trains and hobbyhorses … to be sold at the comforts fund shop in High Street. Do you remember the stringy and nervous kid named Harris who joined us in 1942 after his family had just managed to escape from Rabaul? The anthems of all the Allies at assembly? We sang 'God save the King' and 'Advance Australia Fair' AND 'The Star Spangled Banner,' AND 'The Marseillaise' – in French – and 'The Internationale.' Am I right in remembering that we sang them ALL at every assembly? How was there time for anything else?[47]

That evocative, inquiring tone will be familiar to Inglis readers, the slightly self-effacing way he shared a stream of thought and gently coaxed his audience. The war was not just colourful backdrop in their school days, Ken explained. It made their attendance at school both possible and imperative.

> [We] were the largest Leaving class – 80 strong – in the history of the school. Wartime prosperity enabled more families to let their sons stay on, and there was another reason reported by the headmaster to the advisory council. The minutes record Mr Bishop saying: 'Boys are being kept longer at school to avoid the direction of the manpower to positions not desired by parents.' If you left after form 4 at the end of 1943, you might be manpowered – remember that verb? – into a munitions factory or a canner, and that was not what you'd been sent to Northcote High for.[48]

The war, Ken continued, ruled their lives 'at home' as much as it did at school. And, like the impressions marshalled above, responses to the conflict changed over time and across a vast emotional spectrum. Ken remembered the evening of 1 September 1939 vividly – Hitler's wilful aggression spoiled a night of carefree fun at the pictures.

> [My mother had taken me] to the Planet Theatre, Preston, to see Jeanette MacDonald and Nelson Eddy as *Sweethearts*. The screen was filled with the lovers' technicolour singing faces when a handwritten message slid under them, saying the German forces had entered Poland.[49]

John Ball, another classroom contemporary, evoked a far more traumatic memory. After a day at Northcote High, he was selling newspapers in the city.

> It was pretty graphic. Right across the front page was the headline 'Nazi bombs on Poland' and that was what I was yelling out … I sold a lot of papers. I think I even sold out.[50]

As the initial shock subsided, Preston, like the rest of the country, mobilised for the war effort. Ken recalled rationing ('Rubber was so scarce you [slipped] canvas sleeves under bare parts of [a bicycle] tyre to prolong its life'), patriotic bands (he belted out martial tunes on a drum), and scavenging scrap to support the war effort[51]: 'Our men are fighting for you,' the newsletter in Ken's first year at NHS declared, 'We MUST feed the guns.' Boxes were provided 'for the purpose of receiving floor-polish tins, flat tins, tin foil, paint and tooth paste tubes.'[52] Apparently these stood not far from 'the steel shells of World War 1 mines' that served as the school's rubbish bins.

Ken himself was keen to 'do his bit,' and spent much of his spare time 'swotting' up on the silhouettes of enemy aircraft. 'I don't remember what I planned to do if I was the first observer in Melbourne to spot a ... Zero,' he confessed over 40 years later; 'Aim the pea rifle at it? Grab twopence and rush to the nearest public telephone? All I know is that it was wonderful to have my passion for aeroplanes turned from a hobby into war work.' And war rekindled that frustrated career as a would-be entrepreneur.

> My seven-year-old sister Shirley and I put on a concert, charging the neighbours a penny for admission to the garage, where I did recitations and magic tricks, and Shirley, got up to imitate a Hollywood cigarette girl, sold bags of lollies retailed from GJ Coles and flowers picked from our garden. We carried more than six shillings in pennies and halfpennies to the home of the nearest municipal councillor and saw our efforts acknowledged ... in the *Preston Post*.

Ken was soon writing patriotic verse for the very same local paper:

> The yellow hordes drove southward,
> Toward the fortress strong,
> At least we thought that it was so –
> But sadly, we were wrong.[53]

It was published, he later recalled, with a note that the author was twelve.

Around the same time, brown-outs plunged Melbourne into darkness, the boys of NHS were detailed to dig slit trenches, and families constructed bomb shelters in back yards.[54] 'Ours,' Ken proudly recalled, 'was a beauty, built by Dad and his father, Pa, and myself… With its protective hump of earth, square wooden tower designed to admit fresh air, and water pump sticking out of the tower, the shelter looked at first like a submarine moored behind the house.'[55] Dick's family never finished theirs; nor was Dick in any hurry to use what 'shelter' the school provided:

> We had drills requiring us to run into those smelly, waterlogged slit trenches dug in what had recently been a rubbish tip, so [Ken and I] privately decided we'd stand a better chance of surviving if we ducked down the Merri Creek and hid there among the many trees and bushes, also the slit trenches were just so obvious.[56]

So obvious – and initially at least – so pointless. The hard work of 'countless lads' over many months cut a long straight trench across Merri Park. 'We were informed it was unsuitable,' a much-aggrieved old boy recalled; '[a] zigzag shape was needed to prevent the machine gunners in aircraft lining up a row of victims.' A 'mechanical excavator' promptly undid their labours.[57]

For all these elaborate precautions, fighting so far away had 'an unreal feel to it.'[58] In the early days in particular, most boys 'regarded the war with a sense of detachment.'

> Although the headmaster announced in school assembly each death of a former scholar, and called for a minute's silence, we had not known any of the fallen [Alan Smith recalled over half a century later]. All that changed as the battle zones moved closer

and we then began to feel part of [it]. This latter feeling was confirmed when Mr A. V. G. James, a large, strong, imposing man, walked into class looking absolutely devastated. He felt that we needed an explanation and told us that he had been informed that his son had been killed over Germany, his second such loss. Looking at him, our attitude [to war] was transformed forever.[59]

Boys realised these were 'troubled' times.[60] Even so, for lads like Ken and his mate Dick the war was still less about fear or privation than fantasy and adventure.

> We seemed so remote. We heard about the possibility of Mr Menzies's Brisbane line, and we thought, 'Oh, Brisbane. That's a long way away… I remember us saying 'if the Japs come down here we'll all go down to the Merri Creek'… we knew exactly where to hide.[61]

The Japs never marched into Preston but the Americans did. In 1942, Melbourne suddenly became 'a garrison town' as GIs and marines 'swung through our streets wearing uniforms which, to Ken's and most Australians' eyes, made every private an officer.' But for Ken and Dick at least, Melbourne's occupation by a military force seemed a largely innocuous affair. Dick relished their first encounter with American largesse. The Yanks seemed rather like schoolboys playing at soldiers.

> [Quite close to the school] an American Ack-ack unit and searchlight unit was set up on [Merri] park, and they were out of bounds to us but we used to ignore that and we would get handouts of chocolates and things from the American soldiers who were scarcely older than us. And in fact, opposite, on the other side of St George's Road, was the wonderful Convent of the Little Sisters of the Poor … These American soldiers – I [can] remember them lying back in these special little chairs with their binoculars surveying the convent hoping to find a bathroom window.[62]

Ken's response to the Americans' arrival was similar.

> One morning in 1942 we noticed military activity at the back of
> the Park, on the edge of Merri Creek, and most of the school raced
> over at lunchtime to find a searchlight, a generator, two tents and
> four soldiers. [The] soldiers enthralled pubescent listeners with
> tales of what they did at night when they were not practising to
> light up Japanese bombers.[63]

By the time the two lads ended their schooling at NHS, the Americans
had moved on and Australia inched towards peacetime normality.
Even so, restrictive regulations remained and a regime of rationing
made the peace a parsimonious one. Fewer men had been killed in this
war than the first but Ken still recalled the names of 40 boys painted
in gold on the honour board, and observing a minute's silence in the
assembly hall for every one of them. For all the optimistic talk surrounding reconstruction, and Ken's own hopes for 'a lasting World
Peace' before the Cold War descended, the shadow of 1939 continued
to linger.[64] In 1946, his old school at Tyler Street in Preston removed its
handsome brass bell and installed an air raid siren to summon children
into class. Few filed to their desks with quite the same urgency with
which they rushed to makeshift shelters.[65]

It is at Tyler Street State School that we decided to end this chapter.
Ken is still remembered there, yet another high achiever in a long and
distinguished lineage of publicly funded education. Ken's last memory
of the school was a service on Armistice Day, held on the playground's
baking asphalt, in yet another silent homage to the Fallen:

> The silence must have lasted only two minutes, but it felt lon-
> ger. We... were standing in the sun, bareheaded, and during
> the silence one child, then another, and another, fell down
> in a faint. By the time the bell rang, more than 30 children
> were lying as if dead, and teachers moved along the ranks like
> ambulance men.[66]

But a blazing sun was not the only cause of Ken's discomfort. '[My] chest felt naked as I stood beside boys and girls wearing medals and ribbons won in Turkey, France, Belgium and Palestine.' With a grandfather too old to enlist, and a father barely nine when war broke out, Ken was never among 'the honoured few' who yearly renewed remembrance.[67] Involved but detached, 'critical but respectful' with young eyes ever alert to the meaning and power of symbol and ritual, none would prove better qualified to reveal the meanings of Anzac.[68]

Acknowledgements

The authors warmly thank Susan Harrup and Jocelyn Hill (Principal and Assistant Principal of NHS) for their courteous welcome. The same thanks are due to Janet Paterson and Mark Smith (Principal and Assistant Principal of Preston Primary School) or, as Ken's generation knew it, Tyler Street State School, No. 1494. We are especially indebted to Dick Manuell who kindly agreed to be interviewed and generously provided further access to archival material. We also acknowledge our debt to Gary Israel, Ethek Herenson, Robert Bridges and Hector Gallagher, authors of the official NHS history, and Jayne Regan for careful transcription of the Manuell interview and related research assistance. Gary Israel and Kate Challis kindly facilitated access to the NHS archives. Finally, thanks are due to Rosalie Triolo and Frank Bongiorno for their careful reading and comment.

Endnotes

1   These impressions are based on visits to Northcote High School in February and March 2018.

2   RJW Selleck, *Frank Tate: A Biography*, Melbourne University Press, Melbourne, 1982, pp. 237–240; Frank Tate, *Continued Education*, Government Printer, Melbourne, 1920.

3   G Israel et al, *The Green, the Purple and the Gold: A History of Northcote High School*, Northcote High School, Camberwell, 2010, pp. 18–19; K Derkley, 'The Present Depression Has Brought Me Down to Zero,' *Provenance*, no. 7, September 2008. Around 5000 of Northcote's 42,000 residents relied on sustenance payments in 1933. That same year school fees were increased and extended. By 1934, enrolments at year ten had more than halved.

4   Israel et al, *The Green, the Purple and the Gold*, pp. 18–19; for Tate's support for the war effort see Selleck, *Frank Tate*, pp. 210-30. An illuminating study of the role school honour boards played in fostering cultures of remembrance can be found in R Triolo, *Our Schools and the War*, Australian Scholarly Press, Melbourne, 2012, pp. 227-49.

5   F Bongiorno, 'Vale Ken Inglis (1929-2017),' *Recorder*, no. 291, March 2018, p. 5; T Stephens, 'Ken Inglis, Anzac Historian, Foremost a Storyteller,' *Sydney Morning Herald*, 16 January 2018.

6   A Lemon, *The Northcote Side of the River*, Hargreen Publishing Company, North Melbourne, 1983, p. 63; Darebin Libraries, Local History File: Northcote High School.

7   Ken Inglis to Dick Manuell, 10 August 1992, private papers kindly provided by Dick Manuell, NHS, Class of 1945 (henceforth Manuell papers).

8   Israel et al, *The Green, the Purple and the Gold*, pp. 36–37. Co-education was reintroduced (with strong community support) in the 1980s. Israel, pp. 46–8, 224–8.

9   Dick Manuell, email correspondence to Bruce Scates, 2 March 2018.

10   Ken Inglis to Dick Manuell, 19 April 1997, Manuell papers.

11   Manuell interview.

12   Class List, Northcote High School, 1944, Manuell papers.

13   Ken Inglis, 'An Historian Does Research,' typescript, NHS Archives, p. 3.

14   Recollections of Tom Brenner, 8 June 1985, Northcote High School Archives. Religious instruction was not part of the formal syllabus at NHS, but 'some occasional talks [were] provided by Evangelical Protestants at school assemblies,' email correspondence, Dick Manuell to Bruce Scates, 1 March 2018.

15   Inglis, 'An Historian Does Research,' pp. 1-2.

16   Inglis, 'An Historian Does Research,' p. 4.

17   M Nook (1941) entry in 'Nostalgia Nook,' Northcote High School, *Ex-Student and Staff Association Newsletter*, no 20, 2000 (Winter), p. 6.

18   A Smith, 'Six Great Years as a Student at Northcote High School, 1942–47,' typescript, NHS Archives; Max Morris, 'Meliora Sequamur,' *Northcote High School Ex-Students & Staff Association Newsletter*, no. 5, 1995 (Summer), p. 3.

19   Smith, 'Six Great Years'; M Morris, 'Meliora Sequamur,' *Northcote High School Ex-Students & Staff Association Newsletter*, p. 3.

20   N Ferrier, *There Goes Whatsisname: The Memoirs of Noel Ferrier*, Macmillan, South Melbourne, 1985, p. 4.

21   KS Inglis, 'At War,' in Ann Curthoys, AW Martin and Tim Rowse (eds), *Australians from 1939*, Fairfax, Syme and Weldon, Sydney, 1987, pp. 4, 15.

22   Inglis, 'A Historian Does Research,' p. 5.

23   See recollections by Breemer, Smith and Inglis cited above. Rick Oke, Poppa's son, had stood for parliament on a Communist Party ticket. The boys assumed father and son were fellow travellers.

24 Email correspondence, Dick Manuell to Bruce Scates, 1 March 2018.

25 Dick Manuell, interviewed by Rae Frances and Bruce Scates, Sydney, 21 November 2017.

26 Dick Manuell, Sydney, 21 November 2017.

27 Email correspondence, Dick Manuell to Bruce Scates, 2 March 2018.

28 Inglis, 'At War,' p. 17.

29 G Daws, 'The University of Melbourne' and S Macintyre, 'The 1950s: Journalism and the University of Oxford,' papers presented to 'Ken Inglis in History: A Laconic Colloquium,' Monash University, 24 November 2016. See also contributions to this volume.

30 K Inglis, 'Golden Memories – the Class of 1945,' *Northcote High School Ex-Student and Staff Association Newsletter,* no 5, 1995 (Summer), p. 4. For 'quick and avid,' see Manuell interview.

31 Manuell interview. For NHS prefect, sporting and house structures, see Israel et al, *The Green, the Purple and the Gold*, pp 66–7, 70, 91; for the role of sport and school in shaping middle-class masculinity in the early twentieth century, see M Crotty, *Making the Australian Male: Middle-Class Masculinity, 1870–1920,* Melbourne University Press, Melbourne, 2001, pp. 74–94.

32 Email correspondence, Dick Manuell to Bruce Scates, 1 March 2018.

33 Northcote High resists the specialisation of education commonplace elsewhere, its website honouring both 'a long and distinguished reputation as a high performing sports oriented school' and 'a rich tradition of excellence.' www.nhs.vic.edu.au (accessed 5 April 2018). The school fosters a holistic education, the making of a 'well rounded boy' (and girls, since the reintroduction of mixed classes in the 1980s) its principal object.

34 Manuell interview. For an account of such games and the children's culture that attended them see Jan Kociumbas, *Australian Childhood: A History*, Allen and Unwin, St Leonards, 1997.

35 Manuell interview. For an account of the way bicycles opened up public space for the young, see Simon Sleight, *Young People and the Shaping of Public Space in Melbourne*, Ashgate, London, 2013. The rationing on petrol restricted car usage during the war, freeing the streets for children.

36 Manuell interview.

37 Dick Manuell, 'Ken's 80th, Melbourne, August 15, 2009,' typescript in the Manuell papers.

38 EP Thompson, *The Poverty of Theory,* Merlin Press, London, 1978, pp. 220–1.

39 Manuell interview.

40 For Wally Dey's own reflections on childhood and schooling, see Walter L. Dey to Kate [Challis], 21 June 2010.

41 Inglis, 'An Historian Does Research,' p. 1.

42 'Our Houses,' *Ripples,* December 1945, p. 2.

43 For further insights into the role that river systems, and the Yarra in particular, played in Aboriginal communities, see Peter Read's interview in episode seven of the National Museum of Australia's 'Australian Journey' series. For contemporary commentary see WG Smith, *The History of Northcote: From its First Settlement to a City*, Leader Publishing, Northcote, 1928, pp. 1–4, 11, 41.

44 Israel et al, *The Green, the Purple and the Gold*, p. 87.

45 For the appraisal of Inglis's standing in the profession see Graeme Davison, 'Ken Inglis: Threads of Influence,' *History Australia*, vol. 14, issue 4, December 2017, p. 516. For speculation over the origin of *Ripples*, Ken's role and his mastery of words, see Manuell interview. Also Israel et al, *The Green, the Purple and the Gold*, pp. 38, 88–9.

46 Manuell interview.

47 Inglis, 'Golden Memories,' p. 4.

48 *Ibid*. For an appreciation of Inglis's work as a historian see J Winter, 'Introduction: Ken Inglis on Language, Culture and Commemoration' in J Lack (ed), *ANZAC Remembered: Selected Writings by K.S. Inglis*, Department of History, University of Melbourne, Parkville, 1998, pp. 5–8; and contributions to this volume.

49 Inglis, 'Golden Memories,' p. 4, 'At War,' p. 1.

50 D Crofts, 'Educated in the War Years,' *Northcote Leader*, 10 August 1994, clipping kindly provided by Dick Manuell.

51 Inglis, 'At War,' p. 8.

52 'Our School War Effort,' *Spectator*, May 1941.

53 Inglis, 'At War,' p. 8.

54 K Darian-Smith, *On the Home Front: Melbourne in Wartime, 1939–1945*, Oxford University Press, Melbourne, 1990, pp. 20–5; Lemon, *History of Northcote*, pp. 237–9; Manuell interview.

55 Inglis, 'At War,' p. 7.

56 Email correspondence, Dick Manuell to Bruce Scates, 1 March 2018; Michael McKernan, *All In! Fighting the War at Home*, Allen and Unwin, Sydney, 1995, p. 9.

57 Smith, 'Six Great Years.'

58 Manuell interview; for further comment on the remoteness of the conflict in the popular imagination see K Darian-Smith, 'War and Australian Society,' in J Beaumont (ed.), *Australia's War, 1939–1945*, Allen and Unwin, Sydney, 1996, p. 54.

59 Smith, 'Six Great Years.'

60 'Editorial,' *The Spectator*, n.d.

61 Manuell interview.

62 Inglis, 'At War' p 7; Manuell interview.

63 Inglis, 'An Historian Does Research,' p. 4.

64   Inglis, 'At War' p. 18.

65   WO Clark, 'The Tyler Street School Bell,' Preston Primary School newsletter kindly provided by Dick Manuell. For an evocative description of an air raid drill see Vic Myers letter to Kate Challis, 9 October 2013, NHS Archives: '[Children were required to move quickly] to the lawn area, lie face down, biting on a special rubber mouth guard and hands clasped on the back of your head.'

66   Inglis, 'At War,' p. 2.

67   Inglis, 'At War,' pp. 1–2, *Sacred Places: War Memorials in the Australian Landscape*, Melbourne University Press, Melbourne, 1998.

68   Davison, 'Ken Inglis,' p. 518; B. Scates, 'Letters from a Pilgrimage: Reflections on the 1965 Return to Gallipoli,' *History Australia*, Vol. 14, Iss. 2, December 2017, *passim*.

Chapter 3

THEN AND THERE

Ken Inglis at the University of Melbourne

Gavan Daws

Ken is much more of a historian than I am. What he has done in the profession – and for the profession – is way above my pay grade. For me to presume to do a peer review of the academic work of Professor K.S. Inglis, AO, DPhil (Oxon.), FAHA, FASSA, would be, well, presumptuous. But Ken and I have known each other for going on sixty-five years, so at least I can take a first-person look back at him through a long lens – a kind of historical time-lapse photography.

So, to the first shots, the earliest exposures – Ken at the University of Melbourne. He graduated BA in 1949, with first-class honours in history and English. While he was working on his MA, he tutored full-time in history, making £350 per annum, the basic wage; and for room and board he did night work, tutoring in English at Queen's College, where he had lived in his undergraduate years.

I turned up at university in 1951, a boy from the bush on an Education Department studentship, enrolled by an unseen hand in the same degree course that Ken had taken. It was my great good luck to draw him as a history tutor.

He was only four years older than me, but he was a grown-up. I wasn't, not in any way, and intellectually I was no more than larval. I could read books without having to move my lips on the big words, but that was about all. From Ken I learned how to read for meaning. Also how to listen. Sitting stultified in big classes in the Old Arts public lecture theatre, I could register only one difference between lecturers: Dull or Not Dull. I was sorting with shovels. Ken, though, could sieve and sift whatever it was that various senior history academics were saying, coming up with a fine-grained yield, in words that even I could understand. He was a natural teacher.

He took time with me, and not just in tutorials. We had good conversations over dinner at a classy restaurant he liked, One Swanston Street, upstairs from Young & Jackson's, the pub with Chloé on the wall in oils, life-size and bare-bodied. This was my two-in-one introduction to fine dining and fine art, courtesy of Ken. He also introduced me to stylish three-figure-IQ magazine journalism, sea-mailed from the big world, in the *New Yorker* and the *New Statesman*.

As well as being both interesting and educational, he tolerated me in all my ignorant puzzlements about life. This was not in his history department job description. And there was nothing in it for him personally, no prospect of any kind of return on investment. He was just being Ken.

With his help, I began to be able to identify groupings at The Shop (as the university was universally called). There would have been fewer than 10,000 undergraduates, but this was still a big number for small-country-town me to take on and take in. First, two football teams, Blacks and Blues. That was easy enough. Politics was harder – so many teams, playing by such different rules. On the far-left wing, student communists – not numerous, though ASIO repeatedly published frighteners about the insidious threat of 'pink professors.' When Stalin died in 1953, an undergraduate apparatchik, female, burst into the *Farrago* office wielding a 5000-word eulogy in extremely blunt-instrument prose, demanding publication (resisted). On the right wing, opposite the communists, the Liberal Club. (Their prime minister, R.G. Menzies, a University of Melbourne graduate, banned the Peking Opera from Australia.) In between, the Labor Club. (Four undergraduates from exactly my time went on to be federal cabinet ministers, three Labor to one Liberal; and an economics lecturer rose to be a Labor deputy prime minister.) There emerged the Australian Labor Party (Anti-Communist), which morphed into the Democratic Labor Party. DLP was political code for a determined kind of Catholicism. For other kinds of Catholics there was the Newman Club, and there were clubs for Protestants of differing persuasions: the Evangelical Union, the Student Christian Movement.

Ken was in the SCM, but he did not hold rigidly to any kind of strict doctrine, religious or political, sacred or profane. He was a small-l liberal, open-minded.

And low-key with it. There is a French verb, *s'imposer*, to impose oneself, as in making your entrance with your usual flair and taking over the mic (even when there is no mic). This was not Ken's way. He had a gift for the spoken word, but he didn't need to be the loudest voice in the room. And he was quick-witted, with a quiet sense of mischief, but quite without malice aforethought.

I had heard somewhere about the four classical humours, and I thought I could see three of them coexisting, collegially-congenially, in Ken, without jarring mood swings. He was definitely not choleric – short-tempered, irritable. Quiet and sober, yes, classically classified as melancholic. Also relaxed and peaceful, phlegmatic. And sanguine – sociable and easygoing.

To give just one example of his basic good-naturedness: he did not favour the smart parlour game of parsing people as U or non-U, meaning upper class or non–upper class – a kind of amusing pop sociology, British in origin, that grew to be a big 1950s fad. It was good for getting a laugh at someone else's expense. Ken did not go in for that kind of one-upmanship.

Sociological distinctions were indeed observable at The Shop, some of them U/non-U. There were state school kids on Commonwealth scholarships, as against Harris-Tweeded private school boys and cashmere-twin-setted private school girls with family money. There was a hierarchy of private schools. On the boys' side at The Shop, rank was signalled (you could say insisted upon) by the assertive wearing of the old school tie, distinctively striped, with Geelong Grammar the top knot. Private school girls at The Shop went tieless, but there were other markers – differentiating, for instance, St Catherine's, Toorak, from Methodist Ladies' College, Kew. Here is a call-and-response ritual at the end of a school hockey game. MLC captain: 'Three cheers for St Catherine's! Hooray! Hooray! Hooray!' St Catherine's captain: 'Three cheers for MLC, hoorah, hoorah, hoorah.' U in the form of a hockey stick.

As to gender, what used to be called sex: among students, more males than females, and among faculty, many, many more males. There might be women tutors, even lecturers (history had a few from time to time, even an associate professor); but mostly, if you saw a woman in a corridor at The Shop, of workforce age and employably dressed, she would be the department secretary.

Next, ethnicity, what used to be called race. Multiculturalism was not even a word, much less an issue. You could go for days without hearing a European accent. And there was only a two per cent chance of sighting an Asian face. I happened to run across a Chinese medical student by the name of Chin. A young Filipina woman, Minda Feliciano, was a one-of-a-kind tropical orchid; *Farrago* put her on the front page, photo by Helmut Newton. (I don't know if she finished her degree, but years later she was in the London papers for being 'romantically linked' with Michael Caine.) Then there was Ng, where from I didn't know, who went to a first-year orientation camp at the beach and got lost. Search parties fanned out, calling after him, struggling to project his vowelless name into a blustery wind – '*Ng! Ng!*' – in competition with swirling flocks of squawking seagulls – '*Ng! Ng! Ng!*' Ng was found. But what kind of an un-Australian name was that, only two letters and both of them consonants?

More sociological distinctions, these among Shop white faces. City sophisticates, as against country bumpkins like me. Some free-thinkers and free-lovers, though not remotely in the league of the Sydney Push. A closet of homosexuals, with a few out and about. A small cast of theatricals, strutting and fretting their hour upon the Union Theatre stage. And – distinctivissimo – Barry Humphries.

I remember Humphries declaring his candidacy for election to the Student Representative Council. His main campaign event was in the Old Arts public lecture theatre. He drew a crowd, including Ken and me. In between dada-oid manifestations by his acolytes, he spoke of many things, fools and kings – passionately, though in no apparent order and with no perceptible bearing upon student government – and he had flanked himself with electric toasters incinerating slices of white bread and discharging copious smoke. He failed to be elected.

Besides all the different schools of thought and behaviour – and Humphries, who was several schools of his own – there were schools of Shop drinkers, at pubs only one up from bloodhouses, if that. Naughton's was the closest, just across Royal Parade. The bar ambience, if you could pronounce the word, was all-male-all-Australian. At peak hour, a confused roar of competing exaggerations, randomly punctuated by high-decibel expletives. Air thick with cigarette smoke and alcoholic exhalations. Concrete floor, for ease of hosing down expectorations. An SP bookie out by the horse-trough urinal, for your race-day convenience. Plausible blokes offering for sale items that had fallen off the back of a truck, anything from wristwatches to steaks wrapped in old newspaper (the *Sun*, or the *Sporting Globe*, or the *Truth*, never the *Age* – another sociological marker). And once, on a Friday, just before last call, a cognitively dissonant apparition – a squad of Salvos, among them the only women I ever sighted at Naughton's, uniformed anti-Chloés, devotedly-determinedly elbowing through the foul-mouthed scrum, with collection plates a-jingle to lure drunken small change to Jesus.

Coming off the six o'clock swill, the thing to do, especially at the weekend, was to kick on into the night at parties, where the cultural imperative was to get pissed beyond reason, in the process raising the existential question: which would give out first, brain or bladder?

Ken was all for a party beer or a sherry or three, but not to wretched excess – he was never the one wearing the lampshade or peeing on the potted plant. There were plenty of others with show-off tricks. One bloke, a law student big on the SRC, was apt to drop his daks (though only if there were women present – nothing abnormal about him). Another bloke, a redheaded med student, could and would drink a glass of beer standing on his head. His technical medical term for this procedure was 'reverse peristalsis.' (Attempts at replication were self-gendered – women in skirts did not try it.) Another bloke, a history postgraduate of Ken's time, might stage what nowadays would be called, in academic-speak, a performative intervention – tapping his cigarette ash into your beer. That bloke grew up to be Geoffrey Blainey.

Not Ken. I remember a mannerly evening in his company at a better class of gathering, chez a history academic in North Carlton – après-dinner red wine (a naive domestic claret) and Schubert lieder, agreeably rendered by a (private school) mezzo-soprano, with considerate piano accompaniment by a friend of Ken's (school of Gerald *Am I Too Loud?* Moore).

At the common-or-garden-type party, Schubert lieder were not heard, but there were gems from other musical genres, sung a cappella (always by males). Canonical dirty ditties, like 'Good Ship Venus.' More sophisticated, 'The Doctor's Lament,' about the private parts of women, performed (with women present) to the melody of 'When a Felon's Not Engaged in His Employment' from Gilbert and Sullivan's *The Pirates of Penzance*, featuring flawless Gilbertian scansion and polysyllabic rhyming:

> *Doctors of distinction have examined these phenomena*
> *In numbers of experimental dames,*
> *And given to these ornaments of feminine abdomena*
> *A number of delightful Latin names.*
> *There's the vulva, the vagina, and the jolly perineum,*
> *And the hymen in the case of certain brides …*

Also sophisticated, a Shop version of Noël Coward's 'Don't Put Your Daughter on the Stage, Mrs Worthington,' about the perils of university life for susceptible young ladies, at hazard of falling prey to lecherous academics:

> *In tutes she'll sit upon their knees,*
> *And won't know when to stop,*
> *So be sure, Mrs Worthington,*
> *Keep her pure, Mrs Worthington,*
> *Don't send your daughter to The Shop.*

Ken was not that kind of tutor.

The top song for mass male bellowing at parties was Chad Morgan's big hit, 'The Sheik of Scrubby Creek':

> *I've been loved by the poor and the wealthy,*
> *Loved by the good and the bad,*
> *Loved by the fat and the skinny,*
> *Because I'm a lovable lad …*
> *They say I'm just like Casanova,*
> *I drink, I smoke, I swear,*
> *They say I'm the Sheik of Scrubby Creek,*
> *And–I–don't–care.*

With, between verses, eight bars of yelping and yowling, like a pack of degenerate dingoes, rendering the suburban night hideous for blocks around. Which was, of course, part of the party point.

Some years ago, Ken and I were reminiscing about those long-gone Melbourne times. Ken's memory, short-, medium- and long-term, has always been orders of magnitude better than mine – a major social history archive, saved on his high-capacity mental hard drive, with date-stamped files, instantly retrievable. In a split second he could reach back close to seven decades and call up the name of the woman from The Shop who got it on with a touring Marx Brother (and which Brother it was – Chico). Virtuoso stuff, vastly superior to the ordinary run of party tricks. But here's a curiosity: when I referenced the imperishable collective folk memory of the Sheik, with yowling, Ken drew a blank. Unaccountable.

41

The Sheik was all-Australian, absolutely, unregenerately, triumphally, and he was all over the wireless. Countervailingly, there was a lot of colonial cultural cringe in the air. It took many forms. Speaking reverentially of England as 'home.' Looking forward to a royal visit as a visitation all but divine. Elocuting in what was called the King's (and then the Queen's) English, cultured aping of a 'BBC' or 'Oxford' accent. (The reductive real-Australian term of contempt for this affectation was 'plummy' – but even that word was of British origin.) In Shop circles, there was one particular cringe – deference to a Pommy person who presented himself as the original of Lucky Jim from Kingsley Amis's British-university-based social-comedy novel, which had a cult following. This Pommy person was beyond reasonable doubt a fake, but his bald and unconvincing narrative was enough to keep credulous Melbourne colonials inviting him to dinner. He ate off them.

Even if he had been the real thing, real Australians, meaning of the Sheik persuasion, would not have given him the time of day. For them, England was nothing but 'bloody abroad.'

On the map of history courses at The Shop, though, Britain stood out, the only place in the world strongly coloured in. There were spatters and speckles of various shades on a few other Western European countries. Australia had a growing number of patches, but next to nothing in black. Eastern Europe, Russia, the Near and Middle East, Asia, Africa and Latin America were effectively blank.

What about the United States? In the real world, the Second World War in the Pacific was recent, the Korean War was in the immediate present, and the Cold War was ongoing. All of these were dominated by the United States. But in history at The Shop, the United States was seriously under-represented. And among the general run of Shop students, America was not really real; it was mostly in the movies and on the hit parade – with a select audience for LP cast recordings of Broadway musicals. (Ken's all-time number-one musical was *Kiss Me, Kate* by Cole Porter, from Shakespeare's *The Taming of the Shrew*. I was more for Frank Loesser's *Guys and Dolls*, from Damon Runyon's stories of low-life New York.)

Later, there was an even more discriminating audience for Tom Lehrer and his intelligently funny songs at the piano. Ken and I were big fans, and when Lehrer toured Australia, Ken wrote a concert review for *Nation*. (Ken did not include it in his bibliography, but Lehrer carried the clipping in his wallet for years – his offer of proof, so he Lehrerianly said, that his following was worldwide.)

Lehrer, who graduated from Harvard at eighteen, had an irresistible pièce de résistance, 'The Periodic Table, or The Elements Song,' to the melody of 'The Major-General's Song' from *The Pirates of Penzance*:

> *There's antimony, arsenic, aluminum, selenium,*
> *And hydrogen and oxygen and nitrogen and rhenium,*
> *And nickel, neodymium, neptunium, germanium,*
> *And iron, americium, ruthenium, uranium …*

Ninety-plus elements in under ninety seconds, at more than 200 beats per minute, *prestissimo*, with a scrupulously scholarly endnote, *largo rallentando*:

> *These are the only ones of which the news has come to Har-vahd,*
> *And there may be many others but they haven't been discah-vahd.*

Around The Shop generally, Harvard would have been the only recognised name in American higher education (with Yale perhaps a long-odds possibility). I have a memory of some postgraduates sitting in the Union caff, sniggering over their stewed tea at the very notion of a 'University' of Chicago. What conceivably could be taught there – the theory and practice of gangs, school of Al Capone?

For doctoral study in history, Oxford and Cambridge were the magnetic poles. Ken got a scholarship to Oxford, and he did his DPhil on a topic in British church history.

He did not stay in British history, or in England. Dr K.S. Inglis came home to Australia the same Ken who had gone away, cringe-free and with his vowel sounds unplummified – but now able, as he said, to look at 'the actual and figurative landscape of my country with eyes freshened by absence.'

'My country.' Ken is a very Australian historian. In his long and productive academic life, he has spent stretches of time at a range of universities in different parts of the world: in Australia, Melbourne, Adelaide, the Australian National University, Monash; elsewhere, Papua New Guinea, Oxford, Cambridge, Cork, Harvard, Brown, Hawaii. All along the way, he has devoted himself to understanding and explicating his own country, its institutions, and its people, their preoccupations, their ways of expressing themselves socially.

He played a major part in conceptualising and managing the huge project of an Australian bicentennial history – ten years in the making, 500 contributors. His own single-handed books and articles are interestingly conceived, carefully thought through, well structured. And extremely well written, 'plain style' in the best sense. Ken writes to be read, and he is very much worth reading. His is a distinguished body of work.

Being an academic has suited him. In his words, the profession gave him more freedom than any other occupation he could see himself in. As a journalist, he would have been edited, column inch by column inch, day after day. As a schoolteacher, he would have been constricted by a bureaucratically imposed curriculum. But as an academic, in a small-l liberal democracy, he has been as free in his thinking and teaching and writing as anyone could ever expect to be – and this on an adequate salary, with superannuated security.

So Ken's professional life has been very satisfying to him personally, as well as very valuable to his country. Some years ago, he said he couldn't think of anyone he knew who would have been happier and more fulfilled in their work. I will drink to that.

In the academic world, it is a real bonus when an excellent professor of humanities is also a good human being. Ken is both, and I am one among many to have benefited greatly from his freely offered goodwill. He wrote me two letters of reference – the first in 1958, for an entry-level graduate assistantship at the University of Hawaii, with the possibility of a future path to tenure, the second in 1974, for a professor-and-head-of-departmentship in the Research School of Pacific Studies at the Australian National University. I got both jobs, and each turned out to be good for fifteen years. So I owe Ken for thirty years of interesting, gainful employment, in two hemispheres. And Ken being Ken, he has never called in the debt.

That is Ken, Ken to the life, all the way from the University of Melbourne. That was then and there. In the here and now, as I write, he continues to be Ken, observing Australia – and he lives once again in Melbourne, on Rathdowne Street in Carlton, less than a mile from the Old Arts Building.

Chapter 4

GOING DOWN FROM MELBOURNE

Oxford, scholarship and journalism

Stuart Macintyre

Especially in his later life, Ken Inglis pondered how it was that he found his way from Tyler Street State School to an academic career. The question was at the back of his mind as he exchanged emails with contemporaries, followed the suburb's changing fortunes and recalled formative moments in his childhood. One such moment occurred in 1937 when the teacher of fourth grade carefully wrote the word 'noun' on the blackboard and then explained its grammatical function. Some days later Miss Kinnane followed that revelation with another, equally arresting – 'verb.'[1]

Ken had a preference for nouns and verbs, though he was no slouch with adjectives and adverbs, and appreciated the effects that could be achieved by variations of structure and rhythm. An early influence was George Orwell, whom he discovered through the 1945 essay 'Notes on Nationalism.' The rules of composition that Orwell laid down in the following year in an essay on 'Politics and the English Language' were already apparent in Ken's writing: never use a stale figure of speech; never employ the passive when the active is available; never use an unnecessary word, or a long one when a short one will do, or jargon when there is an everyday English equivalent. Orwell added a sixth rule – to break any of the above rather than say or write anything outright barbarous – though it is hard to find instances of that escape clause in Ken's prose.[2]

He grew up in a house with books and was an avid reader of the press from boyhood. Another writer who influenced him was the American journalist A.J. Liebling, whose contributions to the *New Yorker* spanned politics and popular culture, and who also wrote a pungent monthly survey of the American press. Ken later sent a copy of his book *The Stuart Case* to Liebling in homage and was delighted to receive an acknowledgement.

Ken's interest in journalism was established when he transferred from Northcote High School to Melbourne High in 1945 so that he could progress from his Leaving certificate to the new qualification of Matriculation; it was in his second year of Matriculation studies in 1946 that he resurrected the school newspaper, the *Sentinel*. Already fascinated by broadcasting, he also worked after school on the radio program *Junior 3AW*. Towards the end of the year his father arranged an interview with the editor of the *Age*. Harold Alfred Maurice Campbell – generally known as 'Ham,' though he became Sir Harold in 1957 – was a courteous and kindly man, yet unfamiliar with the *Sentinel*. 'Oh, we all do that,' he said when Ken referred to his editorship, clearly thinking it was another of those school magazines that record deeds in the classroom and triumphs on the sporting field. The sixteen-year-old was too shy to explain that his was a fortnightly publication of much greater substance and purpose. In any event, Campbell said that it was not a good time to be embarking on a newspaper career when so many able reporters were returning from war service; he led Ken to understand that distinguished military correspondents were reduced to emptying wastepaper baskets. So the youthful aspirant's hopes were dashed. 'If the *Age* had taken me on as a journalist in 1946,' he subsequently stated, 'I'd have gone there.'[3]

By this time there was another possibility. Northcote High did not teach history beyond the first few years, but at Melbourne High he was able to pursue a rich variety of history subjects as well as literature and French. Too young to go to university, he did a second year of Matriculation, this time winning a general exhibition and sharing first place in the state for English literature. A friend who accompanied him from Northcote to Melbourne High had meanwhile commenced an arts degree as a resident of Queen's College. Ken visited him there in 1946 and was persuaded to sit for a resident scholarship. Having secured one, he embarked in 1947 on an honours degree in history and English, and found his vocation. As he recalled nearly fifty years later in a retirement address, 'From almost the moment I arrived at the university, I knew *that* was where I wanted to spend my working life.'[4]

Gavan Daws's contribution to this volume attests to Ken's presence in student life and the lasting impression of his intellectual distinction. Having obtained a first in his combined honours degree in 1949, Ken became a temporary tutor in history in 1950, senior tutor in 1951, assistant lecturer in 1952, and in 1953 was appointed to a tenured lectureship. Meanwhile he took over a history of the Royal Melbourne Hospital from Max Crawford in 1952 and submitted it as an MA thesis in the following year as he began doctoral studies at Oxford.

While an undergraduate and for two years after graduation he was a resident of Queen's College, the third of the men's residential colleges attached to the university and at that time probably the most lively. Contemporaries included Geoffrey Blainey, Herb Feith, Sam Goldberg, Murray Groves and Arthur Huck; the economists Max Corden and Murray Kemp; and the legendary George Nadel, a *Dunera* boy of boundless ambition whose silhouette was always visible through the curtain of his study window, working at his desk, until someone discovered he had imitated Sherlock Holmes and rigged up a dummy. Beyond College Crescent, Ken was involved in the university film society, theatre and music but not politics until 1949, when he helped form the ALP Club as an alternative to the communist-dominated Labor Club.[5] This coincided with his joining the Student Christian Movement (SCM) after his boyhood Presbyterianism had lapsed. It was here that he met Judy Betheras, a philosophy student. They married in 1952 and had their first child shortly before leaving for Oxford.

Ken's religious interests informed both his doctoral research and his subsequent understanding of Anzac remembrance. They also stimulated some of his first public statements of what he believed. He was attracted to the SCM, I think, because of the way it bridged faith and reason. Arthur Burns, that gifted but wayward ordained academic who returned from England to the history department in 1949, introduced him to the new theology with its rigorous reading of the scriptures and commitment to public engagement. 'I am a democratic socialist and a Christian,' Ken told an SCM conference, and said that he shared communists' anger at the economic organisation of capitalist society but could not subordinate his conscience to 'the God of the party.'[6]

The Cold War had brought the world perilously close to destruction and it was the zealotry of both camps that created the danger. In a series of articles written for the Victorian branch of the Institute of International Affairs, Ken refuted the polarised claims of the combatants in the Korean War and other flashpoints in the region.[7] 'We live in a secular age,' he preached in the Queen's College chapel in 1950, an age that saw the forms and adherents of Christianity falling away. Ken's was a form of Protestantism that affirmed the personal conscience of the believer, 'the voice of God' finding expression through the individual bearing witness in public endeavours.[8]

He was also involved in student journalism. We find him in the pages of *Farrago* reviewing the 1949 *Melbourne University Magazine*, edited that year by Max Corden and Henry Mayer, who were destined for distinguished careers in economics and political science. They were a mettlesome combination – Max said that at one point he challenged Henry to a duel – and Ken observed that their arguments could have been resolved by both turning their weapons on the cover designer.[9] When he and Murray Groves became editors of the 1950 edition they immediately approached William Ellis Green, better known as WEG, the chief cartoonist for the Melbourne *Herald*, to provide a more arresting cover. The 1950 *Melbourne University Magazine* was redesigned in a smaller format based on the lively British pocket monthly *Lilliput*, and the editors sought contributions that displayed 'passion and a point of view.' 'Hack-work,' they warned, was 'unacceptable.' It was here that A.D. Hope's *Dunciad Minor* had its first outing.[10]

One of Ken's early contributions to the *Age* was aimed at the hack-work that appeared in its Saturday literary section. Assuming the identity of the Reverend T.J. Ransome, he submitted a lengthy essay on 'The Fascinating Bee,' strewn with bogus literary allusions and sonorous analogies. 'Poets have sung of it, and philosophers seeking to discover the elusive truths which, if found and believed, would enable men to live in concord, have been drawn to study and wonder at the harmony of the hive.' Ken's sister, Shirley Lindenbaum, writes in more detail of this ingenious hoax elsewhere in this volume. It appeared with a photograph of busy bees, and Ken worried when he became a regular contributor to the newspaper that someone would say, 'I see you've fooled them again.'[11]

The first of his *Age* pieces that I've been able to find (not all are identified) was a review of two recent productions of Elizabethan plays in 1949, and he continued to write on literary and historical publications. But as early as 1950 there was a striking discussion of the English comedian Tommy Handley, who had died in the previous year. Handley's weekly radio program, *It's That Man Again*, was recalled for its 'verbal cartooning' of wartime sacrifice and postwar austerity, 'conjuring up a crazy world in which his listeners could forget their worries for a half-hour.' Ken drew attention to the distinctiveness of Handley's humour, noting that he did not rely on a stooge, as American comedians such as Bob Hope and Jack Benny did. 'It was a craziness,' he observed, 'made possible by the medium of broadcasting.'[12]

He contributed also to a short-lived quarterly, the *Port Phillip Gazette*, modelled on the *New Yorker*. An early piece for its equivalent of 'The Talk of the Town' related a pipe-smoking contest at the Town Hall where a field of twelve each loaded 3.3 grams of tobacco (weighed out by the city council's weights and measures department) and were given two matches to light up. At ninety-four minutes and thirty-five seconds (measured by technicians from the Chronological Guild of Australasia), the record held by a native of Schenectady in New York, which was the headquarters of the International Pipe-Smoking Fellowship, fell and a veteran pipeman, Bill Branfield, finally stopped puffing after 107 minutes and nine seconds. Ken's deadpan report concludes that it might have been as well to have the weather bureau people present to check the humidity in case Schenectady ruled that local conditions gave too much assistance – and I concluded that this must be another hoax until Trove provided newspaper reports of the event. The *Age*'s reporter asked the winner if he was concerned by the British Medical Association's recent warning against smoking, to which Bill Branfield replied, 'BMA, never heard of 'em.'[13]

It was probably inevitable that Ken would go to Oxford, as so many Melbourne historians did. By my count, eighteen of them were there in the postwar decade, against three who pursued postgraduate studies in London, three in Cambridge, one at Columbia, one at Smith College and one at Harvard. It is noticeable also that three of the five women, Dorothy Crozier, Pat Gray and Dorothy Munro (Shineberg), went elsewhere to train in anthropology, sociology and Pacific history. The men followed a well-beaten disciplinary track, whereas the women felt it necessary, or perhaps desirable, to be more adventurous.

'No Melbourne person, particularly a history graduate, need feel a stranger in Oxford,' Owen Parnaby wrote in 1950 after Hugh Stretton, Laurie Baragwanath and Sam Goldberg welcomed him and his partner Joy upon arrival, and soon John Legge and Frank Crowley called on them. The Australian colony at Oxford sent back intelligence on college admission practices and expenses to guide those who were to follow; Max Crawford provided the references, helped secure the scholarships and on several occasions obtained additional money for those who needed it. When he noted at a departmental farewell to the 1951 contingent that John Mulvaney was headed for an archaeology degree at Cambridge, he added, 'We have nothing against Cambridge, it is just that we don't know it.'[14]

There was a joke among the Melbourne graduates who taught in the history department and undertook a local master's thesis while preparing for their time abroad: 'Which aspect of the Australian labour movement are you going to write your MA on?' The expectation attests to the progressive sympathies of staff and students, many of whom cut their political teeth in the Labor Party, if not the Labor Club. Ken expected to do the same but was happy to take up the hospital history, for he was interested in the way Australians had adapted social policies and institutions to their circumstances.[15]

In formulating his doctoral research project he was strongly influenced by Alan McBriar, who returned from Oxford at the end of 1948 after completing a DPhil thesis on Fabian socialism. A gentle and witty man with a memorably distinctive laugh, McBriar had abandoned his wartime membership of the Communist Party (when he had recruited Amirah Gust – later Amirah Inglis – even though her parents were party members) but remained 'wistful' about the Marxist legacy. Ken tutored for Alan and gave his first few lectures under his sponsorship.[16] On Alan's advice Ken wrote in 1952 to his former supervisor, G.D.H. Cole, asking for guidance on a suitable topic among the social movements of the late nineteenth century. He had the Socialist League in mind, but Cole advised him that a man called E.P. Thompson was working on that and suggested he might instead consider the arguments between socialists and the philanthropic organisations, or perhaps the endeavours of the Labour Churches and other ethical movements of the period. This combination of socialism and religion sparked an interest, and soon Ken settled on a study of 'religion and the social question, c.1880–1900.'[17]

Admission to Oxford was through a college and Ken chose University College, which made few demands on its postgraduates, since he was a married man with a baby and would live in rented accommodation in Summertown. Initially he and Judy had the company of his sister Shirley, who interrupted her Melbourne degree in English for fifteen months abroad, first as a governess in Paris, then as a waitress at the

Lyons buffet at Wimbledon for the tennis, and finally working in Oxford (she borrowed Ken's gown to sneak into lectures).[18] His friends Jamie Mackie and Kit McMahon were pursuing undergraduate degrees as college residents and were more fully exposed to college life. Ken, who hated exams, thought they were the heroes. Judy chose the examination path, though, for a postgraduate diploma in anthropology – the course that Murray Groves had taken and Shirley Inglis would follow. The Inglises were supported by a scholarship Ken had obtained from the Australian National University, which during its early years sent Australians from across the country abroad to obtain higher degrees. The catch was that the scholarship lasted just two years.

At least initially, he found Cole a satisfactory supervisor. In an early letter back to Crawford, he said Cole knew 'an enormous amount about the subject' and professed great interest in it. That favourable impression did not last. Cole was in his mid-sixties and in poor health. He came up from his London residence for just a few days each week during term, and was always busy. When Ken gave him a draft chapter, he would return it promptly but with little comment on its substance. Most worryingly, Cole failed to see what Ken was trying to do, for he was an old-fashioned institutional historian with little interest in a social history of religion.[19]

Ken was enrolled in the faculty of divinity rather than modern history (for his topic was deemed too modern to be history) and no seminars were given in modern history except for one on imperial history, which did not interest him. He found his stimulus among other doctoral students at a cafe near the Bodleian Library. Over grey coffee and Woodbines they would compare their supervisors. An American remarked of Cole's minimal assistance that 'Ya put in a nickel and he plays.' Chushichi Tsuzuki spoke warmly of the assistance he received from his supervisor (and mine at Cambridge) Henry Pelling, and Henry would take a keen interest in Ken's work. Peter Cominos, another American, gave glowing praise to Asa Briggs, the unstuffy, energetic and pioneering young reader in recent social and economic history. Ken had read Briggs's short sketch *1851*, published by the Historical Association in 1951 and foreshadowing his 1954 re-evaluation of *Victorian People*. Through Cominos, Briggs invited Ken to drop in and discuss his research. 'He saw at once what I was trying to do.'[20]

The principal outlet for Ken's journalism during this period was the Sydney-based magazine *Voice*. It began at the end of 1951 as *AIM*, the *Australian Independent Monthly*, an anti-communist, social democratic forum aligned with the Fabian Society and Workers' Educational Association, which attracted contributions from Heinz Arndt, Macmahon Ball, John Burton, Sol Encel, Peter Russo and a young Don Dunstan. Ken's first recorded contribution came in 1954 after he, Murray Groves and Kit McMahon attended a conference in Brighton organised by the Quakers, where the successor of the jailed Jomo Kenyatta defended the nationalist uprising in Kenya. It was a sympathetic but measured report of the violent insurgency.[21]

That was followed by an equally sympathetic but more stringent review of a book by Adlai Stevenson on world affairs, in which Ken drew attention to the way that 'Mr Stevenson's language' went 'foggy' when the politician prevailed over the egghead. A subsequent account of Moral Re-Armament made the same point: 'Ideology is MRA's favourite word. It is modern, versatile, and sounds solid. Again and again it is used to introduce a string of commodious nouns and adjectives' that remained airy and rhetorical generalities. Finally, in 1956 he wrote a 'London letter' on the displeasure of Geoffrey Fisher, the

Archbishop of Canterbury, with the anti-apartheid activities of Father Trevor Huddleston in South Africa, contrasting the 'diplomacy of Dr Fisher' with the decline of his church's membership.[22]

I say finally because a London letter had appeared in *Voice* in September 1953, just as Ken arrived in England. It discussed the division in the British Labour Party between the Bevanites and the 'powerful trade union bosses,' and was followed two months later by a discussion of the BBC.[23] The author of these and subsequent London letters was 'Preston,' a pseudonym that someone who went to Tyler Street State School in north Preston might have adopted. 'Preston' first appeared three months before Ken left Australia, writing on what was likely to happen to Sir Keith Murdoch's newspaper empire following his death at the end of 1952, when Rupert was studying in Oxford (it was his tutor, Asa Briggs, who broke the news to him).[24] Then, in 1954, 'Preston' wrote a feature article on the implications for the *Argus* newspaper of a change in the management of its British proprietors.[25] The correlation of interests between Ken and 'Preston' is marked.

By 1954 Ken's friend Kit McMahon had taken over the London letter and soon Jamie Mackie would begin writing a regular column on 'The Asian Scene.' From January 1955 'Preston' reappeared, this time as the author of reports on 'The European Scene'; indeed, he was identified as 'our correspondent in Europe.' We know from a letter Ken wrote to Max Crawford that he had travelled in Europe during 1955, 'buzzing around France and Italy on a motor scooter.' 'Preston' discussed French politics at length, but in subsequent reports he referred to time spent in Germany and Yugoslavia.[26] This seems to stretch the resemblance too far – and I learned when speculating on the identity of this peripatetic 'Preston' that he was, and always had been, Max Corden. Max worked for the *Argus* after completing his Melbourne degree and then proceeded to doctoral studies at the London School of Economics.[27]

Ken did not intend to become a British historian. Rather, as many other Australians did, he thought of his research as a preparation for writing about Australia. He had no desire to stay on in England and recoiled from its class-bound distinctions – 'If you did stay you would have your children talking like toffs or cockneys.'[28] A fellowship at Nuffield College after his ANU stipend ran out was more congenial, and he taught extension classes in Kent and Gloucestershire, but he was not going to stay. In May 1955 he submitted an application for a newly established chair at Melbourne, at the insistence of colleagues there. Even after Kathleen Fitzpatrick decided not to seek it, there was little chance with John La Nauze and Manning Clark in the field; but almost immediately Hugh Stretton sent him a copy of the advertisement of a senior lectureship at Adelaide. Soon it was agreed that he would take up that appointment in the first half of 1956.[29]

His thesis title had by this time become 'English Churches and the Working Classes 1880–1890, with an Introductory Survey of Tendencies Earlier in the Century' and had grown to more than 150,000 words, for one advantage of enrolment in the faculty of divinity is that it set no word limit. Cole had little to suggest on the final draft but did invite Ken to suggest who should examine it; hence his viva with Asa Briggs and R.H. Tawney in May 1956. Cole apologised for not seeing Ken before he departed but thought he should succeed in finding a publisher; Asa Briggs was more practical and passed a revised version of the thesis to Harold Perkin, then a young lecturer at Manchester University who was assembling a series of studies in social history for Routledge and Kegan Paul. Perkin was greatly impressed but wanted a book that would take in 'the sweep of the Victorian age,' so Ken rebuilt the study to open with a survey of the failure of the churches to reach the working classes and then an examination of their efforts between 1850 and 1900. Interruptions and other tasks such as *The Stuart Case* delayed completion until 1962; 'the trouble with contemporary history is that it goes on happening,' he remarked when apologising for a further delay. But Perkin was a patient and sympathetic editor, his series impressive and influential.[30]

During their time at Oxford, Ken and Judy expected to return to Melbourne, where they owned their home and he had a tenured lectureship. 'I'm still not used to the idea of not coming back to Melbourne,' he wrote to Crawford in July 1955. Crawford assured him that 'people should not be dissuaded from moving to other places, rather the reverse.' In moving on, Ken told Crawford of what he had taken from Melbourne – and I read his tribute as something more than filial respect, for it carries with it an implicit criticism of what he had missed while in Oxford. 'One of the things I've seen more clearly for being away from Australia,' he wrote, 'is that an education as good as we were given is very rare. We knew we were in a very good history school, but we (or at any rate I) didn't realise how rare its virtues were.' He named three of them, and all read oddly in the current lexicon of higher education: first, 'to have such an emphasis on shortish periods and primary sources'; second, 'to have such close relations between teachers and students'; and third, 'to make its students worry about why they are studying history.'[31] Ken went down from Melbourne but he carried those virtues with him.

Endnotes

1 'Ken Inglis Interviewed by Edgar Waters,' 16 October 2006, ORAL TRC 5718, National Library of Australia.

2 George Orwell's 'Politics and the English Language' first appeared in the British magazine *Horizon* in April 1946.

3 'Ken Inglis Interviewed by Neville Meaney,' 1986, ORAL TRC 2053/11, National Library of Australia; and his paper on 'Editors' given at an RMIT conference on journalism, 26 November 2004, Papers of Ken Inglis, MS 10165, Box 17, National Library of Australia.

4 KS Inglis, retirement dinner speech, 2 December 1994, Australian National University, Papers of Ken Inglis, Box 12, Folder 'Retirement,' National Library of Australia.

5 Manning Clark recalls Ken as a 'middle-of-the-road man' who 'had the strength to hold the middle ground without giving offence to the would-be engineers of the human soul': M Clark, *The Quest for Grace*, Viking, Melbourne, 1990, p. 171.

6 KS Inglis, 'God, Creed or Chaos,' paper for SCM conference, 13 August 1951, Papers of Ken Inglis, Box 12, National Library of Australia. Noted by Renate Howe: R Howe, *A Century of Influence: The Australian Student Christian Movement 1896–1996*, UNSW Press, Sydney, 2009, p. 270.

7 'And Another from Mr Inglis,' *Farrago*, 12 July 1950; KS Inglis, 'Korea Since 1945,' *Australia's Neighbours*, no. 3, September 1950, pp. 1–4; KS Inglis, 'Stalemate in Korea,' *Australia's Neighbours*, no. 17, February 1952, pp. 2–4; Papers of Ken Inglis, Box 15, Folder 'Korean War 1950–1952,' National Library of Australia.

8 KS Inglis, sermon, 17 September 1950, Queen's College, Melbourne, Papers of Ken Inglis, Box 12, National Library of Australia; Inglis, 'God, Creed or Chaos.'

9 'M.U.M. On Sale Next Week,' *Farrago*, 3 August 1949.

10 Murray Groves and Ken Inglis to W.E. Green, 15 March 1950; 'Circular,' 3 February 1950, Papers of Ken Inglis, Box 12, Folder 'MUM 1950,' National Library of Australia.

11 TJR [KS Inglis], 'The Fascinating Bee: Inspirer of Poets and Philosophers,' *Age*, 28 July 1951, p. 7.

12 KSI, 'Elizabethan Playwrights,' *Age*, 16 July 1949; KSI, 'A Morale Builder: Tommy Handley and ITMA,' *Age*, 4 February 1950, p. 8.

13 *Port Phillip Gazette*, vol. 1, no. 2, Summer 1952, pp. 4–6; 'Veteran Bill Branfield Shatters Pipe Record,' *Age*, 30 August 1952, p. 3.

14 I base these calculations on correspondence in the R.M. Crawford Papers, 1995.0044, Box 22, University of Melbourne Archives; Owen Parnaby to Crawford, 13 May 1950, R.M. Crawford Papers, Box 22, File 'Correspondence with Former Students 1950–1951'; 'Ken Inglis Interviewed by Neville Meaney.' See also F Anderson, *An Historian's Life: Max Crawford and the Politics of*

Academic Freedom, Melbourne University Press, Carlton, 2005, pp. 226–30; J Poynter, '"Wot Larks To Be Aboard": The History Department, 1937–71,' in F Anderson & S Macintyre (eds), *The Life of the Past: The Discipline of History at the University of Melbourne*, History Department, University of Melbourne, 2006, pp. 60–70.

15 'Ken Inglis Interviewed by Neville Meaney.'

16 'Ken Inglis Interviewed by Neville Meaney'; K Inglis, 'Alan Marne McBriar 1918–2004,' *History Australia*, vol. 2, no. 3, 2005, pp. 92.1–2.

17 Ken Inglis to G.D.H. Cole, 12 March 1952; Cole to Inglis, 6 October 1952, Papers of Ken Inglis, Box 9, Folder 'Oxford,' National Library of Australia; Ken Inglis to Max Crawford, 1 November 1953, R.M. Crawford Papers, Box 22, File 'Correspondence with Former Students 1952–1953,' University of Melbourne Archives.

18 'Variety,' *Age*, 17 March 1954.

19 Ken Inglis to Max Crawford, 1 November 1953; K Inglis, 'Recollections of Asa Briggs,' n.d., Papers of Ken Inglis, Box 17, National Library of Australia. Alan McBriar described Cole's overwork and ill health in a letter to Max Crawford, 29 November 1947, R.M. Crawford Papers, Box 22, Folder 'Correspondence Former Students 1945–1949,' University of Melbourne Archives.

20 Inglis, 'Recollections of Asa Briggs'; see F Bongiorno, 'Asa Briggs and the Remaking of Australian Historiography,' in M Taylor (ed.), *The Age of Asa: Lord Briggs, Public Life and History in Britain since 1945*, Palgrave Macmillan, Houndmills, Basingstoke, 2014, pp. 90–107.

21 K Inglis, 'Mau Mau: A Response to British Injustice,' *Voice*, vol. 3, no. 8, May 1954, p. 20.

22 K Inglis, 'The Way of the Egghead,' *Voice*, vol. 4, no. 3, January 1955, p. 24; 'Salvation by Rhetoric,' *Voice*, vol. 4, no. 7, June 1955, p. 25; 'The Diplomacy of Dr Fisher,' *Voice*, vol. 5, no. 6, June 1956, p. 9.

23 'Preston,' 'London Letter,' *Voice*, vol. 3, no. 1, September 1953, p. 5; vol. 3, no. 2, November 1953, p. 5.

24 W Shawcross, *Rupert Murdoch: Ringmaster of the Information Circus*, Chatto and Windus, London, 1992, cited in Bongiorno, 'Asa Briggs and the Remaking of Australian Historiography,' p. 91.

25 'Preston,' 'The Murdoch Succession,' *Voice*, vol. 2, no. 10, June 1953, pp. 13, 15; 'The "Argus Story",' *Voice*, vol. 3, no. 5, February 1954, pp. 20–21, 23.

26 Ken Inglis to Max Crawford, 28 September 1955, R.M. Crawford Papers, Box 22, Folder 'Correspondence with Former Students 1955,' University of Melbourne Archives; 'Preston,' 'The European Scene,' *Voice*, vol. 4, no. 9, September 1955, pp. 10–11; vol. 4, no. 11, November 1955, p. 8.

27 Max Corden identified himself as 'Preston' when I presented my paper to the Ken Inglis Colloquium on 24 November 2016; see M Corden, *Lucky Boy in the Lucky Country: The Autobiography of Max Corden, Economist*, Palgrave Macmillan, London, 2017.

28 'Ken Inglis Interviewed by Neville Meaney.'

29 Hugh Stretton to Ken Inglis, 8 June, 16 July 1955, Papers of Ken Inglis, Box 9,
    Folder 'Correspondence Ken – Hugh Stretton,' National Library of Australia.

30 G.D.H. Cole to Ken Inglis, 1 June 1956; Harold Perkin to Ken Inglis, 6 July
    1959; Inglis to Perkin, 28 October 1960, Papers of Ken Inglis, Box 9, Folder
    'Churches and the Working Classes,' National Library of Australia.

31 Max Crawford to Ken Inglis, 27 June 1955; Inglis to Crawford, 28 July 1955,
    R.M. Crawford Papers, Box 22, Folder 'Correspondence with Former Students
    1955,' University of Melbourne Archives.

Chapter 5

THE PRESENT
IN THE PAST

Ken Inglis on hospitals and churches

Janet McCalman

It was characteristic of Ken Inglis that his Master of Arts thesis was a brave response to an invitation from the committee of management of the Royal Melbourne Hospital, the city's leading hospital. The bright idea that perhaps a clever young history student could write an institution's history – for no payment, of course – occurs all too often to cash-strapped committees of management, and could only be proffered by people without any idea of the immensity of the task involved: the poring over minutes of meetings, the disentangling of parliamentary debates, the painstaking pre-Trove and pre-*Argus Index* reading of newspapers, the pursuit of biographical details before the arrival of the *Australian Dictionary of Biography*, the judicious juggling of scandal and criticism, vanity and achievement, the writing for a general and interested audience rather than just examiners, and finally the historiography of the field itself. Many are called, few respond, and perhaps only Ken Inglis was gifted enough as a raw graduate to succeed. He hadn't even written an honours thesis and it was to be his first extended piece of historical research and writing.

The thesis was passed in 1954 and the finished book appeared under the imprint of Melbourne University Press in 1958.[1] Ken acknowledged the guidance of Max Crawford in setting the themes, and it is a marvellous exercise in synthetic history, compressing more than a century of change, when hospitals and medicine were transformed from a paradigm that now survives only in the delusions of complementary medicine. Ken had to do this without the immense bank of scholarship in the history of science and medicine that has amassed since Thomas Kuhn's *The Structure of Scientific Revolutions* appeared in 1962, or the discovery of the patient and medical history by Roy Porter or, particularly, the explication of the history of clinical science and practice in teaching hospitals by John Harley Warner.[2]

A high point of Ken's narrative is the debate over antisepsis: introduced to the Melbourne so early by the hospital's senior surgeon, William Gillbee, only to be discarded by his peers before general acceptance by the late 1880s. It was a contest of egos, heightened by the brashness of the self-made men of this frontier city. This hospital history is in fact a colonial drama, a story of a hospital and its place in a community. Makers of this new society grappled with questions of medical provision, medical and university education, poor relief, new knowledge and how to apply it, fierce, corrupt elections for prized positions on the honorary staff and, above all, how to do it: how to build and run a hospital that could meet the medical needs of a colonial outpost that was rapidly becoming one of the most vibrant cities of the New World.

These self-made men brought with them various models of voluntary and teaching hospitals, as in England, Dublin and the Scottish cities, sustained by charitable foundations or subscribers who in some cases maintained the right to recommend patients for admission. Yet the Melbourne hospital was different from the start in that the largest contributor was a colonial government that paid like a charitable donor rather than a controlling funder. The unspoken contract was between the bodies of the poor and the profession of medicine: charity patients were treated for nothing on condition that their diseases and cadavers were clinical material for teaching and research. This gift relationship – which still exists, although couched in more modern ethical terms – meant that while public or charity patients did not pay, neither had they rights to demand therapies that doctors considered wrong or worthless.

This principle had freed the Paris Clinic to observe and measure sickness, evaluate interventions, appreciate that most illnesses are self-limiting and, from the middle of the century, begin to support the sick body in the process of recovery rather than sabotage it with depleting remedies, as in old paradigms of pluralist medicine. What we now understand better about the history of medicine in the nineteenth century is the painfulness of intellectual change: how Lister developed antisepsis without understanding germ theory; how distinguished medical men schooled in the complexity of humoral medicine – disease as a state of over-excitement and heat – found it difficult to accept the germ theory explanation of infection because of its simplicity. Much of this Ken intuited before the field developed as it has, and his interpretations are remarkably close to the mark.

Hospital and Community is a compact, elegantly written book, yet it has to cover an immense range of topics: the politics of hospital provision, honorary staff, and building and development. But there is much more: the emergence of nursing from the rough men and women who had traditionally tended the sick into a trained, ladylike profession. Florence Nightingale, through her colonial agent, Lucy Osburn in Sydney, was critical to the change, but so also, we now know, were the nursing nuns of the Sisters of Charity and the trained nurses and unofficial midwives emerging as early as 1862 from what was then known as the Lying-In Hospital.[3] Nurses and their lady superintendents and matrons became the managers of the modern hospital, the front line in the war against the germ, a battle fought with military precision in the pre-antibiotic era.

The coming of a medical school to the University of Melbourne, even though small, also changed the hospital, as clinical teaching developed from apprenticeship to a university-supervised process, led by clinical staff with university appointments. If I disagree a little with Ken, he perhaps did not appreciate how good the general medical profession was in colonial Victoria. The *Australian Medical Journal*, founded in 1856, reveals a profession reading British and French journals and alive to new developments (Gillbee's early experiment with antisepsis was not unique: others were using chloroform and advancing abdominal surgery apace with London).[4] Most of the leading doctors had walked the Paris hospitals, read French, and, like Scots such as James Jamieson, would bring germ theory to Melbourne from their reading of German scientific literature.[5] It was no colonial outpost.

The quality of medical investigations and clinical meetings reported in the journal through to the First World War was high. Richard Stawell conducted outstanding work on infant mortality from diarrhoeal disease at the Children's Hospital in Melbourne. The Lying-In Hospital had reduced its maternal death rate dramatically with the introduction of antiseptic midwifery by the early 1890s. The major regression was the growing eugenicist preoccupations of the medical elite and their 'syphilisation': it was joked that Professor Harry Allen filled his pathology museum with examples of syphilis that were discovered by his successor, Peter MacCallum, to have been wildly misdiagnosed, and that the only genuine case was one that Allen had missed.

These developments, and the modern hospital, cost far more than the original founders and contributors envisaged. Ken ends his history by discussing a renegotiation of finances with the state government and the allocation of funding from Tattersall's lottery revenue to the cause of public medicine. The great opportunity of an Australian National Health Service was buried by the defeat of the Chifley government in 1949 and the Cold War domination of Australian politics for the next quarter century. It would be a painful political struggle, still under way, for Australians to accept that complex medical care – and the research, training and clinical infrastructure that enables it – is beyond the capacities of the private market and private individuals.

* * *

Churches and the Working Classes in Victorian England appeared in 1963, an early volume in Harold Perkin's innovative Studies in Social History series.[6] It had begun life as Ken's Oxford DPhil under the official supervision of G.D.H. Cole and the unofficial inspiration of Asa Briggs, and as with the Melbourne hospital history, it was a brave and ambitious choice. His two main English reviewers, John Saville and Henry Pelling, acknowledged that it filled a yawning gap in the scholarship of Victorian England, but each quibbled that Ken could have gone further.[7] The title implied that it covered the entire Victorian period, when it concentrated on the final two decades of the nineteenth century, according to one complaint, though this was probably a result of the publisher's not wanting it to sound too much like a thesis; the book should have covered Wales and Scotland, according to another, though it was specifically focused on England, which was more than enough to cover; and it was said that he had neglected working-class religious communities like the Primitive Methodists, except that it wasn't a study of working-class religious life but a study of the leading religious institutions and their response to the challenge of religious indifference and mass poverty. And, when it came to the crunch, he was an Australian.

Ken began with the 1851 census, which revealed the extent of the failure of religion to interest the vast bulk of the growing urban working classes and even many of the rural poor. He argued that it would be wrong to think of this as a recent consequence of rapid urbanisation: the churches had never captured the hearts and minds of the urban poor, and the ragged rural poor were intimidated by the display of class and caste in the church parade. As Keith Snell showed later, the only institutional intervention to penetrate the class barrier was the Sunday school, which by the twentieth century was embraced by parents who needed the children out of the house, and the marital bed, for a few precious hours of privacy.[8] Nor at the mid-century did many in the Church of England actually care about the absence of the poor; those who did were anxious about social disorder more than Christian welfare.

As for the other churches (whose combined attendances on census Sunday exceeded those of the Church of England), the Congregationalists had always been middle-class; the Wesleyans, propelled by Methodist discipline, had prospered and become middle-class; and while some Bible Christians and Primitive Methodists remembered their roots, others indulged in Anglican vices like pew rents. Of the large churches, only the Catholics continued to connect with their largely Irish immigrant and refugee flock. Catholicism,

Edmund Campion once reminded us, provided poor people with not just hope of earthly salvation but also a glorious cast of heavenly friends in the Saints, who held your hand through life's travails and filled your head with colour and wondrousness.[9] Early Methodism had similarly lit up the lives of people shivering with cold, damp and darkness, with visions of Christ as their dearest friend, bringing a warming 'great flame' 'kindled by a spark of grace' that would 'set all kingdoms ablaze.' The Primitive Methodist movement would match that fervour late in the century with its close involvement in trade unions, as would, for a time, the Salvation Army. But evangelistic religion flamed and died, and seemed not to penetrate the deep indifference of the poor to the promises of a better life afterwards. Their interest was a real improvement in their lives on earth.

The core of the book is the emergence of a social conscience among the educated and comfortable classes in the last two decades of the nineteenth century, a conscience that confronted the materiality of poverty. It is the story of the churches grappling with the contradictions between institutional Christianity and earthly misery. It is a complex and nuanced exploration, sensitive to theological developments and conflicts of interest. Organised religion was facing challenges from the presence of the poor, the advancement of science and secularist thought, and what Ken called 'the problem of pleasure.'[10] The problem of pleasure involved more than the new amusements for Sunday recreation, such as excursion trains and bicycles; the more insidious problem was the spiritual threat from worldly pleasures that organised religion labelled vices to be suppressed and stamped out.

The advancing culture of respectability, which offered deliverance from shame to ambitious skilled working men, impecunious clerks, shopkeepers and small businessmen, was a secular path to goodness.

You did not need to believe to be good. The Puritan conscience prohibited dancing, card playing and temperate drinking, but guilt about pleasure and frivolity permeated all levels of society: Ken reports that Sir James Stephen once smoked a cigar and enjoyed it so much that he never smoked again. Methodists characterised themselves as Christians in earnest, but the social consciousness of the better off was also an embrace of a serious life, as was most clearly evidenced when the High Anglican Oxford Movement, having been excluded from respectable parishes, developed a powerful critique of British social policy from its enforced ministries in the slums.

But the churches were also 'doing the numbers.' If they failed to enfold the ever-expanding urban masses they would die, as indeed they have in the century since, especially once the middle classes in the 1960s found Sunday drives more attractive, and their lovingly Dr Spock–raised offspring went on the pill. Therefore, the churches' problem with the working classes was existential as well as spiritual and political, and the responses were various, from Tractarian High Anglicans, to Christian Socialists, to the missionary work of the East End settlements and the Wesleyan urban missions. But who benefited most from missionary outreach? Perhaps it was the young gentlemen themselves who passed through Toynbee Hall and moved in later life into positions of influence and power with a transformed social sensibility? Then there were the secular Labour churches that flourished briefly but failed to attract many, let alone hold them.

The great exception was the Salvation Army, and Ken's account of General Booth is both brilliant and painful: this gifted evangelist, full of imagination and entrepreneurial flair, was none the less incurious and limited. His embrace of the material needs of the poor was superficial and opportunistic: it was his followers who turned the noisy Christian

Army into the saintly and beloved Salvos, which succeeded as a social welfare service rather than as a spiritual force.

What infuses *Churches and the Working Classes* from beginning to end is Ken's historical imagination, his capacity to get inside the worlds of others, to draw on the cadences of the church, to take seriously the theology and doubts of working-class men and women. Yet, in the end, the book reads to me as an examination of class relations and contradictions as mediated by the religious institutions. And it is a story of failure: the failure of the educated and self-enlisted leaders of thought and culture to capture the hearts of the poor. As Snell and Ell later demonstrated with a careful statistical analysis of religion, land holding, urban growth and population change, the deep drivers of increasing secularisation were cultural and economic. The established church was strongest where land ownership remained in the hands of a visible gentry, where tradition and parish obligations endured, and where cultural conformity dominated. With economic pluralism came social and geographic mobility, weakened traditional cultural ties, increased diversity of belief and unbelief – in other words, modernity and the steady erosion of the impact of organised religion, even among nonconformists.[11]

To replace spiritual faith came political faith: the emergence of radical class politics and the rise of socialism in late Victorian England. The book is an innovative exploration of discursive change, which set up the politics of the twentieth century – the contest between left and right that is still playing out in our time, with a return in developed economies to the degrees of wealth inequality that appalled the socially aware more than a century ago.

Secular Labour, not a Labour church such as that of the Unitarian John Trevor, which flourished briefly in the 1890s, became the twentieth-century political religion of the poor. (And, of course, as Inglis's later work explored, war memorialisation assumed the character of a secular faith.) Perhaps we are now in a similar state of political failure as that in which the morally earnest found themselves at the end of the nineteenth century. The alliance of middle-class progressives and mass labour that did so much to remake both Britain and Australia in the wake of the Second World War is breaking down. It appears broken in Britain; it could crumble in Australia as the politics of middle-class progressives become ever more cosmopolitan and detached from the lost jobs and futures of those facing dispossession from structural economic change. And what can the intelligentsia, their good jobs intact, offer to people enraged by the feeling that they are being lectured and talked down to? Some of the contradictions of our own plight are similar to those faced by earnest Christians in the late Victorian period.

The historical questions that animated Ken as a postgraduate student in the early 1960s were to be overwhelmed by the emergence of the new social history, or history from below. His own trajectory reflected this shift of interest to the culture and mental worlds of ordinary people, and he never lost his fascination with belief and faith, religious or secular. Nonetheless, since the 1960s historians have been rather less interested in the ideas and culture of the ruling classes than is healthy. We ignore them at our peril, because they continue to exercise disproportionate political power and because inexorably they incorporate the intelligentsia, whatever their class origins. Thus this lack of interest is also a lack of reflexivity: a failure to see the cosmopolitan intellectual class for what it is – a privileged elite, protected from the dislocations of postmodernity by institutions, money and cultural power.

In 1958 Michael Young published *The Rise of the Meritocracy*, a satire that was rejected for publication by eleven publishers and the Fabian Society.[12] Eventually it became a bestseller, but in 2001 Young was shattered when Tony Blair gormlessly upheld the meritocracy as a Labour ideal. While advancement by merit rather than birth has become more achievable, Young argued, it has since hardened into 'a new social class without room in it for others.' He expected the poor and uneducated to be 'done down' and so they have been by a reform ideology that places individual academic achievement at its core. If some rise, many others are cut down at a young age and many never recover their self-confidence. The successful determine that their progeny will succeed them. Sixty years on, leaders of the left no longer stand in opposition to the rich and powerful, but have joined them at Oxbridge and live next door in unaffordable neighbourhoods, while the poor remain poor and have become disenfranchised and disengaged.[13]

It took the terrible losses of two world wars and the miseries of the Great Depression to build a moral middle class that did care sufficiently about the poor, the homeless and the sick to relinquish some of its privileges. In the postwar reconstruction they shared leadership with politicians whose formation was outside universities and good schools: Bevin, Morrison, Curtin, Chifley. Since the Second World War, the meritocracy has vastly expanded, and it has depended above all on the expansion of the state to provide higher education and secure employment in place of business and the professions. Now, with the neoliberal shrinkage of the state and rising tax unfairness, the younger generation, no matter how good its education, is finding itself joining the precariat of other insecure workers immiserated by deindustrialisation and inherited disadvantage.[14] Perhaps this can provide the shared experience that can cross class lines and forge a new, reforming solidarity. With its questions about the obligations of faith, the nature of the good society, the duties of citizenship and social relationships, *Churches and the Working Classes* continues to resonate in this secular, post-industrial age. The mark of a good history, however long since it was written, is that it continues to make you think about the present as well as the past.

Endnotes

1   KS Inglis, *Hospital and Community: A History of the Royal Melbourne Hospital*, Melbourne University Press, Carlton, 1958.

2   TS Kuhn, *The Structure of Scientific Revolutions*, Chicago University Press, Chicago, 1962; R Porter, 'The Patient's View: Doing Medical History from Below,' *Theory and Society*, vol. 14, no. 2, March 1985, pp. 175–98; JH Warner, *The Therapeutic Perspective: Medical Practice, Knowledge, and Identity in America, 1820–1885*, Harvard University Press, Cambridge, 1986.

3   S Nelson, *Say Little, Do Much: Nurses, Nuns, and Hospitals in the Nineteenth Century*, University of Pennsylvania Press, Philadelphia, 2001.

4   J McCalman, *Sex and Suffering: Women's Health and a Women's Hospital*, Johns Hopkins University Press, Baltimore, 1999.

5   W Anderson, *The Cultivation of Whiteness: Science, Health and Racial Destiny in Australia*, Basic Books, New York, 2003.

6   KS Inglis, *Churches and the Working Classes in Victorian England*, Routledge and Kegan Paul, London, 1963.

7   J Saville, 'Review,' *Sociological Review*, vol. 12, no. 2, July 1964, pp. 214–16; H Pelling, 'Religion and the Nineteenth-Century British Working Class,' *Past & Present*, vol. 27, no. 1, April 1964, pp. 128–33.

8   KDM Snell, 'The Sunday-School Movement in England and Wales: Child Labour, Denominational Control and Working-Class Culture,' *Past & Present*, vol. 169, no. 1, August 1999, pp. 122–68.

9   E Campion, *Rockchoppers: Growing Up Catholic in Australia*, Penguin Books, Ringwood, 1982, pp. 55–8.

10 Inglis, *Churches and the Working Classes in Victorian England*, pp. 74–85.

11 KDM Snell & PS Ell, *Rival Jerusalems: The Geography of Victorian Religion*, Cambridge University Press, Cambridge, 2000.

12 M Young, *The Rise of the Meritocracy, 1870–2033: An Essay on Education and Equality*, Penguin, Harmondsworth, 1961.

13 M Young, 'Down with Meritocracy,' *Guardian*, 29 June 2001.

14 G Standing, *The Precariat: The New Dangerous Class*, Bloomsbury Academic, London, 2011.

Chapter 6

THE SECULAR
AND THE SACRED

Ken Inglis in Adelaide

Robert Dare

Ken's first lecture in Adelaide was memorable, less for what it contained than for what happened after it. The lecture, in Hugh Stretton's course on nineteenth-century history, was on *Rerum novarum*, the 1891 papal encyclical on the respective duties of capital and labour. It was territory familiar to him from his doctoral research, and with customary care and patience he examined the difficulties of interpretation it presented.[1] Ken spent a lot of time recounting other people's often-conflicting views of what it meant. He concluded that it was a deliberately ambiguous document, intended to give comfort to Catholics with very different understandings of the social purposes of their religion. The text of the lecture survives among those of Ken's papers kept at the University of Adelaide. On the folder containing it, he later wrote, 'My first lecture in Adelaide 1956. At the end, Professor Stretton asked, "Was it a *good* encyclical?"'[2]

I take three things from this story. The first is evidence of a remarkable personal and intellectual friendship that enriched Australia for more than half a century. The second is a sign that Ken heard Hugh to be telling him that he shouldn't sit on the fence, especially on issues where his scholarly precision and moral engagement intersect: things like encyclicals aren't merely functional components of complex institutions, and must be understood by their moral purposes and moral effects. The third is that Hugh was urging Ken to know what his point is, and get to it.

Hugh had applied for the Adelaide chair from Oxford in 1953, nine days after his twenty-ninth birthday. He was appointed within days – the university had done its due diligence before he applied – and arrived in Adelaide in October 1954. While he was in Melbourne over the Christmas break, he consulted Max Crawford and John La Nauze on what he called 'the terrible problem of first-year curricula.'[3] He had earlier sent a job advertisement to Ken, the scholar he thought could solve his problem – Hugh too had done his due diligence – but had been disheartened by Ken's reply. The occupant would run the large first-year course, under the stipulation that it would not be concerned with the nineteenth century, or Australia, or the Pacific. Ken explained to Hugh that he hoped to go back to Melbourne and teach a nineteenth-century course of the kind his mentor Asa Briggs excelled in – not, he hastened to add, that he thought he'd been offered the job. No, you haven't, Hugh replied: applications do not close for a week, 'so it is too soon to be certain that neither Briggs nor [Lewis] Namier will apply.' Ken's application went off 'in about five minutes.'[4] Duly appointed, he and his family arrived in Adelaide several months before his twenty-seventh birthday, in time to give the lecture on *Rerum Novarum*. The combined ages of the professor and his new senior lecturer were well short of the age of retirement.

Inside its parklands, and to the south and east of them, Adelaide in the 1950s remained what Beatrice Webb, ever the snob, had described in 1898 as 'the pleasantest' of Australian cities. 'The luxuriously laid out city surrounded by beautiful hills,' she effused, 'the pleasant homely people, the air of general comfort, refinement and ease give to Adelaide far more amenity than is possible in restlessly pretentious Melbourne, crude chaotic Sydney, or shadily genteel Brisbane.'[5] But to the north, and the more distant south, Adelaide was changing. Describing the changes, a New Zealand geographer appointed to the university shortly after Ken, couldn't contain his excitement. He predicted a 'dramatic industrial expansion' around Adelaide, which would result in 'a rapid and significant transition from a predominantly primary-producing state to one with a balanced agricultural-industrial economy.'[6] 'Adelaide is really two cities,' Hugh Stretton wrote a little later. 'A provincial capital fattens comfortably through the second century of its slow growth. But through it like a cable, from twenty miles north to twenty miles south of it, deft men lately threaded a Detroit.' The leader of the deft men was premier Thomas Playford, the conservative orchardist who happily nationalised key industries to promote industrialisation. Playford cared nothing for ideological niceties. 'He was,' Hugh explained, 'a total abstainer from alcohol, education and tobacco.'[7]

The University of Adelaide was eager to participate in the transformation. Soon after Ken joined the university, the Murray committee, appointed by the Menzies government to make recommendations on the future of higher education in Australia, began its visits to the states. It reported that Australia had seen a 'phenomenal growth in recent years of Australian industry, particularly in manufacturing.' To foster that growth, it reasoned, Australia 'must have more than its share of expertise and "know how" in all its enterprises.' The economy would become increasingly reliant on universities for that know-how – in other words, for science and technology graduates. So, it hinted, would national security: the United States and the United Kingdom produced far more science and technology – what we now call STEM – graduates but, ominously, Russia did too. 'What makes the strength of a nation to-day,' the committee urged, 'is its professional and scientific man-power.'[8]

The University of Adelaide heard the message. For years to come, the mantra of a succession of annual reports and speakers at graduation ceremonies was 'we must have more science and technology graduates.' Ken had arrived in a university determined to transform itself into a centre of science and technology, the better to make its contribution to winning the Cold War.

The Murray report also said that history was one of the disciplines in Australian universities that was gravely understaffed. When Ken joined the department he had a handful of colleagues teaching hundreds of students. Tutorials were a rarity. Most lectures were given in the evening to cater to students from the neighbouring teachers' college.[9] Only one of his colleagues, Douglas Pike, was publishing. Ken's first teaching assignment was to master world history, no less, and impart it to first-year students.

The range of topics in his lectures through the following years is astonishing. He covered all periods from 1500 to 1800, and all continents: English, European and American history; Europe's engagement with India, China, Japan and the far east; war, revolution and terror; and the history of religion. One outcome of this punishing regime of reading and writing was a shift in Ken's angle of vision, an adjustment visible in his scholarship thereafter. He encountered historians who announced the end of European history, and he took notice. The proposition came in two forms.

The first turned the world upside down: to the colonial subjects of the growth of empire, Europeans were the barbarians rather than the bearers of civilisation. Ken read and gave a radio talk on Jawaharlal Nehru's massive prison history of the world, and told his students about the rancorous K.M. Panikkar's *Asia and Western Dominance*. He noticed Panikkar's 'distaste for the hypocrisy and arrogance of Europeans'; since 1918, Panikkar judged, Europe had been in inevitable and justifiable retreat. Ken was enlivened by the confidence with which these scholars turned the telescope of discovery back on Europe, to find morally primitive societies that had debased the advanced civilisations they conquered. Demolishing the moral hegemony of Europe helped destroy its claim to pre-eminence in the history of the world.

The second form of the proposition that European history is dead was both more subtle and more dialectical. Ken found it in Geoffrey Barraclough's *History in a Changing World*, published in 1955. Barraclough, he told his students, was critical of the view that the expansion of Europe was 'an inevitable and conclusive process.' That view, in Ken's paraphrase of Barraclough, 'ignores the impact of other peoples on Europeans; and ... it makes it hard for people to realise that the phase of European dominance was temporary and has now passed.' A global history worthy of the name studies the reciprocities of influence and effect as societies separated by vast distances came into contact.

We can see the distinctiveness of Ken's insight in a contemporary exchange on the teaching of European history in Australia. In 1961 the Dutch historian Ivo Schöffer announced that 'European history deserves a central place in the teaching programmes of all history departments in Australian universities.'[10] Two prominent historians working in Australia were invited to comment. In support of Schöffer's argument, W.K. Hancock quoted the Asian historian visiting Adelaide in 1958 who said, 'You cannot be of much use to us ... unless you remain yourselves.'[11] The other respondent was J.H.M. Salmon, a New Zealander and historian of France then at the University of New South Wales. In what was intended as a dissent from the majority view, Salmon drew on Barraclough's declaration of 'the end of European history.' He saw it as 'not merely a call for the replacement of nation-alistic history in a European context by new global categories: it was also a plea to study the overlapping histories of races, cultures, and nations.'[12] This injunction, he went on, was as applicable to Australian as to any other national history. It was a lesson Ken took to heart very early in his career.

Even as he coped with his taxing schedule of teaching, Ken embarked on what amounted to a second career as a journalist, beginning in the pages of the new magazine *Nation*.[13] We can discern a number of themes in this early journalism. The first was the conservative and puritanical cast of South Australia's politics and culture. In an early article for *Nation*, subtitled 'How It Feels to Be South Australian' – if a freshly minted one – Ken reckoned that being half an hour behind the eastern states was metaphorically as well as literally true, as the easterners kept telling South Australians. In a never-ending war of words, South Australians said the east was immoral, to which the east replied that South Australians were soft, and poor at all sports. One jeering journalist announced that in South Australia 'pugilism is non-existent, even among footballers.' As balm to their wounded feelings, South Australians assured themselves that they were '*conservatively* progressive.' They clung to customs such as the pie floater, 'a pie, broken and sauced, sitting in thick pea soup.'[14] Need he say more?

Ken dwelt with fond relish on two Toms. The first Tom was Thomas Playford who, in Ken's wicked phrase, had been premier of the state 'since Munich' – though he added that, for Playford, 'foreign affairs consist mainly of disputes with the big powers, NSW and Victoria, over the water in the Murray.'[15] In a lengthy, unsigned portrait of Playford under the headline 'The Cherry Orchardist,' Ken noted that his conservatism had a contrarian side to it that set it apart from the doctrinaire postures of organised politics. Playford was hostile to universities but also to the Adelaide Club. He thought government was about economic rather than political affairs, and was not frightened to be tagged as a socialist for promoting growth through the takeover of private industries such as electricity supply and coal mining to fuel power stations. But, Ken went on, in a pre-echo of Hugh's remark a decade later, 'he is no more likely to touch socialism than booze or tobacco.' Playford thought the job of government was to increase wealth, not redistribute it, in pursuit of which he would pinch a good idea from whoever has it.[16]

The second Tom was Tom Lehrer, the rogue Harvard mathematician turned musical satirist. Lehrer appeared in the Adelaide Town Hall as part of the inaugural Adelaide Festival of Arts in 1960. As a condition of his appearance, the relevant government minister required him to sign an undertaking not to sing five of his songs that the minister deemed too naughty for South Australian sensibilities. Lehrer agreed, preferring, as he said much later, to ditch the songs rather than go to prison.[17] Anyway, he relished the free publicity, and watched the Town Hall fill to capacity. Audiences, Ken noted, laughed at Lehrer, but even more at the censors. 'They savoured Mr Lehrer,' he wrote, 'and took part in a joyful demonstration against the sour and mindless puritanism of their rulers.' Ken let Lehrer be the historian. 'South

Australia,' Lehrer judged, 'has one of the finest governments of the eighteenth century.'[18] None of this, Ken added in another article in the same issue, would have bothered Playford, who 'draws his orchard spray at the mention of the word culture… With a senile Labour [sic] Party, gerrymandered electorates, and a firm devotion to lower middle class prejudice, he can brush off the civilised element in South Australia like a blowfly.'[19]

These are some of the sharpest remarks Ken made in his many articles for *Nation*, and they are uncharacteristic. What we usually see in his journalism is his refinement over time of a public voice that encourages the hope that we might improve – become fairer, kinder, better educated, more tolerant, more receptive to ideas, less credulous, less cruel – but knows we probably won't, not tomorrow anyway. He favoured irony over condemnation. He let public figures speak for themselves – he was as adept at finding the revealing quotation as his old mentor Asa Briggs – because he knew they usually did themselves more harm than he ever could. His interest was less in voicing disap-proval than in observing the rituals, frequently arcane, usually ancient but occasionally in the process of formation, that structure our lives. That required him to be sensitive to idiosyncrasy and self-delusion, paradox and contradiction, change and continuity, all of which have something to tell us about the peculiarities of our culture – and make great copy to boot. Through the pages of *Nation* he found a way to bring the methods of the historian to an understanding of how we live now. I'll return to this project in a moment.

Ken's second theme was the state of the Australian media, particu-larly newspapers, broadcasting and the emerging television industry. His first article on the media for *Nation* examined the rivalry between the *Advertiser* and the *News*, between the establishment and the young, insurgent Rupert Murdoch. The article contained his first mention of the irreverent editor of the *News*, Rohan Rivett. It would not be the last.[20] His next article on the media, on Anzac Day 1959, anticipated an 'epoch in the cultural history of South Australia,' but he didn't mean anything related to rituals of memory: he reported that television sets would go on sale there in nine days' time.[21] And it's worth noting that Ken's interest in the trial of Max Stuart, dealt with elsewhere in this book, grew out of his surveys of the media. The story first appeared on 18 July 1959 under the headline 'The Hanging of a Man: A Police Association's Extraordinary Campaign.'[22]

The industry Ken brought to these media surveys is breathtaking – he had a day job, remember. For his article of 13 August 1960, which surveyed newspaper responses to the federal Minister of Immigration's opposition to changes in the White Australia policy, Ken read the *Sydney Morning Herald*, the *Advertiser*, the *Age*, the *Canberra Times*, the Melbourne *Sun*, the Brisbane *Courier Mail*, the *West Australian*, the Melbourne *Herald*, the Adelaide *News* and the Sydney *Daily Mirror*. This particular survey is significant for another reason. In it, Ken reported that the article in support of Minister Downer in the Adelaide *News* was identical to that in the Sydney *Daily Mirror*, and contradicted an earlier *News* editorial that had been published on 6 July, just before Rohan Rivett was replaced as editor. Both papers were controlled by Rupert Murdoch.[23] Issues around the independence of editors in the Murdoch press are now well over half a century old, and Ken was watching.

In October 1960 Asa Briggs delivered the annual Joseph Fisher lecture at the University of Adelaide, hosted by the department of economics. His topic was the origin of mass entertainment.[24] The first volume of his history of the BBC appeared a few months later. By then, Ken was already well primed to follow his friend in becoming the historian of the Australian equivalent of the BBC.

Ken's third theme was his most cherished project in journalism, as it later became in his scholarship. By following it we can see how the separate arcs of Ken's work, always converging, finally met in his interest in the shift from organised religion to what he called 'civic religion.'

The first arc was his interest in the vigour, or lack of it, of organised religion. It was the subject of his Oxford doctorate, which he prepared for publication while he was in Adelaide. Among the many sources he drew on to resolve the issue was a unique religious census carried out in the United Kingdom in 1851, which he was the first historian to subject to close analysis. The census revealed that a sizeable majority of people in England did not attend worship, and that urban labour was predominant in this abstinence.[25] The decline in worship in the twentieth century, frequently celebrated or lamented, had its roots deep in the industrial revolution.

Ken returned to Australia intending to sustain his interest in religious practices by studying our own history of worship. From Adelaide, he produced a steady stream of scholarly articles on the history of religion in England and Australia.[26] He set about documenting contemporary religious observance in the pages of *Nation*. He wrote on the Catholic Church's war against godless communism and its hold on the Labor Party; on evangelism and Billy Graham's campaigns here (he doubted Graham's claims to have triggered a religious revival, documenting a string of similar claims stretching back into the nineteenth century); on the hope that migrants would aid the churches in 'replenishing the flocks'; on Jehovah's Witnesses; and on the gulf between the Catholic hierarchy and the laity over adherence to the church's teachings on contraception and divorce.[27] Declining religious observance and the fruitless attempts to reverse the trend were as much true of Australia as of England.

The second arc of Ken's work also drew on his knowledge of the history of religious observance in England and Australia. While he was writing about organised religion in the pages of *Nation*, he began to notice something else: we do things in matters unrelated to theism and churchgoing that look remarkably like religious observance. In July 1960, writing under the pseudonym 'John Kemp,' Ken used the centenary of the Melbourne Cup to show the humorist and sceptic Cyril Pearl and the sternly moral NSW Methodist Church agreeing on one thing: the Melbourne Cup was the climactic event in a nationwide calendar of quasi-religious observance. 'Hippolatry, or horse worship,' he quoted Pearl, 'is the most widely professed religion among Ordinary Australians.' Methodists called the Cup Australia's 'greatest "religious" festival,' with scare quotes around 'religious.' They struggled to plug the holes in the leaking dyke of moralising Protestantism. At their radio headquarters in Adelaide, Ken wrote, 'the only horse likely to be mentioned is John Wesley's.'[28]

Ken documented the ways in which secularism and commerce were hollowing out our most important religious festivals. He pondered the 'long torpor' of Australian Christmas. Rather than a religious festival, it was now a holiday washed down with beer. He noticed a sign outside a Melbourne pub that read 'Avoid the Christmas rush. Drink now!' Again, he traced this deformation back to the Victorians. None of the trappings we set such store by, things like decorated trees and Christmas cards, pre-dates their Queen. Victorians had been captivated by 'a wholly untheological story about petty commerce in industrial England, not one about a manger in Bethlehem.' In writing *A Christmas Carol*, Ken said, Dickens was expressing his hatred of

Catholicism, his disapproval of the established church and his dislike of dissenters. In our time, the core business of the Christmas period, managed by the ubiquitous Santa Claus, was 'to heighten the capacity of children to consume.'[29]

One element remained to trigger a remarkable outflow of Ken's scholarship charting the sacralisation of secular practices in the wake of the decline of formal religion. Ken dates his interest in war in Australian society, and thus Anzac, to 'around 1956,' his first full year in Adelaide. He had become puzzled, and then frustrated, by the neglect in university history courses of the history of war. Several years later, he ran an honours course on Australian historiography, in which he turned his and his students' interest to the themes embodied in the word Anzac.[30] His earliest publication exploring that interest appeared in *Nation* two days before Anzac Day in 1960 under the title 'Anzac: The Substitute Religion.' RSL meetings, he noted, incorporated a 'distinctive ritual' devised by people 'not really convinced by orthodox Christian assertions about what happens when people die.' 'Rarely,' he wrote, 'do the tributes to dead comrades sound as if their authors believe in the doctrine of resurrection.' He later thought the subtitle an oversimplification but it did convey his sense that the rituals and monuments commemorating Australians at war 'constituted some kind of cult,' one that bore comparison with phenomena that were being given 'such labels as civic religion, secular religion, spilt religion.'[31] And that last phrase, Ken must have known, was coined by T.E. Hulme, killed in Flanders in 1917. The outpouring of Ken's many luminous essays and books on the subject had begun.

Towards the end of 1961 Ken took study leave from the University of Adelaide to spend time in the United States. There he read the cultural anthropologists whose work later informed his studies of the monuments and rituals of memory. He did not return to the university, instead taking up a post at the Australian National University in 1962. 'I never planned or even intended to leave Adelaide, and part of me has stayed here, in this town, in this university, in this department,' Ken told an Adelaide audience in 1989 on the occasion of Hugh Stretton's retirement.[32] And part of Adelaide stayed in Ken, without which I don't think he'd have been the historian, mentor and moralist we knew.

Three things stand out in Ken's Adelaide legacy. The first was his realisation that national history treated in isolation was poor history, as was world history conceived as the expansion of Europe. A historian of war could hardly think otherwise.

The second was his distinctive authorial voice. Listen to it and you understand that for Ken writing history was not a passionless pursuit of truths that stand outside him, but an outgrowth of his universe of values and experience. The first sentence of the book of his Oxford doctorate, which had been supervised by a scholar he found 'cold and uninterested,' reads 'A listener to sermons, and even a reader of respectable history books, could easily think that during the nineteenth century the habit of attending religious worship was normal among the English working classes.'[33] Teaching in Adelaide, working with Hugh Stretton, and recording in *Nation* and elsewhere the wondrous ways his fellow Australians thought and acted released him to become as visible to us in his histories as he was in life, and to affirm the view that the historian and his scholarship do not inhabit separate worlds.[34] The first sentence of *Sacred Places* reads 'The Shrine of Remembrance was a new and mysterious presence in the Melbourne of my childhood.'[35]

The third thing Ken took from Adelaide was a way out of a puzzle he had encountered in both his scholarship and his journalism. His work on religion and the working class in England taught him that conventional religious observance has been in steady decline throughout the industrial period. Later he discovered that much the same was true here. Yet he observed a whole range of activities Australians valued that looked to him remarkably like religious practice. Ken's discovery of what he called civic religion while he was in Adelaide yielded some of the richest and most rewarding scholarship we have.

Endnotes

1   KS Inglis, *Churches and the Working Classes in Victorian England*, Routledge and Kegan Paul, London, 1963, pp. 313–19 discusses English responses to the encyclical.

2   KS Inglis, 'Lectures in History, University of Adelaide 1956–1959,' MSS 0067/2, Rare Books and Special Collections, University of Adelaide. Ken retells the story in KS Inglis, 'Hugh Stretton's University of Adelaide, 1954–56,' *Journal of the Historical Society of South Australia*, vol. 18, 1990, pp. 10–11.

3   Hugh Stretton to Max Crawford, 18 January 1955, R.M. Crawford Papers, 1991.0113, Series 7/33, University of Melbourne Archives.

4   KS Inglis, 'Hugh Stretton's University of Adelaide, 1954–56,' *Journal of the Historical Society of South Australia*, vol. 18, 1990, pp. 8–9.

5   AG Austin (ed.), *The Webbs' Australian Diary 1898*, Sir Isaac Pitman & Sons, Melbourne, 1965, p. 96.

6   GR Cochrane, 'South Australia: A Growing Industrial State,' *New Zealand Geographer*, vol. 14, no. 2, 1958, p. 178.

7   H Stretton, *Ideas for Australian Cities*, Hugh Stretton, North Adelaide, 1970, pp. 141, 151.

8   Commonwealth of Australia, *Report of the Committee on Australian Universities [Murray Report]*, September 1957, pp. 13, 15, 27.

9   See GV Portus's apocalyptic report of 1948 on the inadequacies of staff numbers in his joint department of political science and history: Portus: Family Papers, PRG 204, State Library of South Australia.

10   I Schöffer, 'European History in Australian Universities,' *Historical Studies: Australia and New Zealand*, vol. 10, no. 37, 1961, p. 94.

11   WK Hancock, 'European History in Australian Universities: Comments on Professor I. Schöffer's Article,' *Historical Studies: Australia and New Zealand*, vol. 10, no. 38, 1962, p. 222.

12   JHM Salmon, 'European History in Australian Universities: Comments on Professor I. Schöffer's Article,' *Historical Studies: Australia and New Zealand*, vol. 10, no. 38, 1962, p. 223.

13   Ken republished a selection of articles from *Nation*, including a number of his own, in KS Inglis (ed.), *Nation: The Life of an Independent Journal of Opinion, 1958–1972*, Melbourne University Press, Carlton, 1989.

14   KS Inglis, *Nation*, 11 October 1958.

15   Adelaide Correspondent [KS Inglis], 'O'Halloran's Heirs,' *Nation*, 19 November 1960.

16   'The Cherry Orchardist,' *Nation*, 12 September 1959.

17   'Tom Lehrer,' *The Music Show*, interview with Andrew Ford, ABC Radio National, 8 July 2006, www.abc.net.au/radionational/programs/musicshow/tom-lehrer/3344656, accessed 14 September 2016.

18   KS Inglis, 'Hot Night at Town Hall,' *Nation*, 9 April 1960.

19   South Australian Correspondent [KS Inglis], 'Fester After the Festival,' *Nation*, 9 April 1960. *Nation* always put the 'u' in Labor.

20   KS Inglis, 'Adelaide's Version of the Press War,' *Nation*, 22 November 1958.

21   KS Inglis, 'Aerial Warfare in S.A.,' *Nation*, 25 April 1959.

22   KS Inglis, *Nation*, 18 July 1959.

23   On Rivett's departure, see KS Inglis, 'Final Edition,' *Nation*, 30 July 1960.

24   A Briggs, 'Mass Entertainment: The Origins of a Modern Industry,' in Kym Anderson (ed.), *Australia's Economy in Its International Context: The Joseph Fisher Lectures, Volume 2: 1956–2012*, University of Adelaide Press, Adelaide, 2012, p. 49.

25   KS Inglis, 'Patterns of Religious Worship in 1851,' *The Journal of Ecclesiastical History*, vol. 11, no. 1, 1960, pp. 74–86.

26   KS Inglis, 'Catholic Historiography in Australia,' *Historical Studies: Australia and New Zealand*, vol. 8, no. 31, 1958, pp. 233–53; KS Inglis, 'The Labour Church Movement,' *International Review of Social History*, vol. 3, no. 3, December 1958, pp. 445–60; KS Inglis, 'English Nonconformity and Social Reform, 1880–1900,' *Past & Present*, vol. 13, no. 1, April 1958, pp. 73–88.

27   On the Catholic Church and its political and moral campaigns: 'Catholic Voters at the Crossroads,' *Nation*, 8 November 1958, 'Covering of the Sin,' *Nation*, 2 July 1960 and 'Dissenting Laity,' *Nation*, 25 February 1961; on Billy Graham: 'Sydney, Meet Mr Graham,' *Nation*, 11 April 1959 and 'Evangelism Today,' *Nation*, 16 July 1960; on migrants and religion: 'Replenishing the Flocks: Migrants and the Churches,' *Nation*, 20 December 1958.

28   J Kemp [KS Inglis], 'Horses and Deriders,' *Nation*, 30 July 1960.

29   KS Inglis, 'The Long Torpor: Evolution of Australian Christmas Up to No. 173,' *Nation*, 17 December 1960.

30 KS Inglis, 'Remembering Anzac,' in KS Inglis (ed. J Lack), *ANZAC Remembered: Selected Writings by K.S. Inglis*, History Department, University of Melbourne, 1998, p. 130.

31 The article is reproduced in KS Inglis (ed. C Wilcox), *Observing Australia: 1959 to 1999*, Melbourne University Press, Carlton, 1999, pp. 63–70. It appeared in *Nation* under his pseudonym 'John Kemp': J Kemp [KS Inglis], 'Anzac: The Substitute Religion,' *Nation*, 23 April 1960, pp. 7–9.

32 Inglis, 'Hugh Stretton's University of Adelaide, 1954–56,' p. 12.

33 Inglis, *Churches and the Working Classes in Victorian England*, p. 1; on GDH. Cole, 'Ken Inglis Interviewed by Neville Meaney,' 1986, ORAL TRC 2053/11, National Library of Australia.

34 For the contrary view, see JH Hexter, 'The Historian and His Day' in *Reappraisals in History*, Longmans, London, 1961.

35 KS Inglis (assisted by J Brazier), *Sacred Places: War Memorials in the Australian Landscape*, 3rd edn, Melbourne University Press, Carlton, 2008, p. 1. For a similar creation of a historical masterpiece from childhood memory, see the prologue to W Cronon, *Nature's Metropolis: Chicago and the Great West*, W.W. Norton, New York, 1991.

Chapter 7

KEN INGLIS

An anthropological historian

Shirley Lindenbaum

Ken Inglis has been described as a vernacular intellectual who combined a historian's perspective and a reporter's intuition.[1] His ethnographic sensibility and biography suggests that he should be recognised as an anthropological historian, if we define anthropology as a discipline that is part history, part literature, part natural science and part social science.[2]

This essay begins by drawing attention to a little-known publication with the engaging title 'The Fascinating Bee,' subtitled 'Inspirer of Poets and Philosophers.'[3] Published in the *Age* literary supplement in July 1951, during Ken's fifth year at Melbourne University, it was a spoof of the supplement's genteel and whimsical literary style. Identifying himself as T.J.R., the essayist begins:

> Of all the creatures which have won the attention of men of letters, none has exercised more fascination than the bee. Most insects have remained the province of the naturalist, but not so the bee. Poets have sung of it, and philosophers seeking to discover the elusive truths which, if found and believed, would enable men to live in concord, have been drawn to study and wonder at the harmony of the hive.

The author then turns his attention to the image of the bee in literature as 'a creature living in a happy and well-run community.' Plato, we are told, referred to the bee 'as a model for the life of men.' And when Aristotle wrote that 'the gods themselves deemed nectar to be the finest of all beverages,' he too was said to be directing 'the attention of men to the industry and achievement of bees.'

T.J.R. then discusses the work of four poets. The first is a Professor Mollison, 'to whom,' we are told, 'students of literature owe so much for his work "Aran Islanders and the Poetic Instinct."' After the sea, the moon, the stars and the sun, the image said to recur 'most frequently in the songs of the men of Aran is – the bee.'

Mollison was, in fact, the only fictitious person in the essay, apart, that is, from our elusive author, who in correspondence with the editor revealed his identity as the Reverend T.J. Ransome, with a postal address at our father's timber yard in Geelong, a cover he later said he gave for two reasons – and he wasn't sure which was more disreputable – to establish his bona fides, and to make sure he got paid.

Isaac Watts comes next, a hymn writer and Independent dissenter who was perhaps the model for *Age* literary supplement writers, both in style and in message. The Reverend Ransome notes that Watts's poem 'Against Idleness and Mischief,' written in the early eighteenth century, opens with 'How doth the busy little bee,' a phrase that has become part of everyday speech.

The third poet is Sir John Suckling, who sometimes wrote lewd verse and is introduced as 'that curious figure in the energetic and often bizarre seventeenth century,' and who once penned that 'quaint and envious couplet,' 'Thou happy humming bee, O, would that I were thee!'

And then we learn that James McAuley, the Australian poet and literary critic, 'penned a biting indictment of our nation's "middling standard" in his poem "The Bee-Hive." T.J.R. did not add, although this must have been on his mind, that McAuley, with fellow poet Harold Stewart, concocted sixteen nonsense poems in a pseudo-experimental modernist style, supposedly written by 'Ern Malley,' which they sent to Max Harris, the editor of the magazine *Angry Penguins*, where they were published.

The essay ends on the theme of war, a clue to the author's future scholarship:

> Inside the apparent peace of the hive, it is now known, much of the potential working power is spent on preparations for war. Soldier bees, specialists in the arts of defence, wait in readiness for acts of aggression against the hive … [A]lthough the bee provides safeguards against aggression, he has not yet discovered how to prevent it. May not this hard fact bring our own troubled century even closer to the bee than any of the qualities of his life which men in other ages have admired. Perhaps some poet or philosopher of our time will immortalise this aspect of our industrious and captivating friend.

What can we say about the afterlife of 'The Fascinating Bee,' with its attention to community values, both human and insect, and its uncommon knowledge of history and literature? The essay may have so beguiled its readers that the hoax seems to have passed unnoticed. The prehistory of the essay, however, provides another clue to the kind of historian Ken would become. Four close university friends, Arthur Huck, Jamie Mackie, Kit McMahon and Murray Groves, had discussed with Ken a jape of this sort.

This gang of five would choose paths that reflected their often over-lapping literary, cultural and political interests. Arthur Huck did a master's in philosophy, taught for a while at a school in Essendon, studied Chinese at a top-secret school for spooks, published an article on

Mao Zedong as a poet, and then taught political science at Melbourne University. Ken and Huck, as he was known, trod the boards together in the Queen's College production of Shaw's *The Doctor's Dilemma*, and Ken said that Huck helped him gain an understanding of what the devotees of Ludwig Wittgenstein meant by his aphorism 'Whereof one cannot speak, thereof one must be silent.'

Jamie Mackie chose to study history, but his university days were interrupted by the Pacific war. As a gunner on the destroyer HMAS *Warramunga*, he took part in General MacArthur's island-hopping landings from New Britain to the Philippines, his first exposure to Southeast Asia. He finished his degree and left for Oxford, and then worked with the National Planning Bureau in Jakarta. Back in Melbourne, he established the first Indonesian Studies program, then moved to Monash University where, with colleagues Herb Feith and John Legge, he founded the Centre of Southeast Asian Studies.

Kit, Ken and Murray all studied English and history. Kit had a tutorship in English, and then he too left for Oxford and earned a degree in politics, philosophy and economics, with a concentration on economics. His first job in England was as an information officer at the Treasury. He then became a deputy governor of the Bank of England, and then the chairman of the Midland Bank. Like Ken, he had a love of words. He wrote beautifully about economics and said that economics was like crosswords in colour. He chaired a committee to renovate Covent Garden Opera House, for which work he was knighted, and thus became Sir Christopher. Ken and Jamie visited him in London, and reported that knighthood had not changed him.

Ken's interest in anthropology began with Murray Groves. In 1947 and 1948, Murray was in Port Moresby, living several hundred yards from a cluster of Western Motu villages at Hanuabada, where he taught English to the villagers. Returning to Melbourne in 1949, he resumed his studies of history and English, reading anthropology on the side; anthropology was not then taught at Melbourne. Ken, Jamie and Murray joined a splinter group of the Labor Club, of which Murray was president. Ken and Murray later shared a tutor's room, and Ken recalls Murray talking about Hanuabada, anthropology and history. In 1950 they became co-editors of the *Melbourne University Magazine*.

When Ken left Melbourne for Oxford in 1953, Murray was already there. Murray's mentor, E.E. Evans-Pritchard, was something of an outlier among British anthropologists at the time, writing about the unity and overlapping nature of history and anthropology, a view Murray already shared. In 1954, Murray returned to Papua New Guinea to carry out intensive fieldwork among the Motu. His essay 'Dancing in Poreporena,' which was awarded the Hocart Memorial Prize, showed that historical records and field inquiries are better when measured against each other.[4] Murray became a research fellow in the Department of Pacific History at the Australian National University, then senior lecturer in social anthropology at the University of Auckland, and in 1965 moved to the University of Singapore. His dissertation, *The Motu of Papua*, published just after his death in 2011, reflects his life-long interest, which he shared with Jamie, in social change.[5] None of the five friends, who remained in touch, seems to have contemplated another hoax. I suppose the only person we might have worried about in that respect would have been Kit at the Bank of England.

When Ken and Judy, with baby Jamie, arrived in England in 1953, Murray met them at the boat train, found them their first apartment in Oxford, and became their most constant visitor. Judy had a degree in philosophy, and when she checked postgraduate courses offered at Oxford she found two diplomas that could be completed in two years, one in forestry and one in anthropology. Murray had already prepared the ground, so she too studied with Evans-Pritchard, and Ken sat in on Evans-Pritchard's lectures for pleasure. Judy would later become an activist anthropologist, one of the few people studying urban Indigenous people in the early 1960s.

When Ken and Judy returned from England in 1956, I spent the summer camping with them at Cowes, sharing a tent with Judy. I had recently graduated from Melbourne University with a degree in English, and this was the summer of my discontent. At night in our parallel camp cots, Judy told me about the wonders of anthropology, so I returned to Melbourne and set off for Sydney University; anthropology was still not taught at Melbourne. In Sydney, Mervyn Meggitt, fresh from fieldwork in New Guinea, was giving lectures about the lineage system of the Mae Enga, so I learned a lot more about British social anthropology. Ken was now connected to British anthropology by kinship and marriage.

When Ken first began to cite anthropologists, however, he drew not on the work of the British Evans-Pritchard, but on that of an American, Clifford Geertz. In a 1977 conference paper, Ken drew attention to Geertz's account of the dislocation of a funeral in Java.[6] (He had discovered the essay while visiting Jamie Mackie in Jakarta.) Geertz's essay criticises British anthropology's analysis of rituals, with a simplistic view of the functional role of religion in society that sees it merely as structure-conserving. He also criticises British anthropology's inability to adequately account for the failure of rituals. Historical materials, Geertz writes, could be used to develop a more complex conception of the relations between secular social life and religious belief and practice, and thus to deal more adequately with processes of change.

The debate between British and American anthropologists about the nature of ritual may now seem a little arcane, but it occupied anthropologists for some time, their divergent views signalled by the British concept of society and the American concept of culture. The lineage of British social anthropology is usually traced from Bronisław Malinowski, Alfred Radcliffe-Brown and Evans-Pritchard to Émile Durkheim, with a focus on social structures. The lineage of American cultural anthropology, on the other hand, travels from Franz Boas, Talcott Parsons and Clifford Geertz to Max Weber, with a focus on meaning. American anthropologists are said to have felt at home in studies of material culture, and in the search for patterns, themes, values, styles and national characteristics, but were uneasy in the analysis of social organisation, especially in its power aspect. The British are said to have neglected material culture, and to have felt discomfort with American anthropology's focus on 'value culture' and its embrace of history.[7]

This division of labour between British and American anthropology – reduced here to a 'Twitter history' – was coming to an end by the mid 1960s, when many British anthropologists found employment at American universities. Geertz identified 1963, when a conference in Cambridge brought together British and American anthropologists, as a great transition point. Evans-Pritchard and Geertz were both present. According to Geertz, the four books based on the conference papers, published over the next three years, broke down the sharpness of the division between British and American anthropology.[8]

Historians, however, seem to have adopted Geertz's views more readily than some anthropologists. The British anthropologist Mary

Douglas's review of Geertz's *The Interpretation of Cultures* in the *Times Literary Supplement* begins with a withering observation:

> One of the most persistent preoccupations of his working life, Clifford Geertz tells us, has been to find a satisfactory definition of culture. For American anthropologists, this project must seem central, necessary and probably feasible. For American anthropologists have long been trained within a discipline calling itself cultural anthropology. You can search its records high and low for a satisfactory definition. For all the volumes written about it, the concept 'culture' has not become an incisive tool of thought. It remains a commodious cushion, a category in which anything can comfortably recline ... He would do better to talk about 'systems of meaning' and drop culture altogether.[9]

In several essays, Ken tells us why he and other historians found Geertz's approach so attractive. The essay he read while visiting Jamie in Jakarta, in which Geertz describes how ceremonies go awry or are disrupted, abandoned or peacefully altered, seems to have been seminal. Geertz had shown that what goes wrong is as instructive as what goes right. Working on the sociology of religion in the United States in 1961 and 1962, Ken had been bothered by Lloyd Warner's account of the ceremonies commemorating dead American servicemen, which he later described as 'bland functionalism.'[10] All the rituals appear to work, Ken said, and yet there was evidence of conflict that Warner's approach couldn't accommodate. He also seems to have had Geertz in mind in his later praise for George Mosse's focus on the ceremonial use of myths, symbols and rituals in Nazi rallies, an approach that Ken said required historians to look at a modern society with the eye of an anthropologist.[11]

As a historian Ken adopted a broad array of what might be called anthropological research methods or, perhaps, methods that anthropologists and historians share. He made use of oral history for the updated edition of *The Stuart Case*, the story of the murder trial of Rupert Max Stuart, an Indigenous man accused of the rape and murder of a nine-year-old white girl.[12] The epilogue, based on an interview with Stuart, adopts a form of storytelling that focuses on the history of the life of an individual, using it as a lens through which to describe the historical forces that had produced him, an approach that the anthropologist Sid Mintz had used in his much-praised 1974 book, *Worker in the Cane: A Puerto Rican Life History*.[13]

Of greater interest, perhaps, Ken had two experiences of anthropological fieldwork, one of them when he spent eight years at the University of Papua New Guinea, where he found an interdisciplinary world unlike anything he had encountered before. He described it as 'a kind of village,' because he and his family lived for several years next to the anthropologist Ralph Bulmer and his wife Sue, an archaeologist. The Bulmers provided hospitality for famous visiting anthropologists, and as vice-chancellor Ken attended ceremonies introduced by the colonisers as well as those created and performed by Melanesians.[14]

The big anthropological adventure, however, was in 1965 when he lived with another group of 'villagers,' the more than 300 pilgrims who were returning to Gallipoli fifty years after many of them had landed there in April 1915. Qantas took them all from Brisbane to Athens, where they boarded the Turkish liner *Karadeniz*, and for the next three weeks they cruised around the Mediterranean.

Commissioned to write pieces for the *Canberra Times* (which also appeared in the *Sydney Morning Herald*), he was thrilled to be carrying a press card authorising him to send cables en route, via London to Australia. Becoming a journalist had been his boyhood ambition. As they came close to their destination, he tells us, the 'historian …

got the better of the amateur reporter.'[15] It seems, however, that the anthropologist had also emerged.

Seven dispatches filed en route, republished in 2015 with the title *Letters from a Pilgrimage*, bring to mind the work of the distinguished British anthropologist Victor Turner, who wrote about 'Pilgrimages as Social Processes.'[16] Turner adopted the concept of a ritual structure proposed by the great French ethnographer Arnold van Gennep, who had shown that the rituals marking significant transitions in human lives (at birth, puberty, marriage and death) have a three-part sequence: separation from everyday life; a transitional phase, described as liminal, during which an individual or group acquires a new status; and reaggregation and a return to the everyday world.[17]

Turner used this framework in 1974 for his comparative study of what he called the pilgrimage systems found in the major historical religions and in archaic societies.[18] Ken filed his dispatches in 1965, so Turner's studies were not available, but his first report quickly depicts the pilgrims' sense of separation from home, part one of van Gennep's trilogy:

> In Manila they meet the mysterious East. Each man who goes to the toilet of the transit lounge has a small youth creep up behind him bearing an electric vibrator which he rubs up and down the back. One victim comes roaring with laughter into the lounge where others sip whisky at eight shillings a glass. 'Wait'll I tell the boys about this!' he says.[19]

The final dispatch depicts phase three, reaggregation and a return to the everyday world:

> The pilgrims had come to visit the place where they themselves fought half a century ago and where men they loved were killed. When they had done that, most of them wanted to get back across

the world as fast as Qantas could carry them to the homeland from which the living and the dead had set out in 1914.[20]

Dispatches sent during the liminal phase, however, reveal a different understanding of the pilgrimage process. Turner focused productively on the pilgrim's experience of comradeship, but did not address the conflicts and animosities that sometimes occur during pilgrimage, a ritual feature identified by Geertz that Ken would not overlook. The bond established between Australians and New Zealanders, he writes, had become strained when the New Zealand party was assigned the stark and most crowded cabins on the lowest deck.

The dispatches draw attention also to the power dimensions of social organisation identified in British anthropology's analyses. Questions arose about who should land first on the beach. Sir Raymond Huish, the official leader of the pilgrimage, had fought in the war, but he was not a Gallipoli man, so he should stay on board until the Gallipoli men had preceded him; meanwhile, men who had offered themselves for the war earlier than others, and who considered themselves to be an elite within an elite, felt they should have received a medal.[21]

The newspaper-reading public in Australia would have recognised themselves in the carefully crafted portraits of the travellers. Ken blended the American focus on values and national characteristics with the British attention to social status. 'Australians as a people do not fit easily into the commercial parody of aristocratic living that goes on in international hotels,' he observes. '"What Australian," asks one man, "doesn't like his cuppa tea?"… [and] what Australian really enjoys waiters prancing about with silver serving trays and calling him "M'sieur?"'[22]

Turner proposed that the rituals of pilgrimage, like those of initiation, were performed when individuals or groups were undergoing a change in status. The Gallipoli pilgrims did not experience that change on their journey: that transformation had taken place in 1915. The Anzacs were returning to the place of their initiation, their holy ground, where they encountered themselves in memory. Turner also said that pilgrims choose to participate in a religious pilgrimage for the good of their souls.[23] Whether this could be said about the Anzacs was a question Ken had posed in 1960, when he described Anzac celebrations as a 'substitute religion.'[24]

The secular-sacred nature of Anzac is an important theme in the dispatches, which describe the careful avoidance of religion in ritual and ceremonial events. Two clergymen among the pilgrims had once been army chaplains, but they wore their RSL blazers and ties, and the leader, Sir Raymond Huish, used language drawn 'not from the Bible but from Laurence Binyon and Rudyard Kipling.'[25] Ken's definition of pilgrimage, drawn from the *Oxford Junior Encyclopedia*, now seems to have been a measured choice. A pilgrimage, it says, is a movement of people to a sacred spot where they are able to make at least temporary contact with the supernatural world. Some of the 300 or so Anzac pilgrims who visited Gallipoli would agree with this definition more readily than others, he adds, but all would accept the words 'sacred spot.'

The most profound effect of his experience travelling with the pilgrims, Ken wrote later, was a sense that he was experiencing what he had been coming to think of as Anzac religion: 'not anti-Christian, not at all, but not denominational either, incorporating a common Christian ethic, centring on the veneration of dead comrades whose spirits might or might not be inhabiting the hereafter.'[26]

Talal Asad, an anthropologist who has also been thinking about the place of the secular in religious experience, observed recently that religion and the secular are linked both in our thought and in the way they have emerged historically, and that a variety of concepts, practices and sensibilities have come together over time to form the 'secular.' His genealogy of the concept reaches back to the Renaissance doctrine of humanism and the Enlightenment concept of nature, as he reviews the major historical shifts that have shaped secular attitudes in the modern West and Middle East. The nation-state, he says, requires clearly demarcated spaces that it can classify and regulate – religion, education, health, leisure, work, income, justice and war. The question we should ask is when, and by whom, are the categories of religion and the secular defined?[27]

As if in answer to this anthropological question, Ken observes, in *Sacred Places: War Memorials in the Australian Landscape*, that our culture now subjects the very language of religion to a process of secularisation. He also notes that the term 'civil religion' goes back to Rousseau, who defined civil religion as a body of social sentiments without which no man could be either a good citizen or a faithful subject.[28] He documents the creative interplay of new ideas, practices and claims for recognition by local groups, in the unceasing reproduction of secular life within and beyond the bounds of the nation-state. 'Ever since 1915,' he notes, 'the message embodied in Anzac monuments, ceremonies and rhetoric has been contested by overlapping categories of dissenters – socialists, pacifists, Christians, nationalists unable to believe that the nation was born at Gallipoli.'[29] The Anzac tradition is a sort of civil religion in an almost post-Christian society that no longer delivers ancient certainties to young people in search of nourishment for the spirit.[30]

In *Sacred Places*, the anthropological historian travels beyond the bridge forged between British and American anthropology. Still alert, like the Reverend Ransome, to the historical, literary and sociological dimensions of the topic, his writing is more poetic and philosophical, reflecting the cleric's call for such a development. And perhaps, too, he shows the influence of the gang of five who met at Melbourne University, which in the late 1940s and early 1950s provided a stimulating environment for such disciplinary and intellectual border crossings.

Endnotes

1   C Wilcox, 'A Vernacular Intellectual,' in KS Inglis (ed. C Wilcox), *Observing Australia: 1959 to 1999*, Melbourne University Press, Carlton, 1999, p. 5.

2   E Wolf, *Anthropology*, W.W. Norton & Co., New York, 1974, p. 8.

3   TJR [KS Inglis], 'The Fascinating Bee: Inspirer of Poets and Philosophers,' *Age*, 28 July 1951, p. 7.

4   M Groves, 'Dancing in Poreporena,' *Journal of the Royal Anthropological Institute*, 1954, vol. 84, pp. 75–90.

5   M Groves, *The Motu of Papua: Tradition in a Time of Change*, Webzines of Vancouver, 2011.

6   C Geertz, 'Ritual and Social Change: A Javanese Example,' *American Anthropologist*, 1957, vol. 59, pp. 32–54.

7   Wolf, *Anthropology*, p. 62.

8   R Handler, 'An Interview with Clifford Geertz,' *Current Anthropology*, 1991, vol. 32, p. 604.

9   M Douglas, 'The Interpretation of Cultures,' *Times Literary Supplement*, August 1975.

10   KS Inglis (ed. J Lack), *ANZAC Remembered: Selected Writings by K.S. Inglis*, History Department, University of Melbourne, 1998, p. 239.

11   KS Inglis (ed. C Wilcox), *Observing Australia: 1959 to 1999*, Melbourne University Press, Carlton, 1999, p. 121.

12   KS Inglis, *The Stuart Case*, new edn, Black Inc., Melbourne, 2002.

13   S Mintz, *Worker in the Cane: A Puerto Rican Life History*, W.W. Norton & Co., New York, 1974.

14   C Spark, S Spark & C Twomey (eds), *Australians in Papua New Guinea, 1960–1975*, University of Queensland Press, St Lucia, 2014, pp. 320–1.

15   KS Inglis, *Letters from a Pilgrimage: Ken Inglis's Despatches from the Anzac Tour of Greece and Turkey, April–May 1965*, Inside Story, Melbourne, 2015, p. 5.

16   V Turner, *Dramas, Fields, and Metaphors: Symbolic Action in Human Society*, Cornell University Press, Ithaca, 1974.

17   A van Gennep, *The Rites of Passage*, Routledge & Kegan Paul, London, 1960.

18   Turner, *Dramas, Fields, and Metaphors*, p. 166.

19   Inglis, *Letters from a Pilgrimage*, p. 7.

20   Inglis, *Letters from a Pilgrimage*, p. 52.

21   Inglis, *Letters from a Pilgrimage*, p. 31.

22   Inglis, *Letters from a Pilgrimage*, p. 10.

23   Turner, *Dramas, Fields, and Metaphors*, p. 197.

24   KS Inglis, 'Anzac: The Substitute Religion,' in Inglis, *Observing Australia*, pp. 63–70.

25   Inglis, *Letters from a Pilgrimage*, p. 34.

26   Inglis, *ANZAC Remembered*, p. 237.

27   T Asad, *Formations of the Secular: Christianity, Islam, Modernity*, Stanford University Press, Stanford, 2003, p. 201.

28   KS Inglis (assisted by J Brazier), *Sacred Places: War Memorials in the Australian Landscape*, 3rd edn, Melbourne University Press, Carlton, 2008, p. 434.

29   Inglis, *Sacred Places*, p. 438.

30   Inglis, *Sacred Places*, p. 572.

Chapter 8

HISTORY UNFOLDING

Ken Inglis and the Stuart affair

Bob Wallace and Sue Wallace

'The Stuart affair' is a convenient term for the dramatic events following the rape and murder of a nine-year-old girl, Mary Hattam, on the afternoon of 20 December 1958. The crime took place on the beach below the Hattam family's clifftop home near Thevenard, a port town near Ceduna on the west coast of South Australia.

Two days later, Rupert Max Stuart, a twenty-seven-year-old initiated Arrernte man, was arrested and interrogated at Ceduna police station by Detective-Sergeant Paul Turner of Adelaide's Criminal Investigation Branch. In the presence of five other police, according to the official record, Stuart voluntarily dictated a detailed confession to Turner, which was typed word for word as he spoke. He was charged with the murder, tried by jury before Justice Geoffrey Reed at the Supreme Court, and on 26 April 1959 was found guilty and sentenced to hang on 22 May.

But Stuart's appointment with the hangman was to be deferred seven times, the seventh being permanent when, in October 1959, his sentence was commuted to life imprisonment.

The events following the murder are the subject of Ken Inglis's book *The Stuart Case*, published in 1961 by Melbourne University Press, and reissued in 2002 by Black Inc. with an epilogue in which Ken discusses important developments during the forty years between the two editions.[1] This chapter draws almost exclusively on the book's account of the trials, the subsequent legal appeals and royal commission, and Stuart's life following the commutation.

The story is a complex one, with surprising twists and turns. Despite the voluminous writing on the affair, some issues are still in dispute. Ken warns readers that the saga 'resists composition in a single narrative,' and we do not attempt one here. Our purpose is to explain how Ken, while a member of Adelaide University's history department, came to write *The Stuart Case*, and his significant role in Stuart's survival.

At the trial, the prosecution case was presented by Roderic Chamberlain, the state's solicitor-general. He took the police through their account of Stuart's movements after he arrived in Ceduna on Friday 19 December 1958 with Norman and Edna Gieseman's ragtag travelling funfair. That night Stuart went to the pictures with his fifteen-year-old illiterate whitefella friend, Allan Moir, and chatted up some young Aboriginal women from Thevenard. On Saturday morning the pair went drinking wine by the jetty. Sometime after midday Stuart took a taxi to Thevenard Hotel, drank more, talked to some of the women he'd met the night before, and walked back to the fair, crossing the beach where, between 2 and 4pm, Mary was so brutally killed. Later that afternoon, he worked at the fair; around sunset, he went back to the jetty and resumed drinking. At about 9pm he was arrested by the police as a drunken nuisance and was in the cells when Mary's body was found at about 11pm.

Stuart was released on Sunday morning and went back to the fair, where he was rebuked by Norman Gieseman for his delinquency and drinking. They parted, Stuart to return to Thevenard and a job at the wheat stacks, and the Giesemans (and Allan Moir) to Whyalla, where they arrived on Monday. There, Detective-Sergeant Alexander Phin of the local police spoke with Gieseman and Moir about Stuart's actions and conversations on Saturday, and sent details to the Ceduna police. They went to the wheat stacks, took Stuart into custody and, just before midnight, he signed the damning confession.

We cannot know what impression David O'Sullivan, Stuart's lawyer, formed about Stuart's guilt, but he certainly believed Stuart made the confession under duress and that it should therefore have been ruled inadmissible. Uncertainty about Stuart's competence in English was also a key issue: O'Sullivan could not call Stuart to give sworn evidence because Chamberlain, in cross-examination, might have been able to show that Stuart was capable of making a confession broadly consistent with the typed confession. Further, in cross-examination Chamberlain would have been allowed to reveal Stuart's criminal record.

Instead, O'Sullivan portrayed Stuart as illiterate and lacking the competence in English necessary to have spoken the coherent confession as typed. He asked that an unsworn statement by Stuart be read on his behalf. When the judge ruled against this request, Stuart spoke, but only to say, 'I cannot read or write. Never been to school. I did not see the little girl. I did not kill her. Police hit me, choked me, make me said these words. They say I kill her.' O'Sullivan asked the judge not to ask further questions.

In his summing up, Justice Reed stressed to the jury that they could return a guilty verdict only if they believed the police. After retiring for less than two hours, they returned a guilty verdict and Justice

Reed sentenced Stuart to hang at the Adelaide jail on 22 May. Had the sentence been carried out, *The Stuart Case* would not have been written and the murder would be but a mere footnote in the annals of Australian crime.

But O'Sullivan was far from finished. Ten days later he appealed to the state's criminal appeal court, comprising Chief Justice Sir Mellis Napier and Justices Mayo and Abbott. O'Sullivan must have known there was no possibility they would accept his submission that the jury's verdict was unreasonable and should be overruled. Without retiring, they duly rejected it, but not before O'Sullivan had accused the police of committing perjury and claimed that Stuart, in fear for his life, had been prepared to agree to anything. 'That is absolute rubbish,' Napier responded, confirming his confidence in the integrity of the police.

When the court rejected the appeal, O'Sullivan appealed to the High Court. He could hardly have expected Chief Justice Sir Owen Dixon and his colleagues to accept his plea that they overrule the decisions of the two South Australian courts. But the appeal won a respite for Stuart, first to 19 June and then, when the judges delayed delivering their decision, to 7 July. As expected, they rejected the appeal but, in an enigmatic preface and conclusion to their judgement, observed that 'certain features of this case have caused some concern,' a statement O'Sullivan was later able to put to effective use.

* * *

Ken had followed the events, appalled by the suffering of Mary and her family. But it was not until 27 June that the case took on particular significance for him. That evening, his wife, Judy Inglis, attended a meeting at the home of the president of the Aboriginal Advancement League, Charles Duguid, a medical doctor who had established the successful Ernabella Aboriginal mission. There, about fifty people interested in Aboriginal affairs and prisoners' welfare heard from Father Tom Dixon, a Catholic priest who had met Stuart in the death cell on 10 May, where he had gone to prepare him for the hanging.

Dixon had long experience as a missionary to the Arrernte people. He had sought out Ted Strehlow, who had been brought up among the Arrernte people at the Lutheran mission at Hermannsburg and was a recognised authority on the Arrernte language. Strehlow was well acquainted with Stuart's parents and had known Max Stuart since he was a child. After talking with the prisoner, Strehlow concluded that he was incapable of dictating the confession, and joined Dixon in supporting O'Sullivan's efforts to achieve fair treatment. Both spoke at the meeting at Duguid's home, and Judy took detailed notes. After she told Ken, later that evening, what she had heard, he decided to support the campaign, and five weeks later he resolved to write the book (which, appropriately, is dedicated to Judy's memory).

In the High Court, O'Sullivan had presented Strehlow's affidavits attesting that the confession was a concoction. The judges' comments might have reflected concerns that Stuart's competence in English was insufficient for him to tell his story to O'Sullivan and to follow trial proceedings.

Once the High Court appeal was refused, Justice Reed confirmed 7 July as the execution date. At 12.30pm on 6 July, the government's Executive Council met to consider a plea for commutation; ten minutes later it announced that 'no recommendation is made for pardon or reprieve' and that the hanging would proceed at 8am the next day. Stuart asked Dixon to stay with him overnight.

Three days earlier, the Adelaide *News* had published on its front page a long telegram from the federal opposition leader H.V. Evatt, himself a former High Court judge, prepared after discussion with O'Sullivan and addressed to the government. He referred to the High Court's enigmatic statement and said that the 'just thing' would be for the decision to be reviewed by the Privy Council in London, which was then Australia's final court of appeal. Dixon was with Stuart later in the afternoon of 6 July when they learned that, after his lawyers had followed Evatt's suggestion, Justice Reed had granted a respite to 20 July (later extended to 4 August). O'Sullivan flew to London for the hearing.

After the Executive Council so curtly refused to commute the sentence, the public campaign became even more vigorous. But it brought no response from the state government, and on Friday 17 July, three days before the respite expired, Dixon – who had already baptised Stuart – gave him communion in preparation for his death.

Alongside Evatt's telegram, the *News* had published a statement from the Police Association expressing concern about the attacks on the police officers' reputations. In defending the guilty verdict, the association alleged that Stuart's previous convictions included one for an assault on a girl and that at his trial he conducted his own defence and cross-examined witnesses in reasonable English.

The weekend papers of 4–5 July printed O'Sullivan's response, revealing that Paul Turner, who had interrogated Stuart, was president of the Police Association. O'Sullivan claimed that Turner's reckless statements created doubts about all the police evidence, and that the failure of the government to censure the police raised the 'suspicion the government is determined to hang Stuart and is using the Police Association to do its propaganda work.' Turner, outraged, said that

O'Sullivan was alleging that the six police officers had colluded and committed perjury, and were prepared to send an innocent man to his death.

Ken was in a unique position to describe these events, and wrote an article, 'The Hanging of a Man: A Police Association's Extraordinary Campaign,' for the 18 July edition of the fortnightly magazine *Nation*. It told of the grave concerns that led to Dixon's campaign and Evatt's intervention. He explained the heated exchanges between O'Sullivan and Turner, and quoted O'Sullivan's blistering criticism of Turner's intervention along with a statement by J.L. Travers QC, president of the Law Society, that the Police Association statement had 'surpassed the bounds of decency.' The article was a vital step towards the eventual commutation of Stuart's sentence.

The article attracted the attention of Tom Farrell, a senior reporter with the *Sydney Morning Herald*. He flew to Adelaide on 19 July, sought out Dixon and persuaded him to make a public statement that Stuart could not have dictated the typed version of his alleged confession; that there was further relevant evidence to be discovered; and that the authorities should delay the execution until Stuart's guilt was established beyond doubt. Farrell's report of Dixon's statement was the basis for an article of Tuesday 21 July in the Sydney paper, 'Conflict on Hanging in South Australia.' The Melbourne *Herald* also published Farrell's report, as did the Adelaide *News* in its late edition under the headline 'Impassioned Plea for Stuart: Priest's Doubts.'

Three days later, Rohan Rivett, editor of the Adelaide *News* under its youthful owner Rupert Murdoch, met Dixon at a long Friday lunch in the Adelaide University staff club organised by the student warden, Frank Borland, and attended by Ken. Dixon told Rivett he was trying to locate the Giesemans' funfair, which he knew was somewhere in

Queensland. Rivett agreed to pay Dixon's fare to Queensland to seek out the Gieseman party, and on Monday 27 July Dixon found them and obtained their statutory declarations that, at the time police said Stuart had killed the child, he was back at the fairground operating the darts stall in full view of them – apparently providing conclusive proof for Dixon's belief that Stuart was innocent.

O'Sullivan learned of the alibi on the morning of Tuesday 28 July just as he was to present to the Committee of the Privy Council the case for allowing the appeal against the High Court's decision. He spoke for two hours and, having told the Law Lords of the new evidence, sought an adjournment to enable him to consider it. Without calling upon Chamberlain to present the government's case, the lords told O'Sullivan that the appeal would not be heard. They saw no grounds to interfere with the judgement of the High Court, and any new evidence was not a matter for them, 'however relevant [it] may now be for consideration by the executive authority in South Australia.'

On Wednesday 29 July, in the midst of a wave of public support urging the government to consider the new evidence, 15,000 copies of a pamphlet, *Why Not Hang Rupert Stuart? Some Questions About a Murder*, were printed and distributed by volunteers.

The pamphlet stated it had been prepared by a group, but it was written by Ken, with Dixon's agreement and Judy's assistance, using material from the *Nation* article of ten days earlier. It was written in the form of a temperate dialogue between two people, one putting probing questions about the origin, motives and argument of those campaigning to avert the hanging, and the other giving well-reasoned answers.

That night, in a late edition, the *News* reproduced the text in full, and the next day a near-complete version was published in the *Sydney*

Morning Herald and the Melbourne *Herald*, giving it great impact. That day, Thursday 30 July, proved the critical one. During the morning, 10,000 copies of the pamphlet were distributed with an additional sentence urging concerned readers to contact members of parliament. The poster for the noon edition of the *News* said 'Adelaide Leaders Demand Delay' and the paper reported comments from many influential individuals and organisations. The premier, Thomas Playford, received a letter from Sir John Latham, former High Court judge and federal attorney-general, urging a respite for careful examination of the fresh evidence.

When parliament met at 2pm, the leader of the opposition sought to move a motion that the execution be deferred. But the premier had already accepted that the new alibi evidence had to be taken seriously, and announced that 'the sentence had been suspended for a month, and a royal commission comprising three Supreme Court judges would go into the whole matter.'

* * *

Ken was present when the royal commission began to hear its first evidence on 17 August. As a letter sent three days earlier to Evatt shows, he was already committed to writing the book. 'Dear Dr Evatt,' his letter begins. 'With the cooperation of defence counsel and Father Dixon and Professor Norval Morris, I am writing a book about the Stuart case. This may seem premature, but I think it should be told however it ends.'[2]

In the epilogue to the 2002 edition of *The Stuart Case*, Ken explains that when he learned that defence counsel could not afford a clerk to collate the flow of transcript, he offered to do the job and so came to have not merely a ringside view but a seat inside the ring. He wrote the book very quickly. In writing about events prior to the commission, he drew on the voluminous police and court records, the extensive media coverage and his discussions with many of those involved. He wrote the account of the commission as it unfolded before him. Before the enquiry finished he had sufficient material for Melbourne University Press to agree to publish the book, which it did in 1961.

Ken already had a long-held desire to write contemporary history for a wide readership, using as a model the technique of Lillian Ross, whose long essays in the *New Yorker* showed how contemporary history could be written in narrative form. He took full advantage of this fortuitous opportunity to do so. He had been contributing enthusiastically to *Nation* since it was launched in September 1958, and his fortnightly articles on the Stuart affair became components of the book.

Using Ross's technique, he wrote *The Stuart Case* in the form of a mystery told by an anonymous, omnipresent observer. The device established an intimacy between the narrator and his curious audience without revealing he had played a significant part in the story. The result is a ripping yarn, showing how the chain of events that saved Stuart was made up of multiple links, many of which required an unlikely coincidence of events and all of which had to hold for Stuart to avoid the noose. Chapter headings including 'A Race with Death,' 'Alibi,' 'A Cloud of Witnesses' and 'The Prisoner Speaks' encourage the readers to persist to the climax.

Even for most of the penultimate chapter – 'Guilty or Not Guilty?' – readers do not hear Ken's voice. It is written in the style of a judge summing up the evidence in this complex case to assist us, the jury of readers, before we retire to make our decision. But towards the end of the chapter, a paragraph begins 'In the present writer's opinion, Stuart was probably guilty.' In the next paragraph, though, he writes: 'To the present writer, the evidence of the witnesses from the funfair ... is hard to dismiss with certainty ...' so leaving readers the option of returning the Scottish 'not proven' verdict.

Neither Dixon nor Chamberlain had any such reservations. Dixon never wavered in his belief in Stuart's innocence, and Chamberlain never wavered in his belief in his guilt. In 1972 Chamberlain, believing Stuart capable of killing again, rejected his first application for parole. Each published a history of the affair, Chamberlain in 1973 and Dixon, after years of further investigation, in 1987.[3] Ken discusses both books in 'The Stuart Case Revisited,' a review in *Quadrant* in December 1987.[4] Neither lived to read Ken's epilogue: it would have greatly pleased Dixon and much surprised Chamberlain.

* * *

The Stuart Case gives a detailed account of the commission's long, drawn-out, turbulent proceedings, which are summarised below. It is a classic courtroom drama, and was used by the makers of a television docudrama shown on the ABC and SBS, and the film *Black and White.*[5]

The immediate response to Playford's announcement of the commission seemed promising, with all parties welcoming it. But a few hours later, when Playford named Chief Justice Napier and Justice Reed as two of the three commissioners, Stuart's lawyers were outraged. They might not participate, they said, unless the terms of reference were widened and different commissioners appointed. When parliament next met, Playford gave an unqualified commitment 'that every matter connected with this case will be sifted to the ground.' With this assurance and having recruited Jack Shand, a leading Sydney barrister, Stuart's advisers agreed to cooperate.

The first key witnesses, Gieseman and his party, appeared at the commission on 17 August 1959. In answer to Chamberlain's courteous, seductive questions they said that they had experienced no difficulty in conversing with Stuart in English. Chamberlain put it to Gieseman that his sworn alibi had differed greatly from the statement he had made on 30 December 1958 to Phin at Whyalla, which had led to Stuart's arrest, but Gieseman denied key sections of Phin's account of that conversation.

Shand's technique was the opposite. As Ken writes, 'Shand in court was brisk to the point of rudeness, irritable towards other counsel and not very deferential towards the bench.' In aggressively cross-examining Phin, he pointed to differences between his responses and his record of the statements Gieseman and Moir had made at Whyalla. When Napier interrupted him, saying he had 'heard enough' on that matter, Shand accused him of cutting short the cross-examination. Napier told him he could continue, but Shand was not mollified. At the hearing the next day, 21 August, he said that he and Stuart's solicitors considered that the commission was preventing a thorough investigation and that the further participation of his legal team would not assist Stuart, so 'therefore we withdraw.' He walked out of the hearing room with Ken in tow, leaving Stuart without representation until 16 September.

A week later, Napier, in a calm but emotionally charged statement, claimed that Shand's withdrawal 'had every appearance of an act of deliberate sabotage of this enquiry.' He spoke with pride of a thirty-five-year career on the bench that had won him, he believed, the approbation of the whole community. It was a rude awakening, he said, that this could 'be shattered at a touch by a man of whom I know no more than he knows of me.' He spoke knowing that his wife had just suffered a stroke, but not knowing that Shand was suffering from terminal cancer, and would die a few weeks later.

* * *

Premier Playford's handling of the affair had already been much criticised, but Shand's withdrawal turned the storm of protests into a tsunami, fed by worldwide press coverage and statements by highly respected lawyers, judges and politicians. Particularly damaging was the *News* report on the day Shand withdrew. Before noon its display poster read 'SHAND QUITS: "YOU WON'T GIVE STUART FAIR GO."' Another banner followed later in the day: 'Commission breaks up: Shand blasts Napier.' The paper's front-page headline read: 'Mr Shand, QC, indicts Sir Mellis Napier: "these commissioners cannot do the job."'

Playford's response was intemperate and highly damaging. He saw that he had made a serious mistake when he accepted his chief justice's advice that he (the chief justice) and Reed should be the commissioners, and he was rattled. He had been premier and treasurer since 1938, and the state's healthy economy and staid social mores reflected his dominance. The *Advertiser*, the morning newspaper, was the city establishment's newspaper; its editorials were congenial reading for conservative-leaning middle-class and rural readers, and for his government. Other readers much preferred the spicier evening tabloid, the *News*, though until this affair it had given him no more trouble than had the docile Labor opposition.

Playford was generally respected for his personal integrity, and in turn he respected the integrity of his judiciary, his legal officers and his police force. As he saw it, the state was in the hands of good and wise men – and they agreed with him. They were his men and he would defend them.

In the wake of the walkout, the opposition at last went on the attack with a searing criticism of Playford's handling of the affair and failure to respond to the mass of protests by well-informed people. Playford defended the commission, saying that during a month-long campaign 'the vilest crimes have been charged against the judges, the police and every one of our institutions … My government stands for the maintenance of law by the courts.' And then he went on the attack. Brandishing the *News* poster, he read out its text, pointing out that by using inverted commas it had quite wrongly implied that Shand had actually used those words – so committing 'the grossest of libels' against the judges. 'At the appropriate time,' he added, 'the government will act to protect our judges.'

The next day the *News* conceded that 'the Premier is right. And we were wrong. Mr Shand did not use these words, and the headline should never have been published.' After the commission reported, Rivett and Murdoch were charged with seditious and criminal libel, tried in the Supreme Court and, to Ken's satisfaction, found not guilty by the jury.

Three weeks after Shand withdrew, O'Sullivan decided that it was in Stuart's interests to again be represented, and John Starke QC, another distinguished barrister, accepted the brief to act for him. On 16 September, the commission granted Starke's request for an adjournment for nineteen days to prepare his case, and Stuart's hanging, scheduled for 30 September, was postponed yet again, to 9 November. But then on 5 October, Chamberlain informed the commission that the death sentence had been commuted. When the commission resumed the hearings on 13 October, Stuart was at last able to speak freely. He gave evidence for five hours spread over three days. Though at times contradicting himself, he stuck to the main outline of his defence. But he could not give a convincing explanation of why he had not initially told O'Sullivan of the alibi produced by the Giesemans seven months later.

All other relevant witnesses were heard in orderly proceedings, and on 26 October, after Starke and Chamberlain made their final submissions, the commission adjourned. Its report, submitted to the government on 3 December, four months after its appointment, concluded that Stuart was guilty – so confirming the jury's verdict in April, made after retiring for less than two hours. Stuart went to Yatala to serve his life sentence, and Ken completed his manuscript.

* * *

On publication, *The Stuart Case* was favourably reviewed. The only harsh criticism came later when Chamberlain, in his own history, wrote that 'university intellectuals who knew very little ... about the facts of the Stuart case ... led a newspaper editor to discover the makings of a front-page story, and between them they stirred up emotions that developed into an attack on institutions fundamental to the democratic way of life.'[6] The premier would no doubt have agreed. But Ken, clearly a culprit, saw the case as exposing Playford's complacent belief that he and his men in the police and law were incapable of error. This was the real threat to democratic institutions, he believed, and he paid due tribute to those who worked so hard for fair treatment for Stuart.

It seemed that, for Ken, this was the end of the affair. But forty years later he made another important contribution. He had followed with great interest Stuart's life after he began his life sentence. He had a file of the press stories and was surprised that no one had reported on the fact that Stuart had survived the ordeal of the trials, the commission and imprisonment to eventually become a leader of the Arrernte people, respected and at ease in both black and white societies. Ken believed that Stuart's life after he began his sentence merited a supplementary history, and this became the epilogue to the 2002 edition.

The epilogue is written in the first person, and explains how Ken came to write the book and why he played down his own role. He adds some material and corrects errors in the book and in his pamphlet, and acknowledges that his close links to O'Sullivan and the campaigners influenced his account and that, on some issues, he did not give due weight to the other side. He reviewed much of the voluminous writing by people intimately involved in the affair. And then he turned to his main task: an account of Stuart's life over the past forty years.

After thirteen years in jail, Stuart was paroled to Santa Teresa, the mission where Dixon had worked. But he breached parole on six occasions, resulting in six further periods of imprisonment. It was twenty-five years before he became a free man and, in 1985, got a most fortunate break.

Pat Dodson, who had been a Sacred Heart priest like Dixon, was working in Alice Springs at the Central Land Council. He arranged a part-time job for Stuart, which Ken described as the first step in Stuart's ascent to the position of chair of the Council and a role of political and ceremonial eminence in his Arrernte world. Stuart later acknowledged that it was his rich education in prison that enabled him to take full advantage of this break. There, he became competent in spoken and written English and, as his affectionate letters to Dixon show, developed a healthy self-awareness.

Stuart experienced much kindness from his teachers and visitors, particularly from Isabel Penny, a volunteer prison visitor who, he said, made him believe in himself and gave him hope he could survive to lead a good life. He joined Alcoholics Anonymous and got comfort from recalling the myths and songs he had been taught for his initiation. He learned practical skills in the prison kitchens and on the prison farm, and he kept physically well with good food and outdoor exercise. Over time he was allowed more visitors, and after Don Dunstan became premier he was allowed to give interviews to four cadet journalists from Melbourne who were reading *The Stuart Case* as coursework for a diploma in journalism.

It was hard to reconcile this Max Stuart with the young man Ken describes in 'Tracks to Ceduna,' the opening chapter of *The Stuart Case*. That chapter describes a time when the intrusion of white people into Arrernte lands had undermined a traditional culture that had provided clear rules for behaviour through its rich mythology and ceremonies. For Stuart and many other young Aboriginal men, their greatest contact with the intrusive white culture was through the missions, alcohol, police, courts and jail.

From the age of eleven he had led an adventurous but erratic life, travelling great distances and working on cattle stations and as a boxer in Jimmy Sharman's well-known boxing troupe. When he arrived at Ceduna he already had a long record of drunken misbehaviour and had served several prison sentences for violent crimes. As Ken looked at him facing the commissioners, he saw a sullen, bewildered and incompetent liar.

It was to be forty-two years before Ken again came face to face with him. He knew, of course, that Stuart had played a key role in native title negotiations over vast areas, had travelled to negotiate the return of sacred objects, and had played a role in promoting ancient mythology and ceremonies. As an elder, Stuart had assisted in the initiation of his kinsman, the well-known activist and public servant Charles Perkins. The changed position of the Arrernte people was highlighted in 2000 by two events: when Stuart greeted the Queen and welcomed her to his country; and when the party carrying the torch to the 2000 Sydney Olympics said, 'We come to ask permission to proceed across sacred lands,' and he consented.

So it was with great anticipation that Ken went to the Council's office to talk to Stuart in May 2002. He was greeted by a white-haired, pot-bellied, quick-witted old man, with a droll sense of humour and engaging charm. Ken began by mentioning his friendship with Dixon, and that led into a comfortable two-hour conversation. Stuart spoke with justifiable pride of his accomplishments for his people. After a break for a smoke, he took from his wallet a copy of the press photo used on the cover of Ken's book, and Ken asked him about the murder. He talked freely, maintaining that he was at the fair when the child was murdered and that the cops had bashed the confession out of him. He hoped the truth would come out, and that someone, maybe Ken, would tell the rest of his story. In parting, Stuart shook hands firmly, saying, 'Safe journey 'ome, mate.'

Ken had paid what Stuart saw as the standard fee for such an interview, $350, and it was clearly a bargain. He left feeling he 'had been in the company of a person who had achieved some kind of redemption.' He had escaped the noose against the longest of odds and outlived all the agents of the state who had condemned and punished him. If innocent, he had endured great injustice; if guilty, his survival intact was even more remarkable.

Interestingly, Stuart acknowledged that, had the jury not believed the police, he would have gone free and probably continued the dysfunctional life of so many of his age and background. It was his time in prison that equipped him to ultimately enjoy a family life, respected as a champion of his people. Perhaps through the remarkable chain of coincidences, blind fate, rather than the legal process, had delivered a just outcome.

The Stuart affair is a sensational story, which for a few weeks featured prominently in the world media. Ken was pleased to learn from us that *The Stuart Case* is still used as a major study in the training of journalists. But members of the public are now more likely to have learned of the affair through the television and film versions, which, through judicious selections and omissions and some exaggerated portrayals, divide the characters into black hats and white hats, leading some viewers to tell Ken that Stuart was clearly innocent. To which Ken might well respond, 'Why did I bother?'

We must accept that the remaining uncertainties in the Stuart affair will never be resolved. But there is no question that Ken's direct involvement was a significant factor in averting Stuart's hanging, and that his writing contributed to improvements in police practices and legal procedures, which ensure that today an Aboriginal person in a similar situation, while still disadvantaged, would be treated quite differently.[7]

Endnotes

1   KS Inglis, *The Stuart Case*, Melbourne University Press, Carlton, 1961;
     KS Inglis, *The Stuart Case*, new edn, Black Inc., Melbourne, 2002.

2   Inglis to Evatt, letter, 14 August 1959, Dunstan Collection, Special Collections, Flinders University Library.

3   R Chamberlain, *The Stuart Affair*, Rigby, Adelaide, 1973; TS Dixon, *The Wizard of Alice: Father Dixon and the Stuart Case*, Alella Books, Morwell, 1987.

4   K Inglis, 'The Stuart Case Revisited,' *Quadrant*, vol. 31, no. 12, December 1987, pp. 73–7.

5   *Broken English: The Conviction of Max Stuart*, docudrama, directed by Ned Lander, part 1 of *Blood Brothers*, Film Australia, 1993; *Black and White*, film, directed by Craig Lahiff, Duoart Productions, 2002.

6   Chamberlain, *The Stuart Affair*, p. 303.

7   Michael Kirby, former justice of the High Court, discusses the imperfections of the legal system exposed by *The Stuart Affair*, and the improvements since 1959: M Kirby, 'Black and White Lessons for the Australian Judiciary,' *Adelaide Law Review*, vol. 23, no. 2, 2002, pp. 195–213.

Chapter 9

SYDNEY CALLING

Ken Inglis and the press

Peter Browne

Ken Inglis's role in the pathbreaking fortnightly paper *Nation* began with a phone call from its editor, Tom Fitzgerald, not long before it was launched. 'One evening in August 1958,' he recalled thirty years later, 'the operator there told me that Sydney was calling – a rare event – and I heard the gentle, civilised voice of a man introducing himself as financial editor of the *Sydney Morning Herald* and wondering whether I would consider writing for a journal of opinion he was about to start.'[1] Fitzgerald had seen a piece of Ken's in *Meanjin* and wanted him to be the new paper's Adelaide correspondent.

The twenty-eight-year-old historian was just back from three years in Britain and looking for a way to communicate with audiences outside universities. He had written for Harold Levien's pioneering monthly, *Voice*, earlier in the decade, and occasionally for the *Age* since he'd been at Melbourne University, but since his return he had found 'nowhere really comfortable' to write.[2]

Nation gave many outstanding Australian writers a chance to reach an attentive audience over the next fourteen years. It nurtured new talent, gave a sympathetic welcome (and more space than usual) to established figures, and set new standards in Australian commentary, reporting and reviewing.

But Ken and Tom had more than the usual contributor–editor bond. Each of the two men – lanky, slightly dishevelled Ken, with his fine head of hair, and short, neatly dressed, balding Tom – had been the first in their families to attend university, and in both cases that family had run its own business. Both had spent time in Britain but had been unexpectedly invigorated by the United States. ('I found that I was much more at home in every way in America and an American univer-sity than I'd ever felt in Oxford and England,' Ken told the historian Neville Meaney in 1986.[3] 'The cut and thrust of their conversation, the whole atmosphere... I felt that dear old Australia couldn't offer you that kind of challenge,' Tom told Ken in 1988.[4]) Both were passionate in their interests but cool and questioning on the page. Both had a strong belief in the existence of a readership for a paper like *Nation*.

* * *

By the time *Nation*'s first edition appeared on 26 September 1958, another Sydney-based fortnightly was into its eighth month of pub-lication. The *Observer* was edited by Donald Horne and published by Australian Consolidated Press, the company behind the *Australian Women's Weekly* and the Sydney *Daily Telegraph*. *Nation* was centre-left; the *Observer* was centre-right. *Nation*'s proprietor-editor had no one to answer to but himself; Horne was answerable to the owner of Consolidated Press, Frank Packer, who seems to have kept Horne on a fairly loose leash – at least until the subject matter got too close to home.

In May, the *Observer* had announced that a former press critic for the *New Statesman*, writing under the name Autolycus, would contribute a fortnightly critique of Australian newspapers. The danger sign came in the closing sentences of the announcement: 'The opinions expressed are entirely his own and do not necessarily have any connection with those of Australian Consolidated Press or the editorial staff of this publication. We hope the experiment works; it is a case not only of dog eating dog but of dog eating itself.'[5]

In the same edition, Autolycus (real name Robert Raymond, best known as one of the creators of the ABC's *Four Corners*) reported on how many column inches the main capital city dailies devoted to different kinds of content. He found, surprisingly, that the papers in the smaller cities ran proportionally the most foreign coverage. The pattern of advertising space was less clearcut – the big-city *Sydney Morning Herald* had the highest proportion, at 69 per cent, yet the other Sydney morning paper, Packer's *Telegraph*, had the lowest, at 42 per cent. He couldn't resist a dig at Packer's paper: 'Thus it will be seen that either the Sydney *Daily Telegraph* selflessly devotes nearly twice as much of its space to informing its readers as the *Sydney Morning Herald*... or else its advertising department can sell only a little more than half as much space as the *Herald*'s can.'[6]

Over the next two editions, as he analysed press coverage of the crisis in Algeria, Autolycus took further swipes at the *Telegraph*. Then he offered an appraisal of the afternoon papers in each capital city, in the course of which he made these comments: 'If there is a more unreadable pair of newspapers than the *Courier-Mail* and the *Telegraph* I have yet to come across them. Of the two, the *Telegraph* is easily the more horrible – typographically and in content... [I]t must go a long way towards ruining that glorious Queensland winter for the residents of Brisbane.'[7]

'The editor desires to inform readers,' read a note in the next edition of the *Observer*, 'that we dissociate ourselves from the views expressed by Autolycus regarding those two papers, which are held in high repute by the public of Queensland, and, in our view, measure up to high standards of journalism.'[8] The managing director of the papers, Sir John Williams, had rung Packer and accused him of complicity in the attack, and Packer had told Donald Horne that Autolycus must go.[9]

Seeing a succession of editors subjected to proprietorial interference at the *Sydney Morning Herald* had played an important role in Tom Fitzgerald's decision to launch his own paper. 'There were terrible battles about editorials. Long drawn-out battles,' he told Ken in 1988.[10] He assumed he wouldn't be allowed to combine editing *Nation* with his job at the *Herald*, and arranged in advance to write for Packer as a freelancer once he had tendered his resignation. But Fairfax's managing director Rupert Henderson, keen to hang on to the paper's highly regarded financial editor, persuaded the board to let him stay on while running his own paper.

Tom Fitzgerald had grown up in the inner western suburbs of Sydney, where his father owned a milk run. He was educated in the local convent school, at the Marist Brothers school at Kogarah, and later at the Lewisham Christian Brothers school, and served with the RAAF in Britain's coastal command during the war. After he graduated with a degree in economics from Sydney University, he joined the *Bulletin* as a business reporter and was then appointed editor of *Wild Cat Monthly*. He moved to the *Sydney Morning Herald* in 1950 and became financial editor in 1952.[11]

'He had the round, rosy face of a very shrewd cherub,' writes Gavin Souter, a *Herald* colleague, as well as 'a fearless eye for business chicanery, and a clear prose style.'[12] (The shrewdness can be quantified: at one point, four businessmen who had issued stop writs against him were in jail at the same time.) On the basis of his experience at the *Herald*, Fitzgerald felt that Australia's broadsheet papers underestimated their readers. 'The particular kind of people who determined what went into the news pages [at the *Herald*] varied enormously, but generally speaking there was, shall I say, a low-browish, or a down-to-earth, bread-and-butter matter-of-factness demanded in those pages.'[13]

Inspiration also came from *Voice*, which had appeared from 1952–56. It was further fuelled by the group that gathered around Fitzgerald, often at Lorenzini's wine bar, around the corner from the Fairfax building, as he developed the plan for the fortnightly.[14] Several of them, including George Munster, Sylvia Lawson and Keith Thomas, would go on to play significant roles in the new paper. Marie de Lepervanche and, later, Margaret Fitzgerald, managed the *Nation* office, not far from the *Sydney Morning Herald* bulding.

And so, with around a month to go before *Nation* was launched, Fitzgerald made the shrewd decision to place a call to Adelaide. It was 'a great moment in my life, when you rang,' Ken told Tom in 1988, and recalled 'that marvellous moment when the issue came in an envelope addressed in your hand.'[15] Years later, he described his association with *Nation* as 'life-changing.' Writing for *Voice* had been 'more a series of chores' because of the uncertainty about if and when the next edition would appear; writing for the professional, reliably fortnightly *Nation* felt much more like being a real journalist.[16] Topicality was vital – not only because it suited Fitzgerald's journalist impulses but also because he believed that a larger audience could be attracted by a publication closer to the tempo of events – and Ken was a willing accomplice:

Dear Tom,

3–400 words, reaching you Monday, on Adelaide's plans for an Arts Festival.

Yours,

K.I.[17]

Nation's correspondence files in the National Library of Australia show the paper's eagerly engaged network of supporters feeding information and ideas back to the editor. They reported on stocks of each edition in newsagencies ('One friend of mine tried in vain for No. 4 in Melbourne – at the airport, at Myers, and I think at one or two central newsagents'[18]), critiqued layout and printing quality, subjected the contents of each edition to rigorous analysis, and offered up topics for their own and others' contributions.

Ken was one of Tom and George's closest confidants, sending a stream of ideas and observations by mail, even at one point chiding Tom for his and George's erratic correspondence with would-be contributors. He was in many ways the perfect *Nation* contributor: like Tom and many of *Nation*'s inner circle, he was curious about almost everything and had a keen sense of the audience for which he wanted to write. As he told Neville Meaney, 'I would like to be read by the people I went to school with. And by my parents. And by my children... I think I've never settled comfortably into a communication universe – that's putting it badly – of scholarship alone.'[19]

He joined journalists and academics including Macmahon Ball, Cyril Pearl and Ken Gott in Melbourne, Harry Kippax, Robert Hughes, Maria Prerauer and Claire Wagner in Sydney, Manning

Clark, Ian Fitchett and Don Whitington in Canberra, and many others of a left-liberal bent who'd been waiting for an opportunity to write for a paper like this. The most prolific of all were Fitzgerald and Munster. Fitzgerald wrote most of the editorials – sometimes three to an edition, frequently as critical of Labor as of Menzies's government – and he and Munster wrote numerous signed and unsigned articles and reviews.

Nation was launched at almost exactly the midpoint of the Menzies era. Labor's ineffectual opposition, led by H.V. Evatt, had induced growing complacency within the government, and Menzies's ill-advised decision to back the British during the Suez Crisis in 1956 was fresh in people's minds. Labor was in government in New South Wales, Western Australia and Tasmania; the Country Party governed in Queensland; Henry Bolte was in the early years of his long Liberal premiership in Victoria; and the Liberal and Country League's Thomas Playford was in the twentieth year of his in South Australia. Keynesianism was ascendant, though differing views of what that meant in practice (and what was politically wise) had brought a series of booms and busts. The 1958 federal election – a fifth consecutive loss for Labor – was just two months away.

Elsewhere in this volume Robert Dare discusses the extraordinary number and range of Ken's contributions to *Nation* from Adelaide between 1958 and mid 1961, and Bob Wallace and Sue Wallace look at Ken's coverage of the Stuart case. Here I focus on Ken's later work for the paper, including a feature of *Nation*, almost entirely Ken's work, which was unique in the Australian media at the time, and had its only real precedent in Autolycus's brief career at the *Observer*. But it's worth noting that Ken's reporting of the campaign for a fresh trial of convicted murderer Max Stuart – effectively as a participant observer, with the risks that entails[20] – would have added to his understanding of how journalists and the press work. He saw at close quarters the campaigning role of Adelaide *News* and how an Adelaide cause célèbre rippled across the nation, partly as a result of his own reporting for *Nation*. He also saw the coverage shaped by ambitions (the *News* was Rupert Murdoch's one paper at the time) and marred by errors (the Sydney *Mirror* reporter heard 'tactics' as 'antics' at one point in the royal commission – 'a word which his subeditors understandably raised to the headline'[21]).

Nation had been reporting on the business side of the press and broadcasting since its launch, but the approach Ken made his own was the close reading of the content of newspapers, including their visual style. Tom Fitzgerald was more than happy to give space to this kind of scrutiny: it dovetailed with his intention to use *Nation* to show what better broadsheet papers would give their readers. Ken had seen this kind of criticism done extremely well by A.J. Liebling, in the *New Yorker*, and by Francis Williams, who had revived the *New Statesman*'s coverage of Fleet Street after Autolycus left England for Australia.

Nation's first piece in this style came from an unnamed correspondent in Melbourne, who surveyed reaction to the 'jazzing up' of the front page of the Melbourne *Herald* in late 1958.[22] Ken's first piece on the press, one of three pieces advertised on the front page under the headline, 'Newspapers in Turmoil,' came in the fifth edition.[23] All his characteristic qualities are there in this report about the rivalry between the establishment *Advertiser* and young Rupert Murdoch's afternoon paper, the *News*: a slightly quizzical tone, an eye for the telling detail, and the capacity to show rather than tell. 'The News and the Advertiser usually ignore each other's existence, though they are not inflexible about it,' he writes drily, before describing an early instance of Murdoch's modus operandi: boosting his own paper by relentlessly attacking the *Advertiser*'s news as 'stale.'

Ken returned to the performance of the press in his articles about the Stuart case in the second half of 1959, and covered the opening of the local ABC television station, ABC 2, in March 1960. Then he began contributing a column looking at how newspapers were reporting the issues of the day. 'I took all the dailies then being published in capital cities,' he wrote later, 'and in nearly every issue for a year or so I looked at how the makers interpreted their city, their state, their country, their world.'[24] For readers who were unlikely to see interstate papers regularly – Ken had subscribed to sixteen of them – or even to read the rival newspapers in their own city, this would have put a different perspective on the Australian press.[25]

'On the momentous issue of our policy towards Asian migration, you might think that any statement by the Minister for Immigration would be newsworthy, especially as he makes so few,' was the opening of a typical piece.[26] 'Some editors would agree with you, some not,' Ken went on:

> The 'Sydney Morning Herald,' which gave the fullest report of Mr Downer's Milne Lecture, had a headline: MINISTER AGAINST CHANGE. INFLOW OF ASIANS COULD 'DEFEAT FRIENDLY AIM.' The Adelaide 'Advertiser,' the Melbourne 'Age' and the Canberra 'Times' all reported this part of the lecture. Several other morning papers... printed only the Minister's remarks about the effect of European migration on ties with Britain. The Hobart 'Mercury' appears to have decided that nothing in the lecture was worth passing on.

Of the two papers that editorialised about the speech, the 'Advertiser' felt there was 'much to support' in Mr Downer's view 'that to adopt Asian quotas now' – to increase Asian migration – 'would create new tensions and differences, and so destroy the friendly, helpful relation-ships Australia is trying to create.' Presumably, added Ken, it was an accident that the next day's editorial – 'the regular Saturday essay in Addisonian uplift' – 'reflected benignly on the cultural benefits throughout human history of "the rovings and migrations of people into each other's territory."'

Often, Ken told me in 2017, his *Nation* articles were written 'last thing at night' after he'd been thinking about them during the week. Having finished writing at about midnight, he would take the piece to the overnight-rush mailbox at Adelaide GPO, which delivered let-ters to Sydney the next day.[27] There, at the GPO, it might be George Munster who would open *Nation*'s GPO Box 112, 'in his mind's eye a cornucopia.'[28]

Ken's reports on the press continued until he departed for a year's study leave in the United States. Then, as far as I can tell, he didn't reappear in *Nation* until February 1963, and his articles on the press didn't resume until May of the following year. By then, with the highly publicised launch of Rupert Murdoch's national paper, the Canberra-based *Australian*, just two months away, there was plenty to write about. The *Canberra Times* had already acted to deal with the competition in the local market, where Murdoch hoped to create a monopoly base for his paper. A first piece – 'The Homestead Dog' – discussed the sale of the *Canberra Times* to Fairfax, who its former owner, Arthur Shakespeare, believed would have the resources necessary to fight off Murdoch.[29] As managing editor, Fairfax had appointed John Douglas Pringle, *Herald* editor from 1952–57, who had recently been coaxed back to Sydney after a period in his native Britain.

Ken gave a vivid portrait of the paper itself, including its treasured misprints and blurry photos. He also reported that the improvements under Pringle and his editor, David Bowman, had increased sales to 20,000 – not bad in a city with fewer than 20,000 households. The paper, he wrote, was 'looking a little more comfortable in its broadsheet pages' and its photos were less 'muddy.' Even Murdoch was impressed. 'It was a remarkable achievement. And a pretty rough welcome for us,' he told one of his biographers a quarter of a century later.[30]

Ken's two longest press articles for *Nation* were published after the launch of Murdoch's new paper. 'The *Australian*,' he wrote, 'is, first of all, a clean and handsome thing to look at. Not all the news pages have the "elegant appearance" we had been led to hope for; but compared with those of every other Australian newspaper they are, as promised, "uncluttered."'[31] The double-page carrying editorials, cartoon and features seems to me simply beautiful: a few square feet of black and white fit to place alongside the best-designed newspapers of our language and time – the *Guardian*, say, or the *Observer*, or the New York *Herald Tribune*.'

But the prose turned out to be less elegant: 'Contributions by such writers as Robin Boyd, Jock Marshall, Kenneth Hince and Edgar Waters read as if the layout were designed for them; some other pieces, signed and unsigned, sit there less happily.' Even more worryingly, the paper devoted most of page three to an extended gossip column with a horoscope. Rupert Murdoch's contradictory impulses, and his fear of failure, were on vivid display.

Ken looked at the *Australian* again in a 4000-word piece five months later.[32] 'On Saturdays,' he wrote, 'it seems to me quite clearly the best paper we have. During the week, if I lived in Brisbane or Adelaide or Hobart, I would feel a daily surge of gratitude to Mr Murdoch for giving me an alternative to the stifling parochialism and ugly layout of my morning paper... If I lived in Sydney or Melbourne or Perth, my estimate of the *Australian* would depend on how it happened to be performing on any particular day; for its quality as a provider of news varies much more than its readers were led to expect.'

Much later, Ken told me that Murdoch had complained to Tom Fitzgerald that his paper was being singled out for detailed critique while others were getting let off lightly. But the *Canberra Times* had come in for a fair bit of scrutiny as well during 1964. The battle for Sunday supremacy in Sydney between Fairfax's *Sun-Herald* and Murdoch's *Sunday Mirror* was the subject of another long piece; Ken saw the papers as further evidence that 'the leisure time of Australians is now occupied in reading about the activities that occupy their leisure.'[33]

Ken also wrote about church and registry office weddings in July 1964, and then, for a couple of months in the first half of 1965, he was on loan to the *Canberra Times*, as Martin Crotty describes elsewhere in this volume, reporting on the fiftieth anniversary pilgrimage to Anzac Cove. Back in Australia, his final two pieces for *Nation* were a powerful, implicitly antiwar piece about the repatriation of the remains of fallen soldiers from Vietnam (February 1966), and a historical survey of Australia Day observance (January 1967).

Ken's press commentary during that period provides a vivid picture of an industry that was changing quickly, fighting within its own ranks and against new entrants, including the relatively new TV networks. He was undoubtedly the inspiration for the only other sustained media criticism of this kind, David Bowman's monthly column for *Australian Society* (and later for *24 Hours* and then the *Adelaide Review*). More recently, Max Suich, Gay Alcorn and Jonathan Holmes have briefly critiqued the news media in the Fairfax papers, and the *Australian*'s media supplement has intermittently published that kind of critical writing. Online coverage of the media – notably in *Crikey* and the

Guardian – has rarely featured close comparative readings. It's not the kind of thing that proprietors – and even editors – have felt particularly comfortable with.

* * *

A third strand of Ken's work is closer to what has become the discipline of media studies, though it too is characterised by crisp prose, a quizzical authorial voice and provocative question-posing. It first emerges in his contribution to Peter Coleman's *Australian Civilization: A Symposium* (1962), which arose from Ken's press column in *Nation*. ('In a weak moment, too early one morning,' he told Fitzgerald in January 1961, 'I said "Yes" when Peter Coleman rang & asked me for 7000 words...I'm buggered if I know what I'll say, and when.'[34])

In the event, his contribution to the book is generally regarded as perhaps the best of its fourteen essays. Writing in 2011, the political scientist and media historian Murray Goot still considered it 'the best essay written on the Australian press.'[35] It ranges over the ownership, style and twentieth-century evolution of the Australian press, from the macro ('The daily papers which Australians buy so readily come from remarkably few presses") to the micro ('Would such cheery ignorance [in a book review] be tolerated in a racing writer?'). It looks at the uniformity of the capital city papers, both broadsheet and tabloid, relative to their counterparts in Britain ('The size, character and distribution of our population rule out a paper such as the *Times*, which is written for a small elite, or the *Daily Mirror*, which is designed for working-class tastes').

Two years later, Ken's long review of Henry Mayer's landmark book, *The Press in Australia* in the *Australian Journal of Politics and History*

('There is much to quarrel with in this quarrelsome book. There is also much to admire.'[36]), made a further contribution in the developing field of media history. As well as spelling out the kinds of questions future historians (and he himself) would try to answer, he made a compelling case for students of the press to analyse the words on the page as well as the space they took up. Or, as he put it in response to Mayer's methodology, 'it is not enough to measure the words; one must also read them,' though he acknowledged that Mayer did some of that as well.

Two later essays – 'Does It Matter Who Owns the Press, Radio and Television?' and 'Questions About Newspapers'[37] – offer contrasting examples of the breadth of Ken's interests. The first, for a book called *Questions for the Nineties*, is a brisk survey of the state of ownership of newspapers, television and radio – which had undergone 'more changes in the past three years than in any other similar period of media history' – and of the Hawke government's political favour-trading. The observations are characteristically sharp; the solutions encased in tantalising questions.

'Questions about Newspapers,' meanwhile, opens by asking why were there so many newspapers in late nineteenth century Australia (Townsville alone had three daily papers; so did Bathurst) before moving to a discussion of a kind of weekly newspaper possibly peculiar to Australia,' typified by papers like the *Australasian, Town and Country Journal* and the *Sydney Mail*. On the first matter, the questions – or perhaps sub-questions – multiplied:

> Were rural papers helped by railway-induced increases of local population? How many country readers bought a local paper and one from the city? How much does one's sense of a buoyant rural press in the later nineteenth century rest on the papers of mining

districts? … How far were local papers protected by local advertis-ers? By the ability of their proprietors to subsidise the journalistic side of their business by job printing? By the willingness of a man who was at once proprietor, editor and artisan to work himself long hours for low reward? … Were they more Australian than the city papers, and if so did that give them an edge?

Nearly thirty years after his astringent review of *The Press in Australia*, the essay ends with Ken imagining Henry joining him in praise of the 'informal, irreverent' language of the drama critic of the *Bathurst Sentinel* against the snootiness of British observer Matthew Arnold.[38]

* * *

The launch of the *Australian* in July 1964 made *Nation*'s job much harder. The battle for readers – and contributors – became more intense, and not just because Murdoch's paper, for all its faults, was offering much good-quality writing. The other broadsheet papers were forced to improve, and within a few years new weekly papers began appearing – the *Age*'s shortlived *Broadside* in 1969, Gordon Barton's *Review* in 1970, the *National Times* in 1971. *Nation*, its finances perilous, eventu-ally merged with the *Review* in 1972, and George Munster became Sydney editor of the new *Nation Review*. Tom Fitzgerald was in the middle of a short, unhappy period working for Rupert Murdoch and soon went freelance, working on government inquiries and contribut-ing occasional articles and reviews to the *Sydney Morning Herald* and, later, the *National Times* and *Australian Society*.

After he became foundation professor of history at the fledgling University of Papua New Guinea in 1967, Ken wrote occasionally for the *Canberra Times* about that country's journey to independence.

(*Nation* already had a correspondent, Hank Nelson, in Port Moresby.) There he met John Langmore, who would later serve as federal Labor member for Fraser for almost the full term of the Hawke and Keating governments. A shared interest in media diversity, sharpened by News Ltd's recent takeover of the Herald and Weekly Times, led Langmore to ask Ken to draft a paper for Labor's caucus transport and communications committee on the possibility of government support for a newspaper run by an independent journalists' cooperative.[39]

The undated paper, probably completed by the time of the 1990 federal election, proposes a more pluralistic model, including 'other new publications unlikely to be viable without some public protection and subsidy.'[40] It argues that using public funds is justified 'when one owner has acquired a near-monopoly of the press,' as Murdoch had, and proposes a new government agency that could offer 'grants or loans for venture capital or operating subsidies to new publications' providing they met certain criteria.[41] With an election looming and proprietors and editors considering which party to back, any momentum for a change in Labor policy appears to have faded by the time the paper was written.

After *Nation*, Ken continued to write, though less frequently, for newspapers and magazines. Ten years after *Nation*'s merger, a new fortnightly (soon to be a monthly), *Australian Society*, was launched, and Ken contributed occasional pieces, mainly about the media, between 1986 and 1992, including a thirty-fifth anniversary appraisal of the *Australian* in August 1989. One of his *Australian Society* pieces was about *Nation*, and in that same year, 1989, he published a book, part-history, part-anthology, about *Nation* and its creators.

Tom Fitzgerald had set out to create a paper that would help its readers – and its editor and his contributors – better understand the world. His best writers, Ken among them, approached their work with a curiosity, openness and ability to engage readers that has rarely been matched in the Australian media. It all depended on the enormous freedom that Fitzgerald's ownership of *Nation* gave to him and to his writers. As Tom said in his interview in 1988, 'It's hard for people to realise, Ken, that to a journalist who was in the kitchen of a daily newspaper, having the freedom to produce your own paper, however small, is infinitely more rewarding than to be the nominal editor of any bloody metropolitan newspaper.' I imagine that Ken would add that it was almost as rewarding to *write* for that paper.

Endnotes

1   KS Inglis, *Nation: The Life of an Independent Journal of Opinion 1958–1972*, Melbourne University Press, Carlton, 1989, p. 10.

2   KS Inglis, *Nation*, p. 10.

3   'Ken Inglis Interviewed by Neville Meaney,' 1986, ORAL TRC 2053, transcript, National Library of Australia, p. 40.

4   'Tom Fitzgerald Interviewed by Ken Inglis,' 10 February–3 September 1998, ORAL TRC 2247, transcript, National Library of Australia, cassette 2, side 1, p. 10.

5   'Dog Eats Itself,' *Observer*, 17 May 1958, p. 196.

6   'Our "Remarkable" Press,' *Observer*, 17 May 1958, p. 205.

7   'Eggs In the Afternoon,' *Observer*, 28 June 1958, p. 297.

8   'Observer's Diary,' *Observer*, 12 July 1958, p. 322.

9   D Horne, *Into the Open: Memoirs 1958–1999*, HarperCollins, Sydney, 2000, pp. 18–19.

10   'Tom Fitzgerald Interviewed by Ken Inglis,' cassette 3, side 2, p. 13.

11   KS Inglis, *Nation*, p. 2.

12   KS Inglis, *Nation*, p. 9.

13   'Tom Fitzgerald Interviewed by Ken Inglis,' cassette 7, side 1, pp. 7–8.

14   KS Inglis, *Nation*, p. 8.

15   'Tom Fitzgerald Interviewed by Ken Inglis,' cassette 7, side 1, pp. 7–8.

16   Author's interview, Carlton, 2 November 2017.

17   KS Inglis to TM Fitzgerald, undated, Papers of Tom Fitzgerald, MS 7995, Box 1, National Library of Australia.

18   KS Inglis to TM Fitzgerald, 24 November 1958, Papers of Tom Fitzgerald, MS 7995, Box 1, National Library of Australia.

19   Ken Inglis Interviewed by Neville Meaney, p. 76.

20   Ken combined writing about the royal commission into the Stuart case for *Nation* with unpaid 'clerking" for the defence team of JD O'Sullivan and Helen Devaney, and the fact didn't go unnoticed. 'I'm in a bit of a box,' he wrote to Tom Fitzgerald on 17 August 1959. 'Tonight Helen Devaney suggested to me that while I'm acting as her clerk at the R.C. it might be better if I didn't journalise. The govt and the judges are angry at the way she and O'Sullivan have used the press. So, confidentially, is the council of the Law Society, which has sent them a stiff note about the impropriety of advertising. She agrees she has been breaking professional rules, but believes that if she hadn't her client would be dead.' KS Inglis to TM Fitzgerald, Papers of Tom Fitzgerald, MS 7995, Box 1, National Library of Australia.

21   KS Inglis, *The Stuart Case*, Melbourne University Press, Carlton, 1961, p. 195.

22   Anon, 'Press Swings and TV Roundabouts,' *Nation*, 11 October 1958, p. 5.

23   KS Inglis, 'Adelaide's Version of the Press War,' *Nation*, 22 November 1958, pp. 7–8.

24   Undated draft, Papers of Ken Inglis, MS Acc07_007, Box 9, File 63, National Library of Australia.

25   Ken described the genesis of the series, and subscribing to the sixteen papers, in a talk at the Canberra Wordfest, probably in March 2001. Undated notes, Papers of Ken Inglis, MS Acc07_007, Box 9, File 63, National Library of Australia.

26   KS Inglis, 'Reflections in a Mirror,' *Nation*, 13 August 1960, p. 17.

27   Author's interview, Carlton, 2 November 2017.

28   KS Inglis, *Nation*, p. 19.

29   KS Inglis, 'The Homestead Dog,' *Nation*, 30 May 1964, pp. 12–13.

30   W Shawcross, *Rupert Murdoch: Ringmaster of the Information Circus*, Pan Books, London, 1997, p. 116.

31   KS Inglis, 'Enter the "Australian,"' *Nation*, 25 July 1964, pp. 7–8.

32   KS Inglis, 'Five Months' Baby,' *Nation*, 12 December 1964, pp. 6–10.

33   KS Inglis, 'Brighter Yet,' *Nation*, 13 June 1964, p 9.

34   KS Inglis to Tom Fitzgerald, 5 January 1961, Papers of Tom Fitzgerald, MS 7995, Box 2, National Library of Australia. Coleman, who was a key figure at the *Observer*, told me he considered *Nation* to be 'in many ways the better' of the two periodicals. Author's interview, Woollahra, 30 May 2017.

35   M Goot, 'Stripped Bare: A Short Historiography of the Australian Tabloid,' *Australian Journal of Communication*, vol. 38, no. 2, 2011, p. 3.

36   KS Inglis, 'Review Article: The Press in Australia,' *Australian Journal of Politics and History*, vol. 10, no. 2, p. 248.

37   KS Inglis, 'Does It Matter Who Owns the Press, Radio and Television?,' in
      A Gollan, *Questions for the Nineties*, Left Book Club, 1990; KS Inglis,
      'Questions About Newspapers,' *Australian Cultural History*, no. 11, 1992.

38   KS Inglis, 'Questions About Newspapers,' p. 127.

39   KS Inglis to Paul Chadwick, 14 March 1990, Papers of Ken Inglis,
      MS Acc00_053, Box 5, Bag 3, National Library of Australia.

40   'An Independent Newspaper: The Case for Public Support,' undated six-page
      typescript, Papers of Ken Inglis, MS Acc00_053, Box 5, Bag 3, National
      Library of Australia.

41   'An Independent Newspaper,' pp. 3–4.

Chapter 10

CEREMONIES OF LIFE AND DEATH

Ken Inglis on Anzac and civil religion

Graeme Davison

In January 1964 I drove my FJ Holden up the Hume Highway to Canberra, accompanied by a friend, the fledgling biochemist Barry Rolfe. We were bound for our first academic conference, the biennial meeting of the Australian and New Zealand Association for the Advancement of Science (ANZAAS). It was in a time, long past, when the entire academic world of two nations could meet on one university campus. I was twenty-three, a tutor in the University of Melbourne history department preparing to sail off, as Ken Inglis and others had done, to Oxford. My boss, John La Nauze, had financed the Canberra trip with a small allowance, enough for the conference fee, petrol and a week's accommodation in the local caravan park. It was my first glimpse of the national capital, still emerging from the bush, and of the tribe of historians among whom I would spend my life. Apart from the conversation in the beer garden of the Hotel Rex, just two events lodged in my memory: a magisterial presidential address by the sixty-three-year-old John Beaglehole on 'The Death of Captain Cook,' and a paper by thirty-four-year-old ANU historian Ken Inglis on 'The Anzac Tradition.'[1]

I can still picture young Ken, his beanpole figure clad informally in open-necked shirt and cotton trousers, standing behind the lectern in an upstairs classroom in the Haydon-Allen Building. Unknown to us, he had prepared his address in a hurry shortly before the conference, in response to a request from his colleague Barbara Penny, the organiser of one of the conference's strands. The topic, as well as the reputation of the speaker, however, had attracted a good crowd, including historians from the Australian War Memorial working on the Second World War volumes, and a few still-sprightly Anzacs.

Ken began by chastising a senior member of the profession, Professor J.M. Ward, who had recently published, in the United States, a survey of historical writing in Australia and New Zealand. Ward's was a sin of omission – his failure to mention the Australian historian whose books had reached the shelves, if not the minds, of more Australians than any other. In 1964 Charles Bean – Dr Bean as Ken respectfully called the official historian of Australia in the Great War – was still alive, although fading away in a Sydney nursing home. Ward was not the only academic to have overlooked Bean's writings; in fact, he had been selected for censure on behalf of his fellow historians. In my own undergraduate Australian history course, taught by Allan Martin, we studied Ernest Scott's and L.C. Jauncey's accounts of the wartime conscription crisis, but passed over the events of the war itself and ignored Bean's volumes.[2]

This did not surprise or offend me at the time. As a student, I shared something of the outlook of Hughie, the callow undergraduate in Alan Seymour's 1958 play *The One Day of the Year*, who dismisses

Gallipoli as 'the biggest fiasco of the war' and Anzac Day as 'a great big meaningless booze-up.'[3] Ken had begun his 1960 *Nation* article, 'Anzac: The Substitute Religion,' by mentioning the puzzlement of John Douglas Pringle, the English-born editor of the *Sydney Morning Herald*, about a day that seemed to elicit deep emotion yet quickly collapsed into drunken revelry.[4] In speaking about the Anzac tradition and the histories of Charles Bean, Ken was asking his listeners to set aside their prejudices and to consider whether the seemingly 'meaningless' rites of Anzac might have a meaning after all. 'Peace-loving liberals do not find it easy to believe that the history of war is continuous with the rest of history, and for various reasons do not enjoy examining it,' he observed. Marxists, too, were 'unlikely to see much point in studying the actual *course* of a war which is not a class war.'[5] Since most Australian academic historians were either liberals or Marxists, the neglect apparently was general.

Ken ended his paper with this ringing declaration: 'A study of the ceremonies of life and death performed on Anzac Day should tell much about our society; and a national history which does not explore the meaning of these ceremonies is too thin.'[6] After the conference he submitted the paper to the leading Australian historical journal, *Historical Studies*, published by his old department at the University of Melbourne and edited by two young historians who would later become colleagues of his, Allan Martin and Barry Smith. Surprisingly, they did not accept it, but urged Ken to split it in half and expand his discussion of the historian Bean and the popular poet C.J. Dennis in separate articles. So he took his article elsewhere, submitting it to the nationalist literary journal *Meanjin*, where it appeared in March 1965.[7] There, it was immediately hailed by Geoffrey Serle as 'the first serious modern discussion of Anzac and the digger legend.'[8] The words 'serious' and 'modern' were the operative ones, for Ken's paper had placed discussion of Anzac on a new plane, one that was simultaneously critical and respectful, attentive to the analytical methods of the new 'social history' and to the deep currents of pride, loss and suffering that subsisted, almost unexamined, in Australian culture.

Ken led the revival of scholarly interest in the subject, but others soon followed. With the coming of the Vietnam War, interest in Australia's military history was bound to quicken. Lloyd Robson's *Australia and the Great War* (1969) and *The First A.I.F.: A Study of Its Recruitment 1914–1918* (1970), Bill Gammage's bestselling book *The Broken Years*, published in 1974 but based on research begun independently of Ken almost a decade earlier, and Marilyn Lake's *A Divided Society* (1975) were other early entrants to the field.[9] But each was guided, at least partly, by the furrows left by Ken's essay.

Re-reading 'The Anzac Tradition,' I am struck by how much of the writer of *The Australian Colonists*, *The Rehearsal* and *Sacred Places* is already present. The questions he addresses – about history and national character, patriotism and class, death and the decline of religion – would preoccupy him, and many others, for close to fifty years. The originality of Ken's paper lies as much in the method as the argument, especially his subtle tracing of mythic themes from Bean's history through the popular verse of C.J. Dennis to the iconography of the monuments and memorials of the war. For the audience in the Haydon-Allen Building, its impact was magnified by *hearing* the high diction of Bean's prose – 'Life was very dear, but life was not worth living unless they could be true to their idea of Australian manhood' – and the vernacular of Ginger Mick – 'Blast the flamin' war!/I ain't got nothin' worth the fightin' for' – spoken by a historian with an ear for Australian speech and an appropriately laconic delivery.

I listened to Ken's paper in company with Sheila Fitzpatrick, a fellow tutor in the Melbourne history department, also soon to leave for Oxford. After the talk there were questions, some from the old diggers in the audience who welcomed Ken's sympathetic account of the Anzac tradition, perhaps mistaking the respectful enquirer for a fellow believer. As we left the lecture theatre, Sheila and I exchanged impressions. Was Ken a secret devotee of the tradition or, ever so subtly, against it? Was he just being polite to the old diggers or did he really share their belief?

Some years later, in 1986, Neville Meaney asked Ken a similar question: 'Don't you identify with Anzac and Gallipoli?' 'I don't know whether I identify with it,' he replied. 'I think I resist the word "iden-tify."' (With his usual alertness to shifts in language, Ken had recently observed the migration of the psychologist Erik Erikson's concept of 'identity' into discourse about national selfhood.[10]) 'I find it [Anzac] full of pathos,' he continued. 'You have to respect the attempt to come to terms with death by people who can't get sustenance from traditional sacraments and statements.' Death and comfortless sacraments: here was another clue to Ken's orientation to the Anzac tradition. Some in that audience in 1964 may have recognised its personal resonance, for Ken had himself only recently experienced the crushing loss of his young wife Judy. There were things that had always appalled him about Anzac, Ken continued in the 1986 interview, things that had appalled him as a child and even more as the years went on. Yet as a historian, he was bound to take the tradition seriously.[11] Taking it seriously did not necessarily mean identifying with it. So was Anzac something of 'religious significance,' Meaney asked. 'It's hard to know whether to use the word religious,' Ken replied, again slipping the noose of definition, 'but certainly sacred was in there.' 'Identify' or 'respect,' 'religious' or 'sacred'? In seeking words for Anzac, Ken was hinting at unresolved questions about his own attitudes to life and death and the claims of faith and country.

'A lot of history is concealed autobiography,' Ken writes in *This Is the ABC*.[12] On his eightieth birthday, I joined the Inglis family on a minibus tour of the scenes of his Melbourne childhood and youth. We stopped by the fine brick house on the hill in Heidelberg (now occupied by one of Bob Santamaria's children) that Ken's father Stan built for his bride in the late 1920s. (We had already visited the modest rented State Bank bungalow in King William Street, Reservoir, to which they retreated when the Great Depression almost sent the family's timber business broke.) Here, in the year after Ken's birth, the Inglises acquired their first radio receiver and Ken's life-long devotion to the ABC began.[13] We passed the Presbyterian church where Ken attended Sunday school and Bible class. At Tyler Street State School, No. 1494, we relived the Monday-morning assemblies where he vowed to serve the King while wondering how 'cheerfully' he could 'obey [his] parents, teachers and the laws.'[14]

Stan, born in 1905, was too young to have served in the First World War and too old for the Second, so in the school's Anzac ceremonies – among Ken's 'most vivid memories' of his primary years – he stood outside the circle of boys who wore their father's medals, while absorbing the 'oppressive, moving, strange and unique atmosphere' of a day that seemed, even then, more sacred than the holy days of the Christian year.[15] The small boy, hearing the distant sounds of war, moved by its solemn rituals yet standing a little apart, is a figure who recurs in Ken's writing. He is there in *The Rehearsal*, Ken's account of Australia's response to the 1885 Sudan crisis, in the guise of the 'Little Boy from Manly,' and he appears again in the superb child's-eye view of the Second World War that introduces *Australians from 1939*.[16] History is mostly written from the vantage point of adults: perhaps feminist history should be supplemented by juvenilist history, he once playfully suggested.[17]

From Tyler Street State, our minibus drove south to Northcote High School, where Ken spent most of the war years. There we paused to recall John Forster, the English and history teacher who made him feel that writing was 'something worth doing,' and the modest school library where he first glimpsed the twelve blood-red volumes of Bean's *Official History*.[18] His best friend from North Preston, Wally Dey – one of the envied few who wore his father's medals on Anzac Day – had accompanied Ken to Northcote High. One afternoon, towards the end of the war, they visited the Shrine of Remembrance. Ken says it was during the holidays, but Wally, who contributed his recollections to Ken's eightieth birthday celebrations, insisted they wagged school. They were horsing around, 'as kids do,' Wally recalled, when a guard ordered them 'to behave themselves in this sacred place.' 'It's not a church,' Ken replied, a theological pronouncement that got them both a belt around the ears and a kick up the bum.[19] Among the assorted 'Jews, socialists and atheists' Ken met at his next school, Melbourne High, these youthful certainties began to dissolve.[20] He had begun the intellectual journey that led, via debates in the Student Christian Movement and the ALP Club, to Oxford and a doctoral thesis on religion and the working classes in Victorian England.

* * *

When I heard Ken speak in 1964 I had recently read the book of his thesis, published the year before as *Churches and the Working Classes in*

Victorian England, but I did not immediately recognise the connection between its concluding paragraphs, in which he notes the decline of the churches and ponders what would take their place, and his musings in 'The Anzac Tradition' on the seemingly godless commemorations of Anzac. In a pioneering article on the 1851 religious census, and in *Churches and the Working Classes*, he shows that large sections of the English population, especially the urban working classes, were estranged from the churches. Their alienation had little to do with the so-called 'crisis of belief' among intellectuals struggling to reconcile their faith with the discoveries of Darwin and critical studies of the Bible. 'Any decline of worshipping among the urban working classes since 1900 has only accentuated a pattern which was already apparent in 1851,' Ken argues.[21] While working-class people continued to be married and buried on church grounds and held on to some notion of personal immortality, the ceremonies, he finds, were increasingly secular in character. 'How often, and how profoundly, the participants derived from these ceremonies joy, hope or solace, we shall never know,' he reflects.[22]

Back in Australia, he turned his attention to the local patterns of religious belief and practice, comparing them with those in England and the United States. 'Religious adherence in Australia is stronger than a militant agnostic would think healthy, but not strong enough to please leaders of the churches,' he concluded. While church leaders agreed that religious practice had declined since 1900, Ken was more sceptical: the small proportion of people answering 'no religion' to the census-taker (less than 10 per cent) had scarcely shifted over the half-century.[23]

Like many contemporary students of religion, Ken worked within an implicitly Weberian framework. Max Weber's *The Protestant Ethic and the Spirit of Capitalism,* one of the standard texts at the Melbourne history department, asks questions about the place of religion in a 'disenchanted' world.[24] In 'The Anzac Tradition,' Ken suggests that traditional faiths and sacraments had proved unable to provide comfort in the face of the mass slaughter of the Great War. Noting the absence of Christian iconography in most war memorials and services of commemoration, and the indifference of many diggers to traditional religious practice, he poses a question to which he would often return: was Anzac a kind of secularised religion, a functional alternative, perhaps, to the traditional faiths that seemed to have lost their appeal?

In 1965, in a lunchtime lecture to an Anglican audience, Ken posed the question: 'Anzac and Christian: Two Traditions or One?' He told three stories to illustrate the tension between church leaders – who had often devised and led Anzac Day services, with Christian hymns and prayers – and the leaders of the Returned Services League, who developed their own austerely secular form of commemoration, often in forms borrowed from Ancient Greece. If the returned soldiers wished to keep the clergy out, and the ceremony simple and secular, it was not because they were necessarily irreligious, but because Catholics were forbidden by their bishops from participating in ceremonies of a religious character conducted by Protestants. Sectarianism, not militant secularism or even religious indifference, was the main reason why all but the most oblique references to the Christian God were eliminated from Anzac Day services. Some Christian ex-servicemen were dismayed by the 'trend … to dechristianise Anzac celebrations' and to replace 'worship of God alone' with 'a new religion of ancestor worship.'[25] In 1965 it seemed that the secularised forms of Anzac celebration had all but supplanted older patterns of observance. Today, secular victory seems less assured, for the more elaborate rituals of recent Anzac Days often reintroduce traditional Christian elements.

* * *

The historians who first responded to 'The Anzac Tradition' were more interested in questions of nation, class and party than religion. Geoffrey Serle pondered how a tradition grounded in the radical democracy of the bush and goldfields was taken over by the political right. Noel McLachlan contended that it was a tradition that divided Australians as much as it united them.[26] Bill Gammage read hundreds of soldiers' letters and diaries for his prize-winning book, *The Broken Years*. 'The average Australian soldier was not religious,' he concluded, although judging by the testimony of others quoted in his book, some were.[27] Belief in a wise providence was seemingly incompatible with the senseless carnage of the Western Front.

Yet, despite the assault on their faith, most clergymen and many lay Christians watching from home did not readily surrender it. Michael McKernan, a former Jesuit, reached this repugnant conclusion: 'Churchmen accepted the war as part of God's providence for the world; through sacrifice, suffering and devotion to duty, men would be renewed, lifted to a higher, more thoroughly Christian, plane.'[28] Army chaplains, whose experiences McKernan examined in a later book, were more like their men, often returning with their faith in tatters.[29] If the average soldier was not religious, perhaps it was because, as Ken had shown elsewhere, neither were many of his countrymen.

These studies illuminated one side of Ken's interpretation – the relationship between Anzac and Christian belief and practice – but they did not address the other: the 'religious' dimension of Anzac itself.

Greg Dening, another former Jesuit, was an exception: in the mid 1970s I sometimes accompanied him and our University of Melbourne honours students to dawn services at the Shrine of Remembrance, where we talked with old diggers, searching for the links between public ritual and personal experience. Later I discovered that Ken was there too, observing us from the shadows.[30] Only towards the end of the century, as postwar optimism faded, and the 'memory boom' drew historians such as Alistair Thomson, Jay Winter, Stephen Garton, Joy Damousi, Pat Jalland, Tanja Luckins and Marina Larsson back to questions of trauma and loss, did the study of Anzac return to where Ken had left off.[31]

* * *

After publication of 'The Anzac Tradition' in 1965, a decade would pass before Ken returned to the topic, and then by a route that subtly changed the focus of his inquiry. In 1967 he became foundation professor of history at the University of Papua and New Guinea, a nation-building task that remained invisible to most of his Australian colleagues and inevitably slowed his scholarly output. Observing the place of ritual in the everyday life of Papuans and New Guineans sharpened his ethnographic skills and reinforced his interest in ceremonial life.[32] In 1971–72 he devoted a sabbatical year in Canberra to writing *The Australian Colonists* (1974), the first in a projected series of volumes about 'how Australians thought about themselves' in 1915 and before.[33]

In 1975 he returned to the ANU, as a professorial fellow, later professor, in the Research School of Social Sciences (RSSS), where he joined the recently arrived Oliver MacDonagh. 'My first task,' MacDonagh recalled, 'seemed to be to find some major undertaking which our department – as the only "national" department in Australia, and the only department devoted primarily to research – could promote and nurture.'[34] Ken's most notable contribution to the Australian bicentennial history project – the plan for four slice volumes focused on the years 1788, 1838, 1888 and 1938 – reflected his twin interests in rituals of national celebration and the texture of everyday life, and of how the two interpreted each other. Reaching for models of the kind of history he had in mind, Ken mentioned Macaulay and the *Annales* school, but closer to home, and perhaps also in the back of Ken's mind, was an Australian example: Charles Bean's multi-volume history of Australia in the Great War, still the most ambitious venture in Australian commemorative history-making.

In 1977 Ken took the opportunity, once again, to address the ANZAAS conference – it was to be the last meeting of Section E – with a paper entitled 'Monuments and Ceremonies as Evidence for Historians.' 'Monuments and ceremonies go together,' he began. 'A ceremony is to time what a monument is to space.'[35] In *The Australian Colonists*, he had reviewed the times of celebration in colonial Australia; now, with a nod to Clifford Geertz and the ethnographers, he was turning to the monuments.

A consummate wordsmith, Ken was also a perceptive reader of buildings, pictures and monuments. I recall sitting at the back of one of his classes at the ANU – I suppose it was in 1966 – as he encouraged his students, who had recently visited the Australian War Memorial, to interpret the evidence of their own eyes. Until I heard Shirley Lindenbaum's account of his anthropological education (see her chapter in this book), I assumed that the ethnographer's gaze came to him quite naturally. In 1945, the fifteen-year-old aspiring journalist had contributed an anonymous report of his local Anzac Day celebrations to the *Preston Post*. Patriotism – national and local – was its primary theme; only the occasional phrase – 'the rituals and customs of Anzac Day' – and the author's keen interest in Preston's war memorial hint at the future historian. 'The Memorial Arch, with a floral display of wreaths seldom equalled in Preston, was worth going a long way to see,' he notes.[36] A poor man's version of the famous Menin Gate, Preston's Memorial Arch was only a few blocks south of the Inglis home. It was one of the hundreds of local memorials Ken and his assistants visited and recorded in the national survey of war memorials they began in 1983.

In the final pages of *Sacred Places*, his study of war memorials in the Australian landscape, Ken asks again: in what sense were these memorials sacred? Was Anzac a kind of civil religion? The term 'civil religion' came originally from Rousseau's *Social Contract*, where it stands for that minimal 'body of social sentiments' – including belief in God and an afterlife – that binds citizens to each other and the state. It gained wide currency after the publication of sociologist Robert Bellah's influential 1967 essay, 'Civil Religion in America.'[37]

Since the 1950s Ken had been seeking words to describe the distinctive melding of religious and secular motifs in Australia's national life. 'I found I kept moving away from the formal institutions of Christian religion to what we would now label civil religion,' he recalled in 1986. The title of his 1960 article 'Anzac: The Substitute Religion' was chosen not by Ken but by the editor of *Nation*, the magazine where it appeared.[38] The implication that Anzac was filling a vacuum created by the failure of traditional beliefs, however, was also a thread in 'The Anzac Tradition.'

In the early 1970s, Ken borrowed the term 'civic religion' from the Jewish writer Will Herberg, whose 1955 book *Protestant – Catholic*

– *Jew: An Essay in American Religious Sociology* Ken may have read during the sabbatical year he spent at Brown University in 1961–62 studying American religion. 'The more I learned of [Anzac] and thought about it, the more its ceremonies seemed to me to constitute in some respects a *civic* religion,' he writes in the introduction to *The Australian Colonists*.[39] Herberg had coined the term to describe 'the unacknowledged "religion" of the American people,' the common faith that sustained the 'American Way of Life.'[40] Ken's qualification 'in some respects' may have been significant, for not everything about American civic religion applied to Australia or to Anzac. God is a word, and perhaps an idea, that resides more comfortably in American public speech than Australian, just as biblical tropes of the nation as a new Israel lie closer to the surface of American public rhetoric than Australian.[41]

Only later did Ken adopt the now-standard term 'civil religion' from Bellah's 1967 essay. There were similarities, as well as subtle differences, between 'civic' and 'civil' religion. Herberg and Bellah were both left-wing critics of mainstream America and its religion, but while Herberg believed that 'civic religion' suppressed the prophetic dimension of the historic faiths, Bellah, who had participated in the civil rights struggle and witnessed the soaring biblical rhetoric of Martin Luther King, saw its redemptive potential.[42] 'While not antithetical to and indeed sharing much in common with Christianity, [civil religion] was neither sectarian nor in any specific sense Christian,' Bellah writes. It was not a 'substitute for Christianity,' nor a vestigial form of it. 'Without an awareness that our nation stands under higher judgement,' he concludes, 'the tradition of the civil religion would be dangerous indeed. Fortunately, the prophetic voices have never been lacking.'[43]

The aspect of Bellah's essay most relevant to Anzac is his discussion of the symbolism of the American Civil War. In the sublime rhetoric of Abraham Lincoln, the themes of 'death, sacrifice and rebirth' were woven into 'a new civil religion.'[44] There were many Australians in 1915 and later who regarded the Anzacs' sacrifice in a similar light, linking their deaths to the symbolic 'birth' of the Australian nation. Ken acknowledges the resonance between Gallipoli and Gettysburg: 'The Great War delivered ordeal, achievement and loss comparable to the Americans' Civil War,' he writes.[45] But he is reluctant to endorse such a reading of Anzac. Ordinary Australians, including the Anzacs, he insists, were more resistant to the hope of rebirth, either personal or national. Christian symbolism is more muted in the iconography and ceremonial of Anzac than in American civil religion. In *Sacred Places*, as in 'The Anzac Tradition,' his sympathies are with the 'overlapping categories of dissenters – socialists, pacifists, Christians, nationalists unable to believe that the nation was born at Gallipoli' – rather than the true believers. If, as some recent critics argue, Ken underestimated the influence of traditional Christianity on Anzac commemoration, it was in part because, like Rousseau and Bellah, he was interested primarily in the features of religion that bound citizens of all faiths and of none, rather than those central to traditional believers.[46]

In 1964 the Anzac tradition seemed fated to die, like the Christian churches, but by 1998 it had miraculously revived and the austere ceremonies of the first diggers had been blended with hymns and readings into the rites of a 'civil religion' that seemed to embrace almost everyone. Meanwhile, as Ken observed, the word 'religion' had become so secularised that it was difficult to know what people meant when they either affirmed or disavowed it.[47] The word 'sacred,' on the other hand, coupled now in Ken's mind with 'place' and 'landscape,' hinted at traditions that were more deeply grounded – even, I sense, more indigenous.

Ken's frame of reference now was implicitly Durkheimian rather than Weberian. His paper on monuments and ceremonies begins with Durkheim's dictum: 'There can be no society which does not feel the need of upholding and reaffirming at regular intervals the collective sentiments and the collective ideas which make its unity and its personality.'[48] And his discussion of 'civil religion' in *Sacred Places* invokes Bean's similar affirmation of the enduring power of religion: 'Most nations practise, beside their formally acknowledged religion, the cult of some ideal of manhood or womanhood.'[49]

The revival of Anzac – or is it the metamorphosis? – had altered Ken's perspective. Rather than a 'coming to terms with death' in a time of mass slaughter, its rituals offered a kind of transcendence for a secular multicultural society short of such unifying symbols. Ours is not so much a secular society as a post-Christian one, and in the rituals of Anzac the religious dimension, including its Christian antecedents, is not so much absent as hidden. As Charles Taylor notes, 'the religious reference in our national identity (and/or sense of civilizational order) doesn't so much disappear, as change, retreat to a certain distance. It remains powerful in memory; but also as a kind of reserve fund of spiritual force or consolation.'[50] At what point, one wonders, does the religious reference become so distant that the reserve fund is exhausted?

If Anzac had changed, however, its historian remained the same. Like the schoolboy without medals standing a step apart from his mates, Ken remained the watchful, detached, yet respectful observer of our national 'rituals and customs.' If he were not a true believer, it was not because he was indifferent to the deep questions of life and death, religion and the sacred that Anzac touched in the life of the nation and its people.

In June 2016 I visited Ken in his study at his retirement home in inner Melbourne. He was eager to share a story. A member of staff had been assigned to help residents complete the census forms. One question in particular – the religious one – had provoked a telling exchange. Ken had diligently filled out the form but left all the standard religious categories – Catholic, Presbyterian, Buddhist, Muslim, atheist, agnostic and others – blank. Surely Professor Inglis had made a mistake, the carer decided. (She could not have known that her charge was an expert, having written an article on the very first modern religious census.) So she checked the box 'No religion.' Only later did Ken discover her error. No, he insisted, not that box either. Religion, as he knew better than most, was a matter too complex and mysterious to be answered with an absolute no.

Acknowledgements

This chapter draws substantially on my previous paper, 'Ken Inglis: Threads of Influence' contributed to the colloquium in his honour in November 2016. A revised version of the colloquium paper was published in *History Australia*: G Davison, 'Ken Inglis: Threads of Influence,' *History Australia*, vol. 14, no. 4, 2017, pp. 516–29.

Endnotes

1   J Beaglehole, 'The Death of Captain Cook,' *Historical Studies*, vol. 11, no. 43, 1964, pp. 289–305.

2   E Scott, *Official History of Australia in the War of 1914–1918*, vol. 11, *Australia During the War*, Angus and Robertson, Sydney, 1936; LC Jauncey, *The Story of Conscription in Australia*, first published 1935, Macmillan, South Melbourne, 1968.

3   *Three Australian Plays*, Penguin, Ringwood, 1963, pp. 75, 78.

4   J Kemp [KS Inglis], 'Anzac: The Substitute Religion,' *Nation*, 23 April 1960,
     pp. 7–9; republished in KS Inglis (ed. C Wilcox), *Observing Australia: 1959
     to 1999*, Melbourne University Press, Carlton, 1999, pp. 61–70; JD Pringle,
     Australian Accent, Rigby Limited, Adelaide, 1958, p. 201.

5   KS Inglis, 'The Anzac Tradition,' *Meanjin Quarterly*, vol. 24, no. 1, March 1965,
     pp. 25–44 at p. 34; republished in KS Inglis (ed. J Lack), *ANZAC Remembered:
     Selected Writings by K.S. Inglis*, History Department, University of Melbourne,
     1998, pp. 136–46. Italics in original quotation.

6   Inglis, 'The Anzac Tradition,' p. 44.

7   KS Inglis, 'Remembering Anzac,' in Inglis, *ANZAC Remembered*, pp. 136–46.

8   G Serle, 'The Digger Tradition and Australian Nationalism,' *Meanjin Quarterly*,
     vol. 24, no. 2, June 1965, pp. 148–58 at p. 149.

9   C Holbrook, *Anzac: The Unauthorised Biography*, NewSouth, Sydney, 2014,
     pp. 116–43.

10   K Inglis, 'Multiculturalism and National Identity,' in CA Price (ed.), *Australian
     National Identity*, Academy of the Social Sciences in Australia, Canberra, 1991;
     reprinted in Inglis, *Observing Australia*, pp. 186–218.

11   'Ken Inglis Interviewed by Neville Meaney,' 1986, ORAL TRC 2053/11,
     National Library of Australia. References to this schoolyard experience recur in
     Inglis's writings: see KS Inglis, *The Australian Colonists: An Exploration of Social
     History, 1788–1870*, Melbourne University Press, Carlton, 1974, p. x; Kemp
     [Inglis], 'Anzac: The Substitute Religion,' p. 61; KS Inglis (assisted by J Brazier),
     Sacred Places: War Memorials in the Australian Landscape, Miegunyah Press at
     Melbourne University Press, Carlton, 1998, p. 3.

12   KS Inglis (assisted by J Brazier), *This Is the ABC: The Australian Broadcasting
     Commission 1932–1983*, Melbourne University Press, Carlton, 1983, p. 1.

13   Inglis, *This Is the ABC*, p. 1.

14   'Ken Inglis Interviewed by Neville Meaney.'

15   'Ken Inglis Interviewed by Neville Meaney.'

16   KS Inglis, *The Rehearsal: Australians at War in the Sudan, 1885*, Rigby, Adelaide,
     1985, pp. 63–72; KS Inglis, 'At War,' in A Curthoys, AW Martin & T Rowse
     (eds), *Australians from 1939*, Fairfax, Syme & Weldon, Sydney, 1987, vol. 5 of
     Australians: A Historical Library, pp. 1–19.

17   KS Inglis, 'Young Australia 1870–1900,' in G Featherstone (ed.), *The Colonial
     Child*, Royal Historical Society of Victoria, Melbourne, 1981, p. 22.

18   'Ken Inglis Interviewed by Neville Meaney.'

19   'For Ken 2009' [tributes on his eightieth birthday], unpublished, and compare
     Inglis, *Sacred Places*, pp. 3–4; Inglis, 'At War,' pp. 1, 4, 13.

20   'Ken Inglis Interviewed by Neville Meaney.'

21   KS Inglis, 'Patterns of Religious Worship in 1851,' *Journal of Ecclesiastical
     History*, vol. 8, 1960, pp. 74–86.

22   KS Inglis, *Churches and the Working Classes in Victorian England*, Routledge and Kegan Paul, London, 1963, pp. 332–6.

23   KS Inglis, 'Churchgoing in Australia,' *Current Affairs Bulletin*, vol. 22, no. 4, 1958, pp. 53, 61.

24   Inglis, *Churches and the Working Classes*, p. 325. The phrase 'disenchantment of the world' comes from Weber's lecture on 'Science as a Vocation' (1918), in H Gerth & CW Mills (eds), *From Max Weber: Essays in Sociology*, Oxford University Press, New York, 1958, p. 155.

25   KS Inglis, 'Anzac and Christian: Two Traditions or One?' *St Mark's Review*, no. 42, November 1965, pp. 3–12. In a recent article in the same journal, John Moses accuses Ken of failing to acknowledge the role of Christian, specifically Anglican, clergy in the origins of Anzac Day and of dismissing Christian influence on subsequent commemorations: J Moses, 'Anzac Day as Australia's "Civic Religion"?,' *St Mark's Review*, no. 231, April 2015, pp. 23–38. While Ken emphasised an apparent shift towards more secular forms of commemoration, here and in subsequent writing, he also acknowledged the complex relationship between the religious orthodoxy and the national myth.

26   Serle, 'The Digger Tradition and Australian Nationalism'; N McLachlan, 'Nationalism and the Divisive Digger: Three Comments,' *Meanjin Quarterly*, vol. 27, no. 3, September 1968, pp. 302–8.

27   B Gammage, *The Broken Years: Australian Soldiers in the Great War*, Penguin, Ringwood, 1975, p. xiv, and see index entries under 'religion.'

28   M McKernan, *Australian Churches at War: Attitudes and Activities of the Major Churches, 1914–1918*, Catholic Theological Faculty, Sydney, 1980, p. 110.

29   M McKernan, *Padre: Australian Chaplains in Gallipoli and France*, Allen & Unwin, Sydney, 1986.

30   G Dening, 'Anzac Day,' in G Dening, *Performances*, Melbourne University Press, Carlton, 1996, pp. 224–32; Inglis, 'Remembering Anzac,' p. 140.

31   A Thomson, *Anzac Memories: Living with the Legend*, Oxford University Press, Melbourne, 1993; J Winter, *Sites of Memory, Sites of Mourning: The Great War in European Cultural History*, Cambridge University Press, Cambridge, 1995; S Garton, *The Cost of War: Australians Return*, Oxford University Press, Melbourne, 1996; J Damousi, *The Labour of Loss: Mourning, Memory and Wartime Bereavement in Australia*, Cambridge University Press, Melbourne, 1999; P Jalland, *Australian Ways of Death: A Social and Cultural History, 1840–1918*, Oxford University Press, Melbourne, 2002; P Jalland, *Changing Ways of Death in Twentieth-Century Australia: War, Medicine and the Funeral Business*, UNSW Press, Sydney, 2006; T Luckins, *The Gates of Memory: Australian People's Experiences and Memories of Loss and the Great War*, Curtin University Books, Fremantle, 2004; M Larsson, *Shattered ANZACs: Living with the Scars of War*, UNSW Press, Sydney, 2009.

32   'Ken Inglis Interviewed by Neville Meaney.'

33   Inglis, *The Australian Colonists*.

34 O MacDonagh, 'The Making of *Australians: A Historical Library*: A Personal Retrospect,' in E Russell (ed.), *Australians: The Guide and Index*, Fairfax, Syme & Weldon, Sydney, 1987, vol. 11 of *Australians: A Historical Library*, p. 1.

35 KS Inglis, 'Monuments and Ceremonies as Evidence for Historians,' in Inglis, *Observing Australia*, pp. 115–33.

36 *Preston Post*, 9 May 1945.

37 R Bellah, 'Civil Religion in America,' *Daedalus*, vol. 96, no. 1, Winter 1967, pp. 1–21.

38 'Ken Inglis Interviewed by Neville Meaney.'

39 Inglis, *The Australian Colonists*, p. x.

40 W Herberg, *Protestant – Catholic – Jew: An Essay in American Religious Sociology*, Anchor Books, New York, 1960, p. 74.

41 Although I would argue that biblical narratives continued, often subliminally, to shape Australian narratives of discovery, emancipation and reconciliation: G Davison, *Narrating the Nation in Australia*, Menzies Lecture, Menzies Centre for Australian Studies, London, 2009.

42 R Stahl, 'A Jewish America and a Protestant Civil Religion: Will Herberg, Robert Bellah and Mid-Twentieth Century American Religion,' *Religions*, vol. 6, April 2015, pp. 434–50; and compare Inglis, *Sacred Places*, p. 514.

43 Bellah, 'Civil Religion in America,' p. 8.

44 Bellah, 'Civil Religion in America,' pp. 9–10.

45 Inglis, *Sacred Places*, p. 461.

46 Among critiques from historians of religion: R Ely, 'The Forgotten Nationalism: Australian Civic Protestantism in the Second World War,' *Journal of Australian Studies*, vol. 20, May 1987, pp. 59–87; K Massam & JH Smith, 'Images of God: Civil Religion and Australia at War, 1939–1945,' *Australian Religion Studies Review*, vol. 11, no. 2, 1998, pp. 57–71.

47 Inglis, *Sacred Places*, pp. 460–1; G Davison, 'Religion,' in A Bashford & S Macintyre (eds), *The Cambridge History of Australia*, Cambridge University Press, Cambridge, 2013, vol. 2, pp. 213–14, 233–6; and compare the illuminating discussion in R Ely, 'Secularisation and the Sacred in Australian History,' *Australian Historical Studies*, vol. 19, no. 77, 1981, pp. 559–60.

48 Inglis, 'Monuments and Ceremonies,' pp. 117–18.

49 Inglis, *Sacred Places*, p. 458.

50 C Taylor, *A Secular Age*, Harvard University Press, Cambridge, 2007, p. 522.

Chapter 11

THE BOOK
THAT NEVER WAS

Ken Inglis and the 1965 Gallipoli pilgrimage

Martin Crotty

The 1965 pilgrimage to Gallipoli was the first large-scale visit by Australian veterans to the site of the battles where they had, in a mythic sense, given birth to the Australian nation. Organised primarily by the Returned Services League (RSL), it comprised 231 Australians and eighty New Zealanders, most of them First World War veterans.[1] As part of a series of activities designed to mark the fiftieth anniversary of the landings, the pilgrims flew to Athens, where they boarded a ship, the *Karadeniz*, for a three-week cruise. They toured historic sites and military cemeteries and memorials in a variety of locations – Malta, Tobruk, Alexandria, Cairo, Beirut, Rhodes, Heraklion, Izmir, Istanbul – before finally visiting the Gallipoli peninsula, including Cape Helles and Anzac Cove, on 25 and 26 April. After returning to Athens on 27 April, most of the pilgrims had a brief respite before travelling back to Australia and New Zealand, although twenty-nine of them, all Australian, continued on to visit Israel.[2]

This chapter explores Ken Inglis's writings about the Gallipoli pilgrimage and looks at why, in addition to his published writings, there is work he either did not complete, or completed in draft form but decided not to publish. These documents are held in the Inglis papers in the National Library of Australia, and include two versions of the manuscript for the intended history of the pilgrimage, which Inglis later said he felt 'didn't come out right.'[3] When examined alongside the other notes and documents that form the Inglis papers on the pilgrimage, the drafts suggest that Inglis, not unlike C.E.W. Bean in his work on the Australian Imperial Force (AIF), applied several filters in the process of converting observations to writings, removing or downplaying realities that undermined the images he wished to present to readers.[4]

We have no reason to believe that Inglis's notes to himself were anything other than faithful recordings of his observations and ideas. Alongside the extensive archive he compiled, including surveys of the pilgrims conducted shortly after their return to Australia, these notes make it abundantly clear that he knew the pilgrimage was, for many, a deeply unsatisfactory affair. Yet much is omitted from his drafts, and even more from the pieces that he published – seven articles in the *Canberra Times* in April and May 1965, a 1966 article in the *ANU Historical Journal* and a 1991 article in the *Journal of the Australian War Memorial*. The book drafts that Bruce Scates has characterised as Inglis's 'frank and honest narrative' mention some of the difficulties of the pilgrimage and indicate that some pilgrims were less than satisfied; but Inglis was curtailed and constrained by his decency, his obligations and his desire to see, and to have others see, the pilgrims and their commemorations in as favourable a light as truthfulness would allow.[5]

* * *

Ken Inglis is rightly regarded as one of the originators of Australian social-military history. His passion for the subject and commitment to studying the Australian veterans, their rituals and the way they were commemorated came from a blend of personal and intellectual influences that he had felt from childhood years, and which coalesced early in his career as a professional historian. After an early focus on the way people engaged with formal religion, he increasingly turned his attention to Anzac, which he explored as a 'substitute religion' and which he termed, in 1974 in his introduction to *The Australian Colonists*, a 'civic religion.'[6]

Inglis considered Anzac an underestimated force in Australian life and implored his colleagues to take it more seriously. At the 1964 Australian and New Zealand Association for the Advancement of Science (ANZAAS) congress in Canberra, he raised the question of why more Australian historians were not concerning themselves with Anzac. Why did they hold the work of C.E.W. Bean in such low regard? And why did they have such little interest in exploring the lingering effects of war on Australian society?[7] In this, Inglis was something of a pioneer, as has been frequently noted.[8] He recalled later that a number of people expressed to him some surprise that an academic historian should be interested in the topic, and an article based on his paper was rejected by *Australian Historical Studies*.[9]

But if he was a loner at the outset, he soon had more company. Inglis's paper was published in *Meanjin*, a left-leaning intellectual journal published in Melbourne, in early 1965 as 'The Anzac Tradition.'[10] The reaction was sufficient to prompt the editor to solicit contributions on the topic from other historians, and Inglis's piece was followed in the next edition by a similarly influential article by Geoffrey Serle titled 'The Digger Tradition and Australian Nationalism.'[11] Inglis's 1965 article is still generally regarded as the first instance of an academic historian taking the Anzac legend and the effects of the First World War on Australian society as a serious object of study rather than a cultural curiosity.

It was far from the last. As well as Serle, Inglis was soon joined and succeeded by a number of other historians who have, collectively, turned the study of war and its multifarious effects into one of the richest seams of Australian historiography. Inglis himself continued to publish regularly on Anzac matters, even as other research interests and responsibilities absorbed the greater part of his time. He became increasingly interested in memorials and monuments, and the publication of his highly acclaimed *Sacred Places: War Memorials in the Australian Landscape* in 1998 represented the pinnacle of his career.[12] The study of Anzac was Inglis's enduring obsession, and his most profound legacy. He defined Anzac for a following generation of historians and for a wider public who read his books, listened to his talks, studied in his classes, or merely picked up the *Canberra Times* between 15 April and 1 May 1965.

Inglis's 1965 pilgrimage writings are a key element of this legacy. Over the seven articles published in the *Canberra Times*, Inglis took his readers with him to Gallipoli and bestowed on the diggers a collective persona that included elements of the bemused tourist, the dignified old veteran, the troublesome character and the Anzac larrikin. There are shades of Ginger Mick and Barry McKenzie in some of his imagery – and imagery it is, for, as others have noted, Inglis was a 'consummate wordsmith,' with the rare ability 'to show a story rather than tell it.'[13] Most of all, he reminded his newspaper audience, just as he had reminded his academic audience in his conference paper a year previously, that the diggers were to be taken seriously and not to be written off as old boozers living in the past. Inglis's pilgrimage writings were an important waypoint in the growing academic and popular interest in Anzac.

* * *

It could have been very different. What Inglis saw on the pilgrimage, which is recoverable from his drafts, his notes and other records, as well as what he published, might well have resulted in much more disparaging portrayals. The pilgrimage could easily have been rendered as an appalling, tragicomic farce, and many of the former diggers as rather sad old men who were still trapped in a wartime mindset, indulging in racism, disorderliness, drunkenness and other vices – still 'bad characters,' as Peter Stanley might have termed them, even fifty years after the initial landings.[14] Inglis saw and heard it all. But he kept his critical voice restrained, and never showed his readers more than a glimpse of an image that could have been further developed.

When he became aware of plans for the 1965 pilgrimage to Gallipoli, Inglis saw an opportunity to talk to the veterans in a leisurely fashion and to observe their rituals and their reactions as they returned to old battlefields and to cemeteries and memorials that commemorated former foes and dead mates. Inglis obtained support from his employer, the Australian National University, to undertake the pilgrimage and arranged with the *Canberra Times* for it to publish his dispatches, the university and the newspaper contributing half each to his costs. Over the course of the three-week pilgrimage, Inglis wrote seven articles for the *Canberra Times*, published between 15 April and 1 May 1965, and a longer piece for *Nation*, published as 'Diggers in Antiquity' on 29 May 1965.[15]

Throughout his reports Inglis generally adopts a positive, sentimental and sympathetic tone, although he does not paint an entirely rosy picture. In his first report, published on 15 April 1965, he alludes to the fact that the pilgrims were less than impressed with the food they were served in Athens and that there was an 'undercurrent of racial hostility' in the expression of their distaste. He also hints that they reverted to their old ways in their attitudes to the locals, but portrays the behaviour as relatively harmless, even humorous. He mentions the veterans' objections to the fact that Sir Raymond Huish, president of the Queensland branch of the RSL and national deputy president, was leading the pilgrimage, and how they reacted with some hostility to Huish's alleged remoteness. Inglis's reports also refer to the New Zealanders' unhappiness with their accommodation, the difficulty old men had getting from deck to deck, the disappointment that some felt at being unable to take part in the landings on the morning of Anzac Day because of limited space in the ship's lifeboats, the diggers' frustration at the short time spent at Anzac Cove, and the Turks' insistence that the bus fares on the peninsula be paid ahead of schedule, partly because some hotel bills were left unpaid in Athens.[16]

The tone of Inglis's reports is deeply respectful of men from a different time and worldview. Despite difficulties and discontent, the pilgrimage emerges as a generally successful enterprise – and far from the chaotic, poorly planned circus that he might equally have portrayed. Perhaps the positive tone was partly a function of his role on the pilgrimage as a newspaper correspondent. There was much to relay in a limited number of words, and sending back reports that exposed the less pleasant sides of the pilgrimage would have caused some difficulty with his hosts and might have been regarded as something of a betrayal by the old diggers. Inglis would also have been well aware that one of the goals of the pilgrimage was to generate positive publicity about the Anzac tradition – a cause for which he had some sympathy – and negative reports would have cast him in the unsought role of Anzac spoiler.

Longer writings after the pilgrimage gave Inglis more scope to report on what he had observed. His first attempt to deal with the pilgrimage as a whole – relatively short at 3500 words, and limited in its scope – appeared in *Nation* in May 1965.[17] Inglis concentrates on the diggers' reaction to being in the lands of the ancients and some of the birthplaces of Christendom. He notes that for the most part the pilgrims were uninterested in ancient history, hostile to religion and frequently bored by their sightseeing. 'Didn't they ever build anything in these parts except ruins?' asks one.[18] The pilgrimage to holy lands coincided with Easter, but only one pilgrim commented, lamenting that 'we've missed our hot cross buns.'[19] Perhaps not surprisingly, given the times in which they had been born and raised, they were parochial and often uneducated, regarded everything non-British as somewhat inferior, and took little interest in other cultures.[20]

There is a hint of disapproval in Inglis's tone throughout the article, but he avoids condemnation. Indeed, at points he attempts to qualify their remarks and attitudes. He explains their apparently philistine attitudes as resulting from most of them having finished their educations by about 1910, and he suggests that they are representative not of Australians and New Zealanders as a whole, but of those who were given a rudimentary education over half a century beforehand and were then asked to fight in a world war. Inglis even qualifies the comments of one pilgrim who said that every city in the region, because of its squalor, should be bulldozed flat or atom-bombed, by noting that he was a humane man, and that he would certainly have wanted the inhabitants removed 'before this detergent operation.'[21]

In all of these publications, Inglis writes with pathos about the pilgrims and the pilgrimage. He draws out the gentle humour and the dignity of the old diggers, and teases out their stoicism in the face of some of the pilgrimage's difficulties. He never pronounces judgement, never condemns. There is a nobility about the enterprise – a slightly pathetic nobility of men returning fifty years later to a place where they had fought and suffered, to see and commemorate old mates and to relive old battles that much of the rest of Australian society had moved on from. As Inglis later noted, he and others widely expected that the commemoration of Anzac as a significant date and event in Australian history would pass with the old diggers themselves. These men are thus relics – aged, infirm, making one last visit to a place and time where they were regarded as heroes as they, and the Anzac they created, entered their twilight years.

* * *

It was probably soon after his return that Inglis produced a draft for the envisaged book about the pilgrimage, based on material he had gathered, his observations and conversations on board, and his subsequent correspondence with the pilgrims and with the RSL national secretary, William Keys. The Inglis papers in the National Library of Australia contain two drafts of some eighty pages in length, enough for a short monograph with the inclusion of illustrations. Both drafts are marked up in Inglis's handwriting, and it is clear that he wrote one version, then amended it throughout – although generally only with minor changes – to produce the second version.

The second version is not final – there are marginal notes where Inglis appears to have decided on further changes or signified questions that he needs to consider and facts he needs to confirm in producing a final draft. 'Thicken. Too muted!' he writes to himself of his criticisms of the NSW state president, Sir William Yeo, on page five of the second version. 'Mention the climb up the Acropolis? Buses?' he ponders on page twelve. There are intended deletions too – from single words to whole paragraphs.[22] But the drafts are beautifully written and in an advanced state. It would have taken relatively little work to bring them to completion, and Inglis's emerging stature as a historian – and the likely market among veterans – would have ensured easy publication. But he never published the text as a book.

The obvious reasons are somewhat unsatisfying. It may have been that he was too preoccupied with other projects and tasks, and it needs to be remembered that from the start of 1967 Inglis assumed a new role as the foundation professor of history at the University of Papua New Guinea, a role that would have required some upheaval as he took on new responsibilities and moved himself and his family to unfamiliar surrounds.[23] But his academic output remained undiminished for the next few years, and the pilgrimage manuscript was already largely complete, so such an explanation is less than convincing. Nor was he bored by the topic; he continued to write about Anzac and Gallipoli throughout his career, even when other major projects had his primary focus. He certainly did not just forget; in *The Australian Colonists*, published in 1974, he details his ongoing engagement with the veterans, apologising: 'I am sorry it is taking me so long to write about their experiences as I promised them.'[24]

Inglis wrote, many years later: 'I produced a book-length-narrative which didn't come off: somehow I couldn't get the tone right.'[25] On another occasion he said that the manuscript 'didn't come out right.'[26] He cannot have been referring to the quality of the writing, or the structure of the manuscript, or the defensibility of his observations, for considerable portions of the draft were published in an article about the pilgrimage for the *ANU Historical Journal* (*ANUHJ*) in October 1966.[27] Scates has said that his 2017 examination of these drafts 'rescues this remarkable manuscript from virtual oblivion,' but large parts of the manuscript had in fact been published, for they were simply 'lifted' by Inglis to generate the *ANUHJ* article.[28] There are almost no passages in the article that are not in the manuscript – it is, in effect, an abridged version. Large parts of the draft were also published in the *Journal of the Australian War Memorial* in 1991.[29] It, too, is essentially an abridged version.

It may be that Inglis was not happy with the book draft and, having decided not to proceed with it as a book, used it instead for the 1966 *ANUHJ* article, later revisiting it for the 1991 *Journal of the Australian War Memorial* piece. Or, quite feasibly, the *ANUHJ* article might have been intended as a precursor to the book that never was. The latter appears more likely, given that the apology he offered the pilgrims in *The Australian Colonists* is for 'taking … so long to write about their experiences' rather than for not writing about them.[30] But this does nothing to resolve the question of why, at an early stage, he either abandoned plans to produce a book or, more likely, never followed through with the intended publication.

The answer would appear to lie in Inglis's desire to paint the pilgrimage in a more positive light than a full and frank account would have allowed. He knew well that much of the pilgrimage had been a disaster, even a farce. Three of the old diggers died during the trip – a tragic irony in that they survived their war experience as servicemen but not the return as veterans. The standards of healthcare were poor, with the *Karadeniz* providing only Turkish doctors with limited English and very few of the medicines that might – should – have been available to treat more than 300 elderly men and women. Dr Joy Seager, a former repatriation doctor, was on the pilgrimage with her husband, digger Harold Seager, and agreed with the RSL that she would offer her medical expertise in return for a discounted fare.[31] Following the pilgrimage, Seager wrote a scathing report for the RSL about the medical provisioning. She appears to have worked tirelessly throughout the trip, with little support from Huish. She claimed that none of the three pilgrims who died during the voyage need have done so, and that had it not been for her efforts, the illnesses that swept through the ship might have claimed the lives of thirty or forty of the pilgrims. In their later correspondence with Inglis, many of the pilgrims commended Seager and reinforced her verdict on the inadequacy of the medical arrangements.[32]

The conditions on board the ship were entirely unsuitable for the elderly, considerable numbers of whom suffered from war incapacities. The schedule included too many ceremonial functions, yet the time spent at Anzac Cove – the 'holy grail' for the pilgrims – amounted to less than one full day.[33] Huish's unpopularity among the veterans was partly due to the fact that he had never served at Gallipoli and was thus regarded as having lower status than the 'Gallipoli men.' This especially rankled as Huish was thought by some to have made himself far too prominent in the wreath-laying ceremonies. There were even rumours before the pilgrimage arrived at Anzac Cove that if Huish attempted to lay a wreath at Lone Pine, he would be 'counted out.' Huish appears to have fallen out with many of the Australian pilgrims, who regarded him as aloof, and was even less popular with most of the New Zealand contingent, partly because he kept referring to 'Australians' in his speeches. He also fell foul of his Turkish hosts. Max Vickers, one of the pilgrims, told Inglis that a Turkish general liaising with the pilgrimage party had indicated that he was 'cheesed off' with Huish, and that despite his extensive experience as an honorary liaison to visiting parties he had 'never struck a man like this before.' Huish had even informed a Turkish general expecting to attend part of the day's proceedings, 'Your presence will not be required.' Vickers himself called Huish a 'sawdust Caesar.'[34]

The Turkish hosts could be problematic too, and the pilgrims themselves often reverted to less than seemly behaviour. There was a great deal of complaining on board the ship, considerable drunkenness at some functions, and an undertone of racial hostility and contempt towards many of the people the pilgrimage encountered. One pilgrim recorded, in response to Inglis's post-pilgrimage survey, that 'quite a large number of men could not forget that fifty years had elapsed since they were in the A.I.F. and reverted to the rough life and language of those times.'[35] Some left Athens without paying their full hotel bills, one described the less than satisfactory plumbing on board ship as 'too Islamic,' and many made derogatory racial remarks throughout the pilgrimage.[36] The survey revealed high levels of general dissatisfaction. One man lamented that morale on the pilgrimage was lower than in the war and described it as a 'swindle.'[37] Another responded simply: 'No comment. Least said is easiest mended.'[38]

Inglis is much franker about these problems in his two book drafts than in the material he published. The drafts include discussion of the ill-advised choice of ship, the early and ongoing dissent between the New Zealanders and the Australians, the impatience that many of the pilgrims had with the itinerary and visits to the sites of antiquity, the disappointments of the visits to Anzac Cove, the illnesses that swept through the ship, the hostility and contempt towards many of the local people, the dissatisfaction with Huish, the difficult relations with Turkish hosts who misunderstood what the pilgrims were seeking, and the simple desire, by the end of the trip, to go home. He even quotes Joy Seager's judgement that dozens of the pilgrims might have perished if not for her ministrations.[39]

In the drafts, a worthy but occasionally flawed enterprise has become a rather sad and sorry spectacle. The diggers are shorn of much of their dignity and appear instead as cantankerous old men, more in accordance with the rough caricatures offered by Alan Seymour in *The One Day of the Year* and the controversial *Four Corners* investigation of 1963, while the RSL leaders are recast as bumbling incompetents.[40] There is still a moving pathos and sentimentality around the pilgrims' desperation to engage with their former fighting grounds, to find their old mates, and to walk again over their old battlefields. But the focal point of the pilgrimage – the time at Gallipoli – is now so surrounded by calamity and disappointment that it becomes lost in the failings of the overall enterprise.

This was not what Inglis wanted. We know this because of the much more forgiving tone of his published writings and because of his earlier, fruitless attempts to wrestle with the downsides and disappointments of the pilgrimage in a number of incomplete drafts in his papers, drafts he abandoned when he might easily have continued to follow the damning direction they were taking. We know it from the material that he omitted from both versions of the book draft. In neither does he mention the deaths or the ill-health that some pilgrims suffered afterwards. Instead, the illnesses are a burden bravely overcome, thanks in part to the ministering angel, Dr Seager.[41] Few of the criticisms offered afterwards in the post-pilgrimage surveys are included, and although there is considerable criticism of Huish, it is toned down from his notes. Huish is flawed, not damned.

Close examination of both drafts also reveals efforts within each one, and in the development from the first to the second, to downplay even more of the pilgrimage's misadventures. Inglis is far from explicit about how the RSL had badly failed to meet many of the pilgrims' desires, accepting an itinerary that offered too much of little interest to them and too little of the places they had been in 1914 and 1915. There was, he notes, plenty of 'weariness and impatience' about what one man termed the 'buggerin' about the Mediterranean,' but Inglis always appears as if he is attempting to temper his criticisms – and some of the most damning passages regarding the itinerary were removed in the transition from the first draft to the second.[42] The pilgrims' complaints about the nuisance of having to queue up to change currency at every port and Inglis's reference to this being 'a vexing business for people whose bodies and minds were well past their prime' were scored through in the first draft and omitted from the second.[43] Was it because the complaints made the pilgrims seem like eternal discontents, or was the comment about their minds and bodies, on reflection, too unkind? There are plenty of other examples. On re-reading his first draft, Inglis appears to have felt that it showed the pilgrims and the pilgrimage in too unfavourable a light, and to have attempted to paint a slightly more favourable picture in the second.

The complaint of one former Light Horseman when the pilgrimage reached Heraklion – to the effect that he was 'sick of crawling over bloody ruins. Anyway, half of them have been out there for the tourists' – survived from the first draft to the second but was then scored through in the next version.[44] Likewise, the comment of one 'much decorated man' that the places visited were 'of no interest to pilgrims' survived the transition from the first draft to the second but was then marked for removal.[45] An aside that the New Zealanders on board 'had been seething mildly for three weeks' met the same fate.[46] Other criticisms are included but muted. The allegation of one pilgrim who abandoned the venture after a few days that the pilgrimage was 'seething with discontent' is included, but Inglis adds that such a criticism 'may have put it too strongly.'[47] All other sources suggest that the characterisation was probably justified. Some of the pilgrims' complaints about the lack of ceremony when the Turkish and Australian veterans met on the beach make the first draft and survive into the second – but mention of criticism from external satirists and others is either deleted in transition from the first draft to the second or scored through in the second.[48] But this was a far as the manuscript got. The third version never materialised. The book was not to be.

* * *

All historians wrestle with their material as they attempt to convert sources, notes and ideas into a coherent narrative or argument. It is an attempt to impose sense and meaning onto the chaos of the past, to make a story out of the fragments of source material that are left to historians. It can be tortuous, and the results are not always satisfactory. Historians have a commitment to truth-telling, and at the end of every piece of writing ask themselves (or should) whether they have conveyed the past 'how it essentially was.'[49] But they also have consciences and political and research agendas. With rare exceptions, historians will avoid causing needless offence, will shun unnecessary controversy, and will often avoid writing history that clashes with their inner convictions, ideological commitments and political outlooks. It can be a difficult balancing act when the imperatives do not all point in the same direction.

Inglis's attempt to make sense of the pilgrimage cannot be understood solely through his publications. To understand more fully how he struggled with his material requires some consideration of the surrounding context, his own background, the sources that he had available to him, his notes, his drafts and annotations, and the material that he didn't publish. The inner workings of historians' minds as they attempt to shape their research and insights into publishable writing are usually hidden from view, but thanks to his extraordinary archive in the National Library of Australia, Inglis's struggles are laid uncommonly bare. We can witness and even recreate his gathering of evidence, his selection of aspects of the pilgrimage to write about and publish in newspapers and academic journals, his construction of a draft for a book about the pilgrimage, and his attempts to reshape that draft. And ultimately we witness Inglis's 'failure,' for the draft was never satisfactorily completed, much less published as the intended book. Inglis tried to write an accurate, full and honest account of the pilgrimage, a piece of contemporary history, without producing an exposé, and without embarrassing and causing needless offence to his subjects. It proved impossible.

Despite his repeated efforts and his prodigious talents, Inglis could not get the manuscript for the Gallipoli pilgrimage book to 'come out right.' There are a number of reasons why Inglis's drafts would have left him dissatisfied. He had been invited into the inner sanctum of Anzac, had corresponded extensively with the RSL and had been trusted to accompany the pilgrims. They had confided in him their thoughts and beliefs, both on the pilgrimage and afterwards. To portray the pilgrimage as the farcical mess that it often was, and to write frankly of some of the pilgrims' less than endearing characteristics, would have been an act of betrayal. Inglis was by all accounts a man possessed of 'unfailing generosity of spirit'; he would have known, and would likely have baulked at the fact, that his manuscript would have caused offence.[50] Moreover, he would have been well aware of one of the main purposes of the pilgrimage – publicity for the RSL and a reminder of the service rendered by the Anzacs.[51] A book that exposed the deaths, illness, almost criminal negligence of the organisers, fractiousness, racism, drunkeness and disappointments would have given further ammunition to critics of Anzac and the RSL, and would have defeated one of the pilgrimage's primary purposes.

Perhaps, too, Inglis had an emotional investment in the pilgrimage. As much as he deplored some of the attitudes of the old diggers, he appears to have remained kindly disposed to them and their memories. Although not a devotee of Anzac the legend or Anzac the campaign, he respected the veterans' attempts to come to terms with mass death through their own rituals.[52] And he appears to have been something of a devotee of the diggers, and spent much of his life as a student and historian studying and working alongside peers who had fought in the Second World War.[53] He never really questioned the term 'pilgrimage,' and his papers include cuttings and publications about more traditional religious pilgrimages, suggesting that he was predisposed to seeing the trip as a holy quest and thus to downplaying behaviour and practices that might have undermined the image of diggers on a sacred journey. It also suited his conception of Australian history, announced in the conclusion to *The Australian Colonists*, for Anzac to mark the consummation of nationhood – although he shied away from the 'birth of a nation' phrase. His Anzacs, to be worthy of creating a nation, could be unruly and ill-disciplined at times; but they could not be uncouth bigots who went on a fool's errand not once but twice.

But Inglis was also a professional historian, committed to truth-telling. It was defensible for his newspaper articles to put a slightly glossier light on the pilgrimage than might have been warranted by the realities, and in journal articles such as his 1966 'Return to Gallipoli' he could concentrate on particular themes that did not require full examination of the pilgrimage's most egregious failings. A book on the pilgrimage, however, needed to be more comprehensive. The deaths of the pilgrims, the need to keep the planned visit to Israel concealed from Turkish hosts, the appalling organisation and the litany of complaints could hardly be omitted. This, it would appear, troubled Inglis, for at the end of his first draft manuscript, he left himself questions that he knew he needed to ponder: 'End? Mention Israel? Put complaints later? Deaths? Anti-pilgrimage bits?'[54]

Inglis appears never to have resolved these questions. His drafts remained caught between his commitments as a truth-telling professional historian, his desire to see the pilgrimage and Anzac in a favourable light, and his obligations to the veterans and the RSL. When he said that the manuscript 'didn't come out right,' he meant, in my assessment, that he was never able to satisfy these competing, and perhaps irreconcilable, demands. The manuscript tried to serve too many masters, and eventually served none. Unable to satisfactorily compose his history, unable to create a past he could live with, he chose instead to set it to one side.[55] He preserved all his drafts, scribblings, surveys, annotations and other documents, and later donated them to the National Library of Australia. They remain available to subsequent generations of historians, tempting them, with the advantage of half a century's distance and shorn of some of Inglis's obligations, to try their own hand at constructing a 'frank and honest narrative' of the Gallipoli pilgrimage.

Acknowledgements

I drew on an unusually large number of readers for their thoughts and assistance in the preparation of this chapter. I would like to acknowledge the assistance provided by Kate Ariotti, Frank Bongiorno, Linda Crotty, Romain Fathi, Emily Gallagher, Bill Gammage, Peter Stanley and Craig Wilcox.

Endnotes

1   B Scates, *Return to Gallipoli: Walking the Battlefields of the Great War*, Cambridge University Press, Melbourne, 2006, p. 125; KS Inglis, *Letters from a Pilgrimage: Ken Inglis's Despatches from the Anzac Tour of Greece and Turkey, April–May 1965*, Inside Story, Melbourne, 2015, p. 21. The Australian government supported the pilgrimage to the tune of £20,000, although pilgrims still had to pay a substantial sum – some £600 – for a place.

2   R Huish, reports to RSL federal executive on pilgrimage to Gallipoli and visit to Israel, Papers of Ken Inglis, MS389, National Library of Australia. See also Scates, *Return to Gallipoli*, pp. 125–9.

3   C Wilcox, 'A Vernacular Intellectual,' in KS Inglis (ed. C Wilcox), *Observing Australia: 1959 to 1999*, Melbourne University Press, Carlton, 1999, p. 8.

4   On Bean, see DA Kent, '*The Anzac Book* and the Anzac Legend: C.E.W. Bean as Editor and Image-Maker,' *Historical Studies*, vol. 21, no. 84, April 1985, pp. 376–90; and A Thomson, '"Steadfast Until Death"? C.E.W. Bean and the Representation of Australian Military Manhood,' *Australian Historical Studies*, vol. 23, no. 93, pp. 462–78.

5   B Scates, '"Letters from a Pilgrimage": Reflection on the 1965 Return to Gallipoli,' *History Australia*, vol. 14, no. 4, December 2017, p. 533.

6   See KS Inglis, *Churches and the Working Classes in Victorian England*, Routledge, London, 1963; Wilcox, 'A Vernacular Intellectual,' pp. 4–5; C Wilcox, 'A Bibliography of K.S. Inglis's Writings,' in Inglis, *Observing Australia*, pp. 251–8. Inglis's own accounts of his childhood influences are in KS Inglis, *The Australian Colonists: An Exploration of Social History, 1788–1870*, Melbourne University Press, Carlton, 1974, p. x, and KS Inglis (assisted by J Brazier), *Sacred Places: War Memorials in the Australian Landscape*, Melbourne University Press, Carlton, 1998, pp. 1–4.

7   Wilcox, 'A Vernacular Intellectual,' p. 7; KS Inglis, 'The Anzac Tradition,' *Meanjin Quarterly*, vol. 24, no. 1, March 1965, pp. 25–44. See also G Davison, 'Ken Inglis: Threads of Influence,' *History Australia*, vol. 14, no. 4, 2017, pp. 516–18.

8   Wilcox, 'A Vernacular Intellectual,' pp. 1–17.

9   Inglis, *The Australian Colonists*, p. x; Davison, 'Ken Inglis: Threads of Influence,' p. 518; KS Inglis, 'Remembering Anzac,' in KS Inglis (ed. J Lack), *ANZAC Remembered: Selected Writings by K.S. Inglis*, History Department, University of Melbourne, 1998, p. 234.

10   Inglis, 'The Anzac Tradition.'

11   Wilcox, 'A Vernacular Intellectual,' p. 8.

12   For a full list of his Anzac-related writings to 1998, see KS Inglis (ed. J Lack), *ANZAC Remembered: Selected Writings by K.S. Inglis*, History Department, University of Melbourne, 1998, pp. 261–4.

13   Davison, 'Ken Inglis: Threads of Influence,' p. 524; P Browne, '"Sydney Calling": Ken Inglis and *Nation*,' paper presented to Ken Inglis in History: A Laconic Colloquium, Caulfield Campus, Monash University, 24 November 2016.

14   P Stanley, *Bad Characters: Sex, Crime, Mutiny, Murder and the Australian Imperial Force*, Pier 9, Sydney, 2010.

15   KS Inglis, 'Diggers in Antiquity,' in KS Inglis (ed. C Wilcox), *Observing Australia: 1959 to 1999*, Melbourne University Press, Carlton, 1999, pp. 71–80.

16   Inglis, *Letters from a Pilgrimage*, p. 18.

17   Inglis, 'Diggers in Antiquity.'

18   Inglis, 'Diggers in Antiquity,' p. 73.

19   Inglis, 'Diggers in Antiquity,' p. 76.

20   Inglis, 'Diggers in Antiquity,' pp. 73–4.

21   Inglis, 'Diggers in Antiquity,' p. 75.

22   KS Inglis, 'Return to Gallipoli,' draft manuscript 2, Papers of Ken Inglis, MS389, Box 9, File 1, National Library of Australia, pp. 5, 12.

23   Davison, 'Ken Inglis: Threads of Influence,' p. 522.

24   Inglis, *The Australian Colonists*, p. xi.

25   Inglis, afternote to 'Diggers in Antiquity,' p. 80.

26   Wilcox, 'A Vernacular Intellectual,' p. 8.

27   KS Inglis, 'Return to Gallipoli,' *ANU Historical Journal*, no. 3, October 1966, pp. 1–10.

28   Scates, '"Letters from a Pilgrimage",' pp. 533–4.

29   K Inglis, 'Gallipoli Pilgrimage 1965,' *Journal of the Australian War Memorial*, no. 18, April 1991, pp. 20–7.

30   Inglis, *The Australian Colonists*, p. xi.

31   Keys to Seager, 14 December 1964, Records of the Returned Services League of Australia, MS6609, Series 21, File 4893c, National Library of Australia.

32   Dr Joy Seager, 'Medical Report of the Anzac Pilgrimage 1965,' pp. 1–4, Papers of Ken Inglis, MS389, National Library of Australia.

33   R Huish, report to RSL federal executive on pilgrimage to Gallipoli, Papers of Ken Inglis, MS389, National Library of Australia.

34   KS Inglis, undated diary notes, Papers of Ken Inglis, MS389, National Library of Australia.

35   Kelly, survey response, Papers of Ken Inglis, MS389, National Library of Australia.

36   KS Inglis, undated diary notes, Papers of Ken Inglis, MS389, National Library of Australia.

37   Barrie, survey response, Papers of Ken Inglis, MS389, National Library of Australia.

38   Pickett, survey response, Papers of Ken Inglis, MS389, National Library of Australia.

39   KS Inglis, 'Return to Gallipoli,' draft manuscripts 1 and 2, Papers of Ken Inglis, MS389, Box 9, File 1, National Library of Australia.

40   A Seymour, *The One Day of the Year*, Angus and Robertson, Sydney, 1962; R Pullan, *Four Corners: Twenty-Five Years*, ABC, Sydney, 1986, pp. 38–49.

41   Inglis, 'Return to Gallipoli,' draft manuscript 1, pp. 35–6; draft manuscript 2, pp. 38–9.

42   Inglis, 'Return to Gallipoli,' draft manuscript 1, pp. 33–4.

43   Inglis, 'Return to Gallipoli,' draft manuscript 1, p. 34.

44   Inglis, 'Return to Gallipoli,' draft manuscript 2, p. 35.

45   Inglis, 'Return to Gallipoli,' draft manuscript 1, p. 32; draft manuscript 2, p. 36.

46   Inglis, 'Return to Gallipoli,' draft manuscript 2, p. 73.

47   Inglis, 'Return to Gallipoli,' draft manuscript 1, p. 34.

48   Inglis, 'Return to Gallipoli,' draft manuscript 1, p. 56; draft manuscript 2, pp. 61–2.

49   The phrase – and imprecation – originated with nineteenth-century German historian Leopold von Ranke. See R Evans, *In Defence of History*, Granta, London, 1997, pp. 16–17.

50   Davison, 'Ken Inglis: Threads of Influence,' p. 517.

51   Inglis, *Letters from a Pilgrimage*, p. 34.

52   Davison, 'Ken Inglis: Threads of Influence,' p. 519.

53   See, for example, his praise for the comradeship and stoicism of the Anzacs in his articles about the Gallipoli experience: KS Inglis, 'The Australians at Gallipoli – I,' *Historical Studies*, vol. 14, no. 54, April 1970, pp. 219–30; KS Inglis, 'The Australians at Gallipoli – II,' *Historical Studies*, vol. 14, no. 55, September 1970, pp. 361–75.

54   Inglis, 'Return to Gallipoli,' draft manuscript 1, p. 82.

55   See Alistair Thomson, *Anzac Memories: Living with the Legend*, second edition, Monash University Publishing, Melbourne, 2013.

Chapter 12

'LETTING THE PENCIL DROP'

Ken Inglis at the Australian National University

Diane Langmore

On 10 June 1962 Ken Inglis returned to Australia from a year at Brown University in Providence, Rhode Island. Four weeks later, on 6 July, his wife, Judy Inglis, was killed in a car crash while driving on the Hume Highway. On hearing of the tragedy, Professor Manning Clark immediately urged Inglis to apply for an associate professorship in his history department in the School of General Studies at the Australian National University, and organised a visiting fellowship for him until his appointment was confirmed in 1963. For Inglis, it would be a 'heady' time to be part of the new School of General Studies.[1] The school had been formed the year before his arrival, merging the old Canberra University College (associated with the University of Melbourne and primarily offering part-time courses to public servants) into the ANU alongside the university's research institute.

Although he was later saddened by revelations in Mark McKenna's biography of Manning Clark, Inglis regarded him as an inspiring head of department and 'a wonderful colleague.'[2] As well as being a stimulating teacher himself, Clark encouraged his staff to pursue their own research interests. He was, Inglis said, good at 'helping lame dogs over stiles,' as he had when he conjured up the visiting fellowship in 1962.[3] Clark was not so enthusiastic about departmental administration, especially after his six-month appointment as acting principal of the School of General Studies. Pat Romans, the formidable secretary of the history department, warned Inglis in 1964 that he would have to be its 'de facto head.'[4] Applying himself diligently to the task, Inglis discovered that the university's staff–student formula entitled the department to two and a half more staff. He took his discovery to the principal of the school, Professor Joe Burton, who responded, 'You may be entitled – you're never going to get it.'[5]

During his academic year in the United States, Inglis had immersed himself in that nation's history. He was pleased when Clark gave him the American history course, offered to second- and third-year students. His class of about thirty was a congenial mixture of public servants, students from the city and its surrounds and others on national undergraduate scholarships. Among his favourite students were Ursuline nuns, who had set up Ursula Hall on campus. Inglis put a strong emphasis on constitutional history. The compulsory first essay introduced students to Charles Beard's analysis of the American constitution and the historiographical debates it sparked. Honours students undertook an additional course on American religious history.

Students from Inglis's first year recall the excitement of undertaking this new course. It had a strong historiographical orientation, with individual lectures frequently centred on the theses of eminent American historians. Lectures started with a summary and then asked questions, sometimes comparing or contrasting America with Australia. One of his students, Ron Fraser, later described the experience as 'electrifying.' Inglis was completely engaged with his subject: he was making discoveries for himself and sharing them with the class. 'There were more questions than answers,' according to Fraser.[6] The close of the lecture would inevitably see a trail of students wending their way to the library to read and find answers for themselves.

One exhilarating aspect of the course in that last year of the Kennedy era was Inglis's ability to link American historical themes to contemporary events. Fraser noted, for instance, that in one lecture, on 25 June 1963, Inglis alluded to the Supreme Court decision on the Lord's Prayer in schools; the forthcoming African-American protest march on Washington; and a recent article on James Baldwin in *Time*. Fraser said that the course opened up the whole world of history to him, with debates relevant to the present.

A lecture on the Gettysburg Address was one of many 'inspirational' lectures that Fraser recalled vividly. Inglis's contention that the speech was one of the first democratic memorialisations of citizen soldiers, giving 'a new tone to funeral oratory,' foreshadowed his emerging interests. In general, Fraser noted, Inglis had a sociological approach to American historical questions. He lectured on symbols of the American nation, discussing Independence Day, Thanksgiving Day and other significant ceremonial days in the American calendar. Again, there were clear links to questions that were to fire his own research.

Fraser described Inglis as a 'great encourager.' He encouraged one brilliant student – Anne Kingston (later Anne Fraser) – to publish her honours essay in the *Melbourne Historical Journal*, and gave generous support when she embarked with fellow students on setting up a comparable journal and a students' historical society at ANU. He later lamented that he had not realised that another former honours student, Bill Gammage, shared with him a then academically unfashionable interest in the First World War and the Anzac tradition.

Later, in 1974, Inglis recalled that in the previous decade 'the ANZAC tradition began to attract me as a theme to write about, a base from which to explore areas of Australian history not yet well mapped. The more I learned and thought about it, the more its ceremonies, monuments and rhetoric seemed to me to constitute in some respects a civic religion.' He revealed the genesis of his fascination with this theme: 'The ANZAC observances at North Preston [Tyler Street] State School, No. 1494, of the Victorian Education Department, are among my most vivid memories of the years from 1935, when I was five, to 1939.'[7] Even before he arrived at ANU, his interest had already been evident in an article published (under the pseudonym 'John Kemp') in *Nation* on 23 April 1960, 'Anzac: The Substitute Religion.'[8]

In January 1964, Inglis gave a paper, 'The Anzac Tradition,' to the history section of the Australian and New Zealand Association for the Advancement of Science (ANZAAS) congress in Canberra. In it, he later said, he aired his 'puzzlement over academic historians' near-silence on the subject, including the absence of [Charles] Bean from their canon of Australian historiography.'[9] In the audience for the paper was Gavin Long, who had succeeded Bean as general editor of Australia's official war histories. During discussion, as Inglis remembered it, Long observed that it 'was a historic occasion: for the first time in his experience, academic and military historians were talking together about the war and its meanings.'[10] This seminal paper could be seen as the foundation document for what was to become a growth industry within Australian history: in Jay Winter's neat phrase, 'the cultural history of warfare.'[11]

The *Sydney Morning Herald* reported on the paper, giving it favourable editorial comment, and invited Inglis to write two articles on Anzac, which it published on 24 and 25 April 1964, as did the *Age*. The articles stimulated a response from a variety of people who, Inglis noted, 'were surprised that an academic historian should be interested in the subject.'[12] They also led to correspondence and acquaintance with veterans of Gallipoli and with relatives holding soldiers' diaries and letters. In April 1965 Inglis accompanied a group of about 300 Australian and New Zealand returned soldiers on an RSL pilgrimage back to Anzac Cove. Designated correspondent for the *Canberra Times*, he delighted in 'the fulfilment of a boyhood yearning to be a reporter filing despatches,' as his letters from Gallipoli were flown to Australia to be published in the *Canberra Times* and the *Sydney Morning Herald*.[13] He contributed a clear-eyed account of the pilgrimage to the *ANU Historical Journal* for 1966.[14] His later writing on Anzac is infused with his understanding of the diggers whose acquaintance he made and with the insights the expedition gave him.

As he embarked on the three-week voyage to Gallipoli, a cable to the ship told Inglis that he had been appointed to a second chair in the history department. Just before he sailed, his ANZAAS paper was published in *Meanjin Quarterly*.[15] He returned from Turkey to Canberra early in May 1965 and on 19 May he married Amirah Turner. At the end of the year, he applied to become professor of history at the projected University of Papua and New Guinea (later the University of Papua New Guinea). Appointed in 1966, he took up the position in 1967.

Asked why he applied for that position, he said that after three or four years teaching American history he was 'sick of the sound of his own voice.'[16] The thought of doing the same thing for the next thirty years was not appealing. He felt too that perhaps he took the material more seriously than many of his students did: he later found that many Papua New Guinean students, in a country on the cusp of independence, lapped up American constitutional history more keenly than did their Australian counterparts. 'In Canberra I could hardly keep students awake because constitution is a soporific word in Australia,' he recalled. 'When I gave the same lecture in PNG the students hung on every word because the word constitution was connected with nation-making.'[17] There was also an element of challenge behind his decision and, although he might not have declared it, a desire to make a useful contribution to the emerging nation.

Before leaving Australia, Inglis presented a paper on the subject of Australia Day to the ANZAAS congress in Melbourne. It looked back to his work on Anzac Day by extending his exploration to another national day, and anticipated his next book, *The Australian Colonists*, which would include a major section on holidays. Research he had undertaken during his period at ANU resulted in publications after he had left for Papua New Guinea. His presidential address to the history section of ANZAAS 1969, 'The Australians at Gallipoli,' appeared in *Historical Studies* in two parts in April and October 1970; his preoccupation with Charles Bean resulted in his 1969 John Murtagh Macrossan lecture, 'C.E.W. Bean, Australian Historian,' published as a monograph by University of Queensland Press, and an article on Bean in the seventh volume of the *Australian Dictionary of Biography*.[18]

The Australian Colonists, his fourth book, appeared in 1974. He had taken leave from the University of Papua New Guinea in 1971 to complete the manuscript as a visiting fellow at ANU. His introduction makes clear its connection with his previous work on Anzac. Its second sentence reads: 'Chronologically the study begins on 26 January 1788; but as a historical enquiry it starts from 25 April 1915.'[19] As in most of his work, his starting point was not abstract theory or received wisdom but a basic question that had been puzzling him: '25 April 1915 is said to be a consummation. Of what?'[20] This question led to more questions. If it were said that Gallipoli gave Australia its national day, what other days had been celebrated as holidays? What could one learn about Australians from their holidays, rituals and ceremonies? Were there elements in Australia's earlier history that explained the distinctiveness of the first AIF? Such questions, he wrote, sent him further back into early Australian history than he had expected.

In the introduction, Inglis stated that he saw *The Australian Colonists* as the first of four volumes. But it also stands alone as an outstandingly original piece of social history. In Craig Wilcox's words, it 'ignored the customary narrative of discovery, settlement and constitutional development that had hitherto explained nineteenth-century Australia, and instead looked at the everyday struggles, public holidays and self-perceptions of a small, young emigrant society,' using as sources 'poems rather than parliamentary debates, *bon mots* rather than blue books.'[21] Its ninety-one illustrations were drawn from a vast array of sources, vernacular as well as scholarly, and their integration with the relevant material ensured that they were an intrinsic part of the argument. In a later seminar, the art historian Joan Kerr acknowledged Inglis as one of the historians who used works of art as documents to be interrogated rather than simply as illustrations.[22] The historian Russel Ward hailed Inglis as 'the greatest historian in the country.'[23]

In 1975 Inglis and his family returned from Papua New Guinea. He became a professorial fellow in the history department of the Research School of Social Sciences (RSSS) at ANU, on the other side of the campus from his former home in the School of General Studies. The Coombs Building, which housed the RSSS, was to be his workplace for more than two decades, and an optional working space for a further twelve years as a visiting fellow. In 1977 he was appointed professor. His chair – the senior chair in the department – was subsequently named the W.K. Hancock Chair of History.

* * *

The great advantage of the RSSS, as of the wider Institute of Advanced Studies, in that period was that its academics were mostly appointed to full-time research positions. Any teaching undertaken was voluntary. Inglis was one of the occupants of the Coombs Building who made the most of this opportunity. But despite the freedom from teaching, there were other important claims on his time. Within months of his return, he had begun discussions with Professor Oliver MacDonagh, with whom he rotated the position of head of department, and Professor John Molony on ways of commemorating the bicentenary of European settlement in Australia. These talks were the genesis of what was to become the monumental national project *Australians: A Historical Library*.

Another major national project was also profiting from Inglis's guidance. In 1977 he replaced Professor John La Nauze as chair of the editorial board of the *Australian Dictionary of Biography* (*ADB*). He served in that capacity until his retirement in 1994, working with its general editors to shepherd volumes 9 to 14 through to publication.

Chris Cunneen, who was deputy general editor for much of that period, described him as 'the ideal chairman,' supportive and efficient. He recalls that editorial board meetings 'were conducted with collegiality, dignity and despatch' and that during the course of production of a volume, Inglis was 'always available for advice and assistance.'[24] For his part, Inglis remembered his chairmanship of the *ADB* as a totally happy and harmonious experience. As well as writing entries on Bean, Charles Rowley, Rohan Rivett and Stephen Murray-Smith, and co-authoring the article on Henry Mayer, he was one of a small, select band of individuals to read every volume of the *ADB* from cover to cover.

This Is the ABC: The Australian Broadcasting Commission 1932–1983 was a divergence from his sustained work on Australia's ceremonies, rituals and holidays.[25] Jay Winter identified it as his second outstanding achievement, alongside his body of work on the cultural history of warfare. 'Both show Inglis as a pioneering historian,' he wrote, 'and one who has helped shift the centre of gravity of historical study towards an emphasis on cultural forms and the social action associated with them.'[26]

In a paper delivered to the Australian Historical Association in 1983, Inglis reflected on the long and often fraught process that saw the publication of his book on the ABC seven years after he was first approached by Earle Hackett, at the time its acting chairman.[27] He described the pleasures of a 'broadcasting addict' in plunging into the project – most notably that of interviewing staff, board members and broadcasters, the last including some whose voices he remembered from childhood. But such pleasures were counterbalanced by intense frustrations. A generous contract, which guaranteed him the right to publish independently should the ABC decide not to do so, was not sufficient to protect him from bureaucratic obstruction and ambiguities about control of the project, access to sources, and freedom of expression.

During the process of writing, when the commissioners of the ABC had read about half the text, its chairman, John Norgard, told Inglis that there was some unease among them. They felt that his account was 'light, frothy, gossipy and not what they expected an official history of a substantial statutory authority to be.'[28] Although this judgement was delivered as a criticism, it can be seen as a reflection of Inglis's commitment, from which he never deviated, to write in a style that was scholarly but straightforward and accessible to general readers as well as his academic colleagues. It also reflected his long attachment to social and cultural history. The main focus of the book is not the institutional machinations of the commission (although they are there), but rather the contributions of the ABC to everyday Australian life.

The tensions continued. Inglis recalled his encounter with Sir Charles Moses, general manager from 1935 to 1965, at the launch of the book:

> On a sunny Sydney winter morning of 1 July 1983, as guests gathered in the north foyer of the Sydney Opera House, glorious venue for a launch, I saw the 83-year-old Sir Charles walk across the red carpet, still visibly an athlete though walking with a stick. 'Good morning, Sir Charles,' I said cordially. 'I don't want to speak to you,' he replied. 'You will hear from my lawyers.'[29]

In the event, the lawyers for Melbourne University Press, who published the volume, were able to persuade Moses not to pursue his grievances. The book won the Ernest Scott History Prize for that year.

The Rehearsal: Australians at War in the Sudan, 1885, published in 1985, was similarly written in an easy style and colourfully illustrated.[30] It explores an episode of Australian history largely neglected by historians: the dispatch of Australia's first military expeditionary force to fight in an imperial war. This book, his sixth, formed a bridge linking his earlier social and cultural history with his magnum opus, *Sacred Places: War Memorials in the Australian Landscape*, which appeared in 1998.[31] *Sacred Places* won a swag of prizes, including the 1999 NSW Premier's Australian History Prize; the *Age* Book of the Year and Non-fiction awards; the Ernest Scott History Prize and the Fellowship of Australian Writers Literary Award.

The elegant simplicity and clarity of his prose is one of his greatest gifts to those who have heard Inglis lecture or enjoyed his books. As a Papua New Guinean student once told him, his work was 'clear but good.'[32] In a mischievous paper given on the fiftieth anniversary of the RSSS, Inglis parodied the fashionable postmodernist style. Speaking of the history program, he pontificated:

> Its predominant mode has been narrative, both synchronic and diachronic, and its strategy persistently hermeneutic. There has been a fruitful imbrication with the History of Ideas Unit, whose epistemological orientation has diminished a tendency within the History Project proper towards an empiricism which, however mindful, could tend to isolate the project from productive interfacing with innovative and interdisciplinary discourse elsewhere.[33]

As a colleague and mentor Inglis helped countless doctoral students, young historians and colleagues by generously reading their drafts and 'letting his pencil drop' where he thought the prose or the argument might be improved. During his time in the Coombs Building, this same generosity manifested itself in many ways: his commitment to making the history department a welcoming, harmonious and stimulating place for staff, students and visitors; his willingness to take on responsibilities such as writing innumerable references and offering professional advice when it was sought; his thoughtfulness in producing from his voluminous files a news cutting apposite to one's research or an introduction to a scholar in the same field; his wisdom, humour and kindness.

Inglis retired as an emeritus professor of history in 1994. He had hoped to creep off quietly, pausing, as he said, 'only to pinch enough ANU paperclips to eke out the pension.'[34] Instead, a two-day seminar marked his retirement, and at a farewell dinner his colleagues spoke of him with admiration and affection. *Whose ABC?*, which continued his study of the commission (later corporation) into the years 1983–2006, was published in 2006.[35] During his twelve years as visiting fellow he continued to assist the *ADB* by reading and commenting on articles before publication and by giving unstinting support to its general editor.

In this short survey of a long and illustrious career, it has been impossible to discuss most of Inglis's publications or related activities such as radio talks and lectures to community organisations as well as academic audiences. He was a fellow of the Academy of the Humanities from 1959 and of the Social Sciences from 1975; holder of the chair of Australian Studies at Harvard in 1982; visiting professor at the universities of Cork (1982) and Hawaii (1985); overseas visiting fellow at St John's College, Cambridge in 1990–91; and an honorary doctor of literature (University of Melbourne, 1996). In 2003 he was appointed AO. With Amirah, he left Canberra for Melbourne in 2007, but the work continued.

Endnotes

1   KS Inglis, interview with Diane Langmore, 27 May 2016, Melbourne.

2   M McKenna, *An Eye for Eternity: The Life of Manning Clark*, Melbourne University Press, Carlton, 2011; C Spark, S Spark & C Twomey (eds), *Australians in Papua New Guinea, 1960–1975*, University of Queensland Press, St Lucia, 2014, p. 214.

3   Inglis, interview with Diane Langmore.

4   Inglis, interview with Diane Langmore.

5   Inglis, interview with Diane Langmore.

6   R Fraser, interview with Diane Langmore, 27 May 2016, Canberra. Subsequent observations from Fraser are also from this interview.

7   KS Inglis, *The Australian Colonists: An Exploration of Social History, 1788–1870*, Melbourne University Press, Carlton, 1974, p. x.

8   J Kemp [KS Inglis], 'Anzac: The Substitute Religion,' *Nation*, 23 April 1960, pp. 7–9.

9   KS Inglis, 'Remembering Anzac,' in KS Inglis (ed. J Lack), *ANZAC Remembered: Selected Writings by K.S. Inglis*, History Department, University of Melbourne, 1998, p. 233.

10 Inglis, 'Remembering Anzac,' p. 234.

11 J Winter, 'Ken Inglis on Language, Culture and Commemoration,' in KS Inglis (ed. J Lack), *ANZAC Remembered: Selected Writings by K.S. Inglis*, History Department, University of Melbourne, 1998, p. 7.

12 Inglis, *The Australian Colonists*, p. x.

13 Inglis, 'Remembering Anzac,' p. 235.

14 KS Inglis, 'Return to Gallipoli,' *ANU Historical Journal*, no. 3, October 1966, pp. 1–10.

15 KS Inglis, 'The Anzac Tradition,' *Meanjin Quarterly*, vol. 24, no. 1, March 1965, pp. 25–44.

16 Inglis, interview with Diane Langmore.

17 S Spark, 'Interview with Ken Inglis,' in C Spark, S Spark & C Twomey (eds), *Australians in Papua New Guinea 1960–1975*, University of Queensland Press, St Lucia, 2014, p. 220.

18 KS Inglis, 'The Australians at Gallipoli – I,' *Historical Studies*, vol. 14, no. 54, April 1970, pp. 219–30; KS Inglis, 'The Australians at Gallipoli – II,' *Historical Studies*, vol. 14, no. 55, September 1970, pp. 361–75; KS Inglis, *C.E.W. Bean, Australian Historian*, University of Queensland Press, St Lucia, 1970; KS Inglis, 'Bean, Charles Edwin (1879–1968),' in B Nairn & G Serle (eds), *Australian Dictionary of Biography*, vol. 7, Melbourne University Press, Carlton, 1979, pp. 226–9.

19 Inglis, *The Australian Colonists*, p. x.

20 Inglis, *The Australian Colonists*, p. xi.

21 C Wilcox, 'A Vernacular Intellectual,' in KS Inglis (ed. C Wilcox), *Observing Australia: 1959 to 1999*, Melbourne University Press, Carlton, 1999, pp. 9–10.

22 S Foster, interview with Diane Langmore, 11 October 2016, Canberra.

23 Wilcox, 'A Vernacular Intellectual,' p. 10.

24 C Cunneen, email to Diane Langmore, 21 March 2016.

25 KS Inglis (assisted by J Brazier), *This Is the ABC: The Australian Broadcasting Commission 1932–1983*, Melbourne University Press, Carlton, 1983.

26 Winter, 'Ken Inglis on Language, Culture and Commemoration,' p. 7.

27 KS Inglis, 'The ABC as History,' in Inglis, *Observing Australia*, pp. 134–50.

28 Inglis, 'The ABC as History,' p. 145.

29 Inglis, 'The ABC as History,' p. 149.

30 KS Inglis, *The Rehearsal: Australians at War in the Sudan, 1885*, Kevin Weldon & Associates, Sydney, 1985.

31 KS Inglis (assisted by J Brazier), *Sacred Places: War Memorials in the Australian Landscape*, Miegunyah Press at Melbourne University Press, Carlton, 1998.

32 T Stephens, 'A Place in History,' *Sydney Morning Herald*, 13 May 2000, p. 9.

33 KS Inglis, 'A Brief History of History,' (typescript in author's possession), pp. 1–2.

34 KS Inglis, retirement dinner speech, 2 December 1994, Australian National University, Papers of Ken Inglis, Box 12, Folder 'Retirement,' National Library of Australia, p. 1.

35 KS Inglis, *Whose ABC? The Australian Broadcasting Corporation 1983–2006*, Black Inc., Melbourne, 2006.

Chapter 13

NAMBAWAN TISA NA HETMAN BILONG OL UNI

Ken Inglis in Papua New Guinea

Ian Maddocks

Ken Inglis, by Oseha Ajokpaezi

This portrait of Ken Inglis as vice-chancellor of the University of Papua New Guinea (UPNG) by Oseha Ajokpaezi, a former arts lecturer at the university, hangs in the university's council room in Port Moresby.[1] It is jaundiced only in colour; it is a good likeness and appropriately conveys both informality and a forward-directed determination. Later, most vice-chancellors chose to pose for their portraits in academic dress, and their images display considerably less energy.

The personal characteristics displayed in Ken's portrait were shared by many pioneer staff of the UPNG, who took up the opportunities and responsibilities of building a new university in an unfamiliar land. For most, it was a form of pilgrimage, a shared worthwhile adventure with high intent. Travelling together on an exciting venture, they formed powerful personal bonds.

John Gunther, UPNG's first vice-chancellor, whom Ken succeeded, is celebrated by a bronze bust of his grizzled visage on the far wall of the Council Room, also a fair likeness. The foundation and management of an academic institution was a new experience for Gunther. His university exposure in the 1930s had been in the segregated world of the medical school, where prescribing and anatomical detail were practised and memorised in Latin and where surgery held pride of place among clinical skills. As a student, he had been known for boxing prowess rather than academic achievement. As director of public health in the Territory of Papua New Guinea in the 1940s and 1950s, he had launched grassroots training of aid-post orderlies, recruiting village youths literate in pidgin English to undertake twelve months of didactic teaching and rote recitation. Thereafter, each was deployed to a village to provide basic primary healthcare.[2] Gunther's authority drove this unprecedented initiative, which effected a dramatic improvement in human wellbeing and survival in Papua and New Guinea.

Gunther's style was gruff and peremptory; he did not tolerate fools gladly, made decisions quickly, and reacted vigorously when confronted by what he perceived as bureaucratic interference and ineptitude. While these characteristics had led the minister for territories to bypass him for appointment as administrator of Papua and New Guinea, they did suit his role in the relatively independent university.

What Gunther knew was PNG: its multiple diverse cultures and languages, its lack of adequate communications, and its many deficiencies in the fields of education, healthcare and economic development. He also knew well the internal machinations of the Territory's public service and the frustrations caused by distant control from Canberra. A significant qualification for his appointment was his membership of the Currie commission, established in 1964 to advise Canberra on higher education for PNG. The Currie commission had framed recommendations for the urgent establishment of a university and suggested that it should be free to establish its own academic structures and courses, unfettered by any need to emulate examples in universities elsewhere. Gunther and Inglis proved an effective combination in exploiting that freedom to innovate.

Ken Inglis was appointed foundation professor of history at UPNG in 1966, and took up his appointment the next year, arriving in Port Moresby in January 1967. He brought twenty years' experience of study, teaching and research in universities in England, the United States and several Australian states. He had an established reputation as a historian of British social history and had embarked on critical appraisal of the Anzac story's pivotal place in the concept of Australian identity. He knew universities but could claim no experience of PNG.

Ken's decision to take up the position and to forsake a chair at the Australian National University (ANU) in his mid-thirties seemed incredible to some observers. For him and his wife, Amirah, the move to PNG was a timely adventure to share with their newly melded family of six children. Before their marriage in May 1965, each had been through difficult times in single-parent roles. Port Moresby promised something new, an unfamiliar, exotic and enticing world. The task of preparing a colony for nationhood was also an attraction, offering the chance to make a contribution to a worthwhile cause. Colonial arrivals had commonly been classed as 'mercenaries,' 'misfits' or 'missionaries.' Missionary was the only one of these labels to apply to both Ken and Amirah. Amirah's communist past had fostered an urge to 'do good,' and the same motivation exercised Ken, the residue of a Presbyterian upbringing reinforced by his sympathetic study of religious influence in socialist causes.[3]

The chance to be a pioneer, to contribute to a fresh and stimulating endeavour, was compelling. Ken relished the opportunity to establish an informal UPNG style that avoided stultifying conventions, and was happy to lecture in "Afro" shirt and thongs.[4] Soon after his appointment, he suggested to Gunther that UPNG not use academic titles: colleagues and students would know them as John and Ken, rather than Professor Gunther and Professor Inglis. In reply, Gunther asked Ken to speculate on how their colleagues might respond to the suggestion, and there the discussion ended.[5] Nonetheless, informality prevailed, even without official sanction. Bill Gammage and Hank Nelson, inaugural members of the history department, were Bill and Hank to their students. The desire to build a distinct and different university was widespread among UPNG staff. In many Australian universities, competition rather than cooperation and mutual respect characterised staff relationships. Not so at UPNG. When Bruce Mainsbridge, a physicist newly appointed to the university, visited me at the Papuan Medical College in 1967, he remarked, 'You have no gremlins here!' He recognised high staff morale, friendship and cheerful cooperation and commitment. Academics took an interest in the work of their colleagues and encouraged proposals for the integration of disciplines.

As professor of history (1967–72), Ken focused on the needs of his staff and students. Most staff coming to teach at UPNG were young and relatively inexperienced, chosen as much for their teaching ability as their publication record. They accorded Ken a ready respect, and he led by example. His approach was quiet and considered, and his lucid lecturing style meshed well with their needs. As his UPNG and ANU colleague Diane Langmore says, 'he never used two syllables if one would do.' At the same time, 'there was no suggestion of condescension to the indigenous students because they were learning in a second (or third or fourth) language in a culture of which they had little or no experience.'[6] Ken and his colleagues wanted the content of the courses they were designing to be appropriate both to the future careers of their students and to PNG's need for ready indigenous leadership in many fields.[7] These pioneer UPNG students were fated to be among the nation's first indigenous elite. From them would be drawn the future independent nation's leaders in government, commerce and foreign relations. University staff felt a responsibility to prepare them, as far as possible, for futures that were promising, if unpredictable. This meant devising a history curriculum relevant to PNG's foreseeable needs.

Ken's inaugural lecture in 1967 set down some of the issues involved in promoting the study of history at UPNG.[8] He touched briefly on the tension inherent in tertiary study for PNG students. There were virtually no indigenous scholars or published indigenous writings to provide models or examples; archival materials of any kind were meagre; and almost all existing records concerned the practice of colonial control. Many of the early records about New Guinea were written in German, stored in Europe, or had been destroyed in the Pacific war. Records for Papua consisted of the administration's annual reports, and accounts by government officers of forays into accessible villages or unexplored areas. These documents recorded population numbers, observations on the state of gardens and roads, names of appointed officials and those holding gun licences, recipients of the 'baby bonus' paid to large families, and individual misdemeanours and punishments.

Mission records were limited, too; some were lost, some were held in Europe, and most dwelt on the activities of white missionaries and the processes of proselytising. Ken pointed out the ingrained assumption that Pacific history started with the coming of white people, citing as an example a statement he had read about the Solomon Islands having always been British.[9] This was not the history he wanted to teach, or that his students wanted to learn. Colonial history could be only a tiny component of a national history stretching back thousands of years. How exactly to build that history was a challenge that exercised Ken and his colleagues.

Indigenous perception of time in PNG was a potential problem for teachers of history. Expatriates called it the land of *dohore* (later). Its communities functioned without clocks; time was estimated by the movement of sun, moon and tides, and lacked precision, as did measures of distance, weight and speed. Events from the past were recalled through their association with major happenings – volcanic eruptions, tribal conflict, trading expeditions. Ancestor genealogies, important in matters such as land ownership, provided evidence of the past, but the historian needed to adapt to a local understanding that ancestors were ever present as spirits in a house or village.

I knew this from my own experience. In Pari village, I had found that time was viewed as circular, following the seasons, and non-linear; this obviously complicated the assignment of cause. John Prince, an inaugural UPNG staff member, recounted a student explanation of tardy arrival: 'The bus missed me.'[10] Western culture seeks explanation for sickness or accident in precipitating or predetermining factors, or ascribes the event to chance. For the Motu, and for many PNG cultures, nothing occurs by chance. There is always a cause, perhaps stemming from some magical influence – interference by an ancestor spirit or the operation of sorcery.

Students at UPNG quickly became adept at concurrent appreciation of Western thought, religious teaching and traditional understanding. Many students schooled on missions accepted the literal veracity of the Old and New Testaments. Sometimes there was confusion, even anger, when teaching at university contradicted these accounts, but most students learnt to hold traditional beliefs and religious precepts to one side, ready to be taken up if needed, while accepting the priority of what their lecturers expounded.

Ken recognised the responsibility to build, alongside appropriate texts from elsewhere, a library of locally derived materials that would embrace local art forms, oral history accounts and archaeological findings. Creating this collection would depend initially on the effort of non-indigenous workers, but it was important to prepare local graduates for that future responsibility. In the meantime, the techniques of academic endeavour were presented using available materials drawn mainly from outside PNG. Ken had a huge fund of illustrative anecdotes. Diane Langmore recalls him 'holding us all riveted with his account of Baron Miklouho-Maclay's first contact with a New Guinean chief.'[11] The students were particularly suspicious of local materials that differed from texts used in overseas universities. They worried that the differences might indicate that their courses were of a poor standard, second-rate. Ken aimed to foster an understanding of concepts of history, and hoped this would help them find in local resources a path to their own history.[12]

* * *

Ken, Amirah and their children settled in the suburb of Waigani, then on the outer edge of Port Moresby and home to the new university and many of its staff. They experienced Port Moresby's tropical heat, its sudden squalls and showers, and its long dry season. They became familiar with pidgin English words and phrases, and explored the town's one accessible beach and the sparsely supplied shops.[13] Each grew in confidence in dealing with Port Moresby's physical and cultural environment. Amirah tackled, with characteristic energy, the management of a large household, including the training of domestic helpers. With assistance from a New Guinean labourer, she established a fine garden. The children explored the dusty Waigani valley for war relics, and became familiar with the ubiquitous cane toads and venomous snakes.[14] They bussed daily to a Primary A school, which presented a New South Wales curriculum, and later to the Port Moresby High School.[15]

Both schools were on the far side of the largely European suburb of Boroko, which was supplied with abundant water for green lawns, colourful borders and exotic orchids. The low-cost housing suburb of Hohola was also on the bus route, but few children from there joined the journey to the high school, which had an established tradition of racial disparagement. (Papuan Isi Kevau recalls having the epithet 'black bastard' thrown at him when he attended Port Moresby High School from 1962 to 1966.[16]) Colonial Port Moresby was deeply racist, but UPNG was different. Ken and Amirah facilitated the children's opportunities for exchange and friendship with PNG schoolmates and UPNG students, whom they respected for their intelligence, courtesy and vigour. Papuan and New Guinean friends were welcomed into the Inglis household. The children recall the excitement of a *mumu* prepared by UPNG students in the house garden for a special occasion: a pit lined with stones heated by a large fire, then filled with selected meats and local root vegetables and covered with banana leaves and dirt for insulated, slow cooking. They also participated in campus occasions and, being a lively and humorous mob, added much to the informality.[17]

The rewards and wonders of Waigani in these years were many. University staff dined in one another's houses and supported the formation of a popular staff club. Moresby's church communities and clubs, important to expatriate families housed closer to town, held less appeal for Waigani's residents. Many friendships forged in the early days of UPNG were long-lasting, often life-long. The students were some of the most educated and articulate locals, the staff were determined to avoid colonial attitudes evident elsewhere, and informal exchanges between staff and students was encouraged. Younger staff joined with students in UPNG sporting teams, and encouragement from the boundary was a popular UPNG family contribution. The fact that student numbers were small helped many to be known by name to staff. University life, says Langmore, brought 'a huge turning point in race relations ... a new atmosphere with relaxed, happy barbecues and dinners, where students and staff sat around on Papuan mats, students strummed guitars and sang' – occasions quite unprecedented in Boroko.[18]

Some students achieved wider attention through writing letters or articles for the local press or UPNG's own publications, and by singing and acting in campus productions. Many students were inspired by the visit to UPNG of the philosopher Ivan Illich in 1972, and excited by his iconoclastic proposals for education and development in PNG.[19] He proposed that schooling be delayed until the age of twelve, to allow full attainment of village skills before more rapid passage through primary education, avoiding the creation of unhappy, immature school 'dropouts.' He argued for restriction of motor vehicles to one small, flexible machine able to carry people or goods on narrow rough roads. So moved was student Bernard Narokobi that he asked Illich, 'Sir, will you stay among us?'[20] John Kasaipwalova, president of the student council, found in Illich a message of radical love in action, and led the students in an attempt to establish their own cooperative gardens and to seek a stronger role in university affairs.[21]

Port Moresby, though still a small town, was also the likely capital of an independent Papua New Guinea, boasting trappings to which it was pleased to add the status of university town. Some 'b-fores' (old-timers, or residents from before the Second World War) whom I met expressed suspicions that new academic arrivals from Australia and elsewhere, lacking 'Territory experience,' might undermine established ways and foster dissent. The cultural and geographic isolation of Waigani reinforced these thoughts.

Lois Johnson recalls a wary, if polite, distance between Ken and her husband Frank Johnson, UPNG's first professor of English. Frank came from long experience in PNG education, rising from junior teacher to principal of Goroka Teachers' College. 'When I look back it is strange how little we interacted,' remembers Lois. 'I knew Frank and Ken had some difference of opinion, so we didn't meet much, although [it was] always cordial and friendly. I liked them both [Ken and Amirah] very much. I felt there was a strain or tension between those (like us) who were "locals" and the ANU staff. They seemed too anxious about "standards" and future appointments in Australia.'[22] The few UPNG staff with extensive Territory experience felt a commitment to PNG that newcomers could not share. The b-fores were also more aware of common anxieties, voiced in the town, that students may lose touch with their village origins, leaving behind some Papuans and New Guineans on the path to nationhood. Examples from Africa of elites fomenting violent conflict stoked these fears.

The demands of teaching and assessing undergraduate topics and of supporting postgraduate students limited Ken's opportunity to research PNG history during his term as professor. As vice-chancellor (1972–75) he had even less opportunity. Only in an extended period of overseas leave between the two appointments was he able to return wholeheartedly to scholarship, and his work in this sojourn was not focused on PNG.

Ken did publish work about PNG, including some pithy contributions to Australian newspapers and journals of current affairs, but no major monograph to testify to his important contribution to the country. His inaugural professorial address concerned the teaching of history in PNG.[23] Established interest in matters of national identity and the Anzac story followed Ken from Canberra to Port Moresby, and he wrote on the search for a new name for PNG as an independent nation, racial aspects of the Second World War in PNG, and the first ten years of UPNG.[24] Port Moresby knew him best through a 1972 lecture given to celebrate the centenary of the arrival in Papua of Captain John Moresby.[25] It was a joint effort: Nigel Oram outlined the Motu and Koita side of the encounter; Ken reviewed Moresby's published accounts of his arrival and interaction with the local peoples.

Ken's approach to writing PNG history was based primarily on the appraisal of documents and observations drawn from a wide range of potential sources. He did not explore oral history with Papuans and New Guineans, though he encouraged his students and others to collect the testimonies of village elders. The regular UPNG journal *Oral History* became an important stimulus and repository for this.

I regret that Ken did not draw more on indigenous accounts of Papuan and New Guinean history. His paper on the Pacific war, for example, could have expanded its interest and authority by including reflections by Papuan carriers on their experience of the Kokoda Trail.[26] A score or more of former carriers, then in their forties and fifties, could have been gathered from Motu villages and encouraged to reminisce in Motu, their exchanges recorded and translated. In common with many Australian men who had served, ex-carriers were reluctant to speak individually but proved more forthcoming in groups, where they shared memories excitedly.

* * *

Through the eight years of the Inglises' life in Port Moresby, Ken and Amirah's children progressed from primary school to the high school and then to boarding school in Melbourne. The Australian administration in Port Moresby provided generous support to its officers for the secondary education of their children in Australia, and UPNG made the same provision. In Melbourne, the Inglis and Turner children had each other, and their grandparents and other family members, for support. They were defended against the anxiety and grief of separation that affected many Territory families who felt forced to abandon their children to distant school supervision.

With the children at school in Australia, Amirah found herself with time for other interests. She researched local material for two books on intriguing and dimly lit aspects of Papuan history. The first was a critical review of the 1920s legislation aimed at the protection of white women from sexual attack by indigenous men.[27] With a confidence born, perhaps, of familiarity with communist analysis of class struggle, she confronted racist and sexual fears latent in the black and white populations of Papua. Her second book, published after she and Ken had left PNG, was an outline of a 1938 event with elements of Papuan savagery and magic, which had excited awe and wonder across Port Moresby. *Karo* described the life of a convicted Papuan criminal of that name, who had consistently feigned blindness in Samarai jail, been transferred to Port Moresby 'for treatment' and, through conjuring tricks, gained prison privileges in Koki jail that he used to plan the murders of the chief warder and his family.[28] She located and interviewed Papuan informants to bring a wider perspective to her account.

Amirah's choice of topics, and her enthusiasm in pursuing local informants, displayed her energetic involvement in the Moresby scene. She was a vital contributor to the life of the UPNG campus. Her support of Ken as vice-chancellor was invaluable, since he found the role much less enjoyable and far more taxing than teaching history. Often it entailed off-campus negotiation with politicians and bureaucrats, some of them familiar UPNG graduates who had come to exercise power with satisfaction. They sought to trim UPNG's budget, and were consistently dilatory in responding to the university's requests and proposals. The necessary exercise of authority and discipline on campus made it harder for Ken to form close and warm relationships, particularly with members of the student body, which had become larger, less cohesive, and more willing to complain and strike.

Ken and Amirah left Port Moresby in 1975, a short time before PNG achieved its independence. The country is now moving through its fifth decade of nationhood. Its population has increased threefold in that time, its leadership commonly is self-serving and variably corrupt, and its natural resources are steadily plundered in collusion with overseas interests. The university is kept poor, its maintenance deficient, its student life disturbed by tribal competitiveness, violence and the anxieties of uncertain future employment.[29] What legacy can now be attributed to Ken and Amirah? The university they helped to found continues to function, in spite of all its difficulties. It is led largely by home-grown scholars and teachers. While their task is formidable, they continue to follow the path and example set in UPNG's first decade by Ken and other pioneers. Their example informs graduates and scholars whose work addresses aspects of PNG art, archaeology, language, history, environment, economy and culture. This scholarship is readily available to students at UPNG.

The influence that eight years at UPNG had on the Inglis family, while largely unsung, was considerable. In their pilgrimage to PNG they forged deep friendships with fellow pilgrims and students. Like many who shared a time of colonial service in PNG, they were changed by the journey; back in Australia they looked with refreshed eyes. They did not look back at PNG with tropical nostalgia, the habit of many old Territorians, but with fellow UPNG academics found new opportunity, displaying a confidence born of the freedom to innovate that UPNG had allowed them.

When *Observing Australia* was published, I chided Ken for not having included an observation on PNG among those wide-ranging essays.[30] He replied that a long piece on higher education in PNG was eliminated by Melbourne University Press because of restrictions on length. 'Maybe I'll still indulgently assemble a few old items from those days and look for an indulgent publisher. I'd love to see what memory will yield of that marvellous graduation ceremony and our dinner with the Queen. Sad that she sold the yacht!'[31]

Mention of the royal dinner has already been published; the graduation remains strong in folk memory.[32] In 1973, the university saw its first medical graduation, and PNG's first graduand doctor, Isi Kevau, was chosen to deliver the address on behalf of the graduates. To honour the occasion, a choir from Isi's village, Pari, was invited to perform. They regaled the congregation with Motu *peroveta* songs before the proceedings began. A generous repast was being prepared in the dining room close behind the choir. As the ceremony concluded, the singers were well placed to enter; the men to front the bar with enthusiasm, the women, armed with capacious *kiapas* (string bags), to move along the aisles choosing desirable comestibles to take home, as is Motu custom. Guests for the occasion included Australia's vice-chancellors, meeting in Port Moresby; they drifted into the hall, but by then much of the food had disappeared. One bemused vice-chancellor told me that, confronted by empty platters, he had headed for a large plate of cheese and biscuits, only to be cut off at the pass by a large Papuan lady who swept the lot into her *kiapa*.[33] I wrote in my diary: 'As I said to the Vice Chancellor, though the image of Pari at the University might not be entirely improved, the image of the University in Pari has never been stronger or more favourable. It was a great party.'[34] Ken was able to reflect on this desecration of his graduation with quiet good humour.

Australia's long relationship with PNG has been one of recurring discomfort. It evolved slowly through a colonial century, but with urgent haste through the final ten years before independence. That decade coincided with the first years of UPNG. We might have been better prepared for subsequent exchanges had Ken Inglis written more about his time in PNG. His genius as an observer – ever the provider of thoughtful comment and pertinent anecdote – would have served Australia's scholars and diplomats well in their encounters with PNG's diverse communities and leaders.

Endnotes

1   Photograph by Ian Maddocks, UPNG Council Room, 2003.
2   I met Gunther in 1954, when he was conducting an imperious inspection tour of the Malahang Native Hospital where I had medical-student holiday employment.
3   A Inglis, *The Hammer & Sickle and the Washing Up: Memories of an Australian Woman Communist*, Hyland House, Melbourne, 1995, p. 179.
4   D Langmore, email to author, 30 September 2017.
5   S Spark, information provided to author, March 2018, drawing on conversations between Spark and Ken Inglis.
6   Langmore, email to author.
7   KS Inglis, *The Study of History in Papua and New Guinea*, University of Papua and New Guinea, Port Moresby, 1967.
8   Inglis, *The Study of History in Papua and New Guinea*.
9   Inglis, *The Study of History in Papua and New Guinea*, p. 4.
10 Author's recollection of a comment made by John Prince, 1967.
11 Langmore, email to author.
12 M Morauta, email to author, 24 August 2016.
13 L Inglis, emails to author, 17 November – 29 December 2017.
14 L Inglis, emails to author.
15 Primary A school: 'A' stood for 'Australian.'
16 I Kevau, cited in 'Pioneer Students at UPNG: Early Experiences', in I Maddocks & EP Wolfers (eds), *Living History and Evolving Democracy*, University of Papua New Guinea Press, Port Moresby, 2010, pp. 459–60.
17 Langmore, email to author.
18 Langmore, email to author.
19 Illich delivered a public lecture at UPNG. He was introduced by Ken and described the introduction as the most civilised he had ever received. Ken's introduction was not published. Personal knowledge.

20   Personal knowledge.

21   J Kasaipwalova, email to author, 16 August 2016.

22   L Johnson, letter to author, 2 April 2018.

23   Inglis, *The Study of History in Papua and New Guinea*.

24   KS Inglis, *Papua New Guinea: Naming a Nation*, Academy of the Social Sciences in Australia, Canberra, 1974; KS Inglis, 'War, Race and Loyalty in New Guinea, 1939–1945,' in *The History of Melanesia*, Second Waigani Seminar, University of Papua and New Guinea/Australian National University, Port Moresby/Canberra, 1969; KS Inglis, 'Education on the Frontier: The First Ten Years of the University of Papua New Guinea,' in Stephen Murray-Smith (ed.), *Melbourne Studies in Education, 1980*, Melbourne University Press, Carlton, 1980.

25   KS Inglis and ND Oram, *John Moresby and Port Moresby: A Centenary View*, EC Awo, Port Moresby, 1974.

26   Inglis, 'War, Race and Loyalty in New Guinea, 1939–1945.'

27   A Inglis, *'Not a White Woman Safe': Sexual Anxiety and Politics in Port Moresby, 1920–1934*, Australian National University Press, Canberra, 1974. Republished the following year as A Inglis, *The White Women's Protection Ordinance: Sexual Anxiety and Politics in Papua*, Sussex University Press, London, 1975.

28   A Inglis, *Karo: The Life and Fate of a Papuan*, Australian National University Press, Canberra, 1982.

29   The author was a member of the UPNG Council from 2002 to 2012.

30   KS Inglis (ed. C Wilcox), *Observing Australia: 1959 to 1999*, Melbourne University Press, Carlton, 1999.

31   K Inglis, letter to author, 12 June 2002.

32   I Maddocks & S Spark, '"Taim Bilong Uni": Ken Inglis at the University of Papua New Guinea,' *History Australia*, vol. 14, no. 4, 2017, pp. 545–60.

33   Entry in author's diary. Diary in possession of author.

34   Entry in author's diary.

Chapter 14

THE ROAD
FROM PRESTON

The Australian Colonists
and Ken Inglis's explorations in social history

Frank Bongiorno

Thanks for letting me see it. I needed badly to see some evidence that all we do is not in vain. You see, at the moment, of the three possible reasons for welcoming death – as a union with the world spirit, as a chance to see 'those whom we have loved but see no more,' and as a chance not to fail again, I have long given up hope for the first two, but that third one now seems quite attractive. That is bad. So I was glad to read your manuscript because it was written by someone who had not given way to despair.

— Manning Clark to Ken Inglis, 28 August 1972[1]

Do I want this curious transparent blood of the antipodes, with its momentaneous feelings, and its sort of *absentness*?

— D.H. Lawrence, *Kangaroo*, 1923[2]

The Australian Colonists occupies a vital yet ambiguous place in the body of Ken Inglis's writings. Although Inglis was already a major Australian historian by the time the book appeared, it was really his first extended work of Australian history as a mature scholar. His doctoral work at Oxford had been in British social and religious history, but he later recalled that it had not been his intention to remain in that field: 'I never thought of it as a lifelong movement from Australia to England as a scholar, I thought of it as a preparation for writing about Australia.'[3] So, if Inglis were to secure a place in the front rank of the profession as an author of Australian history, *The Australian Colonists: An Exploration of Social History, 1788–1870* needed to be an acclaimed work – or at least one, like Manning Clark's multi-volume *A History of Australia*, that was widely noticed and debated. To this extent, Inglis placed a lot of eggs in this particular basket, a book completed when he was already in his mid-forties and vice-chancellor of the University of Papua New Guinea.

By the time it was reissued in paperback in 1993 by its original publisher, Melbourne University Press (MUP), the book was being called a 'classic.'[4] But it was different from the small number of other books on Australia by professional historians that anyone would dare call a classic. In the first place, unlike, say, W.K. Hancock's *Australia* (1930) or Geoffrey Blainey's *The Tyranny of Distance* (1966), it was never intended to stand alone as a single volume. *The Australian Colonists* was to be the first in a series of four books of Australian social history, each of about 100,000 words.[5] The completed series would have been a remarkable enterprise, not quite on the scale of Clark's six volumes but with few if any other rivals. Inglis even accepted an advance of $1000 for what would have been the second volume in the series, *The Little Boy from Manly*, which he intended would run from 1870 – the end point of *The Australian Colonists* – up to 1900, the eve of Federation.[6] The third book – *Australia Will Be There* – would have ended on 25 April 1916, the first anniversary of the Gallipoli landing. In his final volume, *Anzac Day*, he hoped 'to write about the world I began to know at North Preston [Tyler Street] State School [in the northern suburbs of Melbourne] and thereabouts.'[7]

As is well known, none of the subsequent three volumes would be published. Interestingly, when the paperback edition appeared in 1993 as *Australian Colonists* (the title now devoid of the definite article and by 'Ken,' not 'K.S.,' Inglis, in line with a less formal academic culture), Inglis declared that he still hoped to complete those volumes.[8] To this extent, while *The Australian Colonists* might indeed be considered a success and even a 'classic,' it was also part of an enterprise that never came to fruition.

Yet, this 'failure' – if that is what it was – is only part of the story. As it happened, *The Australian Colonists* would not be the most important or influential work of Inglis's career – a status that surely belongs to his groundbreaking *Sacred Places: War Memorials in the Australian Landscape* (1998), with its glittering prizes, multiple editions and international reputation as a landmark in the burgeoning field of history and memory. But *Sacred Places* took up many of the themes that Inglis had flagged in *The Australian Colonists*; in some respects, it stood in for all three unwritten volumes. Inglis also picked up some of the themes that would have appeared in *The Little Boy from Manly* in *The Rehearsal: Australians at War in the Sudan, 1885* (1985). And, of course, the monumental *Australians: A Historical Library* (1987), the bicentennial project that Inglis led from the Australian National University, remains a significant if undervalued enterprise. Inglis did in a way 'complete' the project of which *The Australian Colonists* was the first instalment, but not quite in the format that he or his publisher, Peter Ryan, had envisaged. This chapter will explore the background, nature and reception of the book, and assess its place in Inglis's oeuvre and Australian historiography.

* * *

The subtitle of *The Australian Colonists* was a piece of benign deception, although Inglis quickly came clean in his introduction. The book's starting point was not really 1788. It was 1915. 'Chronologically the study begins on 26 January 1788; but as a historical enquiry it starts from 25 April 1915.' By the third paragraph of his introduction, Inglis was discussing war memorials, the subject of his later book; and much of the opening of *The Australian Colonists* is devoted to explanation of how he became preoccupied with the Anzac tradition, beginning with his time at primary school in the 1930s.

So, what did any of this have to do with colonial Australia? '25 April was said to be a consummation,' Inglis explained. 'Of what? ... What had Australians thought about themselves before 1915, as Britons, colonists, and members of their own nation?' In grappling with this subject, Inglis compared his endeavour to that of an early explorer of the continent and, drawing on J.H. Hexter, deprecated historians' habit of splitting the past into 'tunnels': of labour history, political history, religious history, and so on, each seemingly self-contained and cut off from the others. Inglis envisaged social history as an integrating enterprise that would bring various themes together while illuminating subjects neglected by historians pursuing their various specialisms.[9]

In the late 1960s, Inglis believed that he was writing a book about Anzac – its working title was 'The Making of Anzac Day'

– for MUP.[10] 'I won't go on about my latest bout of resolution to write,' he told MUP's director, Peter Ryan, from Port Moresby in June 1969, 'but I hope to keep the Anzac book moving slowly for the rest of the year.'[11] Inglis would ultimately write much of *The Australian Colonists* in Canberra while on leave from the University of Papua New Guinea in 1971–72.[12] By February 1972, he realised that what was supposed to be a 'preliminary section' was already 95,000 words. He told Amirah, his wife, who was in Port Moresby: 'I'm spending 2–3 days trying to pretend to be an imaginary reader, wondering whether it resembles a book in any other respect. If it does, I'll suggest to P Ryan that we publish that first; if it doesn't, it will be (cut a bit) half of a book ending in 1900, to be followed by a book on 1901–16.'[13]

Soon after he had begun to suspect that he might already have a book on his hands, he consulted Manning Clark, who was evidently encouraging about a manuscript that Inglis was now calling 'The Making of Australian History 1788–1870.' He informed Amirah:

> I asked fairly laconically and with poker face, and got from him a response I hardly dared hope for: enthusiastic and encouraging in general and also in particular ways that might have been kindly rhubarb if I had told him what it was I wanted reassurance or guidance about, but I hadn't. I think I can leave it behind by late April. Bill [Gammage] had qualms which it's valuable for me to keep in mind; but the worst that can happen is that I find a couple of bits need carpentry that can't be done out of present drafts and notes; what I'm confident about now after a week's ruminating and Manning's response is that there is a book here, and it isnt [sic] far off being finished. It would be followed by other books: say The Crimson Thread of Kinship 1871–1900, about half-written now, and within a few months of finishing in 1975; then Anzac Day (or Australia Will Be There?) 1901–16, which is more than two-thirds written. Within a year of finishing

at UPNG I should be able to have both of those books done – each, like the present one, a fairly readable length, say 100,000 words – and within another year I should get through the book that begins in 1916, which is the one I first started on. Actually that might turn into two books too. Then, I hope, with a row of four or five on the shelf, the kids may understand why it took so long! God willing.[14]

A book that began as an effort to explain the origins of Anzac Day was now a projected four- or even five-volume series!

Inglis soon felt able to share the whole manuscript with trusted colleagues, such as Clark and Geoffrey Blainey. Blainey liked the book but not the proposed title: 'Is *making* the right word? It doesn't seem quite appropriate in a book which perhaps more than any other previous book on Australian history concentrates on what people thought of their lot and experience.'[15] Inglis replied that he had

> qualms about much in the book. I'd only decided in January to try and make a whole book out of taking the themes as far as 1870 and I wasn't confident that it had come off. If it needed drastic rebuilding, that was going to be frustrating, as I wouldn't have the time to do it within my three years in this job [Inglis was now vice-chancellor of the University of Papua New Guinea]. But your comments encourage me to think that what needs to be done to it can be done in bits and pieces of time, and perhaps finished over next December–January if I stay up here and do it.[16]

The book was divided into four sections and sixteen chapters. The first section – 'The People' – with chapters on 'Convicts,' 'Emigrants' and 'Colonists,' deployed a style of heading that Humphrey McQueen, with whom Inglis socialised while in Canberra, had used a few years before in his iconoclastic 'new left' history, *A New Britannia* (1970), with its references to 'Nationalists,' 'Navalists,' 'Poets,' 'Pianists,' and so on.[17] Those headings immediately drew the reader's attention to people, rather than to abstract concepts, structures or processes.

The second section – 'Holidays Old and New' – took up a set of concerns that had also figured prominently in the work of American social historians in the 1960s: how culture, belief and identity could be examined through public holidays, civic ceremonies and national days. The chapters cover days as diverse as those inherited from the old country – such as the monarch's birthday, St Patrick's Day and Christmas – and those that had emerged in the colonies and expressed colonists' emerging sense of history and identity – Anniversary Day (26 January), Eight Hour Day and Melbourne Cup Day.

At this point, Inglis was beginning to explore the rituals and scripts of the society that would settle on 25 April as the closest thing Australia had to a national day. *The Australian Colonists* took up issues that Inglis had already been exploring at article-length, in both academic and journalistic writing. His work in this line had been powerfully influenced by his wide reading in American history, by a sabbatical taken in the United States, and by his teaching in American history at the ANU before his departure for Port Moresby. Inglis thought at this time that he was researching religion – building on his doctoral work on the relationship of the churches and the working class in Victorian England – but it soon became clear that his work was grappling with a variant of this topic, an Enlightenment concept that American historians were again considering: civil religion. By the time *The Australian Colonists* appeared, he had produced studies of Anzac Day in *Nation* and *Meanjin*, and a two-part study of the Australians at Gallipoli in the flagship Australian journal *Historical Studies*, also the outlet for a lighthearted and groundbreaking study of Australia Day published in 1967.[18]

'War and Peace' – the third section – comprised five chapters dealing with 'Natural Enemies,' 'Bushrangers,' 'Rebels,' 'Diggers' and 'The Sound of Distant War.' Here, Inglis dealt with a theme that increasingly preoccupied Australian historians of the 1960s and 1970s – that of violence – but his central concern was what kind of historical sensibility emerged out of these experiences. Why, for instance, did the violence between white settlers and Aboriginal people not form the basis for commemorative activity? And what of the Eureka rebellion on the Ballarat goldfields? If true nationhood came from the shedding of blood, why had no earlier episode of colonial violence provided the rallying point for nationhood?

Inglis's starting date of 25 April 1915 suggested that he was dealing with an absence, but the history of that absence was replete with historical meaning. As he worked his way through these topics, Inglis was providing a vivid account of what it had meant to be a colonist in Australia. Piece by piece, we begin to see why it would be 25 April 1915 that would come to be seen as the nation's founding moment. The final section – 'The Stuff of History' – examined the idea that Australia's history still lay ahead of it. It comprised one long chapter, on Australian heroes, and one very short one, 'She Is Not Yet,' riffing off an 1877 poem by James Brunton Stephens. Appropriately enough, the book ended with a paragraph on Anzac. Its final sentence set out an unorthodox conclusion to a book about colonial Australia that had ended in 1870: 'In Anzac Day, Australians would create a holiday not transplanted from elsewhere, not confined to one region, not an occasion for pleasure; commemorating the shedding of blood for nation and empire, and honouring heroes as nobody in Australia had ever been honoured before.'[19]

The book was beautifully written; all reviewers would later agree on that, whatever else they had to say. Often anecdotal, Inglis revealed a skilled craftsman's ability to see the shape and purpose of the whole object, and he had an eye for the entertaining story that would reveal something worth knowing about colonial society. His interest in the history of words is often in evidence – how they were used and what that might reveal of a culture – and his approach was deeply biographical; the lives of individuals – some well known, others less familiar –often carry his major themes. He paid tribute in his introduction to the role of the *Australian Dictionary of Biography*, whose editorial board he would later chair, in breaking down the 'tunnels' of which he and Hexter had complained, and he looked forward to the completion of a dictionary of Australian English (which would come, as the *Australian National Dictionary*, in 1988).

Inglis also had an uncanny ability to combine academic seriousness with an accessible and inviting prose style. That owed much to skills honed in his own writing for newspapers and magazines, as well as his reading of others' words in the *New Yorker*, the *New Statesman* and the emerging quality press in Australia, including *Nation*, to which he had been a regular contributor. Inglis had aspired to a career in journalism as a young man, and was already by the 1960s a penetrating commentator in and on the Australian press. He would later – like the British historian who most inspired him, Asa Briggs – become an accomplished historian of the broadcast media, writing two books on the Australian Broadcasting Commission/Corporation.

The word 'exploration' in its subtitle captured the book's tone as well as its content. Inglis was indeed like a rather benign head of an exploring party, gently leading it through territory that he was too modest to claim to know well, and yet inspiring confidence that one was in good hands. Inglis wrote like someone who understood that there was still much to be learned; he was slow to judge; he did not pretend to be turning out either the first word or the last on the subject under consideration. There was both grace and wit. 'Among the transparencies greeting the Duke of Edinburgh in Sydney,' Inglis explained, 'was a picture showing the progress of Aborigines under British rule from barbarism to cricket.'[20]

A further point needs to be made about *The Australian Colonists*: it was an important breakthrough in the presentation of Australian history. A lavishly illustrated hardcover book that had many of the features of a coffee-table production, it was clearly intended to be a 'crossover' book that would engage a wide reading public. Designed by Peter Buckmaster and MUP in-house staff, it received a commendation in the 'Scholarly, Scientific, Technical and Tertiary' category of the Australian Book Publishers Association Book Design Awards. *The Australian Colonists* was a 'popular book which also has all the endmatter expected in a scholarly text.' The judges praised its 'straightforward and elegant' design but had reservations about the width of the text, which they thought excessive. 'The book is thought to appeal to a wide market on both a popular and a scholarly level,' the judges' report continued. 'The jacket and the design are at least partly responsible for this.'[21]

The publisher, at least, seems to have accepted the criticism of the type's width: 'I'm glad the design of *Colonists* is approved,' Ryan told Inglis, 'even if not universally. Looking at it, as I do again and again, it seems to me most open to criticism for being just a little too long in the line for comfortable reading. A whisker shaved off the line length might improve *The Little Boy*.'[22] John La Nauze, professor at the ANU, admired the book but was 'in two minds about the semi-coffee-table format.' He liked the way the well-chosen illustrations had been placed where they related to the text, 'but the book is very difficult to hold while reading, and the line (5½ inches) very long for that size of type.' Nor did he approve of the unjustified right-hand margin. 'It's not an easy book for students (school & university) to use – and they should be using it as soon as possible. This sounds carping – I think my point is that it is such a "fine" book that some will be tempted to skip some of the text, and this is so good that it should not be skipped.'[23]

* * *

An encouraging Blainey, commenting on a draft of the book in 1972, advised Inglis to tell Ryan that 'it will sell for at least twenty years.'[24] Undoubtedly, it did: the book was still listed as preliminary reading for a year-long Australian history course I completed at the University of Melbourne at the end of the 1980s. But it cannot qualify as a bestseller. In its first decade or so – to October 1985 – it sold 5474 of the 6532 copies that had been printed.[25] At $13.80 in 1974, it was not cheap, at a time when the average weekly wage for a male worker was less than $150 and times were becoming harder.[26] Hugh Stretton thanked Inglis for sending him a copy of the book and expressed enthusiasm for the daring format, but with a caveat: 'I think Ryan has found the real way to present The People's Historian. But then, our copy doesn't have a price on it.'[27] Ryan explained the difficulty to Inglis, and in a way that allowed him to blame the customer:

> Economies on books are the first line of defence for the more indispensable budget items of booze and Volvo. This thin red

line is observed by no one with more carefully narrowed eyes than by academics, teachers, etc. etc., whose salaries in recent years have risen to a level adequate to sustain great expectations but not yet quite, alas, high enough to allow some subordinate expenditures of an intellectual nature. That is to say, the natural market for intelligent books has melted under the steady glow of colour TV. And it is getting worse; there is no question that, if *Colonists* had been published six or seven years ago at the same (real value) price we would have sold at least twice the number. On the whole, the new non-intellectuals don't seem *too* unhappy about their privations. As a professor's wife said to me the other day, 'a modern house just isn't *meant* for books, is it? But I tell Harry, he doesn't understand how much dusting it saves for the women.'[28]

While Ryan thus had an opportunity to express his well-known contempt for academics, he also had to bear some of the blame. The gamble on the format and pricing was ultimately his, and their implications for the book's sales might have been foreseen, even if the extent of the downturn could not. But there were other issues in play: Ryan was also in serious dispute with at least one of the country's major book retailers, Angus & Robertson, and apparently others as well. Nick Aboud, Angus & Robertson's managing director, explained the nature of the quarrel to Inglis in November 1974, presumably in reply to a query about the book's not being in stock during the Christmas sale period:

We regret that the publisher of your book 'The Australian Colonists' has refused to supply us on any except 30 days' terms. In these days of credit squeeze and extremely tight liquidity retailers cannot operate on these terms and almost all our suppliers are allowing extended terms. We are not alone in this problem…

Your publisher – we know you will send them a copy of this letter – has also seen fit to do many things over the past nine months in an attempt to discredit this company.[29]

These problems would help explain the reference in a letter that a later MUP director, John Iremonger, wrote to Inglis when negotiating over a paperback version of the book in the early 1990s:

> To continue the discussion about retail price and royalties I must first acknowledge that your concern about how the hardback was published was justified. You are right to feel aggrieved and, given that, we will do what we can to make sure the 'second attempt' has real prospects of success.[30]

* * *

I read *The Australian Colonists* for the first time in the summer of 1988–89, at the end of the seemingly interminable Australian bicentenary. It instructed me, but did not grip my imagination in the way that Russel Ward's *The Australian Legend* (1958) did when I first read it a little later. Some of the virtues that I now recognise in *The Australian Colonists*, as in Inglis's other writings, such as his skilled use of narration to convey historical argument, I then saw as a weakness. We students were taught to make our arguments explicit, that storytelling was not a substitute for stating a case, that the accumulation of anecdote could not stand in place of interpretation. Interestingly, at least one reviewer – Samuel Clyde McCulloch, an Australian-born historian who had made his career in the United States – also judged that 'Inglis lets the facts speak for themselves, and, it is to be regretted, attempts no analysis or synthesis.'[31] This was perhaps taking a legitimate ground for criticism too far, and Inglis himself did not accept it, replying: 'I don't know whether you and I have different notions of social history, as you say in your letter; but if you think I didn't attempt analysis or synthesis, we certainly have different notions of them.'[32]

But by the time Inglis learned of this occasionally lukewarm review, in 1976, he should have been satisfied with the book's critical reception. 'The book is too good to have deserved the review in the S.M.H. [*Sydney Morning Herald*],' La Nauze had written cryptically to Inglis in 1975; but the review to which he referred was, like the others, a favourable one.[33] Academic politics never takes a sabbatical: the author of the *Herald* review was Manning Clark, whom La Nauze could not abide. Inglis himself, or at least his publisher, must have appreciated Clark's review, for a line from it would later be picked up to adorn the cover of the 1993 paperback: 'Inglis has the gift to be a historian of the nation's conscience.' Indeed, having read the manuscript in 1972, Clark had predicted the positive reception to which his own review would ultimately contribute. 'I think you will be lucky in the way the work is received,' he told Inglis. 'I imagine that your contemporaries – men like Geoff Blainey – will not be treacherous and will do justice to all the marvellous material you have discovered. That is to say they will enjoy what you have. I certainly enjoyed and learnt a lot from it. But, I still hope you will show the reader the pattern on the carpet.'[34]

The concern that Inglis had not done enough to draw out that 'pattern on the carpet' occasionally nagged, or more than nagged, at reviewers. As we have seen, Ryan believed the book's sales had been affected adversely by its landing in the straitened circumstances of late 1974. But one might just as readily argue that if the book had been released even a couple of years later, it might have received rougher handling from reviewers. An indication is provided by an essay on 'Rewriting Textbooks,' published in 1976 and therefore some time after most of the reviews, by the Marxist historian Humphrey McQueen. He criticised the book's treatment of frontier violence, if in terms that were gentle by his standards:

Aborigines receive four mentions. On pp. 175–6 there is passing reference to blacktrackers: on p. 170, a leading Aboriginal opponent of the whites, 'Mosquito,' gets four lines although there is no suggestion that he was more than a criminal. Two-thirds of p. 129 is given over to Aboriginal cricket teams, that is to a bizarre sidelight on colonial society. The longest single discussion occurs on pp. 159–176 where Aborigines are included in a chapter on *Natural enemies*, along with flood, fire and drought. Inglis comes very close to picturing Aboriginal resistance when he uses words such as 'defenders,' but he shies off and slips back into the old vocabulary of 'massacres.'[35]

McQueen had reviewed the book more fully at the time of its publication; his is, by far, the liveliest of those published either in Australia or abroad. Under the intriguing title 'Waiting Around for Mr Inglis,' McQueen began: 'It is not possible to say if this book is any good. There are indications that it might be very good. There are hints that it is no more than light narrative. We will have to wait until at least one, and possibly all three of its concluding parts appear.' McQueen believed readers would have to wait to decide whether the approach –beginning with 25 April 1915 and working backwards – represented a new way of treating historical time, or just 'a convenient device' for setting out a prologue before getting down to matters, or 'an interpretative scheme picked up from American historians concerned with national symbols, heroes and anniversaries.' If it were a new approach to historical time, 'then Inglis is poised to make a great revolution in Australian historical writing. If it is either of the others, then he falls back into the run-of-the-mill fact-botherers.' 'Reluctantly,' McQueen explained, 'because I should like Australian bourgeois historians to be as good as their overseas counterparts, I think Inglis is not about to lead his brethren into a better country – but I will continue to hope that I am wrong.'[36]

Neither Inglis nor his publisher is likely to have welcomed this suggestion: 'It might be worth waiting till all four parts are available before starting to read any of them.'[37] As we know, anyone who took that piece of McQueen advice seriously would still be waiting to read *The Australian Colonists*. And it could surely not be argued that Inglis's writing did herald the revolution in the treatment of historical time that McQueen was looking for. Nonetheless, a willingness to experiment remained – most obviously in Inglis's idea for a 'slice approach' in three of the volumes of the bicentennial history project, *Australians: A Historical Library*, those on 1838, 1888 and 1938.

Few of the more critical reviews reached the level of sophistication of McQueen's. A more common response was to praise the book in general, while bemoaning – occasionally at tedious length – the topics that had been left out. While indicative of the broadening of the scope and variety of history, such criticism was rarely constructive. It was one thing to judge that the poor or women received too little attention – valid criticism in view of Inglis's overall goals and the deepening impact of the kind of social history epitomised by the work of E.P. Thompson. It was quite another to provide a long catalogue of neglected subjects – books, buildings, clothing, work, wealth and so on – as if any single volume could deal with all of these coherently while keeping an eye on the main game.[38]

By late 1974 Australian historiography had been shaken up by new radicals such as McQueen, by the impact of protest politics, and by the growing popularity of 'history from below.' But it had not yet been revolutionised. For instance, books had begun to appear on the violence of Australia's frontier, and Henry Reynolds was exploring in articles themes that would figure in a series of influential books in the 1980s. Inglis even visited the Aboriginal Tent Embassy outside Parliament

House in 1972. But the rewriting of this aspect of Australian history was still at an early stage, and Inglis's treatment of the topic did register some of the emerging themes of the new research, such as the strength of Aboriginal resistance.

The impact of women's liberation on the writing of Australian history was also still most easily discerned in this or that brief article, rather than in extended accounts. This would soon change, with the appearance of three landmark books: Anne Summers's *Damned Whores and God's Police: The Colonization of Women in Australia* (1975), Beverley Kingston's *My Wife, My Daughter, and Poor Mary Ann: Women and Work in Australia* (1975), and Miriam Dixson's *The Real Matilda: Woman and Identity in Australia, 1788–1975* (1976). In terms of Australian women's history at least, the political and intellectual landscape was rather different by the end of 1975 from what it had been just a year before.

Still, even before these developments there were criticisms of Inglis for failing to deal adequately with women in *The Australian Colonists*. These came primarily from men; continuing male domination of the profession ensured that there were few opportunities for women to have their say. McCulloch noted the paucity of women in the book, suggesting that it reflected the fact that 'even now most Australians think of women as junior members in a partnership with men.'[39] Michael Cannon, himself an accomplished and prolific Australian social historian, commented acerbically:

> Women ... are practically absent from Inglis's story up to 1870. According to the acknowledgements, no less than eight typistes worked on the manuscript, but even this battery of nimble fingers was not able to get the sole entry for 'women' into its correct alphabetical place in the index.[40]

Jill Roe, a versatile social historian who would be an influential figure in the emerging women's history, did not raise this issue in a review in *Historical Studies*. Instead, she praised Inglis for practising 'a democratic scholarship,' and for the ease with which he had transcended the condescension – 'suitable for mavericks, dilettantes and non-careerist female students' – with which many historians in Australia treated social history. But Roe did express 'anxiety as to where the whole project is really going.' She seemed worried by Inglis's indebtedness to the 'themes and methods' pioneered by American historians, and the resulting implied comparison of Americans and Australians, which she cryptically called 'more disagreeable than inappropriate.'[41]

Roe, however, alighted on an issue that was at once ethical, personal, political and intellectual, a matter that also worried other reviewers. That was the problem of war. It reminds us that even in 1974 the Vietnam War was not yet over, and the spectre of militarism remained a troubling one for a generation of historians who had grown up in the shadow of the Second World War and had been radicalised by Vietnam. And perhaps, too, her hesitation reminds us of the nationalism that influenced historians as they went about their work in the post-imperial Australia of the 1970s. What were the implications of Inglis's preoccupation with war and violence as the basis for Australian nationality? 'It is hard to tell if Inglis thinks militarism has been the central unifying Australian experience or if he intuits it to be a central experience in general,' Roe wondered; and she was clearly perturbed by the idea that blood sacrifice might be the 'premise for historical development.'[42]

She was not alone in such musings. Gavin Souter, a journalist and historian of Inglis's own generation, said that he could understand 'the attraction which Anzac holds for Professor Inglis. Our generation was exposed to the full force of a perfected tradition before war had become a drug in the market. Hiroshima and Vietnam stand peremptorily between our children and Gallipoli, but we ourselves are still mesmerised.'[43] A younger Australian reviewer, David Fitzpatrick, the son of the great radical-nationalist historian Brian Fitzpatrick, wondered (from Nuffield College, Oxford) what hope there could be for a nation that could come together only through 'shared slaughter.'[44]

Inglis would presumably – and with some justice – have responded that he was exploring a historical phenomenon and not celebrating it. Certainly, in retrospect, he seems more prescient about the big themes than his reviewers. What we now call 'historical consciousness' has been a field of considerable and still-developing interest since the 1990s.[45] Inglis's placing of Gallipoli in the foreground of Australian identity also seems more soundly based than Souter's suggestion, by no means unusual in the wake of Vietnam, that it was being relegated to just one episode among many in the national story: 'Viewed from a distance of sixty years – back beyond the complexities of Vietnam, the close shave of New Guinea, and all our shifting alliances of the last half century – Gallipoli seems less a culmination than just one of the more interesting episodes in the continuing evolution of our sense of national identity.'[46]

Still, it is hard not to see in Inglis's treatment of warfare in *The Australian Colonists* an aspect of his own life being narrated by means other than conventional memoir. As he wrote in the introduction – and would reiterate in the opening of *Sacred Places* – he had grown up in the shadow of the First World War. Here, there was a feeling of absence, represented by a child's lapel devoid of medals on Anzac Day. As he told the historian Neville Meaney in an interview for the National Library of Australia in the 1980s:

I'm recalling how I used to envy or feel ashamed in relation to kids who were able to wear their fathers' medals. And my father was born in 1905, so he was thirteen when the war ended … I thought, 'Why couldn't my father have been in the war?' … There was a terrible capacity to inspire shame, if that's the word. A kind of helpless reverence, a sense of unworthiness.[47]

He was himself too young to have fought in the Second World War, too old to have been a candidate for conscription for Vietnam. As was the case for those Australian colonists, war was a troubling absence at the heart of Inglis's being. Yet it was also, as for them, powerfully real, a presence tangible in the monuments built during Inglis's childhood to recall a war fought mainly far from Australia's shores, and hardly less tangible in the minds of the people among whom he lived. This strange yet culturally potent mixture of absence and presence would become the puzzle that most engaged his intellect, imagination and passion.

* * *

It has long been a commonplace to recognise that all history is, to some extent, autobiography by other means. The personal dimensions of *The Australian Colonists* now seem to me more salient than I could have imagined when I first read the book. On my recent re-reading of the work – this time of the 1993 paperback – I was increasingly conscious of the extent to which it operates as a foil to Russel Ward's more famous study of colonial society and national character in *The Australian Legend*. Ward, the former communist, private schoolboy and son of a headmaster, both explored and celebrated the frontier as the place where Australian national character was formed, relying especially on the folk ballad as an expression of that character.[48] Inglis, the state school–educated son of a Melbourne suburban middle-class family, seems to have experienced no strong urge to idealise the bush or its inhabitants, either white or black. Did he have Ward's study in view at the beginning of his section on holidays, when he quoted an American patriot, in 1857, declaring: 'If the ballads of a people are the essence of its history, holidays are, on similar grounds, the free utterance of its character'?[49] As Fitzpatrick remarked in his witty and perceptive review, 'Inglis's quintessential early Australian is not a shearer but a suburbanite, who recited pretentious doggerel at banquets rather than ballads about the camp-fire, and dreamed of beaches and beer rather than rum and the Last Frontier.'[50]

Like so much of Kenneth Stanley Inglis's oeuvre, there are at least two routes connecting *The Australian Colonists* to lands beyond. One, as he explained himself, leads to Gallipoli. But the other winds its way to the modest home and business in suburban Preston that he had known as a boy. It was fitting that the book was dedicated 'To my mother and father, grandchildren of Australian colonists.'

Acknowledgements

I am grateful to Seumas Spark for alerting me to the currently uncatalogued and restricted portion of the Papers of Ken and Amirah Inglis; to Judy Turner for permission to use these papers; and to the Special Collections staff of the National Library of Australia for making them available at short notice.

Endnotes

1   Manning Clark to Ken Inglis, 28 August 1972, Papers of Ken Inglis, MS Acc98.147, Box 5, National Library of Australia.

2   DH Lawrence, *Kangaroo*, Penguin, Harmondsworth, 1986 [1923], p. 165.

3   'Ken Inglis Interviewed by Neville Meaney,' 1986, ORAL TRC 2053/11, transcript, cassette two, side one, National Library of Australia.

4   A Hyslop, 'On Revisiting a Classic,' *ANU Reporter*, 27 April 1994.

5   'Memorandum of Agreement,' 23 July 1974, Papers of Ken Inglis, MS Acc98.147, Box 5, National Library of Australia.

6   Peter Ryan to Ken Inglis, 10 December 1975, Papers of Ken Inglis, MS Acc98.147, Box 5, National Library of Australia.

7   KS Inglis, *The Australian Colonists: An Exploration of Social History, 1788–1870*, Melbourne University Press, Carlton, 1974, p. xii.

8   K Inglis, *Australian Colonists: An Exploration of Social History, 1788–1870*, Melbourne University Press, Carlton, 1993, p. xx.

9   Inglis, *The Australian Colonists*, 1974, pp. ix–xii.

10   Ken Inglis to Amirah Inglis, P.P.S., n.d. (c. early 1972), 'Personal Correspondence Ken Inglis to Amirah Inglis, 1962–1975,' Papers of Ken and Amirah Inglis, MS 10165, Box 2, National Library of Australia.

11   Ken Inglis to Peter Ryan, 4 June 1969, Papers of Peter Ryan, MS 9897/1/1, National Library of Australia.

12   Inglis, *Australian Colonists*, 1993, p. xvii.

13   Ken Inglis to Amirah Inglis, 15 February 1972, 'Personal Correspondence Ken Inglis to Amirah Inglis, 1972–1974,' Papers of Ken and Amirah Inglis, MS 10165, Box 2, National Library of Australia.

14   Ken Inglis to Amirah Inglis, n.d. (c. February 1972), 'Personal Correspondence Ken Inglis to Amirah Inglis, 1972–1974,' Papers of Ken and Amirah Inglis, MS 10165, Box 2, National Library of Australia.

15   Geoffrey Blainey to Ken Inglis, 7 August 1972, Papers of Ken Inglis, MS Acc98.147, Box 5, National Library of Australia.

16   Ken Inglis to Geoffrey Blainey, 15 August 1972, Papers of Ken Inglis, MS Acc98.147, Box 5, National Library of Australia.

17   H McQueen, *A New Britannia: An Argument Concerning the Social Origins of Australian Radicalism and Nationalism*, Penguin, Ringwood, 1970.

18   KS Inglis, 'Australia Day,' *Historical Studies*, vol. 13, no. 49, October 1967, pp. 20–41. For fuller details of these writings, see C Wilcox, 'A Bibliography of K.S. Inglis's Writings,' in KS Inglis (ed. C Wilcox), *Observing Australia: 1959 to 1999*, Melbourne University Press, Carlton, 1999, pp. 251–8.

19   Inglis, *The Australian Colonists*, 1974, p. 277.

20   Inglis, *The Australian Colonists*, 1974, p. 129.

21 *Book Design Awards: 1974–5*, Australian Book Publishers Association, Melbourne, 1974, Papers of Ken Inglis, MS Acc98.147, Box 5, National Library of Australia.

22 Peter Ryan to Ken Inglis, 10 December 1975, Papers of Ken Inglis, MS Acc98.147, Box 5, National Library of Australia.

23 John La Nauze to Ken Inglis, 17 January 1975, Papers of Ken Inglis, MS Acc98.147, Box 5, National Library of Australia.

24 Geoffrey Blainey to Ken Inglis, 7 August 1972, Papers of Ken Inglis, MS Acc98.147, Box 5, National Library of Australia.

25 'Melbourne University Press, Sales Return, Year to 1 October 1985,' Papers of Ken Inglis, MS Acc98.147, Box 5, National Library of Australia.

26 G Withers, AM Endres & L Perry, 'Labour,' in W Vamplew (ed.), *Australians: Historical Statistics*, Fairfax, Syme & Weldon Associates, Sydney, 1987, p. 157.

27 Hugh & Pat Stretton to Ken Inglis, n.d. [c. December 1974], Papers of Ken Inglis, MS Acc98.147, Box 5, National Library of Australia.

28 Peter Ryan to Ken Inglis, 10 December 1975, Papers of Ken Inglis, MS Acc98.147, Box 5, National Library of Australia.

29 Nick Aboud to Ken Inglis, 11 December 1974, Papers of Ken Inglis, MS Acc98.147, Box 5, National Library of Australia.

30 John Iremonger to Ken Inglis, 20 July 1992, Papers of Ken Inglis, MS Acc98.147, Box 5, National Library of Australia.

31 SC McCulloch, book review, *American Historical Review*, vol. 81, no. 2, April 1976, p. 438.

32 Ken Inglis to Sam McCulloch, 29 April 1976, Papers of Ken Inglis, MS Acc98.147, Box 5, National Library of Australia.

33 M Clark, 'Ourselves Writ Large,' *Sydney Morning Herald*, 23 November 1974; John La Nauze to Ken Inglis, 17 January 1975; both in Papers of Ken Inglis, MS Acc98.147, Box 5, National Library of Australia.

34 Manning Clark to Ken Inglis, 28 August 1972, Papers of Ken Inglis, MS Acc98.147, Box 5, National Library of Australia.

35 H McQueen, *Gallipoli to Petrov: Arguing with Australian History*, George Allen & Unwin, Sydney, 1984, p. 114.

36 H McQueen, 'Waiting Around for Mr Inglis,' *Nation Review*, 10–16 January 1975, p. 361.

37 McQueen, 'Waiting Around for Mr Inglis,' p. 361.

38 J Leith, book review, *Labour History*, no. 28, May 1975, pp. 42–4.

39 McCulloch, book review, p. 438.

40 M Cannon, 'In Search of Heroes of Our Own,' *Age*, 30 November 1974.

41 J Roe, book review, *Historical Studies*, vol. 17, no. 66, April 1976, p. 94.

42 Roe, book review, p. 94.

43 G Souter, book review, *Overland*, no. 60, 1975, p. 75.

44   D Fitzpatrick, book review, *Social History*, vol. 2, no. 6, October 1977, p. 822.

45   A Clark, *Private Lives, Public History*, Melbourne University Press, Carlton, 2016, p. 9.

46   Souter, book review, p. 76.

47   'Ken Inglis Interviewed by Neville Meaney,' transcript, cassette one, side one.

48   Russel Ward, *The Australian Legend*, Oxford University Press, Melbourne, 1958.

49   Inglis, *The Australian Colonists*, 1974, p. 64.

50   Fitzpatrick, book review, p. 822.

Chapter 15

AMIRAH INGLIS

Activist, historian and friend

Judith Keene

Amirah once offered me a sure tip for achieving academic success. A meticulous proponent of the gold-standard footnote, she indicated that the information had come to her via Natalie Zemon Davis. If you want to guarantee an outstanding conference paper, so the advice went, it is essential to start with a really good haircut. It still makes me laugh. In my ear, I hear Amirah's warm, low-pitched voice. In the Inglis orbit, the world seemed more fascinating, the issues clearer and one's own self somehow more ready for the intellectual tasks ahead. And, as many have attested, Amirah and Ken were generous in sharing their great gift for friendship.

Amirah and I came to know each other in the 1980s, brought together by an encompassing interest in contemporary Spanish history and politics, in particular as it related to the Spanish Civil War. Amirah was working on what became, and remains, the foundation volume on Australians in the Spanish Civil War, a study to which she brought the specialist skills of a historian and personal knowledge from her long involvement in left-wing politics in this country.[1] I had recently returned to Australia and was continuing to work on Spanish women's history and on Francoism and the Spanish state.

I found Amirah an eminently emulatable figure: confident, opinionated, enormously good company, as well as being an energetic mother of a blended family of six children, and grandmother of their children, all of whom she greatly enjoyed. Equally striking to an aspiring academic was that in the space of two decades she had produced six well-received scholarly books. The backdrop to these accomplishments was the long and successful partnership she shared with Ken, which so clearly nourished their emotional and intellectual lives.

The tenor of their relationship is exemplified in a story Amirah told me, and related elsewhere, about how she had come to begin her Spanish researches. Since childhood, she had been curious about her mother's youngest and favourite brother, Henryk, later Henri, who had set off to Spain in 1937 to join the International Brigades. After the Spanish Civil War, he led a swashbuckling but mysterious life in the elite circles of the international communist movement, including the three years he served in a French military prison on a charge of spying. When Amirah first floated the idea of writing Uncle Henri's biography, Ken insisted that she take her 'long service leave' from the family and spend several months in Europe meeting Uncle Henri and making contact with the remaining members of her mother's family.[2] It was this research, begun in 1968, that deepened her interest in the International Brigades and eventually led to the scholarly study of Australians in the Spanish Civil War.

Amirah's story

In a long and thoughtful interview, in October 1998, Amirah noted that her sense of self and her lifelong preoccupations were bound up in a double conundrum.[3] There was the constant drive to untangle the psychological impact of her Jewish heritage, and the need to understand the ways in which her view of the world had been influenced by her years as an active member of the Communist Party of Australia (CPA).

Though raised in a secular family that 'mixed meat and milk,' ate pork and neither fasted nor observed the Sabbath, her Jewish heritage was rooted in a profound sense of living at the convergence of two extended Polish-Jewish families.[4] Her mother, Manka Adler, was born in 1902 in Sosnowiec in southern Poland, a crossroads of Russian, German and Austro-Hungarian influences.[5] The Adlers, owners of a dry-goods wholesale business and a restaurant, were wealthy, sophisticated and well educated. The four boys and the daughter attended Polish schools. Facing an inexorable tide of anti-Semitism, most of Manka's family fled Poland in the 1920s. The parents and older children settled in the safety of Brussels while several younger Adlers headed to Palestine and New York.

Amirah's father, Itzhak Gutstadt, was born in 1898 in Radom, one hundred kilometres south of Warsaw.[6] His father, a well-off merchant, was the proprietor of an agency that sold Russian tea and German confectionery. Family members were observant though not particularly religious. The population of the town was divided between Jews and Christian Poles, each existing in quite separate spheres. Perhaps unusually, Itzhak never attended a Jewish school. Despite the prevailing *numerus clausus* on the numbers of Jewish students, he had managed to obtain entrance to the local Russian gymnasium. Jewish boys sat apart, and the instruction was in Russian. During the First World War, the Gutstadts were forced to move to Mariupol, a Ukrainian city bordering the Black Sea. Itzhak remembered the two years spent there as among the happiest of his life. It was a cosmopolitan port with a multiethnic population where everyone spoke Russian, as did Itzhak, fluently. Jews were not segregated, school students made friends across national groups, and the revolutionary excitement of the Bolshevik revolution in 1917 was palpable. At the end of the war, the family was repatriated to Radom, which Itzhak found extremely dull, prompting him to set off, with many adventures, to Palestine. The Zionist project left him cold, as did the treatment of dispossessed Palestinian Arabs by Jewish settlers, even those in socialist kibbutzim.[7] He and Manka met in Palestine, and in March 1926 were married. Soon afterwards they moved to join her family in Brussels. Itzhak learnt the skills of leatherwork, then set off again, this time to Australia. Isaac Gust, to use his new name, simplified in Australian parlance, arrived in Melbourne in July 1928. Manka and two-year-old Amirah followed in February 1929.

In Melbourne, Itzhak immediately started work using his Belgian leatherworking skills and in a few short years was the owner of a successful handbag factory. At first, the family lived in various flats around Carlton, Brunswick and Parkville. In 1936, they moved across the Yarra to a flat in Elwood.[8] By 1940, Itzhak had bought a 'maisonette' – a two-storey duplex, where the Gusts lived, up and down, on one side, while renting out the two flats next door. There was a housekeeper – Amirah tells us she was called 'a helper' – and, with the birth of Amirah's brother Ian in 1941, a mothercraft nurse was brought in.[9]

Amirah, a girl with the sort of shining intelligence that cheers a teacher's heart, was happy and successful at school. From Princes

Hill Primary School, she went to Elwood Central School and then to Mac.Robertson Girls' High School, that great Melbourne institution that turns out generations of highly educated and self-possessed young women.

The second important influence that Amirah identified as forging her identity was connected to the first. In Melbourne, the family was surrounded by a close circle of friends who were activists on progressive issues. Manka had joined the CPA in 1932. She was a member of the Brunswick branch and then, when the family moved to Elwood, transferred to the St Kilda branch. As a child, Amirah often accompanied her mother on rounds to deliver to party subscribers the *Guardian*, the *Workers' Voice*, and materials from the Friends of the Soviet Union. For a period, Itzhak was the official distributor of the Soviet classics and literature that came via the Australian Soviet Friendship Society. That organisation sponsored the Workers' Theatre Group, whose members often gathered at the Gust home.[10] In 1932, Russian-speaking Itzhak led an Australian trade union delegation to Moscow. During the three months of his stay, he worked in a state leather-making factory and lived in Soviet workers' accommodation. Although he decided it was not suitable to bring Manka and Amirah to live permanently in the Soviet Union, he took every opportunity, once back in Melbourne, to praise the great future he had seen under construction.[11] As a putative capitalist, Itzhak was precluded from joining the CPA until he divested himself of his business, which he did in 1939, while he and Manka took an extended trip to Europe.

The two connected parts of Amirah's life experience provide the themes of the two volumes of her autobiography. *Amirah: An Un-Australian Childhood* appeared in 1983; *The Hammer & Sickle and the Washing Up: Memories of an Australian Woman Communist* in 1995.

The first is a beguiling book and, unsurprisingly, was enormously popular: reprinted twice in the space of two years, it was chosen as the Australian Blind Society Book of the Year and was read by Amirah on ABC national radio. It follows Gust family history from Amirah's grandparents' generation until the Second World War and her experience as a student at the University of Melbourne. Amirah's authorial voice is clear and engaging, as she tracks the coming of age of a highly intelligent and independent young woman, the much-adored daughter of two beloved parents.

The second volume follows Amirah's personal and political life from her university years until the mid-1970s, when she was living in Port Moresby. Here, the authorial voice is often subdued and the reader held somewhat at a distance. The previous enthusiasms of the child and the young woman are dampened in the telling of her years in the CPA and her marriage to the charismatic Ian Turner, communist and historian. Although the narrative of the Melbourne years is lively and there is a close focus on the detail of events, as in the first volume, the change of tone is notable. On the writing of the two books, Amirah reflected that the first came easily and was compiled almost without diaries and documents in an uninterrupted flow. The second volume left her with 'mixed feelings.'[12]

Amirah joined the CPA in 1945 in her first year at university, when she was eighteen. In her second year, as membership secretary of the CPA's university branch, she arranged Ian Turner's transfer into this branch. 'Turner,' as he was called in those party years, had been conscripted into the army reserve. In 1942 he joined the Australian Imperial Force. He drove trucks and then joined the Army Education Service. Like many in the cohort of returned soldiers who took up university places after demobilisation, he was mature, confident, 'anti-army' and entirely unfazed by authority.[13] As Amirah recalled, he was 'Michelangelo's David in a khaki army greatcoat,' and she fell madly in love.[14] They were married at the end of February 1948 by a civil celebrant from the Rationalist Association, in what Amirah suggested may have been the first such civil wedding.[15] They lived in a flat in Richmond owned by the Gust family, whose generosity to the young family was unflagging. When Amirah gave birth to their first child, Deborah, Itzhak bought them a house in Glen Iris. Fresh from university, Amirah began library training and found a position in the state government. Soon she moved to more congenial work at the *Guardian* newspaper, Victoria's communist weekly.

As a rising star in the Victorian branch of the CPA, Turner was often away from home in the evenings. When he was present, at least in the first years of the marriage, his attention was taken with writing a master's thesis in history, which he was to submit to the University of Melbourne. Later, party business took him further from home. He travelled interstate and, in late 1950, spent six weeks in Europe attending the Second Congress of the World Peace Council in Warsaw. These were not easy times for Amirah, especially with the arrival of three children between 1950 and 1957. Frequently hurt by Turner's remoteness and her isolation at home, she came to resent what she saw as the privileging of male party work over what the party considered to be the appropriate female contribution to revolutionary change.[16] The rawness of her resentment was made more painful by the knowledge of Turner's numerous love affairs.

International events were also testing communist loyalties.[17] Manka left the CPA in 1953 over the Doctors' Plot, in which a group of eminent Soviet doctors, most of them Jews, were arrested and tortured on a false charge of conspiring to kill Stalin. From the first, Manka was sceptical about the anti-Semitic Soviet explanation, and in 1956 came proof that the plot was a fabrication. By contrast, Itzhak remained loyal to the positive memories of his experiences in Stalin's Soviet Union. Post-Gorbachev, he stuck with the renamed Australian Socialist Party and the remaining rump of elderly party diehards.

Amirah and Turner weathered the crises of events in the early 1950s that mortally strained the loyalties of many in the Australian communist movement. Perhaps their experiences in the preceding decade had inured them to hostile criticisms of the party. As the CPA's student organiser at the University of Melbourne, Turner had faced down antagonistic opposition when he propounded Lysenko's 'Marxist science' against the 'bourgeois fallacies' of Mendelian evolution, and when he argued for Zhdanov's ideas on the need for socialist realism in literature and art.[18] In mid-1948, Amirah and Turner had been 'stunned' to discover in the communist press that the Yugoslav party had been expelled from the Cominform, but both accepted the official explanation that Comrade Tito was 'anti-Marxist' and Yugoslavia's new democracy was based on 'false information that denied the sharpening class struggle.'[19] They found Khrushchev's February 1956 revelations about Stalinist crimes disconcerting, but remained loyal to the party edict that restricted discussion of such matters to party circles. Similarly, they seem to have accepted with equanimity the Soviet intervention in Hungary in October 1956. The prompt that led to them severing their ties to the communist movement came from the party itself. In June 1958, Turner wrote a letter to the Soviet magazine *New Times* requesting a proper examination of the circumstances around Imre Nagy's execution; he was expelled immediately.[20] Amirah left the party in 1961, by which time she was living in Canberra. When she suggested to her CPA comrades a discussion of the Soviet–China split, she was reprimanded on the basis that there was no split.[21] She resigned and drifted away from the party. Her marriage to Ian Turner ended that same year.

Although Amirah came to abhor Stalinism, she appreciated the positive aspects of her years in the CPA. There was comradeship with like-minded and committed people, and the selfless dedication of many trade unionists and party organisers. She remembered the CPA in its heyday, when party policies and belief in the model for a new society, as embodied by the Soviet Union, were based on a genuine yearning for a better and fairer future.[22] She remained angry about being the victim of intrusive surveillance by the Australian Security Intelligence Organisation (ASIO). ASIO watched Amirah, her home and her family; and long after she had left the party, ASIO agents and their informants continued to raise obstacles to her employment and travel.

Amirah and Ken in Port Moresby

Amirah and Ken were married in May 1965. Early in 1967, they and their combined six children moved to Port Moresby, where Ken took up the first chair in history at the University of Papua and New Guinea. Amirah was 'blown away by the whole place, everything about it was new, the landscape, the people … the relationships.'[23] In her assessment, the establishment of the university was a 'welcome act of de-colonisation'; education would enable Papuans and New Guineans to take over their own country.[24]

Early on, there were a couple of incidents where Amirah's past membership of the CPA blocked her employment in the Territory (as Papua New Guinea then was). The first, about which she long remained 'infuriated,' took place soon after arrival.[25] She had found a job teaching English to dentistry assistants, but her employment was withdrawn abruptly. The reason given by the head of the School of Health was that the position had been 'localised,' though all involved knew that the directive for her dismissal had come from ASIO.[26] A similar incident took place after Amirah was invited to serve as a community visitor to the Port Moresby prison, an episode she described as a 'bloody nuisance but not a disaster.'[27]

By then she had started research for a Master of Arts from the Australian National University. She had written an investigative piece for *Nation* on racial divides in Port Moresby – the 'brown and the white city' – and her master's extended the study to an analysis of white fears of miscegenation.[28] These fears were embodied in the White Women's Protection Ordinance, which was passed into law in 1926 and allowed for the hanging of black men convicted of the rape or attempted rape of white women. The study was a seminal work. Published under the title *'Not a White Woman Safe': Sexual Anxiety and Politics in Port Moresby, 1920–1934*, it was first in a field that had never received proper attention. Amirah later observed that she could have been more courageous in moving from a 'Marxist interpretation' to one nuanced by feminism.[29] Her second book examined Papuan folk memories about Karo, an almost mythical Papuan figure, whose eventful, criminal life had been memorialised by the Motu in song and verse.[30]

Raising a memorial: Remembering the Australian volunteers in Spain

It was after Ken, Amirah and their family returned to Canberra in 1975 that her research interests began to focus on the writing of a volume on the Spanish Civil War. In November 1986, accompanied by her close friend Netta Burns, she travelled to Spain to attend a gathering to mark the fiftieth anniversary of the arrival of the International Brigades in Spain.[31] A little more than a decade after Franco's death, this was the first such official celebration to take place in democratic Spain. It was also the start of an era of raising monuments to the International Brigaders in the forty-five countries from which they had set off to fight in the Spanish Civil War.

Between July 1936 and the end of 1938, around 40,000 anti-fascist men, and some women, offered support to the democratically elected Spanish Republic in resisting the military uprising led by General Franco and a group of other Spanish generals. Almost one in four of these foreign volunteers perished in Spain. From the very first days of the *pronunciamiento*, Franco and the insurgents received strong military backing from Hitler and Mussolini as well as a ragtag bag of interwar fascists. The International Brigades were withdrawn in late October 1938 at the request of the president of the Spanish Republic, Juan Negrín, in the hope that the departure of these foreign fighters would force the hand of the League of Nations and the major powers, and Franco would be pressured to send home his German and Italian units. By then, the Republic was on the verge of collapse, with Franco poised to occupy Catalonia. In the last week of February 1939, Barcelona fell, and thousands of Spanish refugees fled across the border into France.

Spain remained a military dictatorship until Franco's death in November 1975, the country starkly divided between the *vencedores* (victors) and the *vencidos* (vanquished). The Francoist state was unrelenting in its drive to extirpate all vestiges of the Spanish Republic and obliterate all traces of Republican memory. In subsequent *franquista* histories of the civil war, the International Brigaders were depicted as Reds (*rojos*), the vanguard of 'world communism' bent on a mission to destroy 'virtuous Catholic Spain.'

Amirah and Netta returned to Canberra from their 1986 Spanish trip determined to raise a memorial to the seventy or so Australians who had fought in the Spanish Civil War. There was an urgency to their plans: they wanted the memorial in place before the last Australian volunteer died. A small memorial committee was formed, with Len Fox as president. A cultivated ex-communist and previous editor of the CPA's *Tribune*, he had been a stout activist for the Australian Spanish Relief Committee during the 1930s.[32] Sympathetic leftist groups were lobbied for funds. A dedicated group of long-time Spanish Australians in the Canberra community, including Claudio Villegas and Carmen Castelo, provided strong backing.[33] My job was to write the legend for the sandstone monument, in English and Spanish, and to produce a map of the Iberian Peninsula with information about the locations and dates of the major battles. The final description on the face of the monument includes a 1937 quotation from the Australian writer Nettie Palmer, who wrote that the Australian volunteers in Spain were 'few in number, not powerful and seemed often to be shouting against the wind, but their contribution constituted a truly brave chapter in Australia's history.' The bronze map of Spain was cast in Melbourne by the orthodontist and sculptor Ross Bastiaan, whom Amirah knew and who generously agreed to do the job for no more than the cost of materials.

On a sunny morning on 11 December 1993, in Canberra's beautiful Lennox Gardens, Lloyd Edmonds, the last surviving Australian International Brigader, dedicated the handsome sandstone memorial. Spain's ambassador to Australia, whose father had been a pilot in the Republican air force, planted a row of olive trees. These have grown into the fine grove that now shades the paved area and the seating around the sandstone structure. The Spanish Civil War memorial is a recognised site on the national capital's monumental landscape. For many years, members of the Spanish community and friends have gathered there for an annual picnic.

In November 1996, Amirah and I were invited to Spain as official guests of the Amigos de Las Brigadas Internacionales to attend a celebration to bestow Spanish citizenship on the surviving International Brigaders. The Spanish government's policy fulfilled a promise made by the Republican government on 28 October 1938, when the International Brigades were withdrawn from Spain. At the farewell parade in Barcelona, the Brigadiers in their national battalion formations – the men in tattered uniforms, the injured aided by comrades – marched through streets lined by thousands of cheering and weeping Spaniards.[34] President Negrín greeted the international soldiers as 'brothers and compatriots' and, on behalf of a grateful Spain, promised each of them honorary citizenship to be claimed on their return, when the war was over.[35]

On that day, Dolores Ibárruri also spoke. A communist deputy, and miner's widow, from Asturias, she was best known by the sobriquet 'La Pasionaria' ('the Passionflower') and was the most recognised Republican public figure. She was famous for her eloquence and public oratory, whether rallying soldiers at the front or on the floor of the Cortes. Her long and moving speech of farewell first addressed Spanish mothers and wives: 'when the wounds of war are healed and the sad and bloody days have been replaced by liberty, justice and peace,' they should remember always to tell their children about 'the brave men of the International Brigades.' They had 'left home and

hearth and crossed the world to fight and die for Spanish liberty.' To
the men themselves she said:

> You are history, you are legend … and we shall not forget you.
> When the olive tree of peace is in flower, entwined with the vic-
> tory laurels of the Republic of Spain – return! Return to our side
> for here you will find a homeland … and the love and gratitude of
> the Spanish people who will cry out with all their hearts: Long
> live the heroes of the International Brigades.[36]

In November 1996, the Socialist Workers' Party (PSOE) leader,
Felipe González, issued an invitation to the surviving International
Brigaders to come to Spain to receive Spanish citizenship. This piece
of legislative business was passed in the very last parliamentary session
of his government. The PSOE, with González at its head, had led the
country since the first full Spanish elections in 1982. Under the PSOE,
the constitution was framed and many new democratic institutions laid
down. In elections held in May 1996, the PSOE had been defeated
by the conservative Partido Popular (PP), led by José María Aznar,
but legislation to extend citizenship to the International Brigaders
was passed with bipartisan support in the Cortes nonetheless, under
the aegis of the *pacto del olvido* (pact of forgetting). This pact, in place
since Franco's death, meant that Spanish Civil War matters were off
limits for political debate in the Cortes.

When the new conservative government was sworn in, a couple
of weeks before the International Brigaders were to arrive, Aznar
withdrew parliamentary support for the citizenship arrangement.
The PP added the proviso that, before taking up Spanish citizenship, the foreign volunteers must abjure their existing citizenship.
This requirement effectively scuppered their citizenship, and meant
that these elderly veterans would have to relinquish the pensions and

entitlements available to them in their home countries.[37] While the mean-spirited strategy, intended to insult the visiting veterans, broke the bipartisan parliamentary consensus, it mattered little to most of the foreign veterans. The government's shift in position took place so close to their departures for Spain that many of them were unaware of it. And most were in high spirits, delighted to be welcomed back to democratic Spain after the years of the dictatorship when they were uniformly castigated as 'Red enemies.'

It was an exhilarating experience for all involved. And no less so for two Antipodean historians researching and writing about these heroic and tragic times. As part of the International Brigades entourage, we visited battle sites, listened to reminiscences, and heard everywhere the singing of leftist songs from the 1930s. In full voice, Amirah always joined in. During a week of wall-to-wall receptions, the elderly *brigadistas* and their families were cheered and embraced wherever they went. They were given the keys to Madrid, and RENFE, the Spanish national railway, put on a fleet of trains to take the veterans to former battlefields. One International Brigader died during the celebrations. It was reported that she had always hoped to die in democratic Spain.

In Madrid the *brigadistas* were put up as a group in a 1960s hotel, with plenty of room for welcomes and gatherings. Amirah and I met them there every morning, having chosen to stay on the Puerta del Sol at Hotel Paris, now an Apple headquarters but then a traditional Castilian family hotel. While the accoutrements and the beds had seen better days, the welcome was warm. The whole enterprise was under the careful eye of the *patrón* and his family. Every day, guests filed into the dining room to eat at their designated table. On each the waiter placed the previous night's bottle of wine, the level in the bottle marked with chalk. It was a fitting setting for Amirah's and my engagement with the historical past.

We were overwhelmed to be rubbing shoulders with International Brigaders and the many elderly Republican Spaniards who thronged the events. The latter had either weathered the 'hungry years' in Spain, or had returned after long decades in exile. In the congenial atmosphere of the celebrations, and in the context of the new democratic Spain, these men and women were keen to talk of their lives.

Amirah and I engaged in our own intense discussion about how to write a history of these people and their experiences, past and present. We discussed historical methodology and chronology rather than ideology: what research questions should we ask and where might we find the answers? A nuanced history, we thought, would eschew heroisation without occluding the ambiguities of the civil war and individual experience. Interestingly, Amirah, who had lived a third of her adult life through the prism of communism, was far less forgiving of the shortcomings of the old Stalinist politicos we met, especially among the English-speaking veteran groups. Unreconstructed Stalinism was palpable in their speeches, as it was in their writing about the civil war, much of which we knew from our researches. Having read widely about the horrors of the postwar Franco state, I tended to admire the steadfastness of these old activists and their lifelong commitment to the left as it had been configured between the world wars. For Republicans who had remained in Spain, their savage treatment by the Francoist state was often only outstripped by the violence visited on them by their *franquista* neighbours, who acted with impunity in targeting anyone suspected of Republican sympathies.

Amirah, with her deep exposure to Australian politics and its international influences, went on to write a fine history about Australian volunteers in the Spanish Civil War. The book centred on their experiences, but was scaffolded by a close analysis of Australian politics and trade unionism.

* * *

During our visit to Spain in 1996, Amirah and I chose to travel with the Brigadiers to Barcelona via Albacete, once the headquarters of the International Brigades battalions. When our train pulled into Albacete station, we were greeted by cheering people. A huge red banner carried the traditional words of Spanish welcome: *mi casa es su casa* (my home is your home). At a reception at the University of Castilla–La Mancha, we sat beside a very elderly Spanish couple. The husband explained that after the Republican defeat he had been sentenced to work in a labour battalion for several years. During this time his wife and children had suffered grievously at the hands of vengeful neighbours and *franquista* officials in their Castilian village. The wife held Amirah's hand throughout the reception. At each mention of the valiant foreigners who had come to Spain as members of the International Brigades, the wife raised both their hands and shouted, '*Es verdad!*' ('It's true!'). When I asked Amirah if she would like me to explain to the old woman that her Australian *compañera* had been ten years of age when the Spanish Civil War started, but her uncle had fought in the International Brigades, Amirah shook her head and said the main thing was that they were both there together.

Amirah Inglis died on 2 May 2015, aged eighty-eight. Some of her ashes are scattered under the olive trees at the Spanish Civil War memorial in Canberra.

Acknowledgements

Elizabeth Rechniewski, Phillip Deery, Seumas Spark and the Alchemists Research Group in the History Department at the University of Sydney made helpful comments on this chapter.

Endnotes

1   A Inglis, *Australians in the Spanish Civil War*, Allen & Unwin, Sydney, 1987; L Edmonds (ed. A Inglis), *Letters from Spain*, George Allen & Unwin, Sydney, 1985.

2   'Amirah Inglis Interviewed by Sara Dowse,' 20 October 1998, ORAL TRC 3798, transcript, National Library of Australia, p. 66.

3   'Amirah Inglis Interviewed by Sara Dowse,' p. 8; see also 'Amirah Inglis Interviewed by Peter Biskup,' 6 August 1990, ORAL TRC 2617, National Library of Australia.

4   'Amirah Inglis Interviewed by Sara Dowse,' pp. 17, 66.

5   A Inglis, *Amirah: An Un-Australian Childhood*, Heinemann, Melbourne, 1983, pp. 9–13.

6   I Gust, *Such Was Life: A Jumping Narrative from Radom to Melbourne*, with an introduction by his daughter Amirah Inglis, Makor Jewish Community Library, Melbourne, 2004.

7   A Inglis, *The Hammer & Sickle and the Washing Up: Memories of an Australian Woman Communist*, Hyland House, South Melbourne, 1995, pp. 13–17, 189–90.

8   'Amirah Inglis Interviewed by Sara Dowse,' p. 14.

9   'Amirah Inglis Interviewed by Sara Dowse,' p. 14.

10 My thanks to Phillip Deery for this information.

11 Gust, *Such Was Life*, pp. 120–44; S Fitzpatrick, 'Australian Visitors to the Soviet Union: The View from the Soviet Side,' in S Fitzpatrick & C Rasmussen (eds), *Political Tourists: Travellers from Australia to the Soviet Union in the 1920s–1940s*, Melbourne University Publishing, Melbourne, 2008, pp. 1–39.

12 'Amirah Inglis Interviewed by Sara Dowse,' pp. 69, 82.

13 For Ian Turner's University of Melbourne recollections, see I Turner, 'My Long March,' *Overland*, Spring 1974, pp. 31–4.

14 A Inglis, *Amirah: An Un-Australian Childhood*, p. 157.

15 A Inglis, *The Hammer & Sickle and the Washing Up*, p. 43.

16 See Amirah's bitterly ironic poem for the *Tribune* (the submission encouraged by Turner) about the party's exploitation of women, in A Inglis, *The Hammer & Sickle and the Washing Up*, pp. 148–50; and 'Amirah Inglis Interviewed by Sara Dowse,' p. 30. According to Joyce Stevens, by the end of 1935 there were 2800 CPA members of whom 200 were women; by 1942 membership numbered

about 16,000, presumably with a similar gender division. The party followed the Soviet line, and as Stalinism ossified, the CPA moved further away from any notion of women's role in revolutionary politics; see J Stevens, *Taking the Revolution Home: Work Among Women in the Communist Party of Australia, 1920–1945*, Sybylla Co-operative Press and Publications, Melbourne, 1987, pp. 43, 81.

17   A Inglis, *The Hammer & Sickle and the Washing Up*, pp. 123–44; 'Amirah Inglis Interviewed by Peter Biskup,' reel 2.

18   A Inglis, *The Hammer & Sickle and the Washing Up*, p. 65; Turner, 'My Long March,' p. 33.

19   A Inglis, *The Hammer & Sickle and the Washing Up*, pp. 63–4.

20   A Inglis, *The Hammer & Sickle and the Washing Up*, pp. 172–3; Turner, 'My Long March,' p. 40.

21   A Inglis, *The Hammer & Sickle and the Washing Up*, p. 174.

22   Refer to Amirah's terse dismissal of Biskup's reference to 'wasted years in the CPA' in 'Amirah Inglis Interviewed by Peter Biskup,' reel 2.

23   'Amirah Inglis Interviewed by Sara Dowse,' pp. 53–8. Drusilla Modjeska captures the spirit of the Port Moresby university community in D Modjeska, *The Mountain*, Vintage Books, Sydney, 2012. See also KS Inglis, 'Education on the Frontier: The First Ten Years of the University of Papua New Guinea,' *Melbourne Studies in Education*, vol. 22, no. 1, 1980, pp. 61–92.

24   'Amirah Inglis Interviewed by Sara Dowse,' p. 51.

25   'Amirah Inglis Interviewed by Peter Biskup,' reel 2.

26   'Amirah Inglis Interviewed by Peter Biskup,' reel 2; 'Amirah Inglis Interviewed by Sara Dowse,' p. 50. See Ian Maddocks's statement of regret at his part in this incident in I Maddocks & S Spark, '"Taim Bilong Uni": Ken Inglis at the University of Papua New Guinea,' *History Australia*, vol. 14, no. 4, 2017, p. 553.

27   'Amirah Inglis Interviewed by Peter Biskup,' reel 2.

28   A Inglis, 'A Tale of Two Cities,' *Nation*, no. 245, 8 June 1968.

29   A Inglis, *'Not a White Woman Safe': Sexual Anxiety and Politics in Port Moresby, 1920–1934*, Australian National University Press, Canberra, 1974; republished with revisions as A Inglis, *The White Women's Protection Ordinance: Sexual Anxiety and Politics in Papua*, Chatto and Windus for Sussex University Press, London, 1975; and 'Amirah Inglis Interviewed by Sara Dowse,' p. 58.

30   A Inglis, *Karo: The Life and Fate of a Papuan*, Institute of Papua New Guinea Studies in association with Australian National University Press, Canberra, 1982.

31   A Inglis, '50 Years On, Spaniards Hail Independence [*sic*] Brigadiers: Civil War Veterans Remember,' *Canberra Times*, 3 January 1987, p. 9.

32   N Palmer & L Fox, *Australians in Spain: Our Pioneers Against Fascism*, Current Book Distributors, Sydney, 1948.

33 C Castelo (ed.), *The Spanish Experience in Australia*, Spanish Heritage Foundation, Canberra, 2000.

34 See R Capa, *Heart of Spain: Robert Capa's Photographs of the Spanish Civil War*, Museo Nacional de Arte Reina Sofía, Madrid, 1999, pp. 123–65.

35 J Negrín, 'Amigos de España … Palabras de Despedida,' in RA Vergara (ed.), *La Llamada Española: Homenaje a las Brigadas Internacionales 1936–1996*, Ediciones de las Cortes de Castilla-La Mancha, Toledo, 1996, p. 126.

36 D Ibárruri, 'Despedida a las Brigadas Internacionales,' in Vergara, *La Llamada Española*, pp. 155–6.

37 When returned to government, the Socialist Party in June 2009 invited surviving International Brigaders to citizenship award ceremonies in the Spanish embassies of the veterans' home countries.

Chapter 16

PUBLIC INTEREST AND PRIVATE PASSION

Ken Inglis on the ABC

Glyn Davis

'A lot of history,' writes Ken Inglis in his introduction to *This Is the ABC*, 'is concealed autobiography, and this book more than most.'[1] Ken starts the 521-page volume with his own story. Just three years older than the ABC, he recalls the radio voices of his youth. He listened to the wireless with family, trying out radio sets sold in his father's timber yard, joinery and hardware shop. Ken recalls the unfamiliar British voices, learning about cricket, a coronation and arguments about public policy. Later there would be a world war described each night on the radio, and in adulthood ABC television was part of everyday family life. As a young academic he gave occasional talks on the air and, as professor of history and vice-chancellor at the University of Papua New Guinea, he joined the audience of Radio Australia.

So when the ABC board approached Ken in July 1976 about writing a history of the national broadcaster, it was an entry into a life already deeply entangled with the ABC as a 'listener and a viewer.' Now the professional historian could provide a critical view of a personal passion.

As Bridget Griffen-Foley observes, 'Inglis does not write himself into his histories in a self-conscious or fashionable way. And yet he is a subtle presence nonetheless.'[2]

This paper examines how Ken Inglis explored public broadcasting, and his decision to devote years of patient research to producing two large volumes on the ABC – one as an official historian, the second as an independent scholar. It draws on his writings, critical commentary on the books, and two interviews with Professor Inglis, conducted in March and April 2016, about his historical practice. The paper highlights the professional discipline of a man fascinated by his subject but determined never to play favourites.

* * *

Ken Inglis was unsure whether he heard the first ABC radio broadcast on 1 July 1932, those 'whistles and crackles' that resolved into 'voices and music.'[3] Regardless, his first experiences of the wireless remained 'a thrill in my life.'[4]

Yet the young Ken felt some distance from the new ABC. He remembered that 'ABC voices were all English, not in my world.' The earliest broadcasts were modelled on the BBC, complete with Broadcasting House accents. As Maurice Dunlevy notes in a 1983 review of *This Is the ABC*, BBC broadcasters 'left Great Britain and made a Little England in the ABC. For decades the ABC left Australians with the impression that the way they talked was crook.'[5]

Enchanted by radio, young Ken preferred the commercial stations with their local content and familiar-sounding tones. He listened avidly to *Chatterbox Corner* on 3AW, starring Nancy Lee. The informality in speech rang true – the program could talk to Ken 'in a way I didn't feel the people in the *Argonauts* were talking to me.' A concern with national identity, an important theme in his historical scholarship, was early at work.

For young Ken, broadcasting was not just an interest but a potential career. As he approached the end of his secondary schooling, which had begun at Northcote High and continued at Melbourne High in 1945–46, he and his girlfriend sought work on *Junior 3AW*. The experience proved disappointing. Ken hoped to write radio scripts but instead 'what I ended up doing mainly was reading advertisements for soup!'

Ken began his arts degree as a resident of Queen's College at the University of Melbourne in 1947. During his time on campus, the ABC captured his attention for the first time. He attributed this in part to his roommate at Queen's, who liked to study with classical music on the wireless. Ken liked what he heard, and found himself listening to news and talks. 'I was at the right age to be taken up by radio as a new, cultural form,' he recalled. The ABC was still very British, and 'the BBC was worshipped from afar and I didn't mind – I was indulging those English accents by then.' The university student became a 'devotee of ABC radio.'

Soon Ken would experience the BBC firsthand, arriving at Oxford in 1953 to begin doctoral studies in history. The following year he approached BBC radio about doing some broadcasting. With the Queen on tour in Australia, Ken had remembered an earlier incident in Australian history and thought it worthy of retelling:

> No one was mentioning it at the time, but a mad Irish assassin had tried to knock off the son of the Queen, Prince Alfred, Duke of Edinburgh on his visit to Australia in 1868. I wrote a talk and submitted it to the BBC. I got back a very courteous note, thanking me very kindly. But they said to me that this was not

the time to be recalling such an unhappy event, as Her Majesty was in Australia. That was my career as an author of BBC talks.

On graduating from Oxford, Dr Inglis accepted a role with the University of Adelaide. Now at last came the chance to broadcast. As Ken reflects, 'In Adelaide the relationship between the university and the ABC was rather closer than it had been in Melbourne.' He was 'evangelistic about bringing awareness of Asia to Australia' and used the university–ABC relationship to bring this interest out of the lecture theatre. In 1958 he gave a series of talks on ABC national radio outlining relations between Europe and Asia, building on the first subject he taught at Adelaide, 'Europe and the Wider World.'

There was an invitation to help plan a national television series, *University of the Air.* The project went to air in 1961 but 'suffered from under-preparation and vagueness about intended audience.'[6] It was dropped in 1966, a year before Ken made a major career change, moving to Port Moresby as professor of history and, from 1972, vice-chancellor of the University of Papua New Guinea. During these years abroad his 'interests in all things Australian were deflected.' It would not be until 1976, as a professor at the Australian National University (ANU) and looking for his next big project, that Ken would resume thinking about the ABC.

* * *

Though the ABC had been part of national life since 1932, expository writing on the national broadcaster remained modest in scope and ambition. The Commission featured in newspaper tussles about alleged bias, occasional learned arguments in journals about the role of public broadcasting, and a 1967 biography by Geoffrey Bolton of the ABC's chair from 1945 to 1961, Sir Richard Boyer. There was no detailed chronology available of ABC history and only passing reference in works on Australian life. Few researchers had access to the ABC archives in Sydney.

With the fiftieth anniversary of the ABC approaching, economist Richard Downing, who was appointed ABC chair in early 1973, saw the value of commissioning an official history. The ABC board agreed and during 1975 drew up a short list of potential authors. The list included Ken, along with Allan Martin and Hugh Stretton. Sadly Downing died before the project could begin, felled by a heart attack on 10 November 1975.

Though the ABC was soon enmeshed in political turmoil and budget cuts following a change of government, the acting chair Dr Earle Hackett did not neglect the assignment. As Ken recalled, Hackett approached him in July 1976 'and asked if I would be interested in being commissioned to write a history of the ABC.' Ken was surprised by the offer – such a project had not crossed his mind – but sufficiently interested to negotiate terms. He did not want to be paid by the ABC, since he was a research professor at the ANU, but sought both research assistance and a commitment to editorial freedom. Hackett agreed with a written offer that Ken felt 'guaranteed both independence and support.'

Almost immediately the project came under threat. In July 1976 Hackett was replaced as ABC chair by Sir Henry Bland, a retired senior public servant who had worked under prime minister Malcolm Fraser in the defence portfolio. Bland 'didn't like the look of the contract' Hackett had negotiated and seemed 'suspicious' of Ken because he was not seeking payment for writing the history. The stand-off was brief: Bland proved a controversial chair, quickly enmeshed in arguments with ABC staff, community organisations supporting the ABC, and some government backbenchers. He resigned five months into his role after a dispute with the government over the size of the ABC's governing board. His travails were reported, with careful impartiality, in *This Is the ABC*.[7]

The new ABC chair, J.D. Norgard, a retired BHP executive who would serve until 1981, described himself as a 'low-key operator' who knew how to 'get on very well with people, even if we have to differ.'[8] He confirmed the original terms agreed with Ken, and the history project began.

His agreement with the ABC secure, Ken could now focus his scholarly efforts on the history of public broadcasting in Australia. He was assisted from 1979 to 1982 by research assistant Jan Brazier. As a lifelong fan of broadcasting, Ken found the work 'enormous fun.' He was not just allowed but required to 'snoop around' the ABC. He interviewed ABC staff across the nation and watched them at work. Ken particularly treasured an invitation he received to 'sit up with Norman May at the Sydney Cricket Ground watching a rugby test, which I didn't understand a single move of, but which was great fun.'

This remarkable access to the ABC and its archives allowed Ken to achieve depth and breadth in his history. He could watch, record and observe a national institution at work. 'That I had that access was a blessing,' he recalled. 'The one thing that I enjoyed most about the whole process of writing *This Is the ABC* was the access it gave me to creative processes.'

Though editorial independence was guaranteed, Ken could understand the anxieties of many involved with the ABC. As its official historian he was permitted to study ABC board minutes, and he was expected to comment on key controversies. For some significant ABC figures, such as Sir Charles Moses, who served as general manager from 1935 to 1965, an official history was no place for independent assessment.[9] The historian should record, not pass judgement.

The challenge for Ken was to provide a volume that could navigate the tension between chronicler and academic, official history and critical insight. He chose a chronological approach, a single narrative divided roughly into decades. He starts with the first broadcast on 1 July 1932, then examines the development of the organisation until World War Two, its national role in conflict, arguments with government in the postwar era, the arrival of television and the revolution in radio, the growth of public affairs, and the expansion under the Whitlam government and retreat during the Fraser years. The narrative ends in 1983, a time of transition for the ABC. In that year the chair and general manager retired from their roles and an act of federal parliament transformed the Commission into a Corporation. The author had slightly exceeded his mandate, concluding his book fifty-one years after the first radio shows went to air.

In recording a long institutional history, there are judgements implicit in the choice of material, the emphases and the omissions. Ken is a generous interpreter who uses detail to convey complexity, reporting the argument rather than taking sides. The voices of participants carry the story whenever possible. In the introduction to *Observing Australia*, Craig Wilcox describes Ken as a 'vernacular intellectual' because his 'approach to history has been academic in its rigour but vernacular in its taste and style.'[10] In a 2000 interview with Ken for the *Sydney Morning Herald*, Tony Stephens writes that 'Ken Inglis says the nicest thing ever said to, or about, him came from a student in Papua New Guinea. The student thanked Inglis for a lecture that was "clear but good." Inglis says now: "I'd like to think I was clear but good.""[11]

Geoffrey Bolton found much to praise in the way Ken conveyed his findings about the ABC in accessible language with memorable anecdotes. 'His style,' said Bolton, 'achieves a flair and liveliness which should be a model to others in the field.'[12] In his ability to share extensive detail of a sometimes convoluted institutional history, while bringing alive the internal dynamics of boards and broadcasters and external dramas involving government ministers and program content, Ken's achievement was considerable: *This Is the ABC* is accessible and precise history. His approach to writing the book and decisions about how much detail to include were informed by 'that mythical character of the "general reader,"' he recalled.

While the book describes half a century of change at the Commission, motifs recur in the narrative. Ken suggests that each generation fought the same battles about institutional independence amid government control of the ABC budget. In her review of the volume, Beverley Kingston writes: 'running through this measured history of the ABC … are several gently thought-provoking themes, more powerful in their cumulative effect than the narrative for any particular period seems to suggest. Most in evidence is the story of government attempts to control or use the ABC.'[13] An unsigned review in the *Canberra Times* notes that 'the independence of the ABC from political interference is something [Inglis] examines scrupulously, and no politician who has tried to meddle escapes his radar.'[14]

This Is the ABC, a much-awaited volume, was published in a year of significant change for the ABC. In his speech at the book launch at the Sydney Opera House, Ken declared, 'The ABC is dead, long live the ABC.' Not everyone was pleased. When Ken greeted Sir Charles Moses, who had read the manuscript before publication, his proffered hand was rejected. 'I don't want to speak to you,' he replied. 'You will hear from my lawyers.'[15]

Sir Charles subsequently raised a list of fifty items for which he demanded correction or retraction. Fortunately for Ken, no legal action followed. Melbourne University Press persuaded the former general manager that he 'would be crazy to pursue the issues that he complained about.' Ken concluded that Moses 'still thought of it as *his* ABC, and if I thought I could appropriate it, I had another thing coming.'

While Sir Charles was unhappy with the volume, most reviewers recognised the respect, and often admiration, that guided Ken in writing about the national broadcaster. J.D.B. Miller calls it a 'splendid book on a difficult subject.' Miller had worked for the ABC and marvels at how well Ken understood the organisation:

> The ABC I knew is very clearly recognisable from what Inglis has written. I was continually surprised at this knowledge and insight about something which I joined when he was 10 years old; but that is what happens when one reads the work of a good historian.[16]

Writing in *Australian Society*, Peter White admires the detail in the volume but feels it emphasised the 'administrative edifice' of the national broadcaster. White attributes this focus on bureaucracy to a bias in the archives – 'inter-office memoranda are much easier to store than bulky reels of film and magnetic tape.'[17] In *24 Hours* John Moses – no relation to Sir Charles – wants to read more about the ABC's 'great impact on Australian society.' For Moses this 'detailed and obviously deeply researched history' needed even more content, further discussion of the 1930s broadcasters, and more on music, drama, poetry and literature. Above all, Moses wants the volume to convey the excitement of broadcasting, of 'watching the sweep hand tick off the seconds until the cue comes from the control room and an announcer draws a quiet breath and says … "This is the ABC …"'[18]

Before endnotes and references, the text of *This Is the ABC* runs to more than 200,000 words. It works hard to be fair. Ken did not intend to write a polemic or pass judgement on the failings of individuals. Historians, he counselled, should 'write about people who did not know what was going to happen next.'[19] The text avoids overt criticisms of people, alive to the pitfall of historical writing that sees an author assume that he or she could have done better than the people they are writing about. It is the characteristic stance of this vernacular historian, a way to evoke a world through detail and personal stories. The comprehensive nature of the coverage provides the balance Ken sought.

Not surprisingly, the strongest words came from those who demanded Ken take sides. 'It is a pity,' laments Geoffrey Bolton, that Inglis 'did not spell out his own ideas on the role and opportunities for a public broadcasting authority, particularly on that nebulous quality "balance."'[20] Maurice Dunlevy is more cutting. The book, he suggests, 'shows all the signs of having been written primarily for an audience of ABC bureaucrats.'[21] He continues:

> Impartiality, objectivity and balance are its hallmarks, although it never seriously examines the functional meaning of those terms in the ABC, nor indeed does it indulge in any serious theorising about either the nature of organisations or the nature of the electronic media.

In the 2000 interview with Tony Stephens, Ken reflected on some of this commentary. He noted the critical voices and those seeking more explicit value judgements, but made clear this was not his preferred path. He balances narrative and analysis in his histories. Stephens observes:

> The stories in history and legend have captured Inglis's life. He recalls historian Vincent Harlow saying at Oxford University in the 1950s that every historian had to struggle between the demands of narrative and analysis, and the advice from W.H. Dray that historians engaged in "explanatory narrative." Inglis says: "I am first and foremost a storyteller."[22]

* * *

With the publication of *This Is the ABC*, Ken completed his commission from the ABC. His research focus shifted to war and its consequences, including the widely admired *Sacred Places: War Memorials in the Australian Landscape*, published in 1998. Yet the ABC did not let go of his imagination, and towards the close of the century he returned to the subject.

Whose ABC? The Australian Broadcasting Corporation 1983–2006 was published in 2006.[23] This time Ken wrote as an independent scholar interested in extending his work on the ABC; the volume was not an official history. As Ged Martin observed, sufficient time had passed since *This Is the ABC* that 'the historian had become part of the subject of his own study.'[24]

The style of *Whose ABC?* is instantly recognisable, yet there are important differences in approach and emphasis. As commissioned history, *This Is the ABC* enjoyed access to ABC archives and people, and reflected those sources in its account. In writing *Whose ABC?*, Ken was on his own. He could rely only on interviews and occasional summaries of decisions from the Corporation. He lacked the resources of the earlier project and looked to a commercial publisher, Black Inc., rather than a university press, to reach his audience.

The subject matter too shifts in subtle ways. The risk of political interference to the ABC was always present in the pages of *This Is the ABC*, but the relationship between the ABC and government, and between the Australian people and their public broadcaster, is the central focus in the second book. Though similar in length to the first volume, *Whose ABC?* covers a much shorter period, and so investigates controversies in greater detail. The narrative is chronological, as it is in *This Is the ABC*, and the fairness palpable – Gideon Haigh describes the book as 'limpid and scrupulously even-handed history'[25] – but this time chapters are structured around specific events and people rather than decades or governments.

Whose ABC? offers a greater focus on contextual media and political events. The sense of an ABC under threat runs through the volume, given impetus perhaps by the extensive interviews Ken conducted. As Jock Given notes, 'Inglis has talked to everyone who will talk, and he works over the evidence carefully, sparing neither side of politics.' There is a greater sense of drama in the book, of conflict and high stakes. 'For connoisseurs of boardroom and political dynamics,' concludes Given, 'it's enthralling.'[26] The change in tone owed something to the grave perils facing the ABC, and the different research approach.

Still, for some readers Ken remained too cautious. Dame Leonie Kramer, chair of the ABC in 1982 and 1983, wanted the good praised and the bad blamed. In her review of *Whose ABC?*, Kramer complains that 'throughout [Inglis] refrains from making judgements, and from interpreting or even speculating about the motives of some of the key players.'[27]

For another reviewer, the key challenge was sources. Bridget Griffen-Foley much enjoyed the character sketches throughout *Whose ABC?* but found the narrower range of evidence an 'unsatisfactory element in this book.' The circumstances supporting *This Is the ABC* allowed for close scrutiny of archived material. By contrast, '*Whose ABC?* includes a list of informants and summaries of sources for each section, but researchers wishing to pursue numerous specific points would be hard-pressed. A bibliography is a regrettable omission.'[28]

Ken took a different view. He found that distance from the Corporation allowed a degree of freedom and that the lack of access to ABC boardroom minutes and archival material did not prove a significant restriction. Through contacts and reputation, he created his own networks inside the national broadcaster and found people willing to talk. As he recalled, 'It was much easier for me to get access to primary sources than secondary without any permission the second time.'

In writing *This Is the ABC*, Ken had to seek ministerial approval to quote archives. For *Whose ABC?* he could talk directly with the players and quote the wider array of materials now in the public domain. He could draw on his own quarter century researching and writing about national broadcasting. The result, said one review in the *Canberra Times*, is two volumes that serve as 'the definitive works on the broadcaster and with good reason. Inglis's research is meticulous. He leaves no stone unturned, but more than that, he knows where the bodies are buried.'[29]

* * *

Whose ABC? concludes with a chapter titled 'Towards 2032?' – that is, looking ahead to the centenary anniversary of Australia's national broadcaster. While Ken notes trials ahead – the willingness of governments to curtail ABC independence through legislation, the troubled future of SBS, debates on advertising for the ABC, the move to electronic media, concerns about whether broadcasting will survive the coming decades – he does not despair. He expects that despite the changing nature of media the ABC's mandate to speak to Australian circumstances would make it ever more important amid globalised offerings. 'All in all,' he predicts, 'it is likely that viewers and listeners in the digital age will become ever more reliant on public broadcasters for electronic representations of their nation's character and the human condition.'[30] For only the ABC, and its equivalent organisations elsewhere, can 'address their audiences as citizens, not consumers.' So the Inglis account of seventy-four years of ABC history ends on an optimistic note. Under 'whatever name or nickname,' he writes, 'the ABC will still be enriching Australian lives in 2032.'[31]

This Is the ABC and *Whose ABC?* are important and enduring works of scholarship. They convey a complex institutional history with depth and accuracy. In Ged Martin's words, 'it seems unlikely that a single author will ever again succeed in handling a project of such magnitude.'[32] The two volumes are the standard work on public broadcasting in Australia. The conflicts between government and broadcaster, a key theme of Ken's writing on the ABC, seem unlikely to change or disappear. As Margaret Simons observed in 2006, 'Faced with this future, Inglis's digest of the past is indispensable for the perspective it brings and for its underlining of a simple but indisputable fact: the ABC is far and away our most important cultural institution.'[33]

In a speech to the National Press Club in 1983, Ken wondered whether a historian looking at the first century of the ABC will do anything 'so old fashioned as a book.' But whatever the form of the jubilee history, he noted, 'I like to think that someone reviewing it will say what John Douglas Pringle says at the end of his review of my book about the ABC: "What would we do without it? To some of us, at least, it still represents civilisation."'[34]

A decade after finishing his second ABC history, Ken retained a quiet optimism about the ABC, along with a sense of time passing. As someone who grew up with the national broadcaster, he was superbly placed to understand and explain its trajectory. He knew the journey was not over. The ABC evolves, and will eventually change beyond the recognition even of its most eminent scholar. For, as Ken said:

> I think people were aware, and I'm aware, of changes that took the subject out of my world. When I first heard the word pod-cast from a friend from Radio National in 2004, I knew that whole digital world wasn't for me. I had a sense, and people had a sense, that what I had done, and what I had celebrated, was now something that was over.

Acknowledgements

The author thanks Bill Gammage, Jay Winter and Seumas Spark for their initiative in organising a two-day meeting at Monash University to honour the life and work of a great Australian historian, Ken Inglis. Thanks also to University of Melbourne colleagues Lachlan McKenzie and Gwil Croucher, who helped with research on this paper, oversaw transcription of interviews and provided astute advice along the way. Murray Goot forwarded valuable contextual material about the media in Australia, and Jock Given kindly offered comments and suggestions on the text. Above all, gratitude to Ken Inglis, whom I had known and admired since my days as a doctoral student at the ANU writing about the political independence of the ABC. In his gentle way, Ken encouraged and enthused. Interviews for this paper provided a welcome excuse for two enjoyable lunches with Ken in North Carlton, and Ken also took time to provide detailed editorial comments on an early draft, those careful pencil marks on manuscripts familiar to students and colleagues over a lifetime of scholarly contribution.

Endnotes

1   KS Inglis (assisted by J Brazier), *This Is the ABC: The Australian Broadcasting Commission 1932–1983*, Melbourne University Press, Carlton, 1983.

2   B Griffen-Foley, 'The Complete Adventures of Aunty,' *Australian Financial Review*, 1 September 2006, p. 10.

3   Inglis, *This Is the ABC*, p. 1.

4   All unattributed quotes from Ken Inglis are drawn from two recorded interviews in Melbourne, 4 March and 11 April 2016, with Glyn Davis, Gwilym Croucher and Lachlan McKenzie.

5   M Dunlevy, 'Red Tape and High Culture: 50 years of ABC,' *Canberra Times*, 2 July 1983, p. 17.

6   Inglis, *This Is the ABC*, pp. 209–10.

7   Inglis, *This Is the ABC*, pp. 402–4.

8   Inglis, *This Is the ABC*, p. 405.

9   G Martin, 'Review Essay: *This Is the ABC: The Australian Broadcasting Commission 1932–1983* by KS Inglis & *Whose ABC? The Australian Broadcasting Corporation 1983–2006* by KS Inglis,' *Reviews in Australian Studies*, vol. 2, no. 2, 2007.

10 C Wilcox, 'A Vernacular Intellectual,' in KS Inglis (ed. C Wilcox), *Observing Australia: 1959 to 1999*, Melbourne University Press, Carlton, 1999, p. 1.

11 T Stephens, 'A Place in History,' *Sydney Morning Herald*, 13 May 2000, p. 9.

12 G Bolton, 'Review of *This Is the ABC: The Australian Broadcasting Commission 1932–1983*,' *Australian Journal of Politics and History*, vol. 29, no. 3, 1983, pp. 538–93.

13 B Kingston, 'Review of *This Is the ABC: The Australian Broadcasting Commission 1932–1983*,' *Journal of Australian Studies*, vol. 9, no. 17, 1985, p. 97.

14 'An Epic Tale of Broadcasting,' *Canberra Times*, 23 September 2006, p. 10.

15 KS Inglis (ed. C Wilcox), *Observing Australia: 1959 to 1999*, Melbourne University Press, 1999, pp. 134–50.

16 JDB Miller, 'Effective Account of the ABC's Half Century,' *Canberra Times*, 14 August 1983, p. 8.

17 PB White, 'The Problem of Managing Auntie,' *Australian Society*, 1 September 1983, p. 47.

18   J Moses, 'What Is the ABC?,' *24 Hours*, November 1983, pp. 77, 79.

19   T Griffiths, *The Art of Time Travel: Historians and Their Craft*, Black Inc., Melbourne, 2016, p. 235.

20   Bolton, 'Review of *This Is the ABC*,' p. 538.

21   Dunlevy, 'Red Tape and High Culture,' p. 17.

22   Stephens, 'A Place in History.'

23   KS Inglis, *Whose ABC? The Australian Broadcasting Corporation 1983–2006*, Black Inc., Melbourne, 2006.

24   Martin, 'Review Essay,' p. 1.

25   G Haigh, 'Everyone's Battleground,' *Monthly*, September 2006, pp, 56–58.

26   J Given, 'Everything on the Record,' *Australian*, 6 September 2006, p. 18.

27   L Kramer, 'Review of *Whose ABC? The Australian Broadcasting Corporation 1983–2006*,' *Australian Journal of Public Administration*, vol. 66, no. 1, 2007, p. 122.

28   Griffen-Foley, 'The Complete Adventures of Aunty,' p. 10.

29   'An Epic Tale of Broadcasting,' *Canberra Times*, 23 September 2006, p. 10.

30   Inglis, *Whose ABC?*, p. 384.

31   Inglis, *Whose ABC?*, p. 591.

32   Martin, 'Review Essay,' p. 7.

33   M Simons, 'Travels with Our Aunty,' *Age*, 29 July 2006, p. 21.

34   KS Inglis, Speech to National Press Club, 12 July 1983.

Chapter 17

KEN INGLIS AND THE ART OF SLICING HISTORY

Marian Quartly

It was at a meeting of historians at the Australian National University (ANU) in October 1976 that Ken Inglis first suggested that Australian history might usefully be 'sliced.' Oliver MacDonagh, the head of the history department at the ANU's Research School of Social Sciences, had called together members of the department to consider his proposal to mark the 1988 bicentennial with the publication of a multi-volume, multi-authored history of Australia. The proposal included both reference volumes and narrative volumes spanning Australia's 200 years. MacDonagh remembered:

> The crucial happening of this meeting – for the absence of a decision to smother the infant at birth can scarcely be called a happening – was Ken Inglis's proposal that, instead of four narrative volumes, the histories should be four 'slices' of particular years: 1788, 1838, 1888 and 1938.[1]

MacDonagh claimed that this was the only occasion he could remember in a long academic career when 'a daring, original idea was accepted with excited acclamation within thirty seconds of being set out.' It would be the last time the slicing proposal was received without controversy.

* * *

Graeme Davison has written that 'the Bicentennial History was conceived as the historical profession's gift to the nation.'[2] MacDonagh came to the ANU fresh from working on a multi-volume project for a *New History of Ireland*, and his first proposal to his department was for 'an Australian equivalent.'[3] He and his colleagues were looking for a large, significant project – something that underlined the standing of the history section of the Research School of Social Sciences as the only history department in the country dedicated to research. The reference volumes were readily acceptable as national offerings, but slicing history was a touch radical. It is unlikely that the ANU historians would have been persuaded without MacDonagh's strong support. Inglis may not have suggested the slice volumes without prompting from the departmental head. There was affection between the older and the younger scholar, and a shared interest in history-writing as performance.[4]

MacDonagh characterised slicing as 'a revolutionary type of historiography.'[5] Inglis's presentation was more modest. He argued that where standard narrative models tended 'merely to elaborate' our understanding of the past, slicing would require contributors 'to break new ground in method and substance':

> [We] thought of having a series of groups each working together at a very short period; instead of the traditional relay-race along well-worn tracks, a series of survey camps; instead of a continuous

thread of narrative, we imagined drilling a number of bores, or (to avoid painful senses of that word) cutting a number of slices.

Such an approach could be essentially democratic – 'a group of authors talking to each other and corresponding with each other about how to shape their book.' It could bring together historians with different skills: economic historians with historical demographers and historical geographers. 'What we propose is an essay in collaborative scholarship which will come off if enough scholars think it worth attempting and if they have the wits and the stamina to see it through.'[6]

Inglis toured the universities during 1977 seeking support. His plan was not well received by the profession. Critics objected to the scheme in general as monopolistic and wasteful of research time and money, and slicing in particular as 'eccentric or idiosyncratic in concentrating on arbitrarily selected segments of time at the expense of the historian's proper procedures, which were the use of the narrative method and the linear time perspective.'[7] Long-established departments were not ready to accept a claim to research leadership by the relatively youthful ANU. Davison, then a junior member of the University of Melbourne's history department, remembers the evening when Inglis met with his old department in the Jessie Webb Library, beneath the portraits of 'the greats of the Melbourne School':

> Ken's proposal, advanced with his characteristic charm and modesty, elicited a cool response ... The slice idea was described as idiosyncratic, antiquarian, monopolistic and, worst of all, anti-historical.[8]

By the end of the tour Inglis was 'quite daunted and even dismayed.'[9] For the life of the project and later in its critical reception, slicing would be a lightning rod for criticism from conservatives and radicals alike.

279

In Western Australia, Alan Atkinson and I loved the idea. Historians from the University of Western Australia and the fledgling Murdoch University organised a series of seminars during 1977 for staff and postgraduates on the theme of cultural theory in practice. Rhys Isaac came across from La Trobe to talk about what he called 'ethnographic method.' Isaac was eloquent about the uses of anthropology in the service of social history:

> Anthropologists cross frontiers to explore societies other than their own. Social historians cross timespans to study earlier eras. Whether one moves away from oneself in cultural space or historic time, one does not go far before one is in a world where the taken-for-granted must cease to be so. Forms of translation become necessary. Methods must be found of reaching an under-standing of the meanings that the inhabitants of other worlds have given to their own familiar ways. Social historians have therefore been drawn to anthropology as a source of inspiration in their endeavours to enter into past cultural systems.[10]

Our reading of Inglis's slicing proposal was heavily coloured by Isaac's exposition of ethnographic method. In May 1978 we put in a bid to take responsibility for the 1838 slice by publishing the first issue of *The Push from the Bush: A Bulletin of Social History – Devoted to the Year of Grace, 1838*. In a methodological piece called, with conscious irony, 'On Slicing the Historical Tide,' I summarised Isaac's approach:

> Starting from the premise that the documents available to social historians are essentially the record of 'people doing things,' he shows how these may be read to reveal 'explicit social relation-ships ... expressed in a formalised pattern of action.'[11]

The formal proposal we made to the management committee elaborated these 'patterns of action':

Thinking in terms of both sources and style, one can see as a basic unit of description and analysis the single human consciousness in interaction with its immediate environment, social, economic, political, ideal, emotional and physical. Subjective and object-ive reality meet in the individual mind … in the entrepreneur selecting his next venture, the housewife buying lettuces, the missionary contemplating Aboriginal intransigence, the mechanic reading Bentham by candlelight, the convict plotting escape, the mother of six seeking an abortion. In film-making terms, each is a single frame.

From the frame, 'the next level of complexity' was 'the event, or series of events, involving the interaction of a number of minds in a specific context, and defined by ritual or dramatic convention':

a funeral, a picnic, a massacre, the shearing of sheep, a speech from the hustings, a church service, the hiring of a servant, a family argument, a bargain struck at market.

At 'the most complex level' the series of events morphs into elements of the 'lasting social environment':

the building of a house, a church, a road into the interior; the process of courtship and marriage, conception and birth; the passage of a cargo ship from Sydney to Perth, with an account of its commercial venture and internal social relations; the full round of the seasons on a squatting run, with the movement of stock and servants across the inland …[12]

Ken Inglis was familiar with the sociological and anthropological ideas underpinning our approach. In another paper in this volume the anthropologist Shirley Lindenbaum characterises Inglis as an 'anthropological historian' possessing an 'ethnographic sensibility.' She traces his interest in anthropology back to his friendship with Murray Groves at the University of Melbourne and then at Oxford, where Groves was working with Edward Evans-Pritchard, a pioneer in British social anthropology who taught 'the unity ... of history and anthropology.' Ken's wife Judy undertook a diploma in anthropology with Evans-Pritchard, and Ken sat in on the lectures.

Even before his exposure to British anthropology, though, Inglis was attracted to Weberian understandings of social change through the work of Richard Tawney. He tells us in his retrospective musings in *Observing Australia* that reading Tawney at school 'hooked him on history': 'Can anybody now understand how the very title *Religion and the Rise of Capitalism* excited me?'[13] This interest took him into a thesis at Oxford on the social history of Christianity in modern England, and his first academic article, published in *Historical Studies Australia and New Zealand* in 1957, declared a central concern with 'the act of worship and its social environment.'[14]

Back in Adelaide and then Canberra, he read and thought about religion and society in Australia, a preoccupation that led to a chapter in a volume that self-consciously declared itself to be establishing the science of sociology in Australia – Davies and Encel's *Australian Society: A Sociological Introduction*. Encel's introduction defined sociology as 'an academic discipline seeking to illuminate the results of social surveys ... by systematic thinking about social groups and institutions.'[15] Inglis's chapter, 'Religious Behaviour,' met this criterion by opening with an analysis of the 1961 census's findings on religious affiliation. But it quickly went on to explore territory concealed as much as revealed by the census findings: the range of social interactions that Inglis called the 'encounter of faith and society.'[16] After considering the relationships between denominational affiliation and 'private and public attitudes' to issues like 'alcohol, betting, Sunday observance and censorship,' Inglis turned to what he called 'rites of passage': marriage, divorce, death.[17] His conclusion was prescient:

> A sense of identification with a religious body affects Australian lives in ways not visible if we look only at attendance. The identification is mild, but it persists from generation to generation; and what is done temperately and intermittently in an acquiescent environment might be done more ardently if part or all of Australian Christianity were seriously menaced by an enemy.[18]

While Inglis was considering the mild identification of Australians with organised Christianity, he was also pondering the phenomenon that some saw as an alternative, secular religion – the ceremonies and rituals of Anzac Day. Other chapters of this book examine the process and outcomes of these studies. Suffice it for me to notice that Inglis brought their first fruits to the history profession in a paper called 'Monuments and Ceremonies,' delivered to the 1977 ANZAAS conference. Here, he identified as a particular guide the German historian George Mosse. Inglis wrote that Mosse's interpretation of the making of Nazi ceremonies and monuments, 'in which policies and other verbal components of the movement are seen as less important than its symbols and rituals, requires the historian to look at a modern society with the eye of an anthropologist.' Inglis also cited political scientist Benedict Anderson's study of Sukarno's monuments as 'a form of *speech*,' and anthropologist Clifford Geertz's characterisation of Indonesian holidays as 'ceremonies of integration *and conflict.*'[19]

Ken Inglis's pitch to sell the bicentennial history project to the Australian historical profession in 1977 made no reference to sociology or anthropology. His suggested models for the practice of slicing were all histories: 'Macaulay's third chapter, Halévy's first volume, Hofstadter's *America at 1750*, and Helen Lynd's *England in the 1880s.*'[20]

Australian historians educated in the English tradition in the 1950s and 1960s would have been familiar with Macaulay and Halévy (in translation); less so with the Americans Hofstadter and Lynd, both of them pioneers in sociologically oriented social history. The chosen models are a disparate collection, with little in common methodologically; their time frames are variable, likewise the degree to which they look forward and back. Their main commonality is an unusually strong interest in the role of religion in society. One must assume that Inglis's choice of non-anthropological models was intended to appeal to a profession with narrow disciplinary horizons. And that he didn't want to pre-empt anyone's methodological or theoretical choices.[21]

* * *

Once convenors were appointed for the various volumes and research and writing got under way, Inglis began to speak more expansively about the virtues of slicing. In later years, he remembered the impact of Graeme Davison's paper on 'Slicing Australian History,' published in 1982. Davison mounted a well-theorised attack on history understood as a 'stream'; 'the idea of continuous or linear time, which underlies the narrative method, is ... [essentially] metaphoric.' 'By focusing upon an arbitrarily chosen moment of time,' he argued, 'the slice approach acts as a corrective to the inbuilt teleological bias of narrative history.'[22]

Inglis took up this theme in his preface to *Australians 1838*, published in 1987:

> By writing about one year in people's lives ... historians could avoid creating the most common illusion conveyed by narrative approaches: that history is a stream, carrying people towards a predetermined destination clearly visible to us, if not to them.

The reward was empathy with past lives:

> We might recognise people more easily as our own kind if we met
> them living out the daily, weekly, seasonal, annual and biological
> rhythms of their lives; and we would certainly understand them
> more fully by grasping the truth that the future that beckoned
> or alarmed them was not necessarily *our* past – what actually
> happened – but rather a hidden destiny, a precarious vision of
> probabilities, possibilities and uncertainties.[23]

In the event, the four slice volumes – 1788 (not strictly a 'slice' by the
time of publication), 1838, 1888 and 1938 – employ the art of slicing
in very different ways. *Australians to 1788* includes a dozen essays each
reconstructing the life of a different Aboriginal community on the eve
of white contact, and its conclusion is a slice exploring the first year of
British settlement. *Australians 1838* committed its authors 'to present
the minds of people living in Australia in 1838 as far as possible from
inside'[24]: that is, by limiting the sources to those produced in 1838,
by limiting the language to that of the day, and by writing without
the benefit of hindsight – without knowledge of what was to happen
after 1838. *Australians 1888* looked to the model of Fernand Braudel's
The Mediterranean and the Mediterranean World in the Age of Philip II,
aiming to portray 'the regional and social diversity of Australia in 1888
and the ways in which different environments and regional economies
were mediated in family structures and class relations.'[25] *Australians
1938* sliced by taking as its major source interviews with people living
in 1938, and concentrating as far as possible on that year.

Ken Inglis had a go at writing slices himself. He contributed to
two of the volumes, *Australians 1938* and *Australians from 1939*. In
1938 he wrote a chapter on death, 'Passing Away.'[26] It deals with the
rites and ceremonies of death, but it is not a slice; rather it describes

the changes in belief and practice that produced the experience of bereavement in 1938. In *Australians from 1939* the Inglis slice, 'At War,' opens the volume:

> On the evening of Friday 1 September 1939, my mother took me to the Planet Theatre, Preston, to see Jeanette MacDonald and Nelson Eddy as *Sweethearts*. The screen was filled with the lovers' technicolour singing faces when a handwritten message slid under them, saying that German forces had entered Poland.[27]

It goes on to tell, in nineteen pages, the story of the Second World War from the point of view of a Preston schoolboy. The story is told with irony but also with empathy – for the boy that Inglis was and for his schoolmates, their parents and the wider community. Without intruding on the experience that he describes, Inglis always makes it clear when that experience was shared and when it wasn't. Class, gender and race are active players without being named.

There is one more thing to be said about Inglis's personal approach to slicing. The archives of the bicentennial history project include a typed sheet with extensive emendations and additions in Inglis's handwriting, headed 'Notes for interview with Janet McCalman for Times on Sunday 1 6 87.' Point 3, after 'Genesis' and 'The name,' reads:

> 3. Slices. A time everywhere of dissatisfaction with conventional narrative history. Demands of narrative force historians to leave out 90 per cent of what they notice. One way to describe slicing: leave out a different 90 per cent. Another way: Pausing for a year, the historian can look at a past society with the close scrutiny, perhaps intimacy, achieved by the good social anthropologist.

Then, clearly legible but crossed out:

> I'd long thought of trying to write a book about Australia in one
> year: 1888 had been appealing to me. I remembered that when
> we began to talk about a bicentennial project.[28]

I think that Inglis never spoke of this ambition for the same reason
that he crossed it out here – a deep reluctance to put himself in the
spotlight.

* * *

Australians: A Historical Library was widely reviewed in the literary pages
of newspapers and in academic journals. Most of the reviews discussed
the practice of slicing. Most were enthusiastic about the recreation of
everyday life; like Edward Kynaston in the *Weekend Australian*, they
applauded the attention given to 'the lives of ordinary people, which
seem to grow in fascination exponentially as our distance from them
increases.' But reviewers were mostly not convinced that slicing was
'real history.' Maurice Dunlevy in the *Canberra Times* was intrigued
by the 'detailed examination of life in that year – and of how it got
that way' in one slice volume; but he wrote of another, 'It's one thing
to be popular and another to be mindless … There's too much of the
ephemera of life and not enough of what we have traditionally called
history.' Joseph Johnson in the *Age* complained that a slice volume 'sets
out to celebrate the lives of ordinary people, but too often treats them
as consumers of durables and producers of babies, denying them an
active role in the historical process.'[29]

Academic reviewers had the same problem. In a thoughtful review,
Kay Daniels assessed the volumes as examples of the new social history, and found the whole enterprise wanting. The use of documentary

evidence tended to overwhelm the reader with information of 'an almost trivial kind'; 'too much detail is given and too little is concluded from it.' And 'the burden of confinement to one year' was not worth the effort; 'This is indeed writing history with one hand tied behind the back.'[30] Writing as a contributor to one of the slice volumes, Ellen McEwen agreed. After coming to the enterprise as an enthusiast for slicing, she was deeply disappointed by the outcome. In the absence of 'a definite argument and conclusions,' the volume 'remain[s] a bundle of interesting information still waiting to be moulded into shape.'[31] Even the kindest critic, Janet McCalman, found the refusal to look beyond the chosen year too restrictive: 'These Australians come to speak to us from the past; but it is frustrating that we do not know how these lives turned out.'[32]

Inglis's own venture into slicing, the story of the Preston school-boy during wartime, drew perhaps the harshest criticism of all. Jill Matthews wrote:

> A fifty-nine-year-old male historian tells a story, remembers an adolescent boy's experience of living during World War II: a perfectly ordinary boy, respectable, middle-class, sexist, racist, jingoistic ... The story told is apparently crystal clear, photo-graphic, as it really was ... There is no mention of a white adult male recasting a past and patterning it retrospectively from his present position; there is no acknowledgement of a senior estab-lishment historian patterning a past according to his professional standards of significance. We are presented, rather, with a true story, and not only true, but important.[33]

To a less hostile reader Inglis's account of his war reads not as true, 'as it really was,' but as memory. The fifty-nine-year-old Inglis made no overt intervention to inform the recollections of his twelve-year-old self; the acknowledgement of his class, gender and, yes, his jingoism was in the choice of language and of detail. I can only think that Matthews on this occasion was tone-deaf.

The essential tension within slicing – between engaging the past on its own terms and reviewing it from the standards of the present – was perhaps captured best in an elegant review by Jill Roe. Roe critiqued the slicing enterprise, and showed that she could slice it with the best of them. The review took the form of a letter to the author Miles Franklin, whose biography consumed more than ten years of Roe's life. It was written in a voice at once Roe's and Franklin's, in the idiom and phrasing of the Australian 1930s:

> Dear Miles,
>
> Dunno what you'd think of this lot. They've sent me what they call the slice volumes of the bicentennial history project for review, and a couple of the reference volumes as well … I looked you up immediately of course. You got nine references, including two in the index volume to your literary award …
>
> This mob don't lose a chance to tell you what they're up to. Somewhere we are told that the slice is truly revolutionary. Well, it's novel …
>
> Each of the three slices reflects, quite vigorously, contemporary approaches to history. *1838* reminds me of a well-fired Wedgwood pot, Etrurian swirls and all. In *1888* it's like the patriarchal knife through the Sunday roast. By *1938* it's the shiny amplifier and the blare of popular culture. All very self-conscious, but it means well, Miles.

Roe gave each volume a fair hearing, but overall she wasn't satisfied:

> Trouble is, what I'm getting round to, is that post-slice I am not really much the wiser as to what framework-cum-interpretation is now being suggested to us … To tell the truth Miles, I haven't the faintest idea how to weigh much of the new information from

these 'survey camps.' But it must be good to have it, and I've met some interesting people.

In the end, she thought readers should put the volumes aside and 'get on with making sense of our history.'[34]

Thirty years on, the sense that we can hope to make of Australian history is more complex and contradictory than anything we could have imagined in 1988. The big questions have failed us, and we are the wiser for it. The acknowledgement of many voices as makers of our history – Aborigines, women as well as men, recent arrivals and long-term settlers, to name just a few – has enriched our understanding even as it unsettled so many certainties.

More than most academic historians, Ken Inglis could claim a role in the unsettling and reimagining of Australian history. He never would have done so, of course; modesty forbade it. The senior ANU historians who welcomed the bicentennial history project in 1976 saw it as giving a lead to the historical profession, but Inglis never accepted this role, for himself or for slicing. Looking back at the enterprise, his highest praise for slicing was that it had encouraged its authors 'to be more self-conscious about our prose than is general among academic authors.' This may seem one of the least of things, but it may be one of the greatest, especially when coupled with self-consciousness about the language of our sources. In Inglis's own words:

> I believe that sensitivity to the actor's own vocabulary, idiom or rhetoric gives the historian a better chance of crossing that mysterious line between just chronicling past events and beginning to recreate past lives.[35]

Endnotes

1   O MacDonagh, 'The Making of *Australians: A Historical Library*: A Personal Retrospect,' in E Russell (ed.), *Australians: The Guide and Index*, Fairfax, Syme & Weldon, Sydney, 1987, vol. 11 of *Australians: A Historical Library*, p. 2. By the end of the project the 1788 volume was no longer, strictly speaking, a 'slice.'

2   G Davison, 'Ken Inglis: Threads of Influence,' *History Australia*, vol. 14, no. 4, 2017, p. 525.

3   MacDonagh, 'The Making of *Australians*,' p. 1.

4   Alan Atkinson suggested this: A Atkinson, email to Marian Quartly, 7 December 2017.

5   MacDonagh, 'The Making of *Australians*,' p. 2.

6   K Inglis, 'Australia 1788–1988: A Note on Proposed Approaches,' *The Push from the Bush*, no. 1, May 1978, pp. 4–9.

7   MacDonagh, 'The Making of *Australians*,' p. 3.

8   Davison, 'Ken Inglis: Threads of Influence,' p. 523.

9   MacDonagh, 'The Making of *Australians*,' p. 3.

10 R Isaac, 'Ethnographic Method in History: An Action Approach,' *Historical Methods*, vol. 13, no. 1, Winter 1980, pp. 43–61. Rhys supplied us with an earlier copy of the paper as published in the *Newbury Papers in Family and Community History*.

11 M Aveling, 'On Slicing the Historical Tide,' *The Push from the Bush*, no. 1, May 1978, p. 16.

12 M Aveling & A Atkinson, 'A Modest Proposal: A Proposal for the Writing of "Australia 1838" by Informal Collective,' *The Push from the Bush*, no. 1, May 1978, p. 12.

13 KS Inglis (ed. C Wilcox), *Observing Australia: 1959 to 1999*, Melbourne University Press, Carlton, 1999, p. 22.

14 KS Inglis, 'Churches and Working Classes in Nineteenth Century England,' *Historical Studies Australia and New Zealand*, vol. 8, no. 29, 1957, p. 44.

15 AF Davies & S Encel (eds), *Australian Society: A Sociological Introduction*, F.W. Cheshire, Melbourne, 1965, p. 1.

16 KS Inglis, 'Religious Behaviour,' in AF Davies & S Encel (eds), *Australian Society: A Sociological Introduction*, F.W. Cheshire, Melbourne, 1965, p. 44.

17 Inglis, 'Religious Behaviour,' pp. 51–2.

18 Inglis, 'Religious Behaviour,' p. 74.

19 Inglis, *Observing Australia*, pp. 121–2. Emphases in the original.

20 Inglis, 'Australia 1788–1988,' p. 5.

21 Graeme Davison has suggested that 'slicing was a heuristic device, deliberately chosen for its ideological neutrality': G Davison, email to Marian Quartly, 6 December 2017.

22 G Davison, 'Slicing Australian History: Reflections on the Bicentennial History Project,' *New Zealand Journal of History*, vol. 16, April 1982, p. 12.

23 AD Gilbert & KS Inglis, 'Preface,' in A Atkinson & M Aveling (eds), *Australians 1838*, Fairfax, Syme & Weldon, Sydney, 1987, vol. 2 of *Australians: A Historical Library*, p. xiii.

24 A Atkinson & M Aveling (eds), *Australians 1838*, Fairfax, Syme & Weldon, Sydney, 1987, vol. 2 of *Australians: A Historical Library*, p. xvi.

25 G Davison, cited in MacDonagh, 'The Making of *Australians*,' p. 8.

26 KS Inglis, 'Passing Away,' in B Gammage & P Spearritt (eds), *Australians 1938*, Fairfax, Syme & Weldon, Sydney, 1987, vol. 4 of *Australians: A Historical Library*.

27 KS Inglis, 'At War,' in A Curthoys, AW Martin & T Rowse (eds), *Australians from 1939*, Fairfax, Syme & Weldon, Sydney, 1987, vol. 5 of *Australians: A Historical Library*, p. 1.

28 Bicentennial History Deposit, ANUA1/Box 36, Location A/246/3, Australian National University and Butlin Archives.

29 These examples of criticism are drawn from a compilation, KS Inglis (ed.), *How They Sliced Us Up: Reviews of* Australians: A Historical Library, History Department, Australian National University, Canberra, 1989. Kynaston wrote in the *Weekend Australian*, 29–30 August 1987. The Dunlevy reviews cited were published in the *Canberra Times*, 20 June 1987 and 28 November 1987. Johnson wrote in the *Age*, 12 December 1987.

30 K Daniels, 'Slicing the Past: Review of *Australians: A Historical Library*,' *Australian Historical Studies*, vol. 23, no. 91, October 1988, pp. 130–40.

31 E McEwen, 'Australians 1888: A Very Personal View,' *Australian Historical Studies*, vol. 23, no. 91, October 1988, pp. 114–20.

32 J McCalman, 'Committee Creates Not a Camel but Living Vivid History,' *Times on Sunday*, 19 July 1987.

33 JJ Matthews, '"A Female of All Things": Women and the Bicentenary,' *Australian Historical Studies*, vol. 23, no. 91, October 1988, p. 96.

34 J Roe, 'Letter to Miles Franklin: The Bicentennial History Project,' *Overland*, no. 111, June 1988.

35 KS Inglis, 'Planning a Bicentennial History,' in Inglis, *Observing Australia*, p. 183.

Chapter 18

STILL LEARNING

Ken Inglis as teacher

Joy Damousi

Ken was one of the very first people to welcome me when I arrived in 1984 to begin my PhD at the Australian National University. He knocked on my office door and gave me the biggest handshake I remember receiving before or since. He did so with a characteristically warm smile, with kindness and with generosity.

'Welcome,' he said. 'It's lovely to have you here.'

I have never forgotten that moment, simple as it may appear. It has stayed with me not only for the obvious reason that I was deeply appreciative that Ken was bringing me into the ANU fold, and into the community of historians in the history department. Even more than that, I was struck by the fact that he took the time to seek me out and make me feel like a colleague, even though I was only a week or two into my doctoral studies. This gesture, his greeting me like a grown-up, said that we were historians *together*.

That feeling was very strong throughout my time at the ANU. Ken was always keen to make sure PhD students were introduced to every eminent historian who came to the Coombs building on a visiting fellowship. We were *all* engaged in the historical enterprise, and this was the bond we shared.

I was also taken by the moment because it was not the first time I had met Ken, which made his approach and inclusiveness even more special.

The year before, in 1983, I had been a vacation scholar at the ANU. Over the summer, I had researched the topic of my honours thesis, the Melbourne intellectual, socialist and pacifist Robert Ross and his circle of iconoclasts, which included feminists and rationalists. It was a glorious few weeks, not least because I discovered for the very first time the sheer pleasure of researching blissfully uninterrupted in that historian's mecca, the National Library of Australia.

The history department in the Research School of Social Sciences was very welcoming and supportive, providing a relaxed and friendly environment for a group of earnest, budding historians. Looking back, it was my first entrée into an academic community beyond my undergraduate cohort at La Trobe University, which had also provided a dynamic and engaging environment for its students. In Canberra, though, I was mixing with others from outside my immediate circle and meeting honours students from across the country – some of whom have remained friends ever since. It was a great experience.

Ken was one of the staff members who made that time so special. He took a great interest in our work, loved discussing ideas and, despite his own deadlines and commitments, generously made time for us. His warm, congenial and generous spirit made him very popular among the students. I was keen to return to Ken and to this community, so I was very excited when I was offered a scholarship to come back to the ANU the following year.

But lest you think I am remembering this period through the rosy glow of carefree and idealised youth, I must confess that I also felt daunted by the prospect of working with someone of Ken's stature. Iconic historians abounded at the ANU – Manning Clark, Keith Hancock, John La Nauze. These male historians fitted into a proud tradition, though the names personally meant very little to me. It was Ken who was the towering historian, and with the prospect of being in his department came performance anxiety. I had known some of his work prior to arriving – *The Australian Colonists* and *The Stuart Case* in particular, and of course the majestic history of the ABC, which came out in my honours year. Ken's name was everywhere and the ABC book was being widely discussed. I wanted to be part of the world that produced such work, and much else besides. The history bug had bitten.

* * *

So it was with this mixture of first, delight and excitement, second, terror and anxiety, and third, a sense of great warmth and inclusiveness, that I embarked on my PhD with Ken and Barry Smith. And I was to experience all three feelings in ample measure.

What I want to briefly reflect on in this essay are some of the enduring qualities Ken imparted to me during the time I was at the ANU from 1984 to 1987. The PhD years are formative ones for everyone who goes through them. In mine, Ken played a crucial role, although in ways he may not have realised at the time or since.

I will start with the delight and excitement.

One of the most enduring gifts Ken gave me as a student was the feeling that I *could* write history – that scholarship mattered and what you did as an academic was serious business. This may seem obvious. But being shown how to make a claim for the importance of scholarship and one's own history writing made a deep impression on me, and I try to impart this understanding to my own students. Ken believed that the value of the enterprise should never be underestimated; it was, indeed, something of a calling, demanding of commitment, in which you had an opportunity to make a contribution to the world of ideas and debate. I found this intellectual empowerment sustaining and invigorating. As with everything Ken did, this ethos was never imparted with a heavy hand: the lightness of touch, the nuance and subtlety that shaped his work also infused this underlying, steadfast and infectious principle. He never let us forget that we were engaged in an enterprise of utmost importance.

My second point comes under the heading of both delight and terror. It was a great privilege to be at the ANU in the 1980s when Ken was working on two pioneering works – *Sacred Places* and *Australians: A Historical Library*. It was Ken's capacity as a researcher, original thinker and erudite intellectual that both inspired excitement and created heightened anxiety in this PhD student.

I won't rehearse here the discussion of these iconic works elsewhere in this book, but I do recall just how extraordinarily helpful and instructive it was to witness the evolution and progress of major historical works of national and international significance. At a time when memorials were not the stuff of historical study, *Sacred Places* took a truly original approach to studying the past, pointing to the transformative power of new approaches. Ken showed how fresh sources could be found and, through these, how new stories could be told about war. Of course, this is now all very familiar, but at the time it expanded the horizons of so many of us. He opened our eyes to seeing landscapes in new ways.

I remember, as a regular visitor to the State Library of Victoria at the time, how I caught myself looking anew at the war memorial that I had seen twice daily for a decade or so without giving it any thought at all. After I had heard one of Ken's papers, I stopped to take notice, and I saw it in an entirely different way. It wasn't a new landscape but it was one I viewed with new eyes.

The power of the insights Ken offered in *Sacred Places* is that they never leave you. Years later, and after I returned to Melbourne, I came upon a striking war memorial built of white marble in the park near where I lived (and continue to live), commemorating the local men who had died during the First World War. Residents had raised the money in 1921 to build a statue of a soldier that seemed to glow in the dark. *Sacred Places* had just come out and, as we know, the narrative about Australia and the war was changed forever. What I recalled, looking at this statue, was not so much the book itself but the papers Ken had delivered, accompanied by slides of memorials around the country, in Australian towns I had never heard of. Around each he merged narrative and analysis in a seamless – and mesmerising – way.

Although I had left the ANU by this time, our research interests had come together, in my case through *Gender and War* (1995), which I edited with Marilyn Lake, and my own monograph, *Labour of Loss* (1999), looking at loss and mourning on the home front. Ken had not left my professional life. In that latter year – 1999 – our journeys along this research road were linked in a new way when I met Jay Winter, with whom I have shared a warm and long-lasting connection to Ken.

The bicentennial history project also shaped new narratives and created great interest in the 1980s, but in very different ways. It was, of course, much more controversial. The 'slice' approach to history, sliced at fifty-year intervals – 1838, 1888 and 1938 – had everyone buzzing at the time. It was accompanied by a set of reference volumes, including an atlas, a dictionary, a guide to sources, a book of statistics and a handbook of events and places. This huge undertaking dominated discussion in the ANU history department for the latter years of my time there. It involved a vast number of historians and scholars from across Australia. Whatever you thought of the approach – and everyone had an opinion – it sparked debate, discussion and lots of lively engagement. History was on everyone's lips, if not minds. Even PhD students were heard debating the strengths and weaknesses of slices at the ANU bar. It inspired us to talk about our own methodologies, approaches and analyses. None of us was brave enough to slice up our own theses, but what do you do when your supervisor is extolling this approach? What was the importance of periodisation? What did linear time mean anyway? What were the gaps in this approach? Were they really gaps, or just fragments of time?

While the slice approach didn't gain any adherents in our group, the intellectual excitement of the day did give us the confidence to talk about how we looked at our historical study. We were discussing the historian's craft, in fact, without really seeing it as such. The bicentennial project opened debates and discussions about method in a series of seminars at the ANU attended by historians from around the country, including a historian of religion named Alan Gilbert, whom I met there for the first time. Ken was showing us what historians do, how they understand their enterprise and what was possible when you pushed intellectual boundaries.

The next time the historical enterprise would come under similar scrutiny would be in the 1990s, when the linguistic turn would take us into the territory of language, meaning and representation. This, too, would focus the mind and attention on method and approach, what historians do and how they do it. But that debate was imported: it was an international discussion that challenged not just the notion of 'facts,' which E.H. Carr had asked us to consider, but also of truth. The debate around the bicentennial history focused on the specifics of Australian history, interrogating Australian linear timelines, historical progression and the notion that events flow from one to the next. The story of the Australian nation, it was argued, would never quite be the same again.

* * *

The debate continued in the bicentennial year and followed me back to Melbourne. When I arrived at Monash University to take up a three-year tutorship in March 1988 there was even more discussion of the volumes, which were of course published by then and being reviewed by historians. Now in a position to teach the questions that Ken had provocatively asked us to consider, his line of inquiry remained with me. Historians turned increasingly to themes of culture, rethinking the slice approach in different ways. One of the most successful products of this period was Alan Atkinson's award-winning 1988 book *Camden*, a study of farm and of village life in early New South Wales, which speaks to wider concerns of class, race and gender in colonial Australia. Not quite a slice, it nevertheless took the insights Alan and his fellow contributors had developed in the 1838 volume of *Australians* into a new and inspiring area of Australian cultural history. It was a transformative text and fuelled the discussion that Ken had begun.

My third reflection comes under inclusiveness, but it is also more than that. Ken was the exemplar of an exceptional colleague and mentor. He was a model of collegiality and professionalism, of integrity and generosity in sharing and exchanging ideas, arguments and thoughts. My doctoral thesis looked at women on the left from 1890 to 1920, exploring the emergence and relationship of feminism and socialism, and examining the impact of the war on socialists in particular. I took in recent developments in women's history and labour history, and saw my thesis as part of the project of writing women into the history of the left. It aimed to be a history of ideas as well as to chart the history of activism and social change. I was interested in biography, and how a biographical approach could provide a frame to explore the challenges women faced as activists and political agitators. Limited by the availability of sources, I could only go so far in this pursuit. But no one had looked at it this way before, so that is what I chose to do.

Issues of war and gender increasingly began to occupy me. The conscription debates and the role of women in the contending campaigns – particularly those on the 'no' side – opened an aspect of women's political activism that I found especially compelling. My interest in this debate continues today, but in the meantime I have developed an interest in those who voted for conscription and argued on the 'yes' side of the debate. In a recently published chapter on this topic, in a book I coedited with Murray Goot, Sean Scalmer and Robin Archer, *The Conscription Conflict and the Great War*, I drew heavily on Ken's insightful chapter on conscription during the twentieth century, published in 1968.[1] It remains one of the best overviews of the topic, using a longitudinal approach to bring in the debates during the Second World War and the Vietnam War and produce telling insights.

Women's history and labour history were not areas Ken worked in, but as a prodigious and vociferous reader he had his finger on many pulses and was kind enough to impart all that he read. In 1984 he passed on an article he thought might be useful, and suggested that I might consider integrating some of its insights into my thesis. It was an article by historian Joan Scott, whom I had not previously heard of, titled 'Women in History: The Modern Period.'[2] Ken had a habit of passing on articles of use and interest; this one was to be pivotal when I wrote my thesis, and then again when I recast the thesis as my first book, *Women Come Rally*. In that transition, I continued to follow Scott's work, and of course she went on to discuss gender as a historical category of analysis in a way that revolutionised women's history and set in train many debates, shaping a more theoretical approach of gender history.

This was a crucial reference at a timely moment, propelling my work in new directions. This passing on of references points to how different postgraduate supervision was in those days. Supervision was not the bureaucratic and paper-heavy process it is now. There weren't the compulsory scheduled meetings that we are expected to hold today; annual reviews were unheard of, coursework unimaginable. While students were expected to present a seminar paper, publishing work during your candidature was seen as neither necessary nor desirable. You met your supervisor when you wrote a chapter or two, and discussed them. In the meantime, any items of interest or relevance appeared in your pigeonhole. Pre-Google, the circulation of knowledge about current literature was done manually, so to speak, and Ken was always wonderfully generous in that respect.

If the bureaucracy accompanying a PhD has reached Kafkaesque proportions over the past thirty years, one trait of a good supervisor remains timeless. And this is the capacity to listen to students. One of the most striking and effective ways Ken interacted with my work was to listen. Ken was a great listener. It could be disconcerting when he lent forward and you could feel the full force of his body and mind concentrated in his ears. In giving the time to listen he showed great respect for my work, as he did with other students. The skill of listening, and not just hearing, is an exceptional one. Ken patiently listened as I delivered half-baked ideas, undercooked arguments and, I am sure, circular logic in my efforts to find my way through my topic. And after listening, he would deliver succinct, clear guidance and direction. Without fail, his comments were on the mark, productive and constructive, always moving ideas and arguments forward. He always invited conversation and a dialogue.

It was a two-way exchange with Ken. Even if there was no resolution of how and where to take an idea or a structure, the way he offered advice and posed his suggestions and questions was invaluable. Not only did he listen and deliver the astute observation that could dig you out of an intellectual hole – or create one! – he alarmingly and disarmingly spoke in perfectly rounded sentences with correct grammar. He never swore. His utter respect for the English language was part of his very being. It was about not just writing well, but speaking well. This made Ken a formidable role model.

* * *

Leading on from all of this, perhaps the most important of all Ken's qualities was the very high standards he imposed on his students. He wanted us to do our very best and near enough was never good enough. A scholar had exacting standards, and if we were to make our way into the academy and stay there it was essential these were met. One incident in particular stands out, showing him bringing home this message to the students under his watch.

It was during 1985, and Ken was especially enthusiastic about an outstanding PhD thesis he had just examined – one that he believed all history PhD students should read and emulate. It was a model of fine scholarship and incisive argument that was well crafted and beautifully written. He raised the idea of inviting the author to come and discuss this thesis with us. How could we resist? We wanted to hear more, so agreed to meet with the student who had delighted Ken.

The name was familiar to me, as I had read her first book, but our paths had not yet crossed. Looking back, it was one of those moments we used to refer to as a 'turning point.' And so, in 1985, Dr Marilyn Lake came to the ANU and addressed us. It was the first time I had met Marilyn and she inspired us with her presentation. Archival research, argument and narrative were her key themes. I remember discussing the session later when a few us went for a coffee to mull over Marilyn's advice. Getting through to the end point seemed an eternity away then, but it could be done!

Marilyn's visit was a clever idea of Ken's: he wanted to show us what the standard was and how to go about achieving it, and he was indirectly telling us that we needed to lift our game. What better way to do this than to ask a recently completed student to tell us what to strive for in a piece of scholarship. Two years later, in 1987, the book of the thesis appeared as *The Limits of Hope: Soldier Settlement in Victoria, 1915–38*. It was a shining example of how to translate thesis to book.

Supervisors in those days were under no obligation to organise anything for their students. They didn't have to see them or speak to them or actually read their drafts. Ken did all three with passion and commitment. We, the next generation, were the grateful beneficiaries.

Finally, I want to fast-forward to October 2016, in Melbourne. Ken attended a conference I ran at the University of Melbourne on global histories of refugees. There were almost one hundred papers delivered over three days. The topics were diverse, covering both Australian and overseas histories of refugees, mainly focusing on the twentieth and twenty-first centuries. It was a timely conference, with practitioners and journalists as well as historians in attendance. The discussions were wide-ranging and enormously stimulating.

It was a privilege to have Ken come for some of the proceedings. At sessions on refugees, memory and the aftermath of war, he heard the papers on Leonhard Adam, the refugee anthropologist and polymath, and Seumas Spark's paper on the *Dunera* boys. Ken and I were back in the same research space again, this time in our work connecting themes of refugees and their history in Australia.

Nothing had changed from the Ken I had first met thirty-three years earlier. The sophisticated level of engagement was still there in his questioning, of course. He argued passionately for the relevance of history to the topic of refugees and urged all of us to keep writing about it. His generosity and inclusiveness remained a hallmark of his scholarly interactions.

After one of these sessions a newly enrolled PhD student introduced herself to me. She wanted to tell me how much she had enjoyed the conference and how useful it was to her as she embarked on her research. In particular, the last session she had attended was especially useful. She told me she thought a question Ken asked was the best intervention she had heard during the course of the three days of papers.

'What did you like about it?' I asked.

It was, she said, as if he had opened up an entirely new way of looking at the history of refugees and he had – with clarity, sharpness and astuteness – transformed her understanding of it. Then she said, 'Oh, I wish I had him as my supervisor. I would learn so much.'

I couldn't even begin to tell her how much she would have learnt, for I, too, am still learning from Ken.

Endnotes

1   KS Inglis, 'Conscription in Peace and War, 1911–1945,' in R Forward & B Reece (eds), *Conscription in Australia*, University of Queensland Press, 1968, pp. 33–4.

2   JW Scott, 'Women in History: The Modern Period,' *Past & Present*, no. 101, November 1983, pp. 141–57.

Chapter 19

'THE BOOK ON YOUKNOWWHAT'

War memorials in Ken Inglis's mindscape

Peter Stanley

Sacred Places: War Memorials in the Australian Landscape became one of Ken Inglis's most influential books, and one that took decades to coalesce in his mind before it took shape on the page. One of Ken's techniques for refining and testing his ideas was to speak and write often, trying out and reprising subjects and passages from the book he was thinking about or writing. His interest in war memorials, he explained in the introduction to *Sacred Places*, went back 'some forty years'; that is, to the early 1960s.[1]

Through his British doctoral thesis, Ken had become a historian of Victorian religious social history. He 'forgot Anzac for some years' but, returning to Australia, came 'to wonder what had happened in the twentieth century to religiosity, faith, the sense of the sacred' with the gradual decline of Christianity. Reacquainting himself with Australian history, he 'found in books and the history I had been taught and was now teaching' a gap: 'nothing in my university education had helped me understand Anzac.'[2]

The process by which Ken's curiosity impelled him to research, write and publish entailed reflecting publicly on questions that interested him. Looking back on a sequence of articles and talks, it becomes clear from where the preoccupation came – his concern to trace the evolution of spirituality – even if the destination was not certain at the time. In 1964 he spoke at the ANZAAS (Australian New Zealand Association for the Advancement of Science) congress, a multidisciplinary gathering so popular that its sessions were sometimes televised by the ABC and speakers' papers were reported in the daily press. In his paper, 'The Anzac Tradition,' he prefigured the reminiscences of the Shrine of Remembrance in Melbourne in the 1930s with which he opened *Sacred Places*. But the ideas were not yet mature. In the paper's last paragraph Ken admitted that 'the theme of death and the Anzac tradition is one I can't embark on now.'[3]

What Ken did embark on was the Turkish chartered passenger vessel the *Karadeniz* ('Black Sea'). The 1965 Gallipoli pilgrimage had the thirty-five-year-old historian mingle with Anzacs twice his age, observing men who, he wrote, had been nurtured by a very different Australia. The experience led him to frame questions about that older Australia. Ken's enquiry now was to wonder not just about how Australia saw its past, but also about how questioning that past could illuminate the Australia of the later twentieth century. For a time, it seemed that the answer was 'less and less.' In 1960, in his seminal *Nation* article, 'Anzac, the Substitute Religion,' Ken anticipated that 'in fifty years hardly anybody at present eligible for membership [of the RSL] will be alive'; nearly forty years later he remembered that 'hardly anybody foresaw the endurance of Anzac observance.'[4] By the time he began writing *Sacred Places*, he would note 'the imminent resurgence of commemoration, which continues as I write.'[5]

The weeks among the Anzac pilgrims aboard the *Karadeniz* remained profoundly influential for Ken, much as the relationships with other Great War men were for, say, Bill Gammage and Alistair Thomson. 'Thirty years later,' he wrote, 'I still draw on memories of the pilgrimage when I think and write about the meanings of Anzac.'[6]

As Frank Bongiorno shows in this volume, Ken had become interested in ceremonies and festivals, with *The Australian Colonists* the first in a projected series of studies that would culminate in a fourth volume dealing with Anzac Day. His thinking about war memorials and commemoration impelled him to skip the intervening volumes and to begin thinking, researching and writing about war memorials. By 1967, midway through Australia's Vietnam war, when he published an article on 'Australia Day' in *Historical Studies*, the assumption that Anzac Day would fade (as had other seemingly flourishing festivals) had changed. 'Now it is bound to flourish for a long time,' he decided.[7] Even while working on *The Australian Colonists*, Ken continued to explore the theme of monuments and ceremonies and to ask what they might mean. His 1977 ANZAAS paper, 'Monuments and Ceremonies as Evidence for Historians,' became, as he reflected later, 'a kind of prospectus' for the approach he was taking.[8]

Collating Ken's writings on what might loosely be called Anzac, in the decades from 1970, reveals a recurring fascination with the idea of war commemoration. For some years after his 1977 ANZAAS paper, uncertain of how to develop this enquiry and preoccupied by the demands of *This Is the ABC* and the bicentennial history project, Ken characteristically worked out the problem by delivering more papers and publishing articles, wrestling with ideas and arguments that eventually became sections of *Sacred Places*. A 'Checklist of Writings by K. S. Inglis on War and Remembrance' in John Lack's

1998 collection includes more than sixty entries over thirty-six years from 1960.[9]

In the meantime, Ken thought of creating an archive on which a future book might be based. He conceived the idea of surveying war memorials, he recalled, when listening to a radio news bulletin during the April 1983 Hawke economic summit that mentioned a national local government organisation: 'by God, every town's got a war memorial ... You could actually do a survey of them.'[10] Ken approached the Australian Heritage Commission in June 1983 and immediately met with a favourable response.[11] The war memorials project commenced in October 1983 with the Heritage Commission's support, supposedly for two years.[12] As an initial memo demonstrates, Ken began with many questions. How exhaustively would it survey the memorials that were not obvious, such as those in churches, banks, hospitals or workplaces? How should memorials be categorised, indexed or analysed? He began with Judith McKay's survey of Queensland memorials as a guide.[13]

For several years in the mid-1980s, Ken's survey was coordinated by Jan Brazier, a research assistant who had worked for him on *The Rehearsal* in the Research School of Social Sciences at the Australian National University (ANU). The Australian Heritage Commission's funding 'collapsed' after a year, as Ken's and Jan's reports put it (for reasons that remain unclear), and they had to reconsider whether and how the survey could proceed.[14] The project was kept alive by Ken devoting $5000 in royalties from *The Rehearsal* and gaining the material aid of the Australian War Memorial through the good offices of Michael McKernan, its Assistant Director. Originally expecting to be able to cover thoroughly only New South Wales, the project continued through the involvement of a group of volunteers working in various states, including Judith McKay in Queensland, Ashley Ekins and David

Hood in South Australia, and Richard Ely in Tasmania. Jan essayed a pilot study of the memorials of the Hunter Valley and Ken himself covered many of Western Australia's memorials. Jan, 'a champion researcher,' became centre of the network. When she reported that she had obtained a photograph of the memorial in Montville, Queensland (the only memorial to include the names of 'rejected volunteers),' Ken asked 'I wonder how you got <u>them</u>?'[15]

Jan worked in Sydney, and for much of the project she and Ken were in different countries, with Ken often in Cambridge (Massachusetts or England), Italy or elsewhere. She would receive notes, at first handwritten, later typed, towards the end as emails, as Ken forwarded records and responses he had received, giving her what he called 'puzzles' – often vague queries or particular points. Jan came to see that Ken appreciated her as 'a good rummager' (in a pre-digital era), and, not least, able to read his untidy handwriting. In response, she turned up 'goodies' for the files of the thousands of civic memorials, and increasingly took the initiative in suggesting leads ('What about mentioning the earliest we know of …').[16] She found Ken an undemanding supervisor who rarely issued specific directions: 'I just assumed what I gave him was what he wanted,' she recalled, and it was.[17] From the beginning, influenced by his ANU colleague Barry Higman, Ken had anticipated that entries would be analysed using a computer. With the aid of Jan's partner, Ken McSwain, the responses were collated using early database technology, with funding of $3000 provided by the War Memorial's research grants-in-aid scheme.[18]

Ken was by no means the first researcher to notice war memorials, even in Australia. In his initial memo to Jan Brazier he mentioned, as well as Judith McKay's project, Bill Stegemann's 1982 ANU Honours thesis on war memorials in southeast New South Wales, and Jennifer

Turpin's 1981 Sydney Honours thesis on Australian war memorials and the culture of the Great War.[19] The subject was both novel and, in some minds, uncongenial. Not all of Ken's colleagues, friends or acquaintances could share his curiosity: fifteen years later he could still write that 'even now I find some ... uncomfortable to know that I am writing about war memorials, as if the very act of studying them gives blessing to militarism.'[20]

Ken began with an unduly optimistic idea of the likely timetable. In his initial approach to the Heritage Commission he said that he hoped to finish both a published 'register' and an 'interpretative essay' within two years.[21] By October 1983, assuming that researchers would be engaged in other states by late 1984, he anticipated that the survey would take a year, and that 'I would then do the interpretative essay/ book early in 1986.' He bid Jan 'Good rowing!' and the project began.[22]

Even as Ken and Jan and their volunteers began collecting and collating details of war memorials, what Carolyn Holbrook described as 'the Anzac revival' was beginning, a phenomenon that Ken observed and even helped to foster.[23] In 1993, he advised on and analysed the significance of the interment of the Unknown Australian Soldier, delivering a public lecture at the Memorial on other nations' Unknown Soldiers, a further stage in the evolution of his thinking.[24] The interment, he told the Australian-born American academic Jill Ker Conway, seemed to him to be 'a tender farewell to an old Australia' – the Australia they had grown up in – with Paul Keating's words 'flawlessly apt.' It was a ceremony of which Ken was sure Charles Bean would have approved, 'a last act of homage to his old AIF.'[25] Inevitably, Ken mulled over the evidence he and Jan collected, in a series of talks, papers and articles delivered and published in Australia and overseas, not least on the new traditions – the Unknown Australian Soldier, the inclusion of

311

Indigenous communities in war commemoration, the placement of poppies at the Australian War Memorial.

The files that Ken and Jan assembled grew to become an archive, organised state-by-state and controlled by various files and indexes. While the files formed the basis of the analysis in what became *Sacred Places*, the fate of the records became a matter of importance. Ken's close relationship with Michael McKernan, who would later become Deputy Director of the Australian War Memorial 1981–95, and through Michael, Brendon Kelson, its Director 1990-94, led to an 'understanding' that the files would in time go to the Memorial. Early in 1995, with the manuscript nearing completion, Ken contacted the Memorial to arrange the anticipated transfer. By then McKernan and Kelson had left.[26] Ken's need of the files necessarily delayed the transfer of 9.46 metres of boxes, which took a further three years.[27] Its completion, about which Ken told Jan (on a postcard depicting – what else? – the war memorial at Wellington, New South Wales) made him feel 'a strange mixture of liberation + loss.'[28]

* * *

By the time Ken actually began writing what became *Sacred Places*, Jan had moved on (to become archivist at the Australian Museum), though she maintained contact with Ken. The book took a long time, not least because of the competing demands of other projects. At last, at the end of 1993, Ken wrote to Jill Ker Conway that 'I'm close at last to finishing that book on war memorials,' though this was almost five years before its publication.[29] It had been delayed, he admitted, but explained that it had also been 'I hope enriched, by a few sallies into comparative history.'

One of the most fruitful strands, entering Ken's thoughts through the 1980s, had been that he came to see Australian memorials in an international context. His contact with those sharing an interest had resulted in his attending what were the first conferences devoted to considering the international phenomenon of memorial making, notably in Paris in 1991. Gatherings like these, he told Conway, had been 'a kind of coming out,' at which 'a collection of solitary nutters turned into something like a discipline, or at least a gang.'[30] The first member of the gang had been the German-Jewish-American historian George Mosse, with whom Ken had visited the Australian War Memorial in 1979. In the 1980s other scholars interested in the long memory of the Great War joined the gang, including Annette Becker from France, Jock Phillips from New Zealand, and Jay Winter, whose American-British-French perspectives proved to be arguably the most crucial and the most durable. All opened Ken's Australian questions to an international context and comparison, legitimising a novel field. Sadly, the copy of *Sacred Places* that Ken sent to George Mosse arrived just weeks after his death, early in 1999.[31]

It seems that by the time the war memorials survey began Ken had at least the elements of the book's title. Soon after starting, he published two articles (typically, one scholarly, one popular): 'A Sacred Place: The Making of the Australian War Memorial' (in the journal *War & Society*), and 'War Memorials in the Australian Landscape' (in *Heritage Australia*, the journal of the Australian Council of National Trusts).[32] (Granny Riach's memorial at Thirroul in New South Wales, a leitmotif in *Sacred Places*, seems to have had its first outing in the latter.) Together, they suggest that the ideas of 'sacred places' and 'war memorials in the Australian landscape' had coalesced. A decade later, in 1994, he wrote to Jan that he was 'now on the last chapter of the book on youknowwhat.'[33] But not until 13 October 1998 could Ken write to Jan that 'I really finished the book yesterday': this letter was written almost exactly fifteen years after Ken drafted his initial memo.[34] Jan continued to send 'goodies', and in return received occasional 'puzzles' from Ken, and postcards from exotic locations. She did not comment on drafts of the manuscript and was surprised and pleased to learn that Ken had added to the book's title page 'K. S. Inglis assisted by Jan Brazier.'[35]

Finishing a manuscript was one thing; getting the manuscript published turned out to be quite another. As Frank Bongiorno has shown, Ken's decision not to proceed with the 'Australian Colonists' series had led to a falling out with Melbourne University Press and its longstanding publisher, Peter Ryan. Craig Wilcox (one of Ken's former PhD candidates and the editor of the 1999 compilation *Observing Australia*) recalled that Ryan had 'lavished time and money on [*The Australian Colonists*] … and I don't think he ever forgave Inglis for abandoning the project.'[36] In 1994 Ryan complained of Ken's 'gratuitous slur' against Bruce Ruxton in an article he had published on Anzac Day, though Ryan's note ended 'I like to remember our times in PNG.' Ken replied that he only knew Ruxton 'as a maker of public statements which … make me wince,' but undertook to bear Ryan's comments in mind in the manuscript.[37]

With Melbourne University Press out of contention, Ken had depended on an 'understanding' with the University of Queensland Press, with whom he also had a long association. The Memorial's accession file for Ken's and Jan's war memorials records includes a tantalisingly incomplete exchange of letters that reveals Ken's state of mind as he sought a publisher midway through the year of 'Australia Remembers.' On 26 July 1995, Ken wrote to me. 'Within a week of finishing my book on Australian war memorials' he had discovered that the 'informal agreement' he had with UQP to publish a book of 140,000 words and 200 illustrations had collapsed for want of a substantial subsidy.

Perturbed, Ken again approached Melbourne University Press (as it then was) whose new publisher, Brian Wilder, read about half of the manuscript and offered a contract – but only for a book of 80,000 words and just twenty illustrations. Anything longer, he said, would also require a subsidy – Ken understood that figure would be $10,000. He was reluctant to accept Wilder's conditions, but, characteristically, wondered whether he was 'just sulking.' He asked if the Memorial could provide that subsidy. Evidently I replied, in terms that Ken found heartening – he described my reply as 'a most thoughtfully constructive letter … the more so when you and the mannequins and all are so close to going over the top.' (I headed the Memorial's Historical Research Section but was then detached to curate the exhibition, '1945: War & Peace').[38] As I was a notably inefficient public servant, my reply is not on the Memorial's file, nor, it seems, in Ken's papers. In any case, a co-publication deal proved unnecessary. Jan Brazier received the good news in a postcard (undated) from a triumphant Ken. The card, which he amended delightfully, showed 'Captain Cook announcing that' Melbourne University Press would 'publish … it in the posh Miegunyah series.'

Sacred Places was launched on 17 November 1998 by the Governor-General, Sir William Deane, fittingly at the Australian War Memorial; the event demonstrated Ken's tendency to activism. As well as commending the book generally, Sir William observed that 'there are few memorials to … the Aborigines who were slaughtered in the "Black Wars" of that period.'[39] Ken's suggestion, that the frontier conflict dead should be commemorated in the Memorial, was misattributed to Sir William by what Ken called a 'mug Murdoch reporter.'[40] This sparked both denunciations and agreement, in yet another of the periodic public spats between the Memorial and those advocating change. It confirmed the opposition of the Memorial's senior management to acknowledging frontier conflict, and ensured the matter would persist. Ken pursued that cause, observing that achieving recognition for those who died defending their country would demand 'imagination, candour, tact and consultation, and a breadth of vision'; sadly, attributes so far lacking in the conversation.[41] Returning to the issue five years later in a letter in the *Canberra Times*, Ken urged that the 'time has come to portray our frontier wars.' The call brought, as Ken annotated the cutting, 'Silence!' from the Memorial.[42]

Reviews of *Sacred Places* were overwhelmingly positive, the most thoughtful situating it in Ken's evolution. Tim Rowse saw it as standing squarely in the train of Ken's movement from a historian of Christianity to one seeking to understand 'the sense of the sacred' in a secular society.[43] Given Ken's reputation, positive reviews tended to the effusive: 'nobody who tackles the subject of war memorials will improve upon Ken Inglis's magnificent account.'[44] But even critical readings of the book, such as that by John Moses, who thought that Ken had unduly ignored the Christian dimension of war commemoration, suggested that *Sacred Places* was an important book.[45] Moses, an Anglican priest as well as an historian, argued over several articles that Ken had underestimated and misrepresented the religious inspiration of Anzac.[46]

As Craig Wilcox observed just after the appearance of *Sacred Places*, Ken's books presented 'a broad context and considered reflections that allow readers to understand the subject-matter better and to make up their own minds about it.'[47] It was these qualities which perhaps explain the prizes the book garnered – the *Age* Book of the Year, the NSW Premier's Australian History Award, the Ernest Scott History Prize and the Federation of Australian Writers Literature Award.

Sacred Places was not the first analysis of Australian war commemoration nor, given its scope, the most substantial about particular memorial sites, events or practices. What can explain its enduring impact? Its scope, of course; but also its style. Craig Wilcox observed that Ken's 'approach to history' was 'academic in its rigour but vernacular in its taste and style.'[48] Ken's notes were tucked away at the back of the book, discursive in tone and far from the earnest listing of ambitious postgraduates. His text was conversational but serious in intent, like the Student Christian talks he heard at Queen's College.

The three editions of *Sacred Places* published in 1998, 2005 and 2008 allowed Ken to trace continuing changes in Australian commemoration, apparent even as the first edition appeared. John Stephens of Curtin University observed that when Ken began the survey of war memorials 'Anzac day commemoration was waning but had vigorously re-emerged by 1998.' Stephens, an authority on commemoration in Western Australia, suggested in reviewing the largely unchanged second edition in 2005 that 'a desirable addition would have been an update on the latter-day growth of commemoration.'[49] Ken marked this paragraph in his print-out of the online API Network bulletin in which the review appeared: prefiguring a major addition to the third edition.[50]

At a 'conversation' with Bill Gammage, Hank Nelson, Kate Darian-Smith and Katti Williams, convened by Bruce Scates at the Shrine in Melbourne in April 2008, Ken reflected on 'how perceptions of war were changing,' thinking especially of the 'resurgence of Anzac observance.'[51] 'Those changes are the main subject of my epilogue,' he said, speaking in the place where the introduction to *Sacred Places* opens. The new 120-page epilogue looked 'Towards the Centenary of Anzac,' examining the renewed proliferation of war memorials, new memorials on Anzac Parade, the recent history of the Australian War Memorial, the creation of memorials overseas, and anticipating the centenary of Anzac, at Anzac.

At the Shrine conversation, Hank Nelson, Ken's friend and colleague from their time at the University of Papua New Guinea, reflected on Ken's achievement over the previous forty years. Ken, he said, had made 'what now seem astonishing statements':

> It is now difficult to think that we Australians have not always been conscious of the Anzac tradition, and that serious historians have not always been writing about the relationships between the deaths and experiences in the Great War ... But we were not always conscious of those things: Ken Inglis made us so.[52]

Another of Ken's old Papua New Guinea comrades, Bill Gammage, also spoke at the Shrine. A decade after the publication of the first edition of *Sacred Places*, he delivered what could be the definitive judgement on the book and its author. Ken Inglis, he said, had brought to Australians' attention 'something which we thought we had always known.' Before Ken, 'academics ignored Anzac not because it was unimportant, but because they took it for granted.' Ken's books, Bill said, 'have changed our understanding of Australian minds and hearts.' For any historian, that is no bad epitaph.

Acknowledgements

I am grateful to Judy Turner for granting permission to me to consult the otherwise closed Inglis correspondence in the NLA, and to Jan Brazier and Craig Wilcox for sharing their recollections of Ken and allowing me to read documents in their possession.

Endnotes

1   KS Inglis, *Sacred Places: War Memorials in the Australian Landscape*, Miegunyah Press, Carlton, 1998, p. 8.

2   KS Inglis, Text of a talk at the National Museum of Australia, 7 April 2008, Papers of Ken Inglis, MS Acc10165, Box 11, National Library of Australia.

3   KS Inglis, 'The Anzac Tradition' (draft with notes in response by Arthur Bazley), 1964, Australian War Memorial, 3 DRL2914.

4   KS Inglis, 'Anzac, the Substitute Religion,' and later commentary in KS Inglis (ed. C Wilcox), *Observing Australia: 1959 to 1999*, Melbourne University Press, Carlton, 1999, p. 70.

5   Inglis, *Sacred Places*, p. 9.

6   Inglis commentary on 'Diggers in Antiquity,' in Inglis, *Observing Australia*, p. 80.

7   Inglis, 'Australia Day,' *Historical Studies Australia and New Zealand*, vol. 13, no. 49, October 1967, p. 40.

8   Inglis, Text of a talk at the National Museum of Australia, 7 April 2008, Papers of Ken Inglis, MS Acc10165, Box 11, National Library of Australia.

9   John Lack (ed.), *Anzac Remembered: Selected Writings by K. S. Inglis*, University of Melbourne History Department, Melbourne, 1998, pp. 261-4.

10   Quoted by J Steger, 'Inglis Rewarded for Taking His Time,' *Age*, 3 January 2000. Steger and Ken both misremembered the summit as having occurred in 1984.

11   'HISTORY OF PROJECT,' document in the possession of Jan Brazier.

12   'SURVEY OF WAR MEMORIALS: Ken to Jan memo 11/10/83,' document in the possession of Jan Brazier. This is the Ur-document of the entire project, and, indeed, of *Sacred Places*.

13   J McKay and R Allom's *Lest We Forget: A Guide to the Conservation of War Memorials*, (RSL Queensland, Brisbane), appeared in 1984. Ken had been in contact with Judith.

14   'THE PROJECT' annotated 'to KI 8/10' (1984), document in the possession of Jan Brazier.

15   Letters, KS Inglis to J Brazier, 17 June 1988 and 4 July 1990, documents in the possession of Jan Brazier. Notably, both of these letters date from after Jan's formal tenure on the project.

16 Undated letter ('2/6') J Brazier to KS Inglis, document in the possession of Jan Brazier. Jan stresses that the project focused on outdoor memorials, excluding indoor memorials such as honour rolls in halls or churches, partly to make the researchers' task possible when buildings were closed. In this sense, despite its magnitude, the survey is actually not a definitive account of all public commemoration.

17 Interview with J Brazier, Sydney, 27 July 2018.

18 M to KS Inglis, 17 October 1984, document in the possession of Jan Brazier.

19 Bill Stegemann, 'We Will Remember Them: An Examination of the Significance of World War I Memorials in South-Eastern New South Wales,' BA Hons, Australian National University, 1982; Jennifer Turpin, 'Australian War Memorials and the Culture of the Great War,' University of Sydney, 1981.

20 Inglis, *Sacred Places*, p. 6.

21 'HISTORY OF PROJECT.'

22 SURVEY OF WAR MEMORIALS: Ken to Jan memo 11/10/83.'

23 C Holbrook, *Anzac: The Unauthorised Biography*, NewSouth, Sydney, 2014, p. 215.

24 KS Inglis, 'Entombing Unknown Soldiers,' *Journal of the Australian War Memorial*, no. 23, October 1993, pp. 4–12; 'The Funeral of the Unknown Australian Soldier,' *Journal of the Australian War Memorial*, no. 24, April 1994, pp. 6–7; 'The Rite Stuff,' *Eureka Street*, vol. 4, no. 1, February 1994, pp. 23–27.

25 KS Inglis to J Ker Conway, 30 December 1993, Papers of Ken Inglis, MS Acc10165, Box 5, National Library of Australia.

26 J Waterford, 'War at the Memorial,' *Eureka Street*, November 1995, p. 18.

27 The Memorial's accession file, AWM 371, 90/606 is, inexplicably, mostly still closed but the open parts document the beginning of the Memorial's acquisition of the 'Australian National University Survey of War Memorials,' now constituting PR00944.

28 KS Inglis to J Brazier, 19 February 1998, document in the possession of Jan Brazier.

29 Inglis to Ker Conway, 30 December 1993, Papers of Ken Inglis, MS Acc10165, Box 5, National Library of Australia.

30 Inglis to Ker Conway, 15 August 1993, Papers of Ken Inglis, MS Acc10165, Box 5, National Library of Australia. An undated letter from Ken to Jan Brazier in Jan's possession makes clear that Conway attended the Paris conference and doubtless remembered war memorials at Ivanhoe and Hillston, near her home at 'Coorain.'

31 J Tortorice to KS Inglis, 10 March 1999, Papers of Ken Inglis, MS Acc10165, Box 5, National Library of Australia.

32 Copies of articles and papers sent by Ken to Jan Brazier in folders in her possession: 'A Sacred Place: The Making of the Australian War Memorial,' *War & Society*, vol. 3, no. 2, September 1985, pp. 99–126; 'War memorials in our landscape,' *Heritage Australia*, Summer 1983, pp. 16–20.

33   KS Inglis to J Brazier, 8 April 1994, document in the possession of Jan Brazier.

34   KS Inglis to J Brazier, 13 October 1998, document in the possession of Jan Brazier.

35   Interview with J Brazier, 27 July 2018.

36   C Wilcox letter to unnamed correspondent, 13 August 2013, provided by Craig Wilcox.

37   P Ryan to KS Inglis, 28 April 1994; KS Inglis to P Ryan, 14 May 1994, Papers of Ken Inglis, MS Acc10165, Box 5, National Library of Australia.

38   KS Inglis to P Stanley, 26 July; 6 August 1995, AWM 371, 90/606, Australian War Memorial.

39   W Deane, 'Abiding Memories,' *Eureka Street*, vol. 9, no. 1, January–February 1999, p. 11.

40   KS Inglis to T Rowse, undated (1998?), Papers of Ken Inglis, MS Acc10165, Box 11, National Library of Australia.

41   KS Inglis, 'Media Amnesia,' *Eureka Street*, vol. 9, no. 1, January–February 1999, p. 10.

42   *Canberra Times*, 28 March 2003, Papers of Ken Inglis, MS Acc10165, Box 10, National Library of Australia.

43   T Rowse, 'The Modernity of Anzac,' *UTS Review: Cultural Studies and New Writing*, vol. 5, no. 2, November 1999, p. 129.

44   A Trumble, *Art and Australia*, vol. 37, December 1999 – February 2000, 198–200.

45   KS Inglis to J Brazier, 13 October 1998, document in the possession of Jan Brazier.

46   While Moses did not formally review *Sacred Places*, he contested Ken's interpretation in a succession of articles from the early 1990s. For example, see 'Anglicanism and ANZAC Observance: The Essential Contribution of Canon David John Garland,' *Pacifica*, no. 19, February 2006, pp. 58–77 and 'The Faith of Canon David John Garland (1864–1939): An Australian Gladstonian Imperialist,' *St Mark's Review*, no. 225, August 2013, pp. 71–84. Moses's criticism is important in that it throws into relief the humanist approach from which Ken wrote, one shared by many professional colleagues, but which should not obscure other views of either Anzac or Australian historical experience.

47   Inglis, *Observing Australia*, p. 5.

48   Inglis, *Observing Australia*, p. 1.

49   J Stephens, API Network, Issue 36, August 2005 http://www.api-network. com/cgi-bin/reviews/jrbview.cgi?n=0552851908.

50   Even after the publication of the third edition, Ken continued to take an interest in how commemoration was changing. He kept a file of clippings documenting the opposition to (and eventual demise of) the memorials to

the world wars proposed in 2011–12 for the shore of Lake Burley Griffin in Canberra, which, despite the endorsement of successive prime ministers, were eventually seen off by a community-based campaign.

51 Folder relating to event at the Shrine, 3 April 2008, Papers of Ken Inglis, MS Acc10165, Box 11, National Library of Australia.

52 Folder relating to event at the Shrine.

Chapter 20

LOOKING AT MEMORY

Reflections on *Sacred Places*

Annette Becker

The sacred places that Ken Inglis made his own – war memorials in English, *monuments aux morts* in French, *monumenti ai caduti* in Italian – have been sites of memory for almost a century. He was the first to notice the significance of the difference between the French and English terms for the same sites; every culture has its own language of the sacred. Indeed, one of Ken's achievements was to make us all think hard about both the local and the universal aspects of commemoration. When the historian Bart Ziino asked me to write an essay about commemorations of the Western Front, I tried to say this by dedicating the essay to Ken, 'who taught me to look at memory,' a clumsy English translation of the French phrase *regarder la mémoire*.[1]

It was the precision of his work that enabled Ken's writing about war memorials to approach what the French have called total history, the study of how we make sense of the world, in time and space, through sound and silence. His grasp of the significance of these memorials was unique – transnational while deeply Australian, anthropological in spirit and empirical in form. They constitute 'holy ground' but he looked at them with the eyes of a non-believer, or rather the eyes of someone who was intrigued by the beliefs and sentiments of those who came to them.

His contribution in this field was seminal. We can trace it through four articles – 'War Memorials: Ten Questions for Historians,' 'World War One Memorials in Australia,' 'Entombing Unknown Soldiers: From London and Paris to Baghdad' and 'The Unknown Australian Soldier' – and through the finest book in any language about war memorials, *Sacred Places: War Memorials in the Australian Landscape.*[2]

Anyone in this field needs to address the ten questions he posed in the first of those articles. I will try to pose ten issues of my own about these sacred places, fully aware of the fact that what makes Ken Inglis's work so important is that he not only captured the mood in which these monuments were erected but also remained sensitive to the fact that commemoration is never fixed, and indeed remains controversial to this day. Calling war memorials sites of the sacred is simply to open the difficult and important task of interpreting how different generations have understood the tragic history commemorated in stone all over the world.

1. Tragedy: From industrial sound to silence

In 1917, when the American troops reached Saint-Nazaire, the French poet Jean Cocteau heard jazz for the first time. He called it 'a domesticated catastrophe.' We might adapt the term to the entire First World War, and call it an undomesticated catastrophe, though I generally prefer the word 'tragedy,' probably because the French classical tragedies of the seventeenth century involved blood and death, to be sure, but also a certain humanity and nobility. Tragedy is a term suitable for the First World War; it was a bloodbath in which some men made noble choices, admirable choices, the stuff of legends that have come down to our own times.

In France, trench newspapers knew what tragedy meant. One camouflage unit is captured in a cartoon dialogue between two soldiers. One says, 'You were a painter of theatre sets before the war, what are you doing now?' The other responds, 'I am painting sets for a tragedy.'[3]

Ken was well aware of the tragedies behind each and every war memorial. Every site presents the dead to us, in the words of Hans Belting, 'through their absence.'[4] Or rather absences, since we are not seeing war memorials at the moment they were created, inaugurated or visited. We do not see the families in front of them three generations ago, the broken families, the damaged men and women who had to pick up the pieces of their lives after the war. We do not hear their voices, or their silences. But we know why they were there.

2. Images of mourning: Infinite

In late 1916, Guillaume Apollinaire published *Le Poète assassiné*, a book on which he had been working since before the war. Wounded in battle, trepanned, traumatised by being buried alive in the trenches, this ordinary combatant and avant-garde poet became one of the inventors of modern commemoration. His premonitory poetry of 1913, which described a 'great killing,' had been overtaken by reality. In chapter XVIII of the book, entitled 'Apothéose,' he describes the construction of a commemorative monument to the hero:

'I must create a statue for him' [...]

'What sort of statue? ... Marble? Bronze?'

'No, that's too old-fashioned … I must create a profound statue out of nothing, like poetry and like the war.'

'Bravo! Bravo! … A statue made of nothing, a void, it's magnificent, and when are you going to sculpt this?' […]

Next day the sculptor returned with workmen who built a wall around the well … so effectively that the void took the form of the hero. Indeed, the hole was full of his ghost.[5]

Apollinaire and contemporaries who were equally conceptual understood that the dead combatants of the First World War would be no more than phantoms. For a century now, artists have sought to explore this commemorative duality – how to configure absence as a real presence among us.

There were many ways to do so. In the German military cemetery in Vladslo, near Dixmude in Belgium, the mother and father sculpted by Käthe Kollwitz are brought to their knees by sorrow before the tomb of their son. When it drizzles, they weep. In 1934, the Romanian avant-garde sculptor Constantin Brancusi answered the call of the women of Romania and gave Târgu Jiu a war memorial that encompasses the whole city. In one part, the stone *Table of Silence* is surrounded by twelve empty chairs. Even the Apostles are marked by their absence; there are no guests – and, of course, no guest of honour – at this commemorative feast. Here is a site of empty houses, a tiny and un-heroic triumphal arch, an abstraction of Brancusi's already abstract sculpture *The Kiss*. At the other end of the city, in steel, cast iron and brass, is the giant *Endless Column*. In this commemorative landscape, mourning, like Brancusi's column, never ends. The commemorative form tells us what absence is.

And yet, as Walter Benjamin warned us, 'what gives something authenticity is its materiality.'[6] But what happens when a monument points not to durability but to fragility, mortality – in effect, to absence. Is its power as testimony undermined? In some cases, that is the case, but in many war memorials, the historical testimony given is indirect, neither about presence nor about absence but about the binding together of the two. Mourning occurred there, at the site that speaks of presence and absence as inextricably linked realities. All expressions of the sacred do the same.

3. Time and space

In many representations, broken stone or broken landscapes stand in for the dead. This is true of Paul Nash's painting *We Are Making a New World*, and of the memorial in bronze by Ernest Pignon-Ernest, in Sóyecourt, Somme, where twenty-year-old broken trees represent twenty-year-old broken soldiers. In a sense, the soil of France bore the wounds of war just as much as the soldiers who fought there.

Australian commemoration was different, as Ken Inglis demonstrated. Gallipoli did not stay a present, damaged landscape for the Australian and New Zealand troops who fought there. What Anzacs and later generations have remembered is the courage and endurance of the men who landed there. These attributes did not disappear with the bodies of those who were killed, but rather came to stand for the dead. That is how myths are made. Nobility stands in for the bodies of those who died.

On the Somme, this trading of virtue for absence is harder to achieve. The Battle of the Somme was many things, but noble is not one of them. Resisting the last German offensives of 1918 may have had a touch of nobility, but what the Australians did at Villers-Bretonneux was done by thousands of others from all over the world. There was nothing specifically Australian about holding the line; the Allies did it, and won the war.

The Battle of Fromelles shows the limits of the term 'nobility.' This diversionary action, which aimed to move the German forces away from the Allied attack on the Somme in July 1916, was a complete disaster. 'Pompey' Elliott, the Australian commander in the field, begged for the order to attack to be withdrawn. He, and the Allied forces, had no such luck, suffering 7500 casualties for nothing.

Yet the process of creating a presence to embrace absence happened at Fromelles in a unique way. Some inspired research and DNA testing uncovered nearly 200 bodies that had vanished without trace in July 1916. In 2012 the absent became the present, in the sense that the presence of the dead could be marked by precise names, established through up-to-date science, which could now be attached to specific remains buried under a single Commonwealth War Graves Commission stele. Families in our times wrote epitaphs for men who died a century ago. Among them was the line from today's global hymn, 'Amazing Grace' – 'I once was lost, but now am found' – giving voice to the fundamental binary at the heart of all war memorials, the formulation of something present in the place of someone absent.

4. Gender: From military front to home front

Ken Inglis's deep knowledge of French war memorials enabled him to tell us much about how they contrasted with Australian monuments. In France, women, the old and the very young, non-combatants in general, are often represented on war memorials. The memorials show that soldiers and civilians, men and women, fought the same war, each with the arms at his or her disposal. Without the home front

– without weapons, food or support from loved ones – the war would have come to a halt. On certain monuments this idea is explicit – the soldier fighting, the woman working in the fields or in industry. In formerly occupied territories, the monuments remind us of civilian deportations and the destruction wrought by landmines.

The representations of women also remind us that soldiers fought for families and for individuals, those they left behind. This is an enduring tradition. In 1970 a banner was placed (irreverently) on the Arc de Triomphe that covers the tomb of the unknown soldier in Paris. It read: 'There is someone more unknown than the unknown soldier: his wife.' In 2010, the artist Valerie Bouillon set a performance on the war memorial of Lescouët-Jugon in Brittany, hiding the names of the masculine heroes with pink material and adding: 'To the everyday courage of women, everywhere.'

5. Resurrection

In the years during and after the First World War, women were seen, above all, as emulating the Virgin, as mothers weeping for the loss of their sons. In a Catholic country like France, it was easy to imagine the dead of the war as surrogates for Christ. It then followed that war memorials were new calvaries, new sites of suffering due to the modern ordeals of industrial war. This is evident in particular in stained-glass windows in Catholic and Protestant churches. In many churches, plaques offer thanks 'ex-voto' to the Virgin: 'I put my son under her care. She gave him back to me, 1914–1918. Infinite Gratitude.'[7]

Here is the wellspring of popular beliefs that flared up in the First World War and are far from us today. But the shock of mass death left people very little choice. They had to search and find in their environment symbols that seemed to make sense of the tragedy of the war. Ken was well aware of this phenomenon, and measured the substantial distance between the French cultural landscape and that of Australia in *Sacred Places*. All cultures define the sacred in their own language, and his knowledge of the very different repertoires of commemorative practices in Europe enabled him to describe the specifically Australian features of First World War memorials. He wore his learning lightly, but this comparative element gave his writing great depth.

6. Unknowns

Ken Inglis knew very well that the force of artillery had destroyed half of the soldiers who died in the war. Destroyed in two senses: killing them and making their remains disappear. That is why the tombs of unknown soldiers became sacred places, and remained so long after 1918.

Once again, we are in a field halfway between the particular and the universal. Most combatant countries created memorials to the unknown soldier, but each in its own way. Only in France could there have been a crime novel in which the detective, Arsène Lupin, has to deal with a family convinced that *their son* is the one who lies under the Arc de Triomphe. The mother is defiant:

'Not an hour, not a day, I'll never leave Paris.'

'Why, Madam?'

'Because he is there, in the tomb.'

Already in the 1930s, artists and activists were mocking this 'triumph of the unknown' as a false symbol of the sacrifice of the nation, to which people turned despite the fact that those living victims of war, the war disabled, were left in the lurch. How easy it was to salute absence when the presence of the wounded was embarrassing and expensive. In 1930, the German artist Heinrich Hoerle painted *Monument to Unknown Prostheses*. To him, disability was not sacred; in fact it was just ignored. Unsurprisingly, he was labelled one of Germany's 'degenerate' artists a few years later.

Then came the time, in the former British Empire, when it was no longer acceptable for the unknown soldier in Westminster Abbey to represent the entire community of suffering and mourning in areas of British settlement. The unknown Australians, Canadians and New Zealanders needed ones of their own. Ken Inglis's voice was the one to tell us what was going on when the unknown Australian arrived in Canberra in 1993. 'Out in the cloisters,' he wrote, visitors 'began to make a gesture connecting the revered names with the tomb … Possibly some of them wondered, as they marked a name, whether it belonged to that unknown soldier.'[8]

The historian was there to tell us of the search for bodies to go with names, or names to go with bodies. Here we returned to the spirit of the 1920s when it was unbearable not to know where and when a man died on active service, especially when 'your' combatant died thousands and thousands of miles away. Ken Inglis taught us that the cult of the unknown soldier is powerful because it is based on a reality of modern war, namely, that bodies not only are destroyed but can also vanish from the face of the earth.

7. Race (ethnicity)

There are more absences for us to deal with in this domain. Absence is the right word to use with respect to the colonial or indigenous troops' families, but for them there was not much effort in the mother country to celebrate their specificity. Still today we know little about mourning practices in African villages and towns where soldiers had joined up to fight in the war. Apollinaire spoke about their having a kind of camouflage within the camouflage of war, what he called the 'invisibility' of race. On some French war memorials, in Africa, Asia and the Caribbean, black soldiers are represented, very often side by side with white officers, paternalism lasting well beyond death. But whether and to what extent these are sacred places are questions still needing our attention and our answers.

Colonial soldiers in France had to wait almost a century for specific recognition, in a work by Christian Lapie that was installed on the Chemin des Dames in 2007. It is called *Constellation de la douleur,* 'constellation of grief.' Nine trunks of calcified timber, the faces of men without features – universal faces – stand out very tall and very black, in the horizontality of the white chalk landscape, as if risen from the poem by Léopold Senghor, 'Hosties noires,' written in 1938. In translation:

> Hear me, Tirailleurs from Senegal, in the solitude of the black land and of death
>
> In your solitude without eyes, without ears, more than in my dark skin in the depths of the Province
>
> Without even the warmth of your comrades lying close against you, as once they were close in the trench, or in the village councils
>
> Hear me, black-skinned infantrymen, even though you have no ears and no eyes in your threefold enclosure of night.

The contemporary artist Kader Attia brings into his works the facially wounded soldier of the First World War through photographs of 'mended' soldiers, with scars and striking deformities, face to face with African objects with obvious repairs. The broken faces are like objects in every way, damaged and patched up in the reserves of colonial museums, far from the 'aesthetics of purity' preached at the time. The synthesis is on the broken faces of colonial soldiers. The emphasis of so much contemporary memorial art on damaged bodies, and the effort to represent destruction, reflects that growing recognition of the war's totality, and its globality.

8. Hate and desecration … in the past and the present

When the Nazis reached Reims in 1940, they took the monument to African soldiers of the First World War to show in an exhibit of 'degenerate art.' Afterwards they destroyed it.

War memorials, then, can be sites of hatred. The hate came from the war itself. Near Mont Saint-Quentin on the Somme, a monument shows an Anzac soldier bayoneting an eagle. In 1940, this monument too was destroyed, only to be resurrected in the 1960s. In the ossuary of Verdun-Douaumont, a stone crusader protects the sacred bones lying there, occluding the fact that as many German bones as French ones have been under his guard since the end of the 1920s. Germanophobia is a lingering disease.

Modern desecration also has not vanished. *Ils n'ont pas choisi leur sépulture* ('they did not choose their burial'), a sculpture created by Haïm Kern in 1998, was an imaginative work in the woodland on the Chemin des Dames, where mutinies took place in 1917. Kern intended his work to be an enduring link between the living and the dead. He too was moved by the proliferation of unknown soldiers, pulverised by the unimaginable power of artillery. 'I want this sculpture to be physically close to these men so that they return to us, from the earth to the light, standing out in the mesh of history.' Haïm Kern's sculpture was vandalised several times and finally totally destroyed by unknown assailants – probably partisans of military order and/or from the extreme right, who saw the sculpture, which showed only the suffering of war, as a rejection of heroism and patriotism. They interpreted Kern's intentions correctly, and their rejection of a pacifist war memorial echoed the conflict between pacifists and 'patriots' that has gone on for more than a century.

9. Politics: Between sacrifice and pacifism

Between 1914 and 1918 observers in all combatant countries wondered how it was possible to undergo so much and still continue to fight and suffer while, increasingly, many were convinced of the absurdity, the pointlessness of their sacrifice. Still bewildered by their own violence, for the most part it was only after the war that they became aware of another possible form of messianism, that of the total rejection of all war. In this conception, everyone killed between 1914 and 1918 is indiscriminately described as a 'victim' – as confirmed by the inscriptions on so many war memorials.

In today's commemorative awareness, this status is more acceptable than being an agent of suffering and death. Death is always suffered, always anonymous, never inflicted: the individual is, always, the victim. Unless, of course, we are concerned with the leaders, shown as commanders of the massacre or as executioners. Around the very few pacifist war memorials, with the children left to mourn absent fathers in tears, pacifist ceremonies still take place, in a renewal of the vows of the pacifists of the 1930s. Both they and we know that 'never again' didn't work, but they (we) still have to try.

10. One hundred years: A modern approach to the sacred?

Contemporary artists, architects and museographers of ceremonies perform for us this interplay between absence and presence. These artists bring back to us the preoccupation of the war generation with the fate of the bodies of the ten million men who died in the First World War. Like the combatants of the time, the commemorative wave now spans the globe. The former French president François Hollande gave his blessing to this globalised vision of the centenary of the war. 'It is true that it was one side against the other, for their own nation, that these young men died. It is in the name of shared humanity that they will henceforward be brought together.' One hundred years later, everybody together: the intention is not to offer further accounts of the terrible struggle of 1914–18 but to sanitise it by exoneration. Commemoration has become a sort of reparation, offered by the living to the dead, in a desire to gather together all the sacrifices made in the war and bury them once and for all, together. Why? Because all the combatants were men, and they all died together for a cause that no one now wants to immortalise. These dead soldiers have in common their death at that time, on this war terrain, where they are now the guardians of peace and strong emotion, examples of universal reconciliation.

For example, Philippe Prost, the architect for the French war memorial at Lorette, has been forced into marvels of invention to find enough space for the names of everyone who died, listed in alphabetical order regardless of nationality. He built an immense circular structure with its inner and outer walls entirely covered with the names of the dead, from a Nepalese whose last name began with an A to a Russian whose last name began with a Z. The circle stands as a symbol of the globe, of the world war. At the same time, it circles a void, and is not flat but precariously placed on an escarpment. This peace effort could be destroyed easily; we can topple again into the ravine of war.

Much commemorative art today is replete with presences surrounding absences, with the 'deep holes' and 'ghosts' between rehabilitation and disappearance. The works stumble over the difficulty of representing bodies that have suffered violence and then vanished. Above all, the artists have shown the totalisation of the war, and given us works stamped by the recognition that men, women, children and landscapes were transformed or destroyed, then as they are now.

In his work *Tomb* (2013), the New Zealand artist Kingsley Baird presents the dead of the war to the living. In choosing a material, Anzac biscuits, from an intimate setting, the kitchen, he blends the military front with the domestic front, men with women. Baird knows that these biscuits did not exist during the war, that they are an invented tradition, an act of memory from the 1920s. Each of 18,000 biscuits, cut in the shape of a soldier, represents the uniform, represents a man. One plus one, plus one, each was 'eaten' by the war. In modern warfare, the enemy is not only worn down, he is reduced to nothing. Warfare has become a vanishing act.

Baird brings together layers of memory, history and anthropology to represent the complexity of the war. Were not the fighting men of the Australian and New Zealand Army Corps – men of European origin but also Māori and Aborigines – convinced, like all the British and the Allies with whom they fought, that they were representing civilisation in the face of barbarians, those whom they called the Huns, their German enemies? In its sophisticated composition, *Tomb* shifts from the singular that represents the multiple, the unknown soldier, to the multiple that represents the singular, a single soldier in a single grave. *Tomb* is also full of voids; the 18,000 biscuits that can never fill this absence; it is there, enduring.

The South African artist Paul Emmanuel reflects on the bodies of the combatants, on physical and mental fragility faced with the technology of industrial death. His installation *The Lost Men*, placed at Thiepval in 2014, presents a trail of banners printed with photographs of parts of his body after the names of the dead soldiers have been recorded on them. Matrices of lead print were sunk, like temporary sculptures, into the artist's shoulders, thighs, thorax, face and shaven skull. The naked body – represented by enlarged fragments where the bruise-inscriptions are clearly visible – and the delicate fabric – selected for the reproduction and to quiver in the wind – proclaim human fragility and vulnerability. Emmanuel wishes to reflect on age, the youth of the soldiers, their masculinity, their virility, and on race: this white body, his own, also bears the name of dead black soldiers, and by analogy the process recalls the branding of slaves. The installation is close to the grand architecture of the triumphal/mourning arch bearing the carved names of the missing of the Battle of the Somme. Edwin Lutyens, the architect, designed the Thiepval Memorial in such a way that the summit of the arch, built of brick made in the region, leads only into thin air.

In this sense, nothingness defines the sacred places of the First World War. Today war memorials are spread all over the world, and it is among the gifts Ken Inglis gave us that we understand these structures to be hovering around that which is no longer there – the army of the dead, the lost generation of the First World War. The now-familiar symbolic space that he called sacred is configured in myriad ways. He gave us the definitive study of the Australian variant of the war memorial form, deeply informed by a knowledge of the memorials of other countries. We honour him by following the example of his scholarship.

Endnotes

1   A Becker, 'Museums, Architects and Artists on the Western Front: New Commemoration for a New History?' in B Ziino (ed.), *Remembering the First World War*, Routledge, London, 2014.

2   KS Inglis, 'War Memorials: Ten Questions for Historians,' *Guerres mondiales et conflits contemporains*, no. 167, July 1992, pp. 5–21; KS Inglis, 'World War One Memorials in Australia,' *Guerres mondiales et conflits contemporains*, no. 167, July 1992, pp. 51–8; KS Inglis, 'Entombing Unknown Soldiers: From London and Paris to Baghdad,' in KS Inglis (ed. J Lack), *ANZAC Remembered: Selected Writings by K.S. Inglis*, History Department, University of Melbourne, 1998; KS Inglis, 'The Unknown Australian Soldier,' *Journal of Australian Studies*, vol. 23, no. 60, 1999, pp. 8–17; KS Inglis (assisted by J Brazier), *Sacred Places: War Memorials in the Australian Landscape*, Miegunyah Press at Melbourne University Press, Carlton, 1998.

3   *La Baïonnette*, no. 112, 23 August 1917.

4   H Belting, *Pour une anthropologie des images*, Gallimard, Paris, 2004, p. 185.

5   G Apollinaire, *Le Poète assassiné*, Gallimard, Paris, 1979, pp. 300–1.

6   W Benjamin, 'L'œuvre d'art à l'époque de sa reproductibilité technique,' in W Benjamin, *Œuvres*, Gallimard, Paris, 2001, p. 176.

7   A Becker, *War and Faith: The Religious Imagination in France and the USA*, foreword by Ken Inglis, Berg, Oxford, 1998.

8   Inglis, 'The Unknown Australian Soldier,' p. 17.

Chapter 21

WRITING *DUNERA*

Ken Inglis's last work

Seumas Spark

In 2006, at the launch of his book *Whose ABC? The Australian Broadcasting Corporation, 1983–2006*, Ken Inglis told his audience that henceforth he would write only for his grandchildren.[1] Over decades of public scholarship, many thousands of Australians had read his words. Now, his words would be for this select group of eleven. Questions from his family had led to reflection. His son-in-law, Maurizio Nazari, wanted to know why he had never embraced communism. Ken's grandchildren had their own questions, which they put in a short film, conceived and directed by Nicholas Nazari. As Nicholas remembered, the film roused something in Ken: he 'mentioned that he started feeling like something had been uncorked and a lot of memories had started to flow about things he had not thought about in many years.'[2]

Encouraged by Nicholas, Ken set to work on a memoir. He started, as he always did, by creating archives. Papers and photos were arranged in files ordered by time and theme: life and school in Preston; Northcote High and the Second World War; the University of Melbourne.

Thinking on his time at university sparked memories of a teacher named Franz Philipp. Philipp was one of about 2000 men, most of them German and Austrian Jews, who were arrested in wartime Britain on the basis of their nationality and then deported to Australia in 1940 on a ship called the *Dunera*. Many of these men were refugees from Nazism. All were subject to deplorable conditions aboard the *Dunera*. Eventually, the British and Australian governments came to recognise the injustice of their situation, and that they posed no threat, and from 1941 offered them paths out of internment. These 2000 men are now commonly known as the '*Dunera* boys.'

Philipp found a home at the University of Melbourne, first as a student then as a tutor in Max Crawford's History Department. An essay Ken wrote in 1948 for Renaissance and Reformation History stirred such admiration in Philipp that he suggested his student become an academic. Ken found the prospect thrilling, and remained forever grateful for the suggestion. Philipp set the course of Ken's life.

Finding himself dwelling on memories of Philipp and other *Dunera* men, in 2008 Ken recast his project. Instead of a memoir, he would write a new history of the *Dunera* internees. This suited him, for the idea of himself as subject troubled him. Ken read memoirs and knew their worth, but wasn't comfortable writing his own. Nor did the decision undermine his pledge to write for his grandchildren. The *Dunera* had been part of his life for the sixty years since his defining encounter with Philipp. And so, in the year Ken turned seventy-nine, he set sail on the 'bad ship *Dunera*,' as he sometimes called it.

Ken had known several *Dunera* men at the University of Melbourne in the late 1940s. There were three at Queen's College, where he lived. Dr Leonhard Adam had arrived at Queen's in 1942, his release from internment arranged by charitable organisations sympathetic to the plight of the *Dunera* internees. Fifty years old, he had served the Kaiser in the First World War, found success as a legal scholar and judge in the Weimar Republic, then built a reputation as an expert on primitive art. Thanks to Max Crawford, the university gave him work as an anthropologist. The other two *Dunera* men at Queen's were students whose educations had been interrupted by war and internment. George Nadel started at Melbourne in his mid-twenties, Georg (George) Duerrheim when he was thirty-five. Duerrheim hoped to finish the medical degree he had nearly completed in his native Vienna before the *Anschluss* of 1938 and the adoption of Nazi race laws led to his being barred from his final exams.

Beyond Queen's were other former *Dunera* internees at the university to begin or resume scholarly lives. 'Around the Arts building and the Union,' Ken remembered, 'were three dashing students of philosophy: Peter Herbst, Gerd Buchdahl and Kurt Baier; [and] two terrifying apprentice political scientists, Henry Mayer and Hugo Wolfsohn.'[3] He heard Buchdahl give a 'superb' seminar paper to the History Department on the evolution of scientific thought, Kepler to Galileo to Newton, and what it was that Newton knew that the others didn't. Gerd 'had everything as a lecturer,' Ken recalled.[4] Mayer and Wolfsohn, meanwhile, 'were a fearsome pair, prowling the Arts building and the Union like bears hungry to feast on our dogmas and confusions, especially those deriving from Karl Marx.'[5] Mayer was a vocal member of undergraduate societies, author of firebrand articles for campus publications, and in 1949 a provocative and stimulating editor of *Melbourne University Magazine*. Ken succeeded him, co-editing the magazine the next year. Later, he worked directly with Mayer, contributing a chapter to his 1961 volume *Catholics and the Free Society*.[6] These *Dunera* men offered Ken glimpses of new worlds. They were a 'kind of person he had hardly ever struck,' sophisticated and exotic Europeans whose disparate, rich histories he found fascinating.[7]

Dunera friendships followed Ken beyond the University of Melbourne. In Oxford in 1954, Ken and his wife Judy welcomed Gerd and Nancy Buchdahl and Peter and Valerie Herbst to their flat. Judy had her own links to the *Dunera*. She had studied philosophy at Melbourne, graduating with first class honours in 1950, and was close to Herbst in particular, who had been teacher and colleague. At the Inglis's flat, Buchdahl and Herbst, both of whom spoke perfect English and favoured high diction, fell into an argument and name-calling. 'Nonsense, you stinkpot.' 'Don't talk to me like that, you shitbag.' Ken remembered the scene as vividly as any from his time at Oxford.[8] Two German refugees and Anglophiles, once interned in the Australian bush, mixing profanities and scholarly wisdom in his flat in Oxford. He told the story with relish.

No matter where in the world Ken was, *Dunera* connections were close. In Port Moresby, where he lived and worked from 1967–75, he had dealings with Gerry Gutman, an economist with the Australian Department of Territories, and once a *Dunera* internee. Gutman thought Ken a 'woolly-minded liberal.'[9] Did Ken think of him as Gerhard Ottmar Gutmann, German Jewish refugee from Munich? These connections and other *Dunera* links Ken knew of led him to a theory, one of the few he advanced as an empirical historian. Everyone is connected to *Dunera* one way or another, he would say with a smile.

Personal reasons led Ken to write about the *Dunera* internees, but it was his interests as a historian that sustained him. 'My curiosity about them and their world was never quite satisfied by what I happened to learn about them,' he wrote in 2013. 'Now, in old age, I am drawn to them as subjects for history.'[10] *Dunera* offered the chance to keep exploring topics that had interested him for decades. To what extent was religion important to the internees? In what ways did the men come to mix history and myth in telling their stories? One of Ken's first publications on the subject has the title 'The *Dunera* Boys in History and Memory.' The title tells of another question that interested him. Who coined the phrase '*Dunera* boys,' and when? He was always alert to etymology and idiom.

Ken used a simple gauge to measure the merit of new writing, including his own: does the piece tell us something we don't know? As a *Dunera* historian, he knew he wanted to go further than Benzion Patkin and Cyril Pearl had in their books on the subject and explore the lives of the men before and after internment.[11] What did they do with their freedom? Answering that helped him better to understand the stories of their incarceration. Ken was careful to use the plural 'stories' – there was no single tale to represent the lives of 2000 individuals.

He hoped that his *Dunera* writing might stimulate fresh thought about similarities and differences between the *Dunera* internees and contemporary refugees and asylum seekers. Many *Dunera* men lived long enough to see the *Tampa*, a Norwegian ship, sail into Australian waters in 2001. Its crew rescued Hazara Afghans from a stricken vessel, and in the process waded into a political quagmire. The Afghans eventually were sent to Nauru, the first of many asylum seekers and refugees to be subject to Australia's 'Pacific Solution.'[12] Why, Ken wondered, did some *Dunera* boys reject comparisons between themselves and Asian and Middle Eastern asylum seekers? According to these *Dunera* men, the matter of intent undermines any possible comparisons. They believe that contemporary refugees and asylum seekers have a choice about emigration, whereas they never intended to come to

Australia but were sent anyway, deported in the manner of convicts. Ken knew the argument, but didn't use it. It favours semantics over humanity, and he was a humane scholar. 'The questions we ask about the past always depend on where we're standing in the present', he told an audience at the State Library of Victoria.[13] Australian guards treated the *Dunera* internees with such warmth and compassion that stories of their kindness fill *Dunera* memory still. Would the same happen today, Ken asked another audience.[14] He wanted his study to lead Australians to think on their society, then and now.

Ken began to publish and talk publicly about *Dunera* in 2010, once he had a couple of years of dedicated research behind him. The themes that most exercised him are evident. Musings about the *Dunera* internees as boat people recur. He explores the ways in which *Dunera* children, more than most children, adopted their parents' values and preoccupations. He recounts popular *Dunera* tales, but with the facts teased from the fiction. Of the *Dunera* men Ken knew, most married out of Judaism. What did that tell us, wondered the historian of religion. The question was for his audiences and himself.

These talks and papers, and the enormous research archive Ken amassed, which he kept in filing cabinets by his desk, give a glimpse of the book he planned. In his archive are primary documents, newspaper clippings, interview transcripts, and reams of email correspondence with *Dunera* families. Scattered throughout are notes in his inimitable scrawl, reminders of ideas and details. What did this *Dunera* internee have in common with others? With whom was he close? Why does his story matter?

Physical frailty changed Ken's plans for the book. Though he faced his incapacities with remarkable dignity, and made no fuss, inevitably it troubled him when his body began to fail his mind. For a man who delighted in words and found pleasure in arranging them into elegant, thoughtful prose, it was hard to accept that typing had become a stiff challenge. 'I used to be able to touch type', he rued more than once. It took time to accept that he needed help to finish his *Dunera* project, and more time again to adjust to the realities of collaboration. Though always a collegial scholar and willing editor of the work of others, he preferred to write on his own, as people who write well often do. And yet adjust he did: in his eighties, he changed the habits of a lifetime. When the physical act of writing, by pencil or keyboard, became too much, he worked at shaping the words written by Jay Winter and me, the two of us having joined his *Dunera* project. He ensured that our sentences were accurate and expressed something of what he wanted to say about the men he knew. He had an astonishing ability to remember tiny details of people's lives. Lengthy passages were read aloud to Ken, who held the words in his head while he added, deleted and rearranged to improve rhythm and clarity. He could edit without looking at a page.

Though Ken never warmed to the idea of collective writing, he did enjoy its social aspect. He was pleased to share the topic that had interested him for so long. He delighted in the help and companionship of his old friend Jay, and that of a new friend and colleague, Carol Bunyan. Mutual interests in the *Dunera* brought them together. It was my privilege to be the other member of this collective.

Volume 1 of *Dunera Lives* was published in July 2018, seven months after Ken's death. He saw the first proofs shortly before he died, and was happy. 'Youse done good', he said to Jay, Carol and me. Was it the book he would have written on his own? Not quite. The concessions that collective work demands meant that some of Ken's ideas did not get as much space as he would have wished. For instance, the book dwells on the refugee's lot, but not on the idea of the *Dunera* internees as wartime boat people. Accommodation was the price Ken paid for a complete manuscript. It was a mighty step for a proud scholar to take.

The second volume of *Dunera Lives* was completed after Ken's death. Several chapters are the work of Bill Gammage, who joined the collective after Ken died. Ken would have smiled at the involvement of his old mate. They were friends and supporters of each other's work from 1963, when they met at the Australian National University. Bill, Jay, Carol and I were in firm agreement that the cover of volume 2 should name Ken first, because it is his book. He set its direction and wrote four of the chapters. He knew personally several of the men it discusses, some of whom came from the same scholarly community as he did. They shared friends and interests, politics and causes. *Dunera Lives* is not about Ken – he saw to that – but the two volumes do answer some questions about his life. They are books for the many, and for his grandchildren.

Endnotes

1   Email from Steve Dyer to author, 25 January 2017.

2   Email from Nicholas Nazari to author, 25 February 2019.

3   Ken Inglis, 'The *Dunera* Boys in History and Memory', *Australian Jewish Historical Society Journal*, XXI: 3, 2013, p. 287.

4   Author interview with Inglis, 21 October 2016.

5   K Inglis, 'From Berlin to the Bush', *The Monthly*, August 2010.

6   K. S. Inglis, 'The Australian Catholic Community' in Henry Mayer (ed.), *Catholics and the Free Society: An Australian Symposium*, (Melbourne: Cheshire, 1961).

7   Author interview.

8   Author interview.

9   Author interview.

10   Inglis, 'The *Dunera* Boys in History and Memory', p. 287.

11   B Patkin, *The Dunera Internees*, (Stanmore: Cassell Australia, 1979); C Pearl, *The Dunera Scandal: Deported by Mistake*, (London: Angus & Robertson, 1983).

12   Ken Inglis talk, State Library of Victoria, 14 April 2011.

13   Inglis talk, State Library of Victoria.

14   Inglis, 'The *Dunera* Boys in History and Memory', p. 305.

Chapter 22

KEN INGLIS AND THE LANGUAGE OF WONDERING

Jay Winter

The subtlety of Ken Inglis's writing arises in part from the rhetorical posture of his prose. Leaning back, as it were, he approaches a subject or a problem with his sympathetic gaze, offers relevant evidence and a few remarks, and then says, 'I wonder.' What could be more disarming than that? Not only is he inviting, even demanding, that the reader enter into a conversation with him, he is also abjuring the authoritative authorial voice, pronouncing the truth as he sees it while recognising that history is more often about truths than about truth, about uncertainties and puzzles and those matters impossible to know for sure. If he had written his life story, the title could have been the two simple words 'I wonder.'

And what a wonderer he was. His brilliant strategy of interrogating both the object of study and his own subject position appears starkly in his first major work, *The Stuart Case*, published in 1961. I shall say more about the style in which the book is written, but consider the ultimate question of this whodunnit.[1] Was Max Stuart guilty of the rape and murder of nine-year-old Mary Hattam? The answer Inglis gives is cautious but clear. Probably; on balance, yes. But justice requires more, especially when capital punishment is at stake, and here Inglis is unequivocal. No Aboriginal man in South Australia in 1958 charged with committing the rape and murder of a nine-year-old white girl could get fair treatment from the police and a fair trial, or rather a trial sufficiently fair to determine the guilt or innocence of the accused without the prism of race refracting everything and everyone in the story.

In the second edition of the book, published in 2002, he reflects (once more with Inglisian modesty) that 'a properly informed jury' would have had reasonable doubt about Stuart's guilt. Thus, his conclusion is that 'the case warranted the Scottish verdict "not proven,"' a wonderfully ambiguous legalism: guilty but freed. What made 'proven' impossible in South Australia in 1959 was insidious and ubiquitous racial prejudice, a fog of distortion working so subtly that it had to enter into deliberations about both guilt and punishment.[2]

The entire case turned on language. After Max Stuart was found guilty, an expert on the Arrernte language stated that he could not have made the statements the police said he made voluntarily, because the wording and syntax were foreign to him and to all those who spoke his language. Without the confession, there was only circumstantial evidence that Stuart had committed the crime. In addition, Stuart had been denied the right to address the court with a personal statement. Thus, the matter of language made it impossible to be sure that Stuart was guilty of the crime and to send him to the gallows. After all the controversy, after a royal commission, after heated and protracted political debate, doubts about the words Stuart was said to have spoken to his police interrogators saved his life.

On the topic of Stuart's confession, Inglis once more shows us how to write with ambiguity and moral integrity at one and the same time. He goes through all four elements of Stuart's interrogation: first he said he didn't do it, but had seen a white man kill the girl; then he said he couldn't recall; then he admitted to being so drunk he couldn't have done it; and then, finally, he offered a full confession. This sequence, Inglis writes, shows the tendency of Aboriginal people to 'give verbal assent to whatever whites tell them.' Then comes Inglis the wonderer: 'I wondered,' he writes, 'what Max Stuart would say about that.'[3]

We all wonder, and then in May 2002 Inglis had a chance to ask Stuart directly if he might wonder about it too. 'Yeah, he would talk to me,' writes Ken. 'Not Saturday, when he would be out roo-shootin'.'[4] Reflecting on their conversation, Inglis described Stuart as a 'white haired, white-bearded, pot-bellied old man [who] needed only a red gown and hood to be the Father Christmas who had handed out presents to the children of Santa Teresa.' Then comes this gem, identified as an aside by parentheses. '(Not quite your conventional Father Christmas: between the Ho Ho Hos he had taken a bottle of rum out of a pocket and after several swigs had told the children to fuck off.)' When Inglis turned to Stuart and asked him whether he was looking for a pardon, Stuart answered 'yes,' and 'as long as I am alive, I will say I didn't do it.' The cops had 'bashed' the confession out of him.[5]

When they parted, Stuart asked, half-seriously, why he, Ken Inglis, shouldn't write his, Max Stuart's, life? Indeed that is what Inglis did, by telling the story of the crime, the trial, the appeal and ultimately Stuart's rehabilitation and role as an elder of his people. Here is a classic case of justice and injustice braided together. When, after the meeting with Stuart, Ken's companion on the visit, historian James

Warden, picked Ken up to take him to his plane, Warden opined that there would be no exoneration; the story 'might have no ending, like the Todd River in the desert, it just ran out.' And yet Ken's view was different. He felt he had been in the presence of someone 'who had achieved some kind of redemption.'[6] Stuart's early life, drowning in drink, had dried up; in Yatala prison and after, he had remade himself, and self-fashioning after a death sentence for murder is a rare achievement for anyone, whatever the colour of his skin.

Self-fashioning is a powerful subject, prominent in Ken Inglis's writing. He wrote about it well before Stephen Greenblatt turned it into everybody's subject, though Inglis, like Greenblatt, is a historian with English language and literature in his bones. Consider but one example of the way he drew us into his own life in order to draw us into the lives of others, in his book on Australian war memorials, *Sacred Places: War Memorials in the Australian Landscape*, first published to considerable acclaim in 1998. It is a profound book on the self-fashioning of the Australian nation in the shadow of the First World War.

Just as in *The Stuart Case*, Inglis starts his book with the *eikon* and the *topos*, the trace and the place. And once again, we benefit from the point of view of an insider, someone who has seen and has used his own feet and has thought about these events within his own lifetime, and not only within the life of his society. Here is the seemingly effortless prose introducing us to Ken Inglis's childhood while introducing us to the Shrine of Remembrance while introducing us to the subject of war memorials themselves:

> The Shrine of Remembrance was a new and mysterious presence in the Melbourne of my childhood. Rising from a mound in the Domain, just south of the city, the building proclaimed itself the most important object in the landscape. The king's son, the Duke

of Gloucester, dedicated the Shrine on 11 November, Armistice Day, 1934, when I was five, at a ceremony timed to coincide with the city's centenary celebrations.

So much for time and place; now for meaning. Once again the interrogative poses questions that seem simple on the surface but are the profound subject of the entire book:

> What was a Shrine? In remembrance of what? The makers, sensing that elucidation was necessary, had answers carved into the grey granite wall. Every visitor, everybody who passed along the grand boulevard of St Kilda Road, was addressed by a solemn command.
>
> 'LET ALL MEN KNOW THAT THIS IS HOLY GROUND
>
> THIS SHRINE ESTABLISHED IN THE HEARTS OF MEN AS ON THE SOLID EARTH COMMEMORATES A PEOPLE'S FORTITUDE AND SACRIFICE
>
> YE THAT COME AFTER GIVE REMEMBRANCE.'
>
> The archaic language signalled tradition. What tradition?

What tradition indeed? A self-fashioning one is the answer, unfolded and described scrupulously in all 800 pages of this book. Then, after a few words about Greek structures and Christian words, we return to the world of Ken Inglis, the child:

> My own earliest memory of the Shrine connects it with the occult. I learned with wonder that on Armistice Day every year, at the eleventh hour of the eleventh day of the eleventh month, a ray of light would fall on the stone of Remembrance. Had some capricious supernatural power chosen to stop the war at exactly that moment?[7]

'I learned with wonder.' The wonderer started wondering, and kept doing so for the rest of his life.

In this inevitably brief account of Inglisian English, I must make room for Inglis the critic. I long for those old days when my pigeonhole at the Research School of Social Sciences in Canberra was stuffed with a draft chapter or essay miraculously turned into English by Ken's amputation of useless words and word grafts of better ones than those I had chosen. How many of us have benefited from the same surgical transformation? Hence my personal pleasure in drawing attention to perhaps the most amusing and most penetrating exposé of the weakness of historians' prose, in Ken's essay 'Historians and Language,' written in 1990. In it he cites a sociologist's advice that we historians run our sentences through a computer program called 'Grammatik III,' which searches for grammatical errors. 'I wonder what other historians think of using such aids,' he asks innocently.[8]

If only historians could follow his commonsense rules, then such computer-aided tools would be unnecessary. How can we avoid the 'vices' of writing poorly? Among his answers are these:

> 1. Be alert to the history of words that define periods or styles or movements, because we and our readers can benefit from knowing whether or not our subjects used those words.

> 2. Don't attribute the knowledge or use of words to people who didn't have them.[9]

Evidently, Ken Inglis took the linguistic turn before it became fashionable to do so, and he had the powerful armoury of the *Australian National Dictionary* to help him do so. If only Ken Inglis, armed with the *AND*, had been at a famous meeting in London in 1917 where Ada Holman and her husband, the premier of New South Wales, were pressed by the prime minister, Lloyd George, to explain the meaning of the word 'wowser.' Holman tried 'puritan,' 'killjoy,' 'Tartuffe,' but all were rejected as imprecise. Since no satisfactory synonym was accepted, another member of the group, Sir Rufus Isaacs, offered to pay for a prize in the *Daily Mail* 'for the best definition.' Inglis would have won the prize hands-down, though he would have had to wait until he was born twelve years later to receive it.

Inglis the interrogator, the master of the interrogatory, is known to us all. His taste for paradox and nuance remained as refined as it had been in 1947 when he began his study of history and literature at the University of Melbourne. It is hardly surprising that I give pride of place to the fact that he was the first to study war memorials in a fully comparative framework, and as such his pioneering work has indeed launched an entire field.

In 1992 he spoke to the very first international conference on the subject of war memorials in Les Invalides in Paris. He ended his remarks meditating on Saddam Hussein's two monuments, one to the unknown soldier and the other, the Victory Arch, commemorating those who died in the war with Iran between 1980 and 1988. He then posed a typically Inglisian question: is it, he asked, rational that a monument that should never have been put up should for that reason not be pulled down? As usual Inglis was prescient. In February 2007, the Iraqi government of Nouri al-Maliki started dismantling it. The American ambassador objected, and there it stands, today, resplendent with painful historical messages that later historians will have to try to address. When they do, they will be following in Ken Inglis's footsteps.

I recall well the frisson we shared at the opening of that 1992 conference when, in the middle of Ken's opening paper, a nurse guided a patient on a bed, a very real military invalid, through our meeting room to further treatment. Remembering war and those who suffer in it is everybody's business. This incident, hardly surprising in a state hospital and monument, where Napoleon lies in state, added to our sense of the moment when Ken announced that over decades, as a lonely historian of war memorials, he felt as if he had been practising an art reserved for consenting adults in private. Now in Paris is the time, Ken said, for a coming-out party.

In a way, the colloquium in Melbourne in 2016 at which I read this essay was a collective vote of gratitude for all those moments when Ken Inglis showed us the way to wonder aloud and in print, and presented for all to see the virtues of his curiosity, his humility, his artisan's careful attention to detail, his novelist's willingness to prefer prolonged interrogation to instant publication, and his humane restraint in the face of the temptation to act as an oracle, an author of those once-and-for-all statements, those ersatz authoritative utterances that fly in the face of what we all know to be true but rarely admit – that certainty and finality are the ultimate illusions of our profession. I think this is the longest sentence I have ever written, and for that verbosity, I ask Ken's forgiveness, and simply say to him, with Bob Hope, thanks, Ken, for the memories and the histories.

Endnotes

1   KS Inglis, *The Stuart Case*, Melbourne University Press, Carlton, 1961.

2   KS Inglis, *The Stuart Case*, new edn, Black Inc., Melbourne, 2002.

3   Inglis, *The Stuart Case*, new edn, p. 392.

4   Inglis, *The Stuart Case*, new edn, p. 392.

5   Inglis, *The Stuart Case*, new edn, p. 395.

6   Inglis, *The Stuart Case*, new edn, p. 398.

7   KS Inglis (assisted by J Brazier), *Sacred Places: War Memorials in the Australian Landscape*, 3rd edn, Melbourne University Press, Carlton, 2008, pp. 1–2.

8   KS Inglis, 'Historians and Language,' *Australian Historical Association Bulletin*, nos. 64–65, October–December 1990, p. 6.

9   Inglis, 'Historians and Language,' p. 10.

KEN INGLIS'S
WRITTEN WORKS

Following the lead of Craig Wilcox in *Observing Australia* (1999), we have chosen to list Ken Inglis's published works in chronological order to give an insight into the development of his interests.

The bibliography is testament to his productivity over seventy-five years of scholarly endeavour, yet even then we believe it may be only 85 to 90 per cent complete. It is hard to track his journalism, for instance, especially in the 1940s, 50s and 60s. Some articles went unattributed, or were written under a pseudonym: Stanley Kaye, John Kemp, Rev. TJ Ransome, James Reddup, John Rudolf and K. Stanley are those of which we are aware. We know that Inglis wrote for *The Age* literary supplement from 1951 to 1953, and that he continued to write for the newspaper while studying in Oxford – in 1954 he was Edinburgh Festival correspondent for the paper – but many of these articles are untraced.

Should any readers know of Inglis publications not included here, we would be delighted to hear from them.

'M.U.M. On Sale Next Week,' *Farrago*, 3 August 1949.
'Elizabethan Playwrights,' *The Age*, 16 July 1949.
'Around the Shop' and 'The Vice Chancellor' [both articles co-authored with M Groves], *Melbourne University Magazine*, 1950.
'Korea Since 1945,' *Australia's Neighbours*, 3, 1950.
'Moral Builder – Tommy Handley and ITMA,' *The Age*, 4 February 1950.
'And Another From Mr Inglis,' *Farrago*, 12 July 1950.
'The Fascinating Bee,' *The Age*, 28 July 1951. [Written under the pseudonym TJR (Rev. TJ Ransome).]

'Stalemate in Korea,' *Australia's Neighbours*, 17, 1952.

Unattributed and untitled article on pipe-smoking championship, *The Port Phillip Gazette*, 1, 2, 1952-53.

'Our Pastoral History,' *The Age*, 29 November 1952.

'Mau Mau: A Response to British Injustice?,' *Voice*, 3, 8, 1954.

'A Diaghilev Triumph at Edinburgh Festival,' *The Age*, 25 September 1954.
[Article was written by a 'Special Correspondent,' believed to be Inglis.]

'Salvation by Rhetoric,' *Voice*, 4, 7, 1955.

'Solo,' *The Port Phillip Gazette*, 2, 2, 1955. [Written under the pseudonym 'Stanley Kaye'.]

'The Way of the Egghead,' *Voice*, 4, 3, 1955.

Untitled article on *The Champion* comic book, *The Port Phillip Gazette*, 2, 2, 1955.

'Professor Arndt and the Labour Party' [co-authored with RH Wallace], *The Australian Quarterly*, XXVIII, 4, 1956.

'The Diplomacy of Dr Fisher,' *Voice*, 5, 6, 1956.

'Churches and Working Classes in Nineteenth-century England,' *Historical Studies Australia and New Zealand*, 8, 29, 1957.

'Broadcasting in Australia' [review of *Broadcasting in Australia* by Ian K. Mackay], *Meanjin Quarterly*, XVI, 4, 1957.

'Catholic Historiography in Australia,' *Historical Studies Australia and New Zealand*, 8, 31, 1958.

'Churchgoing in Australia,' *Current Affairs Bulletin*, 22, 4, 1958.

'English Nonconformity and Social Reform, 1880-1900,' *Past and Present*, 13, 1958.

Hospital and Community: A History of the Royal Melbourne Hospital, Melbourne University Press, Melbourne, 1958.

'Notes in Indonesia,' *Varsity* [Adelaide University magazine], 1958.

'The Labour Church Movement,' *International Review of Social History*, III, 3, 1958.

'Clerical Errors,' *Nation*, 1, 26 September 1958.

'Playford and DLP,' *Nation*, 1, 26 September 1958. [Author: 'Our Adelaide Correspondent.']

'Half-an-Hour Behind,' *Nation*, 2, 11 October 1958.

'Pensions for Self-Helpers,' *Nation*, 2, 11 October 1958. [Author: 'Our Adelaide Correspondent.']

'Waiting for Doctor Graham,' *Nation*, 2, 11 October 1958. [Written under the pseudonym K Stanley.]

'Opening Gambits,' *Nation*, 3, 25 October 1958. [Author: 'Our Adelaide Correspondent.']

'Catholic Voters at the Crossroads,' *Nation*, 4, 8 November 1958.

'Two Adelaide Occasions,' *Nation*, 4, 8 November 1958. [Author: 'Our Adelaide Correspondent.']

'Adelaide's Version of the Press War,' *Nation*, 5, 22 November 1958.

'For Growing Heirs,' *Nation*, 6, 6 December 1958. [Author: 'Our Adelaide Correspondent.']

'An Edinburgh in the South?,' *Nation*, 7, 20 December 1958. [Author: 'Our Adelaide Correspondent.']

'Replenishing the Flocks,' *Nation*, 7, 20 December 1958.

'Billy Graham in Australia,' *Current Affairs Bulletin*, 24, 4, 1959.
Reprinted in KS Inglis (ed. C Wilcox), *Observing Australia: 1959 to 1999*, Melbourne University Press, Carlton, 1999.

Why Not Hang Rupert Stuart?: Some Questions About a Murder, Adelaide, 1959.

'Scheming for Health,' *Nation*, 10, 31 January 1959.

'Deep Sleep in Adelaide,' *Nation*, 11, 14 February 1959. [Author: 'Our Adelaide Correspondent.']

'Playford's Genteel Gambit,' *Nation*, 12, 28 February 1959. [Author: 'Our Adelaide Correspondent.']

'Millennial Churchmen,' *Nation*, 13, 14 March 1959. [Written under the pseudonym K Stanley.]

'Bar and Ballot Box,' *Nation*, 14, 28 March 1959. [Author: 'Our Adelaide Correspondent.']

'Sydney, Meet Mr Graham,' *Nation*, 15, 11 April 1959.

'Aerial Warfare in SA,' *Nation*, 16, 25 April 1959. [Author: 'Our Adelaide Correspondent.']

'Saints and Scholars,' *Nation*, 18, 23 May 1959.

'Invisible CAB Men,' *Nation*, 20, 20 June 1959.

'Careful! There's *Odium Theologicum* in that Plate of Weet-Bix,' *Nation*, 21, 4 July 1959. [Written under the pseudonym John Kemp.]

'Mr Boydell Finds a Champion,' *Nation*, 21, 4 July 1959. [Author: 'Our Adelaide Correspondent.']

'The Hanging of a Man,' *Nation*, 22, 18 July 1959.
Reprinted under the title 'The Stuart Case' in KS Inglis (ed. C Wilcox), *Observing Australia: 1959 to 1999*, Melbourne University Press, Carlton, 1999.

'The Spread of Marmite,' *Nation*, 22, 18 July 1959. [Written under the pseudonym John Kemp.]

'Playford's Sense of Justice,' *Nation*, 23, 1 August 1959.

'Bolte Upright, Stark Staring,' *Nation*, 24, 15 August 1959.

'Man Who Walked Out,' *Nation*, 25, 29 August 1959. [Written by Anon. Inglis likely author or co-author.]

'Where the Stuart Case Stands,' *Nation*, 25, 29 August 1959. [Author: 'Our Adelaide Correspondent.']

'The Cherry Orchardist,' *Nation*, 26, 12 September 1959. [Signed Anon, but Inglis the author.]

'They're a Weird Mob,' *Nation*, 26, 12 September 1959.

'Why Travers Followed Shand,' *Nation*, 27, 26 September 1959.

'Stuart for the Box,' *Nation*, 28, 10 October 1959. [Written by Anon. Inglis likely author or co-author.]

'The Tracks to Ceduna,' *Nation*, 29, 24 October 1959.

'Let Them Go Hang,' *Nation*, 31, 21 November 1959. [Author: 'Our Adelaide Correspondent.']

'Ceduna Fadeout,' *Nation*, 33, 19 December 1959.

'Patterns of Religious Worship in 1851,' *The Journal of Ecclesiastical History*, XI, I, 1960.

Untitled [review of *The Ten Hours Parson* by JC Gill], *Victorian Studies*, 3, 4, 1960.

'Jehovah's Rampant Witnesses,' *Nation*, 35, 16 January 1960. [Written under the pseudonym John Kemp.]

'It's that Police-man Again,' *Nation*, 35, 16 January 1960.

'Rohan Rivett in the Dock,' *Nation*, 35, 16 January 1960. [Written by Anon. Inglis may have been the author.]

'Two Viewers,' *Nation*, 39, 12 March 1960. [Written under the pseudonym John Kemp.]

'In Moses' Promised Land,' *Nation*, 40, 26 March 1960.

'Hot Night at Town Hall,' *Nation*, 41, 9 April 1960.

'Anzac: the Substitute Religion,' *Nation*, 42, 23 April 1960. [Written under the pseudonym John Kemp.]
    Reprinted in KS Inglis (ed. C Wilcox), *Observing Australia: 1959 to 1999*, Melbourne University Press, Carlton, 1999.

'Politics, Bench, Journalism,' *Nation*, 42, 23 April 1960. [Author: 'Our Adelaide Correspondent.' Inglis was Adelaide correspondent, but this piece is not in his style.]

'Rustle of Silks,' *Nation*, 44, 21 May 1960. [Author: 'Our Adelaide Correspondent.']

'Stuart's Last Echo,' *Nation*, 46, 18 June 1960.

'Covering of the Sin,' *Nation*, 47, 2 July 1960.

'Evangelism Today,' *Nation*, 48, 16 July 1960.

'The Cross of Lorraine,' *Nation*, 48, 16 July 1960.

'Final Edition,' *Nation*, 49, 30 July 1960.

'Horses and Deriders,' *Nation*, 49, 30 July 1960. [Written under the pseudonym John Kemp.]

'Reflections in a Mirror,' *Nation*, 50, 13 August 1960.

'Catholic Press Month,' *Nation*, 51, 27 August 1960.

'Cancelling Out,' *Nation*, 55, 22 October 1960.

'O'Halloran's Heirs,' *Nation*, 57, 19 November 1960. [Author: 'Our Adelaide Correspondent.']

'Cauldron Bubble,' *Nation*, 58, 3 December 1960.

'The Long Torpor,' *Nation*, 59, 17 December 1960. [Written under the pseudonym John Kemp.]

'The Australian Catholic Community' in H Mayer (ed.), *Catholics and the Free Society: An Australian Symposium*, FW Cheshire, Melbourne, 1961.

The Stuart Case, Melbourne University Press, Melbourne, 1961.
New edition published by Black Inc., Melbourne, 2002.

'A Year of Dailies,' *Nation*, 60, 14 January 1961.

'The Meek People,' *Nation*, 62, 11 February 1961.

'Dissenting Laity,' *Nation*, 63, 25 February 1961.

'The Mirror's Reflection,' *Nation*, 66, 8 April 1961.

'In the Press,' *Nation*, 67, 22 April 1961.

'A Sheltered Existence,' *Nation*, 79, 7 October 1961. [Author: 'An American Correspondent.']

'Lord, Who is My Neighbour?,' *Nation*, 82, 18 November 1961. [Written under the pseudonym James Reddup.]

'Brisbane Fred in the Wild West,' *Nation*, 83, 2 December 1961. [Written under the pseudonym James Reddup.]

'The Daily Papers' in P Coleman (ed.), *Australian Civilization*, FW Cheshire, Melbourne, 1962.

Churches and the Working Classes in Victorian England, Routledge and Kegan Paul, London, 1963.

'The Daily Diet,' *Prospect*, 6, 2, 1963.

'Judgment at Armidale,' *Nation*, 112, 9 February 1963.

'Screen on Bidault,' *Nation*, 115, 23 March 1963.

'Kathleen Fitzpatrick: A Tribute,' *Melbourne Historical Journal*, 4, 1964.

'The Press in Australia' [review of *The Press in Australia* by H Mayer], *The Australian Journal of Politics and History*, 10, 2, 1964.

'The Little Boy From Manly Grows Up,' *The Age*, 24 April 1964. [Also in *Sydney Morning Herald.*]

Reprinted in G Hutton and L Tanner (eds), *125 Years of Age*, Thomas Nelson, Melbourne, 1979.

Reprinted in J Lack (ed.), *Anzac Remembered: Selected Writings of KS Inglis*, University of Melbourne History Department, Melbourne, 1998.

'The One Day Will Endure,' *The Age*, 25 April 1964. [Also in *Sydney Morning Herald.*]

Reprinted in J Lack (ed.), *Anzac Remembered: Selected Writings of KS Inglis*, University of Melbourne History Department, Melbourne, 1998.

'Going National,' *Nation*, 144, 16 May 1964. [Written by Anon. It is thought that Inglis was the author.]

'The Homestead Dog,' *Nation*, 145, 30 May 1964.

'Brighter Yet,' *Nation*, 146, 13 June 1964.

'Gospel of St Mark,' *Nation*, 146, 13 June 1964.

'Snowballing in Canberra,' *Nation*, 148, 11 July 1964.

'Enter the "Australian",' *Nation*, 149, 25 July 1964.

'Down the Aisle,' *Nation*, 154, 3 October 1964.

'Looking Back in Wisdom at the Gallipoli Failure,' *Canberra Times*, 7 November 1964.

'The Great Conscription Row,' *Canberra Times*, 21 November 1964.

'The Last Man and the Last Shilling,' *Canberra Times*, 23 November 1964.

'Why Did Hughes Choose a Referendum in 1916?,' *Canberra Times*, 24 November 1964.

'Archbishop Mannix; The Turbulent Priest,' *Canberra Times*, 25 November 1964.

'Hughes a Contributor to Referendum's Defeat?,' *Canberra Times*, 26 November 1964.

'Moral Division Between Troops and Shirkers,' *Canberra Times*, 27 November 1964.

'Five Months' Baby,' *Nation*, 159, 12 December 1964.

'Anzac and Christian – Two Traditions or One?,' *St Mark's Review*, 42, 1965.

'Religious Behaviour' in AF Davies and S Encel (eds), *Australian Society: A Sociological Introduction*, FW Cheshire, Melbourne, 1965.

Reprinted in S Encel and M Berry (eds), *Selected Readings in Australian Society: An Anthology*, Longman Cheshire, Melbourne, 1987.

'The Anzac Tradition,' *Meanjin Quarterly*, XXIV, 1, 1965.

> Reprinted in CB Christesen (ed.), *On Native Grounds: Australian Writing from Meanjin Quarterly*, Angus & Robertson, Sydney, 1968.

> Reprinted in J Lack (ed.), *Anzac Remembered: Selected Writings of KS Inglis*, University of Melbourne History Department, Melbourne, 1998.

'The Unity of Living and Dead,' *Canberra Times*, 10 March 1965.

'Letter from a Pilgrimage,' *Canberra Times*, 15 April 1965.

'Anzac Diggers see Tobruk and Cheer,' *Canberra Times*, 21 April 1965.

'Why They Came,' *Canberra Times*, 22 April 1965.

'Happy Days Relived by Old Men of Gallipoli,' *Sydney Morning Herald*, 23 April 1965.

'Nasser earns the Anzacs' Admiration,' *Canberra Times*, 23 April 1965.

'Pilgrimage's Climax at Gallipoli Tomorrow,' *Sydney Morning Herald*, 24 April 1965.

'Stepping Ashore Tomorrow on Australia's "Holy Land",' *Canberra Times*, 24 April 1965.

'Anzacs Play to Turkish Rules on Their Return,' *Canberra Times*, 27 April 1965.

'10 000 Miles and Back to Commune with Anzac Dead,' *Canberra Times*, 1 May 1965.

'Not All Tears Were Shed by Women,' *Sydney Morning Herald*, 3 May 1965.

'Diggers in Antiquity,' *Nation*, 170, 29 May 1965.

> Reprinted in KS Inglis (ed. C Wilcox), *Observing Australia: 1959 to 1999*, Melbourne University Press, Carlton, 1999.

'Australians at Worship,' *Canberra Times*, 9 August 1965.

'The Four-Wheeled Christian,' *Canberra Times*, 10 August 1965.

'Three Times as Moral as the US?,' *Canberra Times*, 11 August 1965.

'Funerals of Bad Taste,' *Canberra Times*, 12 August 1965.

'Press Self-Examination an Encouraging Sign' [review of *A Newspaper's Role in Modern Society* by TC Bray, and *The Australian Country Press*], *Canberra Times*, 6 November 1965.

'Poppy Day – The Irony of It,' *Canberra Times*, 13 November 1965.

'Members Exercise Real Powers,' *Canberra Times*, 8 December 1965.

'Language is a Perplexing Impediment,' *Canberra Times*, 9 December 1965.

'A Name, A Flag, An Anthem,' *Canberra Times*, 16 December 1965.

'Remedial English at the Australian National University' [co-authored with WS Ramson], *Vestes*, IX, 4, 1966.

'Return to Gallipoli,' *ANU Historical Journal*, 3, 1966.

> Reprinted in J Lack (ed.), *Anzac Remembered: Selected Writings of KS Inglis*, University of Melbourne History Department, Melbourne, 1998.

'Compassion for Emerging N.G.' [book review of *Parliament of a Thousand Tribes* by O White], *Canberra Times*, 8 January 1966.

'The Digger's Grave,' *Nation*, 188, 19 February 1966.

'Dirty Word,' *Nation*, 191, 2 April 1966.

'The Easter Rising and its Influence in Australian Politics,' *Sydney Morning Herald*, 9 April 1966.

'Anzac Pilgrims: A Self-Portrait,' *Canberra Times*, 25 April 1966. [Also in *Sydney Morning Herald*.]

'Australia Day,' *Historical Studies Australia and New Zealand*, 13, 49, 1967. Reprinted in KS Inglis (ed. C Wilcox), *Observing Australia: 1959 to 1999*, Melbourne University Press, Carlton, 1999.

'Conscription in Peace and War, 1911-1945,' *Teaching History*, 1, 2, 1967. Reprinted in R Forward and B Reece (eds), *Conscription in Australia*, University of Queensland Press, St Lucia, 1968.

'Mark Twain and the Gilded Age: Some Suggestions for Comparative Study,' *Australian Economic History Review*, VII, 1, 1967.

The Study of History in Papua and New Guinea, Inaugural Professorial Lecture, University of Papua and New Guinea, Port Moresby, 1967.

'University in a Hurry,' *Overland*, 36, 1967.

'Twilight Birth,' *Nation*, 211, 28 January 1967.

'Two Papuans Led the March,' *Canberra Times*, 2 May 1967.

'Scrimping at the University of P and NG,' *Canberra Times*, 23 February 1968. [Extract from a talk given to the Papua and New Guinea Society of Victoria, February 1968.]

'Anne Fraser' [co-authored with M Clark], *ANU Historical Journal*, 5, 1968.

'Island Without History?,' *New Guinea*, 2, 4, 1968.

'The University – Progress and Prospects,' *UPNG News: Newsletter of the University of Papua and New Guinea*, 7, 1968. [Publication of a talk given to the Papua and New Guinea Society of Victoria, February 1968.]

'Early Courtship,' *Nation*, 251, 31 August 1968.

'War, Race and Loyalty in New Guinea, 1939-1945' in *The History of Melanesia* (Second Waigani Seminar), University of Papua New Guinea/Australian National University, Port Moresby/Canberra, 1969.

C. E. W. Bean, Australian Historian, The John Murtagh Macrossan Lecture 24 June 1969, University of Queensland Press, St Lucia, 1970. Reprinted in J Lack (ed.), *Anzac Remembered: Selected Writings of KS Inglis*, University of Melbourne History Department, Melbourne, 1998.

'The Australians at Gallipoli,' *Australian Journal of Science*, 32, 9, 1970.
Reprinted in two parts:
'The Australians at Gallipoli – I,' *Historical Studies*, 14, 54, 1970.
'The Australians at Gallipoli – II,' *Historical Studies*, 14, 55, 1970.

Untitled [reviews of *The Victorian Church* by O Chadwick and *The Victorian Church in Decline* by PT Marsh], *Victorian Studies*, XIV, 3, 1971.

'Returned Soldiers in Australia, 1918-1939' in *Collected Seminar Papers on the Dominions Between the Wars*, Institute of Commonwealth Studies, London, 1971.

Untitled [review of *Australia in New Guinea* by LP Mair], *Journal of Commonwealth Political Studies*, X, 2, 1972.

[Speech given at the eighth graduation ceremony, University of Papua and New Guinea, July 1973], in *UPNG News: Newsletter of the University of Papua and New Guinea*, 34, 1973.

Australian Colonists: An Exploration of Social History 1788-1870, Melbourne University Press, Melbourne, 1974. [Reprinted in paperback, 1993.]

John Moresby and Port Moresby: A Centenary View [co-authored with ND Oram], EC Awo, Port Moresby, 1974.

Papua New Guinea: Naming a Nation, The Academy of the Social Sciences in Australia Annual Lecture 1974, The Academy of the Social Sciences in Australia, Canberra, 1974.
Reprinted in *New Guinea*, 9, 4, 1975.

'Rich Universities in a Poor World,' *UPNG News: Newsletter of the University of Papua New Guinea*, 36, 1974. [Text of a paper delivered at the University of Adelaide, August 1974.]

'The Future of Universities in Papua New Guinea' in J Brammall and RJ May (eds), *Education in Melanesia* (Eighth Waigani Seminar), Australian National University/University of Papua New Guinea, Canberra/Port Moresby, 1975.

Australian Politics: A New Ball Game? Eighteen Contributions on the Concept of Politics [editor], Australasian Political Studies Association, Sydney, 1976.

'Through the Looking Glass,' *Politics*, XI, 1, 1976.

'Accas and Ockers: Australia's New Dictionaries,' *Meanjin*, 36, 1, 1977.

'Australia 1788-1988: A Note on Proposed Approaches,' *Australian Historical Association Bulletin*, 10, 1977.

'Bean, Charles Edwin Woodrow' in B Nairn and G Serle (eds), *Australian Dictionary of Biography*, Volume 7, Melbourne University Press, Melbourne, 1979.

'Imperial Cricket: Test Matches Between Australia and England 1877–1900,' in R Cashman and M McKernan (eds), *Sport in History: The Making of Modern Sporting History*, University of Queensland Press, St Lucia, 1979.

'Institutional Planning' in *Spring Seminar 1979*, [Libyan] Higher Institute of Mechanical and Electrical Engineering, Hoon [Hun], Libya, 1979.

Untitled [review of *A Dictionary of Australian Colloquialisms* by GA Wilkes], *Australian Literary Studies*, 9, 1, 1979.

'Education on the Frontier: The First Ten Years of the University of Papua New Guinea' in S Murray-Smith (ed.), *Melbourne Studies in Education 1980*, Melbourne University Press, Melbourne, 1980.

'The ABC and Australian Society, 1932-1982,' The 1979 Eldershaw Memorial Lecture, *Tasmanian Historical Research Association Papers and Proceedings*, 27, 1, 1980.

'The Green Report and the ABC' in D Turbayne (ed.), *The Media and Politics in Australia*, University of Tasmania, Hobart, 1980.

'The Imperial Connection: Telegraphic Communication between England and Australia, 1872-1902' in AF Madden and WH Morris-Jones (eds), *Australia and Britain: Studies in a Changing Relationship*, Sydney University Press, Sydney, 1980.

'Introduction' to CEW Bean, *The Story of Anzac: From the Outbreak of War to the End of the First Phase of the Gallipoli Campaign, May 4, 1915*, [Reprint of volume I of *The Official History of Australia in the War of 1914-1918*], University of Queensland Press, St Lucia, 1981.

'Young Australia 1870-1900: The Idea and the Reality' in G Featherstone (ed.), *The Colonial Child*, Royal Historical Society of Victoria, Melbourne, 1981.

'Inside the ABC,' *Quadrant*, XXVII, 6, 1983.

'Teaching Australian History at Harvard,' *Overland*, 92, 1983.

'The ABC as History,' 1983 Colin Simpson Memorial Lecture, *Australian Author*, May 1983.

Reprinted in KS Inglis (ed. C Wilcox), *Observing Australia: 1959 to 1999*, Melbourne University Press, Carlton, 1999.

This is the ABC: The Australian Broadcasting Commission, 1932-1983, Melbourne University Press, Melbourne, 1983.

Second edition published by Black Inc., Melbourne, 2006.

Untitled [review of *Inventing Australia* by R White], *The Journal of Imperial and Commonwealth History*, XI, 3, 1983.

'War Memorials in our Landscape,' *Heritage Australia*, 2, 2, 1983.
> Reprinted in *Australia We Trust: A Selection of the Best Writings from 'Heritage Australia,'* William Collins Pty Ltd, Sydney, 1985.

'Slicing History to Suit All Tastes' [radio broadcast], *Look & Listen*, 1, 5, 1984.

'What now for the old Parliament House?,' *Canberra Times*, 15 February 1984.

'A Sacred Place: The Making of the Australian War Memorial,' *War & Society*, 3, 2, 1985.

'Ceremonies in a Capital Landscape: Scenes in the Making of Canberra,' *Dædalus*, 114, I, 1985.
> Reprinted in SR Graubard (ed.), *Australia: The Daedalus Symposium*, Angus & Robertson, Sydney, 1985.

'Gambling and Culture in Australia' in G Caldwell, B Haig, M Dickerson and L Sylvan (eds), *Gambling in Australia*, Croom Helm, Sydney, 1985.

The Rehearsal: Australians at War in the Sudan, 1885, Rigby, Adelaide, 1985.

'Father Mathew's Statue: The Making of a Monument in Cork' in O MacDonagh and WF Mandle (eds), *Ireland and Irish-Australia: Studies in Cultural and Political History*, Croom Helm, London, 1986.

'A Rip Van Winkle Survey,' *The Wyvern*, Queen's College, University of Melbourne, Melbourne, 1987.

'At War' in A Curthoys, AW Martin and T Rowse (eds), *Australians from 1939* (Volume V of *Australians: A Historical Library*), Fairfax, Syme & Weldon, Sydney, 1987.

'Australia's Bicentennial Year,' in *1987 Britannica Book of the Year*, Encyclopaedia Brittanica, Chicago, 1987.

Australians: A Historical Library [general editor with F Crowley, AD Gilbert and P Spearritt], 11 volumes, Fairfax, Syme & Weldon, Sydney, 1987.

'Memorials of the Great War,' *Australian Cultural History*, 6, 1987.

'Men, Women, and War Memorials: Anzac Australia,' *Dædalus*, 116, 4, 1987.
> Reprinted in JK Conway, SC Bourque, and JW Scott (eds), *Learning about Women: Gender, Politics, and Power*, University of Michigan Press, Ann Arbor, 1989.
> Reprinted in R White and P Russell (eds), *Memories and Dreams: Reflections on Twentieth-Century Australia*, Allen & Unwin, Sydney, 1997.
> Reprinted in J Lack (ed.), *Anzac Remembered: Selected Writings of KS Inglis*, University of Melbourne History Department, Melbourne, 1998.

'Passing Away,' in B Gammage and P Spearritt (eds), *Australians 1938* (Volume IV of *Australians: A Historical Library*), Fairfax, Syme & Weldon, Sydney, 1987.

'Populate or Perish,' *Australian Society*, 6, 7, 1987.

'Press, Radio and Television' in A Curthoys, AW Martin and T Rowse (eds),
    Australians from 1939 (Volume V of *Australians: A Historical Library*), Fairfax,
    Syme & Weldon, Sydney, 1987.

'The Stuart Case Revisited,' *Quadrant*, XXXI, 12, 1987.

Untitled [review of *Exploring Women's Past* edited by P Crawford et al], *The Journal
    of Imperial and Commonwealth History*, XV, 2, 1987.

'1788 to 1988: Visions of Australian History,' *Overland*, 106, 1987.
    Reprinted in KS Inglis (ed. C Wilcox), *Observing Australia: 1959 to 1999*,
    Melbourne University Press, Carlton, 1999.

'Anzac and the Australian Military Tradition,' *Current Affairs Bulletin*, 64, 11, 1988.
    Reprinted in *Revue Internationale d'Histoire Militaire*, 72, 1990.
    Reprinted in J Lack (ed.), *Anzac Remembered: Selected Writings of KS Inglis*,
    University of Melbourne History Department, Melbourne, 1998.

'Eight Million Words of *Nation*,' *Australian Society*, 7, 9, 1988.

'Planning a Bicentennial History of Australia' in G Shaw (ed.), *1988 and All That:
    New Views of Australia's Past*, University of Queensland Press, St Lucia, 1988.
    Reprinted in KS Inglis (ed. C Wilcox), *Observing Australia: 1959 to 1999*,
    Melbourne University Press, Carlton, 1999.

'Remembering Australia, 1788-1988,' *The Historian*, 19, 1988.

'The Term "Australian" in J Jupp (ed.), *The Australian People: An Encyclopedia of the
    Nation, its People and its Origins*, Angus & Robertson, Sydney, 1988.
    Also in G Shaw (ed.), *1988 and All That: New Views of Australia's Past*,
    University of Queensland Press, St Lucia, 1988.

Untitled [piece on Stephen Murray-Smith], *Overland*, 112, 1988.

'War Memorials' in *The Australian Encyclopaedia*, Volume 8, The Australian
    Geographic Society, Sydney, 1988.

'A tall poppy in history field' [obituary for Sir Keith Hancock], *Canberra Times*, 15
    August 1988.

'Four Thuds at 7am,' *Australian Society*, 8, 8, 1989.

'How They Sliced Us Up: Reviews of *Australians: A Historical Library*,' Unpublished
    collection of reviews, compiled by Inglis, Canberra, 1989.

Nation: The Life of an Independent Journal of Opinion [editor], *1958-1972*,
    Melbourne University Press, Melbourne, 1989.
    'Remembering Australians on the Somme, Anzac Day 1988, *Overland*, 115, 1989.
    Reprinted in J Lack (ed.), *Anzac Remembered: Selected Writings of KS Inglis*,
    University of Melbourne History Department, Melbourne, 1998.

'The Time Has Come to Speak for Ourselves,' *Australian Society*, 8, 11, 1989.

'Does it Matter Who Owns the Press, Radio and Television?' in A Gollan (ed.), *Questions for the Nineties*, Left Book Club Co-operative Ltd, Sydney, 1990.

'Historians and Language,' *Australian Historical Association Bulletin*, 64-65, 1990.

'Hugh Stretton's University of Adelaide, 1954-56,' *Journal of the Historical Society of South Australia*, 18, 1990.

'Kapferer on Anzac Day and Australia,' *Social Analysis: Journal of Cultural and Social Practice*, 29, 1990.

'Monuments in the Modern City: The War Memorials of Melbourne and Sydney,' in D Fraser (ed.), *Cities, Class and Communication: Essays in Honour of Asa Briggs*, Harvester Wheatsheaf, Hemel Hempstead, 1990.
Reprinted in J Lack (ed.), *Anzac Remembered: Selected Writings of KS Inglis*, University of Melbourne History Department, Melbourne, 1998.

'Anzac Revisited: Australia, New Zealand and the Anzac Tradition,' in A Seymour and R Nile (eds), *Anzac: Meaning, Memory and Myth*, University of London, London, 1991.

'Australian Historiography of World War I,' *La Grande Guerre: Pays, Histoire, Memoire. Bulletin du Centre de Recherche, Historial de La Grande Guerre*, 4, 1991.

'Charles Manning Hope Clark, 1915-1991,' in *Academy of the Social Sciences in Australia: Annual Report 1991*, The Academy of the Social Sciences in Australia, Canberra, 1991.

'Gallipoli Pilgrimage 1965,' *Journal of the Australian War Memorial*, 18, 1991.

'Les Memoriaux dans les pays anglophones,' in Mission Permanente aux Commemorations et l'Information Historique, *Monuments de Memoire, Les Monuments aux Morts de la Premier Guerre Mondiale*, Paris, 1991.

'Multiculturalism and National Identity,' in CA Price (ed.), *Australian National Identity*, The Academy of the Social Sciences in Australia, Canberra, 1991.
Reprinted in KS Inglis (ed. C Wilcox), *Observing Australia: 1959 to 1999*, Melbourne University Press, Carlton, 1999.

'Remembering Manning Clark,' *Overland*, 124, 1991.
Reprinted in KS Inglis (ed. C Wilcox), *Observing Australia: 1959 to 1999*, Melbourne University Press, Carlton, 1999.

Untitled [review of *A War Imagined* by S Hynes], *La Grande Guerre: Pays, Histoire, Memoire. Bulletin du Centre de Recherche, Historial de La Grande Guerre*, 4, 1991.

'War Memorials in Australia and New Zealand' [co-authored with J Phillips], in J Rickard and P Spearritt (eds), *Packaging the Past? Public Histories*, Melbourne University Press, Melbourne, 1991.

Black and White in Australia Since 1688: A Survey of Perceptions and Encounters,
   Dwelling on the Years 1688, 1788, 1838, 1938, and 1988, Lecture at the
   University of Hawai'i 12 May 1992, University of Hawai'i, Honolulu, 1992.

'Going Home: Australians in England, 1870-1900,' in D Fitzpatrick (ed.), *Home
   or Away? Immigrants in Colonial Australia,* Australian National University,
   Canberra, 1992.

'Meetings in Moscow,' *Australian Society,* 11, 1-2, 1992.

'Questions about Newspapers,' *Australian Cultural History,* 11, 1992.

'Report of a Panel to Evaluate the Research Funding of Australian History 1981-
   1985' [co-authored with D Horne and J Roe] in *Response by the Australian
   Research Council to Report Number 3, Australian History, 1981-1985,* Australian
   Government Publishing Service, Canberra, 1992.

'Synthesis in Moscow,' *History Workshop Journal,* 35, 1992.

'The Homecoming: The War Memorial Movement in Cambridge, England,'
   Journal of Contemporary History, 27, 4, 1992.

'War Memorials: Ten Questions for Historians,' *Guerres Mondiales et Conflits
   Contemporains,* 167, 1992.
   A version of this article (same title) is in VV Sogrin, LP Repina, NV Strelchenko
   and DA Model, *Social History: Problems of Synthesis,* Russian Academy of
   Sciences, Moscow, 1994. [Publication in both Russian and English.]

'World War One Memorials in Australia,' *Guerres Mondiales et Conflits
   Contemporains,* 167, 1992.

Australian Legends: Anzac and the Bush, The Russel Ward Annual Lecture,
   University of New England, Armidale, 1993.
   Extract published in *Australian Folklore,* 9, 1994.

'Entombing Unknown Soldiers,' *Journal of the Australian War Memorial,* 23, 1993.

'Entombing Unknown Soldiers: From London and Paris to Baghdad,' *History &
   Memory,* 5, 2, 1993.
   Reprinted in J Lack (ed.), *Anzac Remembered: Selected Writings of KS Inglis,*
   University of Melbourne History Department, Melbourne, 1998.

'Men and Women of Australia': Speech Making as History, Barry Andrews Memorial
   Lecture, The University of New South Wales, Canberra, 1993.

'Variations in PhD Examining Procedures,' *Australian Historical Association
   Bulletin,* 74, 1993.

'A New Kind of History,' in P Donovan (comp), *Adventures with Clio: Historians
   Recounting their Memorable Experiences,* Donovan & Associates, Adelaide,
   1994.

'Grabmäler für Unbekannte Soldaten,' in R Rother (ed.), *Die letzten Tage der Menschheit Bilder des Ersten Weltkrieges*, Deutsches Historisches Museum, Berlin, 1994.

'Le 25 Avril en Australie et en Nouvelle-Zélande,' in J-J Becker, JM Winter, G Krumeich, A Becker, S Audoin-Rouzeau (eds), *Guerre et Cultures, 1914-1918*, Armand Colin, Paris, 1994.

'My Debt to Fred Smith,' in P Donovan (comp), *Adventures with Clio: Historians Recounting their Memorable Experiences*, Donovan & Associates, Adelaide, 1994.

'The Funeral of the Unknown Australian Soldier,' *Journal of the Australian War Memorial*, 24, 1994.

'The Premier and the Editor' in P Donovan (comp), *Adventures with Clio: Historians Recounting their Memorable Experiences*, Donovan & Associates, Adelaide, 1994.

'The Rite Stuff,' *Eureka Street*, 4, 1, 1994.
    Reprinted in J Lack (ed.), *Anzac Remembered: Selected Writings of KS Inglis*, University of Melbourne History Department, Melbourne, 1998.

'As the Sun Rises, a Nation Recalls Anzac Day,' *Canberra Times*, 23 April 1994.

'Introduction,' in C Wilcox (ed.), *The Great War: Gains and Losses – ANZAC and Empire*, Australian War Memorial and Australian National University, Canberra, 1995.

'Monuments to Difference,' *Eureka Street*, 5, 9, 1995.

'The Boorowa War Memorial,' *Canberra Historical Journal*, 35, 1995.

Untitled [review of *Commemorations* edited by JR Gillis], *Journal of World History*, 6, 2, 1995.

'Australia' in PJ Marshall (ed.), *The Cambridge Illustrated History of the British Empire*, Cambridge University Press, Cambridge, 1996.

'John Mulvaney's Universities,' in T Bonyhady and T Griffiths (eds), *Prehistory to Politics: John Mulvaney, the Humanities and the Public Intellectual*, Melbourne University Press, Melbourne, 1996.

'Notes of a Retiree' in *The Newsletter of the Academy of the Social Sciences in Australia*, 15, 2, 1996.

'Parliamentary Speech,' in *Poets, Presidents, People and Parliament: Republicanism and Other Issues*, [Papers on Parliament No. 28], Parliament House, Canberra, 1996.

'The Silent Sentinel: War Memorials in the Australian Landscape' [co-authored with J Brazier], *Kunapipi*, XVIII, 2-3, 1996.
    Reprinted in A Rutherford and J Wieland (eds), *War: Australia's Creative Response*, Dangaroo Press, West Yorkshire, 1997.

'ABC Shock Crisis Threat,' *Media International Australia*, 83, 1, 1997.

'Foreword,' in A Becker, *War and Faith: The Religious Imagination in France, 1914–1930*, Berg, Oxford, 1998.

'Foreword,' in D Walker and M Bennett (eds), *Intellect and Emotion: Perspectives on Australian History. Essays in Honour of Michael Roe*, Deakin University, Geelong, 1998.

'Remembering Anzac,' Paper delivered at the University of Melbourne in 1996, published in J Lack (ed.), *Anzac Remembered: Selected Writings of KS Inglis*, University of Melbourne History Department, Melbourne, 1998.

Sacred Places: War Memorials in the Australian Landscape, Miegunyah Press, Melbourne, 1998. [Second edition 2005, third edition 2008.]

'War Memorials in the Australian Landscape,' *Wartime*, 4, 1998.

'Funeral Oration for Geoffrey Serle, 30 April 1998,' *Overland*, 156, 1999.

'Media Amnesia,' *Eureka Street*, 9, 1, 1999.

'Monuments and Ceremonies as Evidence for Historians,' Paper delivered at the 1977 ANZAAS conference, published in KS Inglis (ed. C Wilcox), *Observing Australia: 1959 to 1999*, Melbourne University Press, Carlton, 1999.

'Paul Bourke: An Appreciation,' *Research School of Social Sciences 1999 Annual Report*, Australian National University, Canberra, 1999.

'Right Words' (1996 Stephen Murray-Smith Memorial Lecture), *The La Trobe Journal*, 63, 1999.
> Reprinted in KS Inglis (ed. C Wilcox), *Observing Australia: 1959 to 1999*, Melbourne University Press, Carlton, 1999.

'The Unknown Australian Soldier,' *Journal of Australian Studies*, 23, 60, 1999.
> Reprinted in P Craven (ed.), *The Best Australian Essays 1999*, Bookman, Melbourne, 1999.
> Reprinted in R Nile (ed.), *The Australian Legend and Its Discontents*, University of Queensland Press, St Lucia, 2000.
> Extract published in I Gold (ed.), *The Invisible Thread: One Hundred Years of Words*, Halstead Press, Canberra, 2012.

'Communication Breakdown,' *The Walkley Magazine*, autumn 2000.

London Calling: The Empire of the Airwaves, Menzies Centre for Australian Studies, London, 2000.

'Peace,' *Dialogue* [newsletter of the Academy of the Social Sciences in Australia], 19, 1, 2000.

'Ken Inglis in Conversation with Jill Roe,' *Australian Historical Association Bulletin*, 92, 2001.

'Writing Recent History: The Case of the ABC,' *Australian Historical Association Bulletin*, 93, 2001.

'Rivett, Rohan Deakin,' in J Ritchie and D Langmore (eds), *Australian Dictionary of Biography*, Volume 16, Melbourne University Press, Melbourne, 2002.

'Welcome to Dogura [co-authored with A Inglis]' in RG Ward and SW Serjeantson (eds), *And Then the Engines Stopped: Flying in Papua New Guinea*, Pandanus Books, Canberra, 2002.

'Alan Martin, 1926-2002' in *Australian Historical Studies*, 34, 122, 2003.

'Aunty's Story,' *Meanjin*, 62, 2, 2003.

'Foreword,' in G Briscoe, *Counting, Health and Identity: A History of Aboriginal Health and Demography in Western Australia and Queensland, 1900–1940*, Aboriginal Studies Press, Canberra, 2003.

'They Shall Not Grow Old,' *The Age*, 30 April 2004.

Whose ABC? The Australian Broadcasting Corporation 1983-2006, Black Inc., Melbourne, 2006.

'Donald William Archdall Baker, 1922-2007,' *History Australia*, 4, 1, 2007.

Speechmaking in Australian History, The Allan Martin Lecture, Australian National University, Canberra, 2007.

'Murray-Smith, Stephen,' in M Nolan (ed.), *Australian Dictionary of Biography*, Volume 18, Melbourne University Press, Melbourne, 2012.

'Rowley, Charles Dunford,' in M Nolan (ed.), *Australian Dictionary of Biography*, Volume 18, Melbourne University Press, Melbourne, 2012.

'Dunera Boy Touched by History' [obituary for Roy Thalheimer], *Sydney Morning Herald*, 29 February 2012.

'Interview with Professor Ken Inglis,' in C Spark, S Spark and C Twomey (eds), *Australians in Papua New Guinea 1960–1975*, University of Queensland Press, St Lucia, 2014.

'Mayer, Henry' [co-authored with M Goot], in *Australian Dictionary of Biography*, National Centre of Biography, Australian National University, published online 2014.

'Talk and Chalk,' in B Gammage, BV Lal and G Daws (eds), *The Boy from Boort: Remembering Hank Nelson*, Australian National University Press, Canberra, 2014.

'In Search of Henry Mayer,' *Australian Journal of Political Science*, 50, 1, 2015.

'Return to Gallipoli' [collaboration with K Ariotti], *Wartime*, 70, 2015.

'Reflecting on a Retrospective' in T Frame (ed.), *Anzac Day: Then & Now*, UNSW Press, Sydney, 2016.

'The Odyssey of Leonhard Adam,' *History Australia*, 14, 4, 2017.

Dunera Lives: A Visual History [co-authored with S Spark, J Winter and C Bunyan], Monash University Publishing, Melbourne, 2018.

Dunera Lives: Profiles [co-authored with B Gammage, S Spark, J Winter and C Bunyan], Monash University Publishing, Melbourne, 2020.

INDEX